COLORADO

MOUNTAIN COLLEGE

**Alpine Campus
Library
Bristol Hall
P.O. Box 774688
Steamboat Springs
CO 80477**

DEMCO

MIDDLE EAST MONOGRAPH

SERIES

The Islamic Movement
in
North Africa

by

François Burgat

and

William Dowell

Center for Middle Eastern Studies
University of Texas at Austin

Library of Congress Catalog Card Number: 92-075654

ISBN 0-292-70793-2

Printed in the United States of America

Cover Design: Diane Watts

Editor: Annes McCann-Baker

First appeared as *L'Islamisme au Maghreb*
Éditions KARTHALA
75013 Paris

Calligraphy on cover first appeared in "Harakat al-Ittijah al-Islami,"
on the third anniversary of the student's movement, Tunis, 1984.

TABLE OF CONTENTS

EDITOR'S ACKNOWLEDGMENTS

The American publication of *The Islamic Movement in North Africa* is the result of a joint effort among international institutions. François Burgat's initial volume, *L'Islamisme au Maghreb*, was published by Karthala Press in Paris in 1988. After reading the book, Robert Fernea, chair of the Publications Committee at the Center for Middle Eastern Studies at The University of Texas at Austin, sought to raise funds to make possible an English translation and publication in the Center's Middle East Monograph Series.

As a result of an agreement between the Universities of Texas and Aix-Marseille III in France, the Center had recently entered into a collaboration with the Institut de Recherche et d'Etudes sur le Monde Arabe et Musulman (IREMAM) at Aix-Marseille III. Both groups contacted the French government for a possible subvention to support the translation of *L'Islamisme au Maghreb*. The grant was forthcoming, and the Center hired *Time* correspondent William Dowell in Cairo to do the translation. At the same time, author Burgat continued both to update the book to cover the traumatic events in Algeria through the summer of 1992, and to support its central thesis with more field work, notably, in Egypt and the rest of the Middle East.

The Center would like to express its gratitude to IREMAM, the French Consulate in Houston, and the French research center in Cairo CEDEJ (Centre d'Etudes et de Documentation Economique, Juridique et Sociale), where Burgat has been given the opportunity to update and extend his research. The international collaborative effort has made possible the English-language new version of this valuable and timely text.

Annes McCann-Baker
Editor

FOREWORD

If the relationship between the Western world and the Arab world is not to worsen, a major change must take place in the way contemporary Islamic discourse is understood in Europe and the United States. At the present time, the words "Islamic Fundamentalism" have become so nearly synonymous with terrorism—the killing of the Copts and Western tourists in Egypt, for example—that one might be led to fear that the need to prepare once more for the Crusades is imminent. On the other hand, from a Muslim viewpoint, the rape of Muslim women by Christians in Bosnia, military sanctions against Iraq, the expulsion of Palestinians by Israelis, and the destruction of mosques and burning of Muslim neighborhoods in India are all seen as a single pattern of persecution, tangible reasons for distrusting the non-Muslim world.

A sense of rage and despair is moving across North Africa and the Middle East, feelings of resentment so great that the most outrageous acts against foreign and local Christians, which only a small minority of persons would actually commit, may find passive support among the many educated men and women. Combined with economic hardships, inflation, unemployment and deteriorating standards of living, the threat to internal stability and the peaceful resolution of differences becomes increasingly problematic in many countries. What the Western media have failed to communicate, what scholars are only beginning to address, is the way in which Islamic discourse is articulating opinions about both internal and external problems in a new language, a language that struggles to free itself from the contamination of Western political concepts, which are regarded by many as the symbolic residue of colonial domination.

This book is one of the first to lay before readers the complex, contested nature of this new Islamic political articulation and the practice it advocates. We are invited to overhear and try to understand a new form of political discourse, a discourse which rejects the epistemological foundation on which both Western democracy and Western imperialism have been based and which replaces that foundation with words, concepts, images and metaphors drawn from Islam. By Islam is meant here not only the roots of that tradition, the Koran and its commentaries, but also the local practices and understandings that are part of the cultural expressions uniting and dividing millions of Muslims of all ages and nationalities.

Within this framework of Islamic discourse, there are local differences of opinion about proper government, proper community life, and proper personal behavior. As the authors here demonstrate, the Islamic movement is far from a seamless whole. Power differences of class and gender still prevail; the means of change remain in dispute even where common goals are generally accepted. But it is in this new Islamic discourse that political ideologies and social practices will be proclaimed and practiced. And it is our responsibility to understand what is happening rather than negatively labeling as "Islamic fundamentalism" this new discourse, and in opposition blindly supporting sectarian governments that use familiar terms and make comfortable promises to Western governments.

The authors of the work that follows especially concentrate on Algeria and Tunisia with important observations about the rest of North Africa, and provide us with an opportunity to see Islamic discourse at close range. Their interviews with Muslim leaders, translations from the press, from sermons and speeches and from local media accounts reveal the diversity and complexity of (what we would consider) political and economic considerations, couched in (what we would regard as) religious argumentation. We are here invited to see beneath the "froth of extremism" that captures the attention of the Western press; we are invited to encounter at first hand the political forces that now engage a new Middle Eastern public, a public which for many years has been alienated by the essentially foreign quality of post-colonial political language. The text that follows then is often marked by the movements of concepts and syntax from Arabic through French and into English. A new authority, a new source of legitimacy, infuses public language, but it is only new in the purposes to which it is being put, the issues it addresses. For millions of Muslims, this language has always been present even if confined and restricted by modern (read Western) political institutions. Nor are the problems new which Islamic leaders must face as they take power.

My own sense of urgency over the stereotyping and ethnocentrism of Western thought about the Islamic world has become intensified by fear of the violence that Western interference in the politics of the Middle East may enflame. Treating Islamic political movements as subversive on the one hand and consistently supporting secularly based governments on the other, is not only intrusive interference in the affairs of others; it is also a refusal to examine rationally what is actually happening in the area. Such blind sight is also a way of sustaining and magnifying the already strained relations between the West and the Arab world. No one will finish this book with a sense of comfort about the Muslim Middle East, but readers will come to understand why "Islamic fundamentalism" is as much a new language of political differences as it is a mass movement with common objectives.

Robert Fernea
University of Texas

INTRODUCTION

In this turbulent contemporary period of conflicting ideologies, the industrialized North has recently had to contend with a new force coming from the South, which now threatens its influence and undermines its most deeply held convictions. Addressed in French or English, this new upstart in North Africa replies in Arabic. Confronted with Western notions of a secular society, it sees only "materialism," and openly prefers its own "spirituality." Instead of the Western notion of the nation-state, it proposes the "umma," the Islamic concept of community. In the place of democracy, it prefers "shura," or the principle of consultation.

The arguments that have raged for more than a decade between followers and adversaries of these new references often sound to the casual observer like a dialogue of the deaf. To the modernist elites in the South, the militant language of political Islam—for that is what is being spoken here—sounds threatening. To the North, the "*Allah Akhbar* (God is Greatest!)" of the Islamists is received as both a message of defiance and of rejection.

Against a background of economic uncertainty, political frustration and cultural crises, Islamism, this new voice from the South, shows no signs of abandoning its path. The death of Khomeini; the persistent refusal by Tunisia's President Zine Al Abidine Ben Ali to recognize the Hizb En Nahda (the Party of the Renaissance) of Rached Ghannouchi after it had demonstrated in the elections of April 2, 1989, its strength among the electorate; the recognition by Ghannouchi's now-deposed Algerian counterpart in the Islamic Salvation Front, which quickly became the major force of opposition in the country; the electoral victories by the Muslim Brothers in Jordan;(1) the reassertion of anti-Islamist repression almost everywhere else, have all served to draw attention once again to these new winners on the political chessboard of the Arab world.

Those who wanted to interpret the Islamist surge as nothing more than a momentary phenomenon, more or less tied to the Revolution in Iran, have been forced to reevaluate their assessments. In doing so, they acknowledge

---

(1) During the first free election organized in Jordan since 1967, Islamists obtained 34 (22 for the Muslim Brotherhood) seats in the parliament (out of 80), thus appearing as the largest force in opposition to the regime. See: Pascaline Eury, "Jordanie: les Élections du 8 novembre 1989," *Les Cahiers du Cermoc*, No. 2, Amman, 1991, 131 pages.

1

that the froth of extremism associated with the phenomenon has masked the gestation of political forces that are more serious and consequential than the small activist groups with which they are often identified. The emergence of pluralism, by permitting small clusters of militants to connect with their electorate, has helped to reveal the magnitude of the phenomenon. Whether in Algeria or elsewhere in the region, the themes which permitted the Imam of Qom to break out of the ghetto of clandestine opposition will soon allow Islamist movements to take over all or part of the political heritage of the nationalist parties in power today.

It is only in seeing beyond its extreme expressions to the essence of the Islamist dialectic that it is possible to understand why it has such a remarkable capacity for mobilization, how it is likely to express itself politically, and the potential limits of its early successes.

The inflation in terminology—"Islamism," "Fundamentalism," "Integrism," "Khomeinism," "Muslim Brothers," etc.—created by Western writers intrigued and disturbed by what they see, attests both to the difficulty of coming to terms with the movement's diversity from the exterior, and of grasping the essence of its meaning.

In the West's newspaper headlines, the nationalist movements with their "independences" and their "nationalizations" seem today to be pale figures. Nasser and Ben Bella have been dethroned and placed in the gallery of those great men who have been tamed by history. Even if the media's attention has allowed Kadhafi to hold on longer than most, the once-brilliant new arrival among bogeymen has now been largely overtaken. For more than ten years, in effect, it has been the mirror of Khomeini and his "terrorist orchestra" that the West has used to gauge the difficulties it faces in trying to find its place in a world where it has lost the monopoly on expression, and where some of its most ethnocentric representations have lost their pretensions at universality.

To understand the Islamist surge, one must first be able to measure the pitfalls that lay in the path of the orientalist's approach. The inventory of these has expanded considerably over the last ten years from the writings of Edward Said to Bernard Lewis and from those of Hassan Hanafi to Fouad Zacharia.(1)

---

(1) Edward Said, *Orientalism*, New York, Vintage, 1979; *Covering Islam*, New York, Pantheon, 1981. Pascal Bruckner, *Les sanglots de l'homme blanc*; *Tiers Monde, culpabilité, haine de soi*, Paris, Le Seuil, 1983, (L'Histoire immédiate). Bernard Lewis, *Le retour de l'Islam*, Paris, Gallimard, 1985. Gérard Chaliand, *Mythes révolutionaires du Tiers Monde*, Paris, Seuil, 1980, (L'Histoire immédiate). Hassan Hanafi, notably, *Muqadimat li'ilm al-istighrab*, Madbouli,

To understand Islamism implies first of all that one is capable of remaining alert to the limits of an enterprise of objectification. To observe, one must choose the right focal length, to sufficiently approach the object to be able to reintroduce that irreducible plurality, which too often becomes abstracted when one looks in from the outside. One cannot forget that it is men and women who give the movement its foundation, and not just *suras* of a dogma that may be more accessible to the observer than the millions of individuals who claim it. And it is necessary to remember that none of these are immune to their environment or to human and sociological laws, despite the force of their affirmations. In addition to the pitfall of the simplified generalization, it is also necessary to avoid that of the reassuring "atomization" that leads some to deny the common denominators behind the numerous facets of local particularities.

As with any of the socio-political currents that have defined the history of the planet, Islamism is also crisscrossed by internal dynamics which keep it in constant evolution. More than the discourse of the Islamists at any given moment, it is the sense in which the evolution of this discourse is perceptible that ought to give the analysis its foundation. Taking these internal dynamics into account, one must reject any analysis that in the name of any atavism, religious or not, tries to fix in time once and for all an explanation of what is happening.

This work is the result of research conducted between 1984 and 1988 in the framework of the Centre National de la Recherche Scientifique (CNRS) with the collaboration of the Institut de Recherches et d'Etudes sur le Monde Arabe et Musulman of Aix-en-Provence (IREMAM). It was updated starting in January, 1989, at the Centre d'Etudes et de Documentation Economique, Juridique et Sociale (CEDEJ) in Cairo.(1) It may seem to skip over some of the usual academic approaches. The Islamist leaders questioned in free interviews express themselves at length and in a fairly unrefined state. Instead of

---

Cairo, 1991. Fouad Zacharia, notably, *Al-Sahwah al-Islamiyya fi mizane al-'aqe* (The Islamic Awakening to the Light of Reason), Cairo, 1987.

(1) Created in 1986, IREMAM, a mixed unit of the Centre National de la Recherche Scientifique (CNRS), is one of the most important French research centers on the Arab and Muslim world. CEDEJ (Cairo), which relies upon both CNRS and the social and human sciences administration of the French Ministry of Foreign Affairs, was created after a Franco-Egyptian cooperation agreement signed in 1968.

synthesizing the information in their discourses,(1) we preferred to allow the reader the direct perceptions of these men. This is one way of avoiding the simplification that comes from a unilateral reading. The public outside the university is also given the possibility of hearing the "Islamist activist" express himself without mediation, and thus verifying for those who still doubt it that he was, in fact, really born on the same planet as we were.

For a long time, the West as well as the independent elites of the Arab world itself have seen nothing more in the demands of the Islamists than the jolts of agony of a tradition riddled with archaism. In fact, something completely different has been taking place. Behind the beards and the *hijjabs* are no "Martians." Not even, in most cases, "fanatics" or other "extremists." These are, quite simply, the descendants of the nationalists who have entered the political arena.

The South, after having (through the independences) undertaken to disconnect its political future from the West, and then (through the nationalizations) to win more autonomy in the management of its material resources, has now turned towards the terrains of culture and ideology, domains previously conquered by the North, and which it now seeks to reappropriate. Even if it is very far from representing the outcome, Islamism, "the rocket of decolonization's third stage," manifests the acceleration of this process of repositioning the South in relation to the North. And it is an essential step.

In a non-democratic political environment, that is, one that is unreceptive to protest, Islamism has sometimes opted for the path of a violence that appeared less legitimate than that of the government. Thus, the list of villains, which was seriously reduced by the banalization of nationalist ruptures, has easily found in the "integristes" an indispensable replacement in the imagination of the West. The cracks in the foundations of the "friendly" regimes have been sensed in the West only through the deformed echo of the repressive measures that they have carried out. Marked by a violence practiced more often by the regimes than against them, the extremist froth of the Islamist phenomenon has for too long constituted the unique gateway into a phenomenon which nevertheless remains irreducible.

---

(1) Certain interviews have been lightly edited to eliminate repetitions, silences, hesitations, and other lapses whose meaning could not be interpreted within the limits of these pages. Some of the materials have been translated from Arabic into French by Richard Jacquemond, others by F.B. William Dowell has both translated the book into English and helped F.B. adapt it to the specificity of the English "lectorate."

The terminology employed in 1992 to present the origin of the parliamentary majorities in the South to their partners in the North, resembles that used ten years earlier to describe the mentality of the assassins of Sadat. Fortunately for the West, that same leap in logic is not applied to contemporary political dynamics in our own countries. No one confuses the terrorist group Action Directe with the French Socialist Party; no responsible person confuses the Red Brigades with the Italian Communist Party. In the United States, even though there may be certain points on which members of both groups can agree, it is easy to see the difference between the Republican Party and the Ku Klux Klan. It is worthwhile then to avoid extrapolating—either in time or in space—the mentality of the radical groups who happened to be the first to draw the attention of Western observers. It is a mistake to project the facets of one aspect of the phenomenon onto the process of re-Islamization as a whole, which in fact is very diversified. The extreme weaknesses of the apparatus of knowledge—academic or otherwise—of the North with respect to the South, has accentuated its difficulty in understanding the exact impact of this new distancing on the part of the South.

Between 1960 and 1980, France, which seemed—along with a good part of the West—fixed solely on the economic dimensions of its relations with the Muslim world, had appeared only marginally interested in the cultural realities of what was happening on the southern shores of the Mediterranean. A French-speaking Maghreb, too hastily labeled "Francophile," has masked the emergence of an impertinent new Maghreb, which today wants to use a new language.

Just when this region of the world most needed some kind of reconnection with the symbolic attributes of its precolonial culture, the vast majority of its Western interlocutors, deprived of any linguistic foothold,(1) saw everything aimed at distinguishing Muslim cultures from the West as a mere attack.

The West, which feels a certain measure of uneasiness at these developments, prefers above all to speak to those whose voices are reassuring.

---

(1) How many journalists actually have direct access today to the writing of their hundred million Arab neighbors? How many politicians? Last but not least, given the context of disciplinary segregation in the universities, whose limits are just beginning to become apparent (and which this author has not escaped), how many academics have been able to reconcile the necessity of having a profound base in linguistics, language and history, with the indispensible methodological baggage of the social sciences?

The mediators who shape Western perceptions of the phenomenon, and who are by no means the least significant obstacle to reaching a genuine understanding, have often been precisely those whose convictions are threatened by the new developments. Those whose political futures are tied to the survival of regimes that came into power just after independence have a tendency to mystify developments that do not tend to act in their favor.

To understand the Islamist eruption on the Tunisian scene in 1987, the French media were much more likely to interview Habib Bourguiba's ambassadors than to talk to the spokesmen of the movement that the monarch, who had turned into an aging tyrant, was trying to eradicate.

It is all too often the prince, himself, who one solicits to help us understand the logic of those who are trying to overthrow him. Jean Daniel, the editor of the French magazine, *Nouvel Observateur,* began an interview with Morocco's King Hassan II in 1987 by diffidently slanting his question: "You understand that I would like to begin by asking you about what is most urgent for you, for us, for all of us, in short 'integrism'...!"(1)

In the Western political landscape, the Islamist discourse has thus provoked the same dangerous unanimity, the same refusal to listen to what is being said, that was raised by the nationalist discourse in the fifties. Those very few who understood the nationalists of the past have often paradoxically been convinced that, since they were on "the right side of history" at the beginning, they still know the sole legitimate actors on the scene in the person of the political elites now in power. In "Islam," the "Third World," and the "Arabs," the political right has found the bogeyman it needs to justify its own well-anchored convictions. Supposedly freer to accept the birth of the "Other," the Left has retrenched behind the ramparts of its finicky attachment to secular symbols, and today seems to be a prisoner of its own inability to admit that the universalism of republican thought can be called into question, or that anyone might dare to write history in a vocabulary other than the one that it has forged itself.

But it is precisely the rupture in language and syntax—the discarding of Western political terminology—which is the core of the Islamist recipe. Henceforth, the potential for misunderstandings becomes vast.

From the Islamist crucible, however, it is possible that once the stage of reaction has passed, we may begin to see a new equilibrium—precisely the balance that has been missing in these societies in the colonial and postcolonial decades. Behind the banner of "integrism," a valuable synthesis

---

(1) Interview with King Hassan II, *Le Nouvel Observateur,* March 28, 1987.

may well be in the process of being woven into the fabric of these societies, which neither the violence of colonialism, nor the counter-violence of the nationalists or that of the modernizers who followed them have been able to impose.

CHAPTER 1

ISLAMISM, FUNDAMENTALISM, INTEGRISM: THE DIFFICULTY IN CHOOSING A NAME

For greater convenience and because it is part of the current language, we will refer to the new religious radicalism which embraces the countries of the Orient indifferently under the designations integrists, fundamentalists, extremists and gamaat.(1)

"Fundamentalism," "integrism," "traditionalism," "religious activism," "Khomeinism," "Muslim Brothers," "Arabism," "Salafism": In the press, and more significantly in the ivory tower of the specialists, the designations used to describe the eddies and counter-currents emanating from the Muslim world and troubling the calm waters of Western convictions have fluctuated for too long. At the root of this difficulty in finding a name, is the difficulty of understanding the phenomenon in its specificity as well as its diversity.

Attitudes, conduct, and discourses in which religion and politics support each other are not new to Islam. Certain phenomena that were at first hastily combined can today be more or less completely disassociated from the ultimate amalgamation of politics and religion, which constitutes Islamism.

In less than ten years,(2) some helpful clarifications have been made in the terminology, and a relative consensus appears to be taking shape. If the concept of "Islamism" is imposing itself little by little, there is no longer as great an inclination to have it represent the totality of the social attitudes and political comportment linked to or influenced by the Muslim religion. The distinction, however, is never absolute. To one degree or another, the phenomenon always reattaches itself to those appellations that focus on one or another of its dimensions or affiliations, while failing to describe it in its globalism. Parallel to this "external" rationalization, is an identical process taking place inside the Islamist movement. These two initiatives often collide with one another, which becomes evident in the rejection by the Islamists of certain labels that have been attached to them.

---

(1) Claire Brière and Olivier Carré, "Islam, Guerre à l'Occident," *Autrement,* 1983.

(2) Thanks notably to Olivier Carré, Olivier Roy, Jean-Francois Clément, Jacques Berque, Mohamed Arkoun, M. Al Baki Hermassi, Gilles Kepel, Ali Eddine Hillal Dessouki, Saad Eddine Ibrahim, Bruno Etienne, Mohamed Tozy, Michel Camau, Maxime Rodinson, Jean-Claude Vatin, Bernard Lewis, Leonard Binder and many others.

8

It is this complex web of multiple designations, most of which are at least partly erroneous, which we want to try to untangle here. Beyond just clarifying the terminology, we have another ambition: to begin the objectivization of a phenomenon in which religion and politics, current events and history, the perceptions of others, and our views of ourselves, are intricately intertwined.

Islam and Islamism

It is possible to be a Muslim and not be an Islamist. This first distinction is often not fully appreciated. In fact, what is at stake, as Michel Camau (1) writes,

> is not to operate in confusion between a contemporary political-religious phenomenon and a culture that is more than a thousand years old (...) Tunisian society is "Islamic." There is a dimension there which the events of a decade can neither challenge nor diminish. On the other hand, the modalities of perception, representation and mobilization of Islam in the heart of a society can be affected over the short term. It is from this viewpoint that one can speak of an "Islamic *upsurge*"...

Bruno Etienne and Mohamed Tozy favor the term "Islamist," for the distinction that it allows one to make with the "classical Muslim," and with the followers of certain mystical practices, such as the Sufis. They point out that the term "Islamist" is the one usually used by the interested parties themselves. It is "often claimed by women wearing the *hijab*, and is in all cases preferred to 'Muslim' which is not satisfactory."(2) In effect, the perception of the Islamists themselves usually takes into account the distinction: "Islam (in Tunisia) is ancient, but the Islamist movement is recent," says Rached Ghannouchi, the leader and theoretician of the principal current in Tunisia.

> By Islamist movement, I mean the action to renew the comprehension of Islam. I also mean the action which began in the 70's and which calls for a return to the sources of Islam, far from the inherited myths and a fixation on traditions.(3)

---

(1) "Chronique Politique de la Tunisie, 1979," *Annuaire de l'Afrique du Nord*, Ed. by CNRS, Paris, 1981.

(2) "Femmes Tunisiennes Islamistes" in *Le Maghreb Musulman* in 1979, Christiane Souriau dir., Paris, CNRS, 1981.

(3) *Le Maghreb Musulman en 1979*, page 77. It is not nevertheless the attitude of all Islamist leaders: "In your book" criticises Abbassi Madani, "you must first of all

Although both "Islamist" and "Islamic" have been used in French translations, French-speaking militants seem increasingly to prefer "Islamist." The important point is to take notice of the demand for specificity that the "Islamiyyine" are expressing with respect to the rest of the "Muslimine."

As with all frontiers, the one which separates Islamism and its militants and the community of believers is not absolute. If a thousand-year-old culture cannot be completely reduced to fit the contemporary interpretation given to it by a single group, or to the political uses the group wants to make of it, the group's capacity to expand its influence over the entire community, which may go as far as assuming moral and political leadership, can certainly over a period of time make the distinction a relative one.

Islamism and Sufism

Neither Sufism nor Maraboutism can be confused with the Islamist current. Islamist theoreticians have long been explicitly reticent about Sufism and even more so about Maraboutism. They fret about the alleged "looseness" of morals which reputedly takes place during some of the large popular demonstrations by the brotherhoods and more often the illegal creations of the Sufis toward the basic message of Islam.

> Islam is the way we know it through the Koran, the Hadiths, and the Sira (biography of the prophet). The *tasawuf*, or Sufism, as you say,(...) arrived during a certain period of Islamic history. During the time of the rasidun califs, power and sanctity went together. With the coming of the Omayyads, sanctity began to diminish. It was at that moment, then, that voices were raised to bring people back to the right path. This movement gradually transformed itself afterwards, until it pretended that beyond the clear information contained in the Koran and the sunna, there were secrets which the Prophet left only to certain of his closest followers, and that these had since undertaken to transmit them. It is on this belief that Sufism developed. (...) Well, for us, none of that exists. It is simply a deviation. Islam is what is found in the Koran and the hadith. It is in the comportment of the Prophet as related by his companions, and it is nothing else (1).

---

change the title! Why 'Islamism'? It is Islam which is at work in Algeria, nothing but Islam. We are Muslims ...!" (Interview with the author, Algiers, June 1990).

(1) Interview with Abdallah Benkirane, a young dissident of the Chebiba Islamiyya, now the leader of a legalistic group in Morocco (Rabat Salé, October, 1987).

10

The Islamists are generally even more critical of the Sufis' apolitical nature, which is to say its passivity in front of the decadence of the Umma, and, in most cases, the recuperation of the grand brotherhoods by the authorities, i.e. colonial power during the colonial period and local regimes since then. Traditional Islam (they often prefer the term "archaic") appears to many to be a brake on the development of their thought, and its manifestations are seen as obstacles to their action. "(The Islamist message) has encountered internal obstacles due to the traditionalist image of inherited Islam," says Rached Ghannouchi. "I mean by that the spiritualist teachings, the cults that were produced late in history and which have no relation with Islam: Sufism, the Dervish movement, visits to ancestral tombs, the *hadra,* or seances of the Sufis, the cult of saints, etc."(1)

Regarding the cult of saints, Malek Bennabi, a major reference for the Algerian trend, has demonstrated since 1954 in his *Vocation de l'Islam* this reticence to consider it as anything other than an expression of disarray in a society that has lost its structure.

History begins with the whole man, adapting his efforts constantly to his ideal and to his needs, and accomplishing his double mission in society as actor and as witness. But history finishes with man disintegrated, the body deprived of a center of gravity, the individual living in a dissolved society that no longer furnishes either a moral or material base to his existence. That is when the escape into maraboutism or into no matter what other nirvana occurs, which is nothing more than the subjective form of a social "every man for himself."(2)

For Ahmida Enneifer, one of the founders of the Tunisian movement, it is Sufism which is in a large part responsible for the immobility from which the Islamist movements are trying to free the Muslim world today. His plea recaptures the principal chapters of the case generally made against the contemporary expressions of Sufism by modern Islamist thinkers.

"LET HIM GROAN" OR "AGAINST SUFISM"

Can one blame Sufism for the failure of the Islamists, for their deviations, and their paralysis? And if yes, why? (...) Three marks have been left on contemporary Islamic thought by the Sufi deviation: First of all there is the profoundly anchored belief in asceticism as an ideal in the education of

---

(1) Interview with Christiane Sourian in *Le Maghreb Musulman en 1979,* op.cit.

(2) Malek Bennabi, *Vocation de l'Islam,* Le Seuil, 1954, 168 pages, page 27.

the militant; then (...) this unshakable faith in the group to which one belongs, which is turned into the unique source of truth and which drives one to consider all others as being in a state of error; the absolute and unconditional obedience, finally, to the Sheikh who directs the group.

1. The vitality of the ascetic ideal—which makes a vision of the world on earth as an endless trial and malediction the principle of the education of the militant—is at the root of the malaise towards life felt by the committed Muslim militant who belongs to these groups, and of the pathological fear that he has of committing a sin or of showing disobedience towards God. He sees religious prohibitions everywhere, and only feels at peace with himself when he is praying, practicing the *dhikr* or other religious devotions of the same order, anything else being only a trial or leading directly to one.

It is not with this kind of pedagogy that one will be able to invent anything or to arrive at surpassing oneself (...) One cannot validly base an education on the renunciation of the world. It means depriving it of anything that it can have that is positive. It gives birth to a divided morality which eulogizes abstinence and neglects ambition; which turns reciting the Koran into a virtue and confidence in oneself a vice. This truncated morality emphasizes "qualities" such as avoiding laughter, and being chaste to the point of prudery, to the multiplication of superfluous acts, and it considers a taste for perfection, for challenge, and for awakening, to be "secondary" virtues. But an education which wants to be positive must be based on moral integrity. Virtue cannot take the place of valor. The recitation of the Koran cannot replace discipline, nor can evening prayers replace scientific research.

2. Turning in on oneself in the interior of the group. Not one Muslim, I believe, will contest the importance of the principle of community in Islam. The modern period, which has seen the emergence of so many Islamist groups has been struck as I see it by a Sufi type of listlessness, which translates itself by the fact that all those who involve themselves in an Islamic action, no longer consider themselves to be members of a group, but see themselves to be the group, the sole possessor of the truth. The division of the world which certain jurists of the classical period made between the "land of Islam" and "enemy land" [*dar Islam wa dar harb*] has just aggravated that listlessness. This distinction could have been justified at a period when Islamic society possessed a high degree of doctrinal, intellectual and material truth. In our time, this type of critical interpretation (*ijtihad*) no longer has a place: the balance of forces is reversed, and the economic, cultural and political factors have changed completely. But, like the members of a Sufi association, the members of the community continue to make a systematic distinction at the heart of men and institutions between "Muslims" (us) and wayward "infidels" (them). Such a division is the sign of a sick psyschism, in which the community is allowed to understand and apply Islam, while the others are irremediably dedicated to vice and evil. It is extremely damaging in that it gives the community an assurance which is never denied and which distances it even further from the others and leads it to close in on itself. Turning in on oneself is a sign of an approaching end, either softly or

with violence. The murder of Sheik Dhahabi in Egypt is not so far from us.(1)

3. Blind obedience to the "Sheikh." This blind confidence in the "guide" is another characteristic of Sufi influence on contemporary Islamic action. Command is certainly an essential element in the Islamic structure; but it has been transformed by the trickery of medieval and contemporary Sufis into a pathological symptom called "tagging along" (al imamiyya). Tagging along consists of developing a human model who is outside the corruption that is rife everywhere in society, but which is incapable of freeing himself from the interior of the community. Crushed before joining, he is crushed again afterwards. The Prophet also commanded, but he never crushed the personality of his companions. Never did he turn anyone into a servile imitator. (...) Our epoch is one in which every Sheik-guide constitutes, in the name of command, a "school" in which he imprints his own way of thinking, his temperament, and is followed by disciples who are most often either dominated, rebellious or sometimes dissident, who almost invariably finish by deviating after the death of the sheik-master.

Ask a Sufi the origin of this dhikr where the "disciple" tries to outdo himself repeating the word "Aah," considered to be one of the most beautiful names of God. He will answer: "There is a tradition of the Prophet (that prayers and salvation be with him) according to which while visiting a sick invalid and finding him in the process of moaning and repeating the word, 'Aah', he did nothing to stop him and on the contrary said to the others, 'Let him moan, for his moan is one of the names of God which is very high....'." Put aside any debate over the authenticity and the sense of this tradition; what matters is that from this simple argument in favor of this dhikr which they are the only ones to practice, they have created a conceptual framework, a way of acting in society: "Let him groan," has become of itself an attitude towards illness and misfortune. All through the centuries of decadence, the Sufis guaranteed their followers an elevated spiritual life and authentic brotherhood, while injustices and darkness built up in successive waves, toward which no one made the slightest gesture, and society moaned, left to itself. Such is the approach of the Sufis: spiritual elevation while society sinks deeper into neglect, and moans. It is this approach which, in its essence, has passed to the contemporary Islamic movements. They understood the existence of the illness, but the cure was not easy... And when one asked them, "What do you recommend to cure the patient?" they invariably responded, "Let him moan. He is only a heathen. Educate ourselves first; we'll see about him later." And society continued to groan. "Let him groan." "It is a contagious disease. Don't go near him!" It is like that that one holds on to easy slogans, "Corruption is everywhere," or "Only one solution, Islam!" The slogans are like sedatives; their effect is

---

(1) Sheikh Dhahabi was kidnapped and then "executed" in June, 1977, by members of a group known as Takfir wa Hijra.

13

limited over a period of time, and when they cease to act, the patient realizes that his condition has grown worse.

Al Maarifa (Tunis) No. 3, Year No. 4 (1976)

Here, as elsewhere, the frontiers, nevertheless, are not hermetic. The political mobilization of traditional religious mystics is not without rapport to Islamism. A simple recollection of the role of the Sufi brotherhoods in the resistance to colonialism, from Algeria to Sudan to the Libyan Senoussi, is enough to justify the first nuances. There is no lack of examples of rebellion against government power by traditional religious groups. If most Islamists condemn the contemporary organizational expressions of Sufism and its recuperation by the regimes on all sides, certain Islamist militants have also a relationship with Sufi mysticism that has been much more ambivalent; Abdessalam Yassine, one of the principal leaders today in Morocco, returned to militant Islam himself via the *tariqa* of Haj Abbas, to whom he remained loyal until his death. Today, Yassine still retains this specificity, which he considers to be an intrinsic part of his personality. And he recalls that he shares this with some of the most prestigious "founding (Muslim) brothers." In fact, his personal itinerary illustrates both the contribution of Sufism to Islamism and, on the other hand, the need to move beyond the narrow paths of the tariqa to accede to the universe of Islamism.

ABDESSALAM YASSINE: FROM SUFISM TO ISLAMISM

Let's say, before anything else, that personally, today, where I am, I conceive of Islam as a form of militancy. You are not unaware that the word *jihad* is a privileged word in the Koran and the Sunna. But Muslims have lost this inclination for jihad. They have lost it by the wearing away of history, by the inducement of sleep. They slept for centuries under the yoke of successive regimes, which have all been more or less Islamic, more or less violent against anything said in opposition to them. They are now rediscovering this energy which reappeared in the world... which expresses itself in many different ways, and which the West sometimes calls terrorism and sometimes calls fundamentalism, integrism, etc., mere words. Words cover the truth. The truth is that in man, in every man, there is this divine spark which waits to be lighted, to be put back into action. Well, in my case, let's say that in 1965, I had what we can call a "spiritual crisis," a spontaneous awakening, like that, in the measure in which spontaneity always has some significance for someone who believes in God and in divine destiny. No, I was not cut off from religion. I had learned the Koran as a child. I studied in the Ben-Youssef medersa, a traditional Koranic school in Marrakesh, and my education was above all traditional: Koran, *fiqh*. I did not begin to learn French until I was 19, when I was already preparing to enter the normal school for teachers. But this traditional education meant that I lived my Islam... very gently. That is to say, that I practiced it; I said my prayers, I occasionally read the Koran so as not to forget it completely, since I had learned it by heart. I was known in the circles I moved in as someone who was reserved. At 20, I became a civil servant, then a professor of Arabic, education inspector, etc. During all that time, my Islam was very gentle, let's say very nice, an Islam that did not ask questions. I did not have, let's say, any preparation to launch myself into a protest, or a challenge to the realities which the *umma* lived as a fait accompli. And then in 1965, I was 38 years old then, and suddenly, all at once, I lived through this crisis. You have no doubt read biographies of Christians, of Muslims, of Buddhists, who experience this kind of spiritual awakening at around the age of forty. I immediately abandoned the books I was reading, books of a foreign culture, to launch myself into the search for God.

In my conscience, it was a pure quest for God. Very simply. I am someone who asked himself existential questions, who told himself: "Here it is. I am forty years old, what have I done with my life? Where am I going?" Anxiety over death, anxiety over having lost something. (...) So I began this spiritual quest. I read books on Sufism. I even read books on yoga, strangers to Islam, and everywhere I read the testimony of people who said they had found something... and I told myself: "You, you haven't found anything..."

Then I had an encounter. Someone told me: "There is a Sufi master in Morocco. If you go to see him, he will guide you." And in effect, I met a master named El Haj Abbas, and I saw him for six years. He was not illiterate, but he only had a traditional rural education. On the other hand, I, I who was imbued at that time with my own self sufficiency—I was an important person at the Ministry of Education—I became his disciple, his humble disciple, and I understood what was Islam, what was God. Very humbly, I recognized that this man gave me a great deal. I went to see him for six years.

After that, he left this world. He left and he departed and he left behind him a group of people who preferred to follow the tradition of the Sufi *tariqa* that everyone knows. There is a master who everyone venerates, and then there is a group which has...no project...in a traditional framework...like that...more or less conforms to the Sharia. I tried, not to reform it, because it was not really constituted into a group, but to simply give it a direction which was more in line with my conception of Islam, that is to say a synthesis of my encounter with Sufism and my knowledge from books. So for two years after the death of my venerated master, a transformation took place in me. I meditated for a long time on the itinerary taken by my friends in the tariqa. And then I began to read the books of the Muslim Brothers...a little bit of everything...I took from this and that. Hassan al Banna, Sayyid Qutb—not a lot—a little of Mawdudi too.

Hassan al Banna, as you know, was a Sufi. In his books I found this special spiritual taste that is not found with the others. It is not so much my reading of Islamic or Islamist books which determined my action, nor the despair of ever seeing the tariqa become something other than a tariqa, but an internal logic which holds that Islam must lead to the *imane*, and the

15

imane must go to the summit of *ihsan*, and the summit of ihsan is the jihad. I had no personal ambition. I had this ambition which goes beyond limits, which transcends death, life and death: I wanted to please God.

In 1974, I decided to do something...to, how shall I put it...to go out from the ambience of the tariqa, and then...to go out...to begin my action. I did not leave Islamic logic. Sufi logic? It is true that there are Sufis...and I think they are the majority—who have fixed a ceiling, a limit, in telling themselves: we do not want to dialogue with rulers. If they have closed themselves within a certain logic, not all have. There are Sufi movements which have been born during important historical movements, the Libyan Senoussia for example, or Mahdism in Sudan, or Ahmed Chahid in India, to list only a few. There are thus Sufis who remained faithful to a logic which is Islamic...not Sufi. Sufism is something which came afterwards. It is something that is a retreat from the first thrust, people who have decided to remain in the terrain of the spiritual, while no longer paying attention to the world... I am not going to start criticizing them...It is not the right moment...

(Interview with the author, Rabat-Salé, October, 1987)

Nevertheless, the once paradoxical relation between Sufis and Islamists is not shielded from evolution. First, because the Sufi brotherhoods have themselves entered a phase of modernization and their cadres, notably in Sudan but also in Egypt, no longer belong to the most traditional or rural area of the social landscape, which once was their principal characteristic.(1) Then, because, especially in the areas (Sudan mainly but also Egypt, Jordan, etc) where the brotherhoods still benefit from a high level of popular support, most Islamist leaders are ready to work out compromises with their former enemies and have started restoring some relations with those rural elders, whom their urban elites had once made the mistake of ignoring. Nothing prevents Sufis from voting for an Islamist candidate in the future: in the final analysis there is absolutely no reason to assume that Sufism and Islamism are necessarily condemned to eternal enmity

Islamism, Piety, and Proselytizing: The Case of Jemaat at Tabligh

The Jemaat at Tabligh, an association which was founded in Pakistan and has crisscrossed the world for several decades trying to convince believers to practice more intensely, is often mentioned by the Islamists, themselves, as one

---

(1) On Egypt, see Pierre Jean Luizard, notably in "Le role des confréries soufis dans le système politique égyptien," *Maghreb Machrek* 131, January-March, 1991, page 26.

of the forerunners of their mobilization.(1) After reaching the limits of strictly religious proselytizing, a good number of them sought to extend themselves more effectively through political action, thus, strictly speaking, crossing the line into Islamist action. In 1970, the year the Tunisian movement was founded, Jemaat ad da'wa [another name for the Jemaat at Tabligh] began approaching the Islamists in Tunisia. "In the beginning they only included Pakistanis, but afterwards there were Tunisians who were trained at their school," explains Ahmida Enneifer today.

The Jemaat ad da'wa are people who travel around the Muslim world in order to preach a return to Islam, to religious practices, etc. It was their simplicity which influenced us, their life-style which seemed old-fashioned in Tunisia. There were two ways of thinking then. One, which could be called "apolitical," that of the Jemaat at da'wa, which taught how to announce the good news to people and asked them to return to the right path. And then there was another trend, much more intellectual, in the framework of the Association for the Preservation of the Koran, in which conferences were given, meetings organized, and a small laboratory created for scientific research. There were two absolutely different approaches: on the one hand, the side that was popular, populist, militant, etc., and on the other, intellectual research which touched a much smaller number of people. That is how we operated up until 1972 or 1973. They were years of groping. We didn't know exactly what to do. We were, nevertheless, certain of one thing. That was that we could not get by without a certain religious ideology. The religious side had become essential. On the other hand, the political side was still very vague."(2)

"For Morocco, it was exactly the same thing," says Yassine.

It was they, the Tablighi, and not the Muslim Brothers, who were the first. Before them there were a few rare missionaries from the Muslim Brothers, but they didn't produce any offspring. The people from the Jemaat at Tabligh talked to laborers and doctors in the same language. Without subterfuge and with no political or economic dimension. Those people represented the profound voice of Islam, which spoke to the heart before addressing the brain and intelligence. They preached by example before preaching with words. They had and continue to have the healthiest influence on the

(1) This observation, valid for a large number of leaders, does not contradict the validity of the distinction proposed notably by both G. Kepel and Olivier Roy, between an Islamization "from the top" (which would have founded the Islamist demarche) and an Islamization "from the bottom" (which would before the failure of the first strategy have "taken the relay" in the eighties). (Cf for instance *La Revanche de Dieu*, Le Seuil, 1991); but it does pose the problem of its chronology.
(2) Interviews with the author, Tunis Beni Khiar, August, 1985.

Islamic movements. Their non-political nature is a plus for them, since it allows them to travel freely and more easily. Even the West, which is, I believe, spiritually arid, found in the Tablighi what it missed... With this simplicity, this pure religiousness, they made conquests in Italy where people came up to them in the street to ask, "Who are you?" and discovered Islam for the first time in their life, and in Japan, in Canada or in South Africa, and even in South America. Their annual assemblies today gather millions of people. I believe there were four million last year in Bangladesh....(1)

Islamism and Traditionalism

In the Islamic world, there have always been political discourses linked to tradition. But not all have a direct connection to Islam, and even less to Islamism. The comportment of the traditionalists needs to be clearly distinguished, and most often disassociated, from the Islamist movement.

The desire to fix society to the memory one has of a father's or grandfather's society has always served as a reference for certain fringes of human society: "Everyone knows very well, that since schools have existed, there have been voices that have cried that the level of the students has dropped," Olivier Roy says ironically.(2) But it is not the brutal development of conservatism and this type of longing for the past that has nourished the sudden explosion of Islamism.

In contrast to Islamism, traditionalism "does not create political projects." Instead it leans "towards everything that is conservative." "Its nostalgia for the past is also more moralizing than influenced by a desire for social justice." Thus, this theme is a favorite of the Islamists.

The privileged relationship that traditionalism has with religion comes from the fact that "the stakes naturally influence customs: the veiling of women, education of girls, filial piety, a respect for hierarchies,"(3) all values close to the natural normative sphere of religion.

The comportment of the traditionalist more easily fits a rural environment than an urban one, and it is much more at home in social levels which have not opened up to Western culture than those who have already discovered it. Tradi-

---

(1) Interviews with the author, cited.

(2) Olivier Roy, *L'Afghanistan, Islam et Modernité Politique*, Le Seuil, 1985, and training seminar for professors of geography and history of l'Académie d'Aix Marseille, Aix-en-Provence, April 23, 1986.

(3) Olivier Roy, *L'Afghanistan*, op. cit.

tionalism is also more at ease among the relatively uneducated fringe (or where the education is primarily religious), rather than in science faculties, and among those who are at a mature age rather than the young. But all of this is clearly very far from the social and political criteria of the Islamists. The village elder, who is close to the religious establishment and knows little of Western culture (from which he refuses technology a priori), cannot be confused with the young science student who is more than able to deliver a criticism of Western values, with which he is familiar and from which he is able to appropriate certain dimensions. The traditionalist will reject television, afraid of the devastating modernism that it will bring; the Islamist calls for increasing the number of sets...once he has gained control of the broadcasts.

When political discourse is mixed in, it adds to the confusion. The Islamists' first demands were systematically dismissed by the media in the Maghreb as well as the West, as being the reactions of those longing for the past, which, from the evidence, they are clearly not.

When in 1975, Hind Chelbi, a young student of theology, publicly contradicted Habib Bourguiba's reformist vision of the role of women in Islam by draping herself in a *hijjab* (which in fact had no connection to local tradition) and refusing the paternal kiss of the old leader, the political class radically misunderstood the episode. Although the incident is remembered today as one of the first demonstrations of the Islamist movement aimed at the media, politicians at that time were only capable of seeing in the movement another example of a traditionalism "destined to disappear before the latest advances of modernity." The error was not only one of terminology.

Islamism and Fundamentalism

Contrary to traditionalism, fundamentalism plays an important role in the ideas and approach of the Islamists, since it provides a major reference for their doctrinal plan. The fundamentalist attitude nourishes itself on the idea that it is necessary to effect "an absolute return to the Word, as the only foundation for any critique and all renovation."(1) No doubt, it represents a return to the past, and, from that, often comes an abusive assimilation of traditionalism and fundamentalism. But this return is only justified in so far as it carries the "original purity." "The enemy is not modernity...but tradition," Roy emphasizes. "It

---

(1) Olivier Carré, *Mystique et Politique, Lecture Révolutionnaire du Coran by Sayyed Qutb*, Paris, Ed. Cerf Presses of the FNSP, 1984.

therefore concerns reform."(1) In sharp contrast to traditionalism, fundamentalism produces active militants and not passive followers. With a project for transformation that is far less diluted than simple conservatism, it can even prove to be revolutionary. "Perhaps it is necessary to say more precisely that regardless of the system of thought in question, the fact of preaching a "return to the sources" (...) has an influence which is nothing less than innovating," adds Tareq al Bishri.(2)

> This return permits the "lifting of immunity" for a certain number of beliefs, and of breaking down the foundations of the doctrinal constructions and inherited practices of the Middle Ages. It authorizes a direct contact, an effective interrelation between the original text and the reality of the moment. This return to the sources also permits the unraveling of all the quibbling over doctrine and the schools imposed during the Middle Ages on dogma, which considerably favors the unification of thought.
>
> Marxist thought also, when it tried to renew itself or a new school appeared, expressed itself through an invitation to "return to Marx" to make a "re-examination of Marxist thought," etc.

If the principle of return is admitted, it is still nevertheless necessary to determine with precision exactly to what one is returning. The goals vary, depending on the personality of the initiators (and of their reading of the texts) and they are also affected by the local political and cultural context. Colonel Kadhafi's fundamentalism is, thus, particularly radical since he sweeps away the tradition (sunna) of the Prophet, which he considers impractical and perverted by the body of critical interpretations, along with the whole of the *sharia*, which is founded on juridical interpretations of Koranic texts. He instead relies on the Koran alone. Kadhafi's approach has aroused the opposition of conservative and orthodox circles who dismiss the Libyan leader purely and simply as an apostate. His vigorous interpretation of verses dealing with the condition of women, on the other hand, has won Kadhafi sympathy in more modern urban circles, which have little inclination for a literal application of the Koran, which they feel has been cut off from its true meaning. In contrast, in societies like Afghanistan (which Roy describes as being still largely organized according to Muslim laws) and in the rural fringes of Arab society, fundamentalism that calls for a classic return to the traditions of the Prophet does not entail a significant break with current customs. By supporting practices which are already in use, it even seems

---

(1) *L'Afghanistan*, op. cit.

(2) Interview with the author, Cairo, April, 1991.

somewhat similar to traditionalism. But in more Westernized urban environments, which is to say in most Arab cities, the same message challenges the nationalist elites who have committed themselves to modernization, and it automatically takes on a connotation of defiance, bringing it closer to Islamism.

Islamism and the Ulema

In the landscape of the 1970s, the Islamist upsurge often reshaped the frontiers of action of institutional Islam's ulemas. In fact, a distinction naturally separates those actors of the religious establishment from the Islamist protesters who come from outside institutional Islam.(1)

Politics, which are at the heart of the Islamists' program, are largely outside the ulema's field of action. The ulema basically support the regimes, and their power of mobilization is therefore deprived of the "oppositional" dimension which characterizes the Islamist discourse. This is why they most often limit themselves to the moral sphere and do not count, at least explicitly, on political action to make the content of their doctrinal message prevail. And therein lies the difference between the ulema vision and that of the Islamists, whose program's core is this passage to politics, the conquest of power from above, this recognition of the State as a necessary step in the establishment of a program. Evoking the difference that he sees between an *'alim* (singular of ulema) and an Islamist, Abdessalam Yassine explains the limits of the ulema's action since 1979:(2)

> It is very interesting, what a few ulema are doing, but it is not enough. They are (no doubt) in the opposition, (but it is) an opposition based on principle, which is eternal. They only point with their finger at the things which they consider immoral. This is not sufficient. It is necessary to move to the next step, which is to have a program. (...) With a few rare exceptions, they never speak about economic problems, and rarely about politics, when what is essential is to realize that there exists a close relationship between immorality and the economic and political system... We demand power (...) that is permitted by democracy, that is what we want.

---

(1) According to the distinction which is at the center of the analysis of Gilles Kepel in *Le Prophète et Pharaon*, La Découverte, 1984; see also "The Ulemas, the Intelligentsia and the Islamists in Egypt," *Modes Populaires d'Action Politique*, Ceri, 1984.

(2) In an interview with Mohamed Tozy in "Croisement du champ politique et du champ religieux au Maroc," D.E.A., Aix-en-Provence, 1982, page 124.

In an explicit articulation of economic and political policy, and the will to proceed from a mere language of rejection to the elaboration of an alternative global, social, political and economic program, Yassine traces clearly here the frontier between the old discourse of the passive and moralizing clerics of official Islam (which in the cases of some had already been discredited by their immobility in the face of the colonial authorities), and the program of the Islamists, which is active and—even if it does not necessarily consider the conquest of the State to be a priority—explicitly integrates all the tools of modern politics.

Here and there, this one-time, very clear border between institutional Islam and Islamism tends nevertheless to attenuate and becomes more and more relative. First, because part of the Islamist trend does not concentrate their proselytizing on the political level and therefore may appear to keep closer to the "non oppositional" Islam of the religious establishment. But, also and maybe even more, because some of the ulema who are aware of their growing power in the society feel the danger of getting too close to the secularist discourse of the regimes, and thus too far from their more and more powerful Islamist challengers. In Egypt notably, they tend more frequently to seek some recognition from those who—although they do it from a different compartment of the political scene—use basically the same anti-secularist language as theirs and promote the same values. Therefore, their relations with the regimes slowly evolve to a point where it is difficult to know who really is mastering the political game.

Islamism and Salafism

In Arabic, the evocation of the "Salafiya" is polysemous. It may for instance refer to the generic notion of orthodoxy disengaged from any precise affiliation. "In Morocco there were two (other) Islamist currents," explains Abdelkrim Moutti, leader-in-exile of Morocco's Mouvement de la Jeunesse Islamique.

> There was first of all a group whose action consisted of an appeal in favor of Islamic customs through the wisdom of good words, without entering into political affairs. That was the Jemaat at Tabligh, which we respect and with whom we fully agree. After that there is a group which has consecrated itself to purifying Islamic references (*ibadate*) from the additions and contributions which have no connection to religion, and which has studied in an academic manner the dispositions of the *fiqh* without becoming in-

volved in political or doctrinal causes. That is the Salafiyya, with whom we have good relations.(1)

The notion of Salafiya is also occasionally used to recall the great reformist movement (Salafi) at the end of the 19th century, which today often appears as the historical antechamber of the Islamist mobilization. The perception that the Islamists have of the movement of Al Afghani (1839-1897); Mohamed Abduh (1849-1905), founder of the magazine *Al Manar* in Cairo; and Rachid Ridha (1865-1935), who started, in fixing its doctrine, the movement's transition towards the conceptions of the Muslim Brothers, is not at all uniform.

If, for Hassan Hanafi,(2) all that the Salafi's project missed was the militant apparatus that the Muslim brothers added to it, for Rached Ghannouchi, the Salafi are guilty of unacceptable concessions to the West. "During the early days of our relationship to the West," he writes,

> the duty of Muslim thinkers was to prove by any means that Islam was in conformity with modern civilization. It followed from that, that Mohamed Abduh, as Albert Hourani (3) writes, "conceded to Europe its pretension that it had discovered the laws of progress and social happiness, and went so far as to say that these laws were in conformity with Islam." The duty of intellectuals and politicians was then to put the Islamic world on the path of the West, to "march in the footsteps of the advanced nations."(4)

For Yassine, the contribution of the Salafi, which he refuses to identify with, must, nevertheless, be seen in the context of the period in which they acted:

---

(1) Interview given to Bernard Cohen for daily *Libération* (unpublished) and presented to the author. In this sense of the term, Salafiyya clearly opposes "political" Islam: "In Algeria, one can say that there are two major tendencies," explains an Algerian preacher who is close to Mustapha Bouyyali, the leader of the fugitive Mouvement Islamiste Algerien, dismantled by the police between 1985 and 1987 (cf infra), "the Salafists (fundamentalists) and the Ikhouanistes (literally brotherists, a reference to the Muslim Brothers)." Interview with the author, Marseille, October, 1986.

(2) Cf. infra.

(3) *Arabic Thought in the Liberal age, 1798-1939,* Oxford University Press, 1962.

(4) Rached Ghannouchi, "Nahnou wal-gharb," *Maqallat*, Dar al-Karouane, Paris, 1984.

To make a balance sheet means making a list of profits and losses. For me, there was no loss. There was only gain. In my opinion the best way to criticize people like the Salafiyya, like Ridha, etc. is to situate them and to see what their projects were, and what were the limits that prevented the evolution of their thought. In a large measure, I share the opinion of Ghannouchi with respect to a generation which found itself suddenly faced with a West that was superior, invading, violent, colonizing, and different from us. Great men like Abduh believed that they had to make concessions on articles of faith. For example, there were dissertations on the existence or non-existence of angels or genies. I don't know by what desire for conciliating, people who were otherwise quite sensible, pious and intelligent, pronounced judgments on these things which conform neither to the spirit nor the letter of Islam or sacred texts. Let's say that in the history of every people there are surprise movements, and that it is the surprise that tore judgments like that from those people. It's over, and overtaken. We are living in a different period. We have other means of understanding the West, which they did not have, and I remember very well a phrase from that venerable old man who was Abduh, when he said, "Europe is Islam without Islam. It's Islam without Muslims... You, you are Muslims without Islam." He understood that the values which he had discovered in the West, such as liberty and cleanliness—for he mentioned these details—the organization, the technology, the social peace, all that, that is Islam, and for us too. So, things have evolved since then. The West has become less moral, more technical. The central question remains: Will the West one day want to look and think about its interests over the long term, and not let itself be entangled in the turbulences of the world?! (1)

The Salafiya may also finally evoke the image of the followers of Wahabism. Founded by Mohamed Ibn Abdelwahab on the territory of the future Saudi Arabia, it is sometimes considered the ancestor of reform movements, of which it was one of the first expressions despite the fact that its heritage is not uniformly appreciated by the Islamist leaders. "The Wabhabis are not the Salafiyya," considers A. Benikrane.

They are a Salafiya among others. In the modern sense, the word can be misused, because there is Mohamed Abdel Wahab, but there is also the regime in Saudi Arabia which has one comportment or another, and there are the ulema, who also have their position. The Salafiyya, for us, is the way to look objectively at the texts of Islam. Abdel Wahab is only one of those who called for that.(2)

---

(1) Interview with the author, cited.

(2) Interview with the author, Rabat-Salé, October, 1987.

24

CHAPTER 2

ARABISM AND ISLAMISM, MUSLIM BROTHERS, KHOMEINISM: THE DIFFICULTY IN CHOOSING A NAME

Arabism and Islamism

From the intransigence of Gamal Abdel Nasser and Muamar Kadhafi, to the explicit rejection by the Islamists, the status of Arabism has evolved in Muslim countries in a way that has been difficult to grasp for outside observers, who occasionally still mistakenly assimilate the two.

In the beginning there was Arabness, or the quality of being Arab. It came from the lap of Islam, which first united the tribes and cities that had been dispersed and enabled them to carry out the imperial conquest of the Umma of the Golden Centuries. Arabness, nevertheless, distanced itself little by little from its religious references and in the process it became "Arabism" (*qawmia arabia*). Used at first in the mobilization against the Ottomans (which is to say against religious domination), it was then partially appropriated by the Christian Arab elites. Reactivated by the Arab left at the end of the first half of the century, Arabism was crystallized by the acceleration of the Palestinian question and the creation of the Jewish state. Flavored more and more by socialism and notably by the founders of the Baath, Arabism was then elevated to the rank of state discourse by Gamal Abdel Nasser, before being consecrated yet again by the accession to power of the Syrian Baathists. Egypt, in advance of most of its neighbors on the path to nationalism and basking in the glow of its successful confrontation with Western armies at Suez, occupied the front rank of the political scene during the period of Nasser. Arab nationalism, which served as Nasser's ideological emblem, was equally successful, at least in the Machreq (the east of the Arab world). In the Maghreb, its impact was less clear. Although it indisputably marked the popular consciousness, Arabism was welcomed and used with more reticence by the regimes. Because Arabness, "provincial, socially and culturally inferior, and therefore condemned to disdain"(1) evoked

---

(1) Given the absence of Christian minorities, Arabism has always had a more Islamic connotation in the Maghreb. "In the Maghreb," writes Hichem Djait, "and the more one moves towards the West, Arabism gives itself a dose of Islamness. In contrast, in the East, it has a tendency to liberate itself, although without losing its mystical dimension." It is that Arabism, "political ideology derived from Arabness is partly a tributary of Christianism and oriental Shiism,

25

an idea of bedouin ruralism, it had a status for a long time that was ambivalent.

It was the great movement of renaissance (the Nahda) which, according to the beautiful formula of Hichem Djait, "readjusting the vision of Arabness with a retrospective movement, extended its hand to the glory of the first Arabs."(1) In that way, Arabism won the hearts of the Maghreb, even if this success owed more to an awakening of historical conscience than to any adherence to a program for political unity, as it did in the Machreq. After 15 years of increasing power, Nasser's Arabism reached the limits of its political effectiveness in June, 1967, when the Rais' discourse suffered the blow of the brutal defeat of his armies. From that time on, the Islamist alternative, which Nasser fought against so violently, has challenged bit by bit the place of the fallen leader in the hearts of Arabs. In repossessing the mobilizing contents of Arabness, while redefining the hierarchy of a new relation between Arabness and the quality of being Islamic, the Islamist alternative attempts to reappropriate the capacity for mobilization of Nasserism and uses it in the service of a program in which secularism is gradually losing its place.

In this process, Kadhafi has played a transitional role. More Arabist than Nasser, but also more Muslim, he managed to reintroduce Islamic references in the discourse of unity. Rejected today by most of the Islamist movements, the spiritual son of the Rais appears, paradoxically, to be the first Arab leader to have begun to displace the center of gravity of Nasser's Arabism by reinforcing the Islamic component of his discourse.

The precocious reintroduction (from the beginning of the 1970s) in Libyan politico-juridical language of several categories of Islam even made him seem to be the first Islamist head of state. But admiring Nasser too much, Khadafi took the Egyptian leader's enemies as his own, and thus cut himself off from the Muslim Brothers. They had organized a plot against Nasser, which in Khadhafi's eyes amounted to attempted patricide. Beyond this initial reticence to the Egyptian Brothers, which he has expressed in a more nuanced fashion by distinguishing the educational role of Al Banna from the later political action of the movement, Kadhafi has also distanced himself from the movement's successors and from the majority of

and it takes its support, its birth, from the hostility to Turkish domination, which was a Muslim domination," in *La Personnalité et le Devenir Arabo-Musulman*, op. cit., page 27.

(1) Idem.

contemporary Islamist movements. Without worrying too much over the similarity of goals between many of their ideas and his, he persists today in seeing them only as enemies of the Arabism that occupies the heart of his universe even more than Islam. In 1973, he declared, "The movement of the Muslim Brothers is at the present time a natural extension of the Chuubiya Movements [a movement of Iranian origin, which contested the preeminence of the Arabs in the eighth century], full of bitterness against the Arab Umma."(1) It is not by chance, if the opponents of the Jamahiriyen regime—whatever their ideological affiliation, from modernists asking more of the economic infitah to soldiers concerned about expansionist adventurism, and all those disappointed by post-petroleum reality—are systematically dismissed as "Muslim Brothers."

> They are clergy who want to use religion to resolve problems that are political. They say that the solution to a political crisis can be found through religion. In 1928, Hassan al Banna created a *jemaa* that was educational and religious. But what is called the Muslim Brothers today is different. They are the valets of imperialism. They are the reactionary right, the enemies of progress, of socialism and of Arab unity. They collect all the hoodlums, liars and misfits, the hashish smokers, the drunkards, the cowards, and delinquents. That is the Muslim Brothers. And all of that has made them into the valets of America. Anyone who belonged to the party of the Muslim Brothers is ashamed to admit it today. It has become synonymous with something that is rotten, dirty, detested in all the Arab world and throughout the Muslim world. No, even if their intentions were good, I think that they ignored the reality of the Arab world.(2)

More fundamentally, Arab unification—which remains at the heart of Kadhafi's political program more than any illusory unification of all Muslims who are too diverse as a group—cannot be conceived on the basis of religion. It is there that the explicit limits of the Islamic element of his Arabism are to be found.

> There cannot be unity of the Arab world on a religious base. One can unite Arabs as Arabs who have a Muslim spirit. But if one tries to unite them as Muslims, ignoring that they are Arabs first, it will be a vain

---

(1) Cited by M. Majzoub in *La Libye et l'Unité Maghrébine*, DES de droit public, Aix-en-Provence, 1982, page 54.

(2) Interview with the author, Tripoli, Bab Azizia, December 6 and 10, 1987.

effort. It will fail one hundred percent. We are not living the century of religion. We are living in the century of space, of science.

And pressed on the possibility of maintaining relations with the Islamist movements today:

> That said, I think that with people like Ghannouchi or Habib Mokni, dialogue is better than prison or repression... if they are Arabs....If they belong to the non-Arab minorities, the problem is no longer a religious one. That becomes a question of defending a minority against a majority. An attempt to impose religion (1).

In the understanding of Kadhafi, the relation between Islam and Arabness is almost ethnic. It has led him to reaffirm more than once the assimilation that he would like to see operate between the two.

In August, 1980, on the eve of a visit to Lebanon, he recommended all Arabs to convert to Islam. "Christian Arabs," he pleaded,"have a Western spirit in an Arab body. It is aberrant to be Christian and Arab at the same time." Kadhafi is also the partisan of a categorization which in order to better emphasize its privileged relationship with Arabness, tends to nuance the universal vocation of Islam. There is, for him, a substantial difference between the Mohamedia, the religion of Mohamed, revealed and destined for the Arabs and which can really only be understood by them, and Islam of universal appeal, whose teaching can be appropriated by all the nations of the world. Contacts with the Black Muslim community in the U.S. may well have been at the origin of this unorthodox critical interpretation. The practices of the Black Muslims, according to some of his close aides, ended by somewhat disconcerting the Guide of Libya, and finally convinced him of the structural incompatibility between the religion of the bedouin tribe of Quraysh and the urban culture of the underproletariat of the black ghettos in the great American cities.

The massive integration of Islamic references in the Nasserian discourse (of which the proclaimed adoption of the Koran as "the law of society" is the most spectacular) is not usually perceived by the Islamists (even if the sincerity of the Libyan Guide is not always put into question) as anything more than a dangerous deviation, or a vulgar maneuver destined to stabilize the "Jamahiriyen" sinking ship. Even when bedecked with a strong Islamic coloration, the Arabism advocated by Nasser or the Baathists has long incited a negative reaction among most Islamists. And its expression by

---

(1) Idem.

Kadhafi, after having once aroused sympathy for the vigor of his cultural and political rejection of the West, and its support to Khomeini's Persian and Shiite Iran against Arab and Sunni Iraq, today provoke among the Islamists a similar reticence everywhere. From Rached Ghannouchi to Abdessalam Yassine, Nasser is accused of having led the community of believers astray in reducing the Umma to its Arabness alone, and thus masking the fundamental character which constitutes its Islamic nature. "It is Islam that gave force to the Arabs, and not the reverse," says Yassine.

It is suitable then, to separate the "good Islamic seed" from the "nationalist chaff," and to underline the legitimacy of such an enterprise, it is enough to recall that Arab nationalism was in many respects the creation of men who were living in Muslim lands, and therefore could not seek in religion a vocabulary for their political program. Weren't they, with Michel Aflaq (the founder of the Syrian Baath party) at the head, Christians?

"What makes us bend before challenges," says Yassine (1)

> is the weakness of the borrower's personality, which a certain lay Arabist culture has succeeded in imposing on our true personality, which is summed up in the word, Islam. At the head of States, (are) politically aware nationalists conscious of the necessity of Arab union. At the base, there are people who identify themselves with Islam above all else. The political and ideological Islam of the leaders...is nothing more than a demagogic concession to the convictions of the people. Deep down, the agents of Arabism sap the foundations of faith in presenting our Arabness as our only dimension and in trying to associate in people's minds greatness of soul with secularism. These agents are in the minority, Christian in origin, roughly seven percent of the Arab population, who first made contact with the West and managed to occupy a privileged spot in contemporary Arab culture. This minority, which is active and intelligent, moves towards an open divorce between Arabness and Islam. It supplies the ideologists and the militants initiating the pan-Arab movement. The few Arab chiefs who pretend to escape the ideology of the ancients and still possible associates of the Jahiliya, our Christian brothers, only propose quixotic ideologies and instant and frenetic programs.

More recently, a reevaluation of the Arabist project has begun to take place in the ranks of the Islamists. Its development is measured by the contacts with the secular national movements, which previously were for a long time considered impossible. One of the symbolic moments of this new

---

(1) *La Révolution à l'Heure de l'Islam*, Gignac-la-Nerthe, 1981, page 37.

process was a seminar organized in Cairo in September, 1989.(1) Representatives and opinion leaders among the Islamists and the nationalists showed, in a relatively new development, that from now on a questioning of their references would be accepted. They then sketched out the line along which their discourses were entering more naturally into ideological contact, thus removing the limits on an eventual political rapprochement.

Islamism would eventually admit the complementary value of the Arabist approach to the unification project in comparison to a solely religious reference (something which Rached Ghannouchi invited the participants to do), and thus recognize an Arabism which would accept for its part that it no longer considered its secularizing dimension to be an intrinsic component.

Regardless of the contents of its discourse of legitimization, the unification project maintains a mobilizing force. But this "oummist" internationalism nevertheless has limits which merely show the good health of this reprieved prisoner on death row, which is what the nation-state would become in the logic of a resurgence pure and simple of classical Islamic thought (to which nevertheless Islamism is not reducible).

If it is true that the review *Al Maarifa* of Tunisia's Islamic Group was banned for the first time in 1974 for having criticized Bourguiba's retreat from the union with Djerba, other regional events—and notably the affair of Gafsa in 1980(2)—have given the Islamists the occasion to show the limits of their adherence to indiscriminate regionalism, and the emergence in the register of their references of what must be called a form of national conscience.

Little by little, the framework, if not strictly doctrinal (for the "doctrine" Ghannouchi and Yassine insist, "is unique. It is intangible. It is contained in the Koran and the Sunna") but at least tactical and methodological, has increasingly taken into account the specific

---

(1) *Al -hiwar al -qawmi al -dini* (The nationalism and religion dialogue), Centre d'Etudes pour l'unité arabe), Beirut, December, 1989, 381 pages. The Popular Arab and Islamic Congress founded by Hassan Tourabi in Khartoum, the first session of which was held April 25, 1991, also emphasized this trend for reconciliation between secular Arabism and Islam. Cf. Hassan Tourabi, *The Popular Arabic and Islamic Congress,* Al-Insane, Paris, No. 5, July 1991. See also Ghannouchi, "Arabness and Islam" in *Maqalat,* Dar al-Karouane/Paris, 1984.

(2) A commando of Tunisian nationalists, trained in Libya, took control of the city of Gafsa, and tried to create an uprising of the people against the regime.

circumstances in different national settings. Although transnational "oummists" refused for a long time to acknowledge national differences, irreducible national characteristics and the state structures which they imply, have increasingly become reference points for the Islamists. This evolution balances the supranational and anti-state image which is sometimes rigidly coupled to the Islamist movement. "Thus one sees," writes Olivier Carré, "Islamic radicalism, once it is sure of its roots, will enter modern politics, even if it doesn't say so explicitly. The secular State is being naturalized Islamic."(1) It is this process which illustrates beyond the ritual appeals to dogma the interpretation of A. Yassine on the place of the State in the Arab and Muslim world today.

ABDESSALAM YASSINE: ISLAM, ARABNESS, THE STATE (2)

F.B. Is it true that the process of re-Islamisation leads inescapably to a questioning of the borders of national-states? Is is written in the dogma?

Yes. In the dogma, the Umma can only be one.

F.B. In the larger sense?

Yes, the Umma in the larger sense. Indonesia, included. But the national fact, the national State, is the most rebellious "concretization," and the one which will be the most difficult to dilute. You would be completely ignorant of God's law as revealed in the Koran, and revealed in the cosmos, if you wanted to annihilate these frontiers, to wipe them out from one day to the next. In re-Islamizing themselves, the Muslim states will come little by little in the medium and long term to destroy first of all the frontiers which exist in the way they speak and feel. It is a question of method, and also of education. It is not a question of doctrine, it is one of method. Do I consider myself an Arab? Certainly. Even though I have Berber ancestry, I am Arab. I speak Arabic, and I am an Arab in heart, soul and language. Those who are not Arabs feel the importance and the essence of Arabs, the Arabic language, and the quality of being Arab. God said in the Koran that God, alone, knows for what end and for what reason he revealed his law there and not elsewhere. So the entire Umma surrounds the Arabs with a respect that they have inherited from their ancestors, because it was they who propagated the faith. In contrast, Arab intellectuals, Arab nationalists, make Islam into an outgrowth of Arabism. We are Arabs. We have Islam as one of our attributes among others... I believe that that is an attitude that is nothing less than satanic. It is an attitude which is blind to the light of Islam. It is also blind to the simple study of history: the Arabs were peoples, scattered tribes who tore themselves apart in wars, guerrilla

(1) *Radicalismes Islamiques*, vol. 1, page 17.

(2) Interview with the author, Rabat-Salé, October, 1987.

wars and interminable raids. And it is Islam which suddenly revealed... them to the world as a "nation"—I put "nation" in quotation marks—which was carrying an eternal message. What gave value to the Arabs was Islam, and not the reverse. It is said in the Koran: "They impress on thee as a favor that they have embraced Islam. Say, 'Count not your Islam as a favor upon me: Nay, God has conferred a favor upon you, that He has guided you to the faith, if ye be true and sincere'."(1)

This declaration was addressed to the bedouins, who were not very converted to Islam, and who had just told the Prophet, "It is we who have defended you, it is we who have taken you in, etc." The Koran addressed them, saying: "It is the good work of God who saved you from the Jahiliya, to have welcomed you into the fold of Islam. It is not for you to presume to have achieved that."(2) Now, this nationalism, which is, I believe, the *nec plus ultra*, as you say, of Western evolution, of the unsurpassable horizon, well, even Marxist-Leninism has retreated from it. The Communists have changed their opinions concerning nationalism, with Italian Eurocommunism, Communism in France, etc. This nationalism is an invention. The Nation-State is a Western invention. It is a Western fixation which was imposed on us, and which we inherited from colonialism.

Yes, certainly we had instances of particularisms before colonialism. They were inherited from our history. Islam is descended from Saudi Arabia, where there were very sharp particularisms. To belong to a tribe was something that was more narrow, more down to earth, more vital, than belonging to a nation-state. Islam did not try to destroy these tribal or family ties. On the contrary, it used them as the underpinnings to support a new structure. The particularisms of race, language and religion are facts which are spread throughout the entire world. In the history of humanity, all the misfortune and good fortune that humanity has known are due to this tribal or racial collective. All the wars, all the deviations, all the civilizations, too. It is not in vain that one now talks of European civilization, because there is a race that is European, and languages that are related to one another. There is something in common, isn't there, that has supported this civilization. There is also an Arab civilization which has assimilated other civilizations. There is a Turkish civilization, a Chinese, etc. So particularisms are a common fact in history. Islam does not fight against them. It does not fight against particularities. It wants these particularisms to support that which is more noble. To give you a point of reference, the nation-states after the Second World War gathered in San Francisco to build something that was more noble. It was a higher inspiration. They wanted to surpass this nationalism from which they had suffered a great deal. You can ask me: "Was this nation-state imposed by colonialism, or not?" I will tell you that on this substrata, on these

---

(1) The Koran, Sura 49, verse 17, translation by Yusuf Ali.

(2) Idem.

particularisms, which colonialism found itself facing, it imposed nation-states which were badly marked out and ill-defined. For example, the Ottoman Empire, in Muslim countries under the authority of Istanbul, there were no rigid borders. These particularisms were a bit diluted in this Islamic fraternity. Even Morocco, which did not belong to the Ottoman Empire and which had a character that was quite distinct throughout Islam, did not feel completely apart or different from the Muslim world. Frontiers were open. Free passage was permitted. There was no customs. The fraternity was lived. The gathering in Mecca united everyone, all these brothers, to renew the pact of community.

You find that I am idealistic. Yes, certainly. But on the whole, despite these particularities and in spite of the fratricidal wars which have always existed in Islam, despite these tribal turbulences, the continual wars in and outside of Morocco, in spite of all that, people did not feel that they belonged to a specific place. If you had asked a Moroccan 100 years ago if he were Moroccan, he would have been astonished. He would have replied: "I am a Muslim. I am a Jew" or something else. This nationalist identity did not find a foothold with us or attitudes ready to welcome it. But it gained all its force, it produced negative effects after colonialism. Now, to reopen these frontiers, it is not in twenty years, in fifty years or even in a near future that we will be able to do it. But is it desirable, is it something to hope for, that this be ordained by the world of God? Yes. How to do it? Gradually. By what means? Education. When? When God will permit.

F.B. But for the moment, the question of state is not a priority?

No, no, we can live for another century within frontiers. I say a century in taking a large view. I do not see how it is possible to step over these borders in passing a law as though they did not exist. Because they will always exist, and in spirits and souls, in practice and habits, etc. I absolutely do not share these Kadhafiesque whims which try to achieve unity to the left and right. These are really laughable vacillations.

The demand to join the European Economic Community?... The King is trying to recall the role that Morocco has always played. The Common Market is the number one outlet for Morocco. Our exports might as well be tossed into the sea if we do not have access to the Common Market. The King, in his role as head of the family, does what he can... It is not a question to be examined from an Islamic point of view. It is a circumstantial necessity, as you say. It is a commercial transaction which obviously has political implications, but it won't be like drinking an ocean for us. We've already filled up on European culture and European nationalism. Commercial contact with the European Community will add nothing to our misfortunes.

Islamism and the Muslim Brothers

"The Islamic resurgence is often attributed to the Muslim Brothers, commonly known as the 'Khoangi'," notes Michel Camau in reference to the situation in Tunisia.(1)

> That is an over simplification. It gives the impression of an organization that is highly structured, when what one really finds is less a party or sect than a movement of ideas which takes on multiple forms.

The assimilation of Islamism into the single movement of the Muslim Brothers (which is also current in Arab opinion) is indisputably false. Nevertheless, it is not difficult to understand when one recalls the origins of the movement. It was in Egypt that the Islamist spark was ignited. Egypt marked a turning point when followers of the movement that was to become the Muslim Brothers began to demand a return to the orthodoxy of classical Islam as a solution to the problems of the century. Hassan Al Banna, and later Sayyed Qutb, provided the missing political ambitions and organizational logistics to a reform movement which up until then had lacked a political structure. Regardless of whether they placed the conquest of the power of the state at the top of their list of objectives or simply stopped considering politics as a field outside their preoccupations, the movement was born. "We are brothers in Islam, we are Muslim Brothers."(2)

The name earned its place in history, but the Islamist movement has largely overflowed the original doctrine and objectives of its founders. The Muslim Brothers were the first to want to take power and to bring logistical organization to the reformist project. "The novelty of Hassan al Banna," underscores Hassan Hannafi,

> is that he dedicated an organization to carrying out the project of Al Afghani whose movement was in the process of dying out. It re-launched the spirit of reform. And that is why it was a great success. Hassan al Banna realized to what point our (reform) project had begun to decline. As if it wasn't enough to see our entire culture dying out. Even our latest hope, reform, had also started to die. He came to

---

(1) "Chronique Politique Tunisie 1978," *Annuaire de l'Afrique du Nord*, op. cit. 1979.

(2) Olivier Carré et Gérard Michaux, *Les Frères Musulmans,* Paris, Gallimard/Julliard, 1983 (Archives).

complete the project of Al Afghani. Al Afghani also wanted to mobilize the masses and to found an Islamic party capable of carrying out the project. To say the truth, the ideas of Hassan al Banna probably may not amount to much: an Islam that is simple and clear... everyone knows that. The Koran, the Hadiths, etc... He was very open to Arabism, to nationalism, etc... His ideas were very clear, very pure and there was no ideological complexity, but... as an organizing power.. he was something else.(1)

Hassan al Banna, Sayyed Qutb and their successors exercised such a doctrinal domination over the Maghreb that it is not astonishing that their disciples have been able to preserve the name chosen by the founding fathers to this day. The principals, Ghannouchi, Mourou, Enneifer, Moutii the Moroccan, etc.—all have at one time or another established contacts with the "Brothers," and the links are openly admitted by the "descendants" themselves in Tunisia, Morocco or elsewhere. "The second element which strongly influenced Tunisia," emphasizes Enneifer,

> was the liberation by Sadat of the Muslim Brothers which Nasser had imprisoned. It was then that the production of books by the Brothers started up again. Actually, even before then the phenomenon of reading books coming from Egypt was important. We were in a period of groping. The sheikhs of the Zitouna were disappearing more and more. Finally, we no longer had the Ulema. Zitouna University was completely closed, and as far as religious sciences went, we no longer had any references. That explains the importance which the production by the Muslim Brothers took on for us. And it was precisely this current which pushed us to engage more directly in political action as well as in a certain "underground" formation. It was then that we began to form secret groups to train them, a sort of political training, even if there was always a spiritual dimension which distinguished them. Above all else, we read everything that had to do with forming a brotherhood, how the Muslim Brothers in Egypt formed their first cells, etc.(2)

A certain amount of confusion resulted from the fact that it was only in the later evolution of these movements, especially the ones in the Maghreb, that an internal diversification developed on the one hand and a partial doctrinal "autonomization" on the other. Today, the existence of both elements justifies putting an end to confusion over terminology. Very early

---

(1) Interview with the author, Cairo-Héliopolis, January, 1988.

(2) Interview with the author, cited.

on, in fact, national characteristics were taken into account. As Enneifer puts it,

> That said, certainly there were changes... We couldn't do exactly the same thing. We were living in a country that was completely different from Egypt. (...) We had different opportunities for working than the Egyptians. At that period, the government was not concerned with what was happening in the mosques...and it didn't care what was going on in the high schools. We could easily hold weekly conferences, or hold meetings and distribute literature to students during recreational periods in the high schools.(1)

And in fact, the movement of the Muslim Brothers as it was in Egypt, is no longer representative of the totality, or even the majority of the movements in existence today as far as organization, tactics and doctrine are concerned. In Egypt, itself, its former monopoly is contested by the non-legalistic movement of the Jemaat Islamiyya and by the reformist Labour Party of Ibrahim Choukri and Adel Hussein. Elsewhere, the degree of autonomy with respect to the Egyptian founding fathers has even become one of the criteria for telling the differences between the movements themselves. The original relationship to the Muslim Brothers, however, remains essential to the understanding of the Islamist movement today.

Islamism and Khomeinism

Although the adaptation is not perfect, Khomeinism manages to a large degree to match the contours of modern Islamism. For Khomeinism more than anything else is "Islamism which has succeeded." Just as Libya managed to do for Arabism after Nasser's Egypt, the Iran of Khomeini has become in effect (with the exception of Pakistan) the first state to have translated an Islamist program into government practice and applied concepts that had previously been consigned to speeches of opposition groups . It is seen as the doctrine which proved sufficiently fertile to win the fruits of a stunning political victory over a regime that had been presented as one of the most powerful in the region. At the height of its victory, Khomeinism was, nevertheless, certainly not solely responsible for the creation of the Islamist movement, which is by definition polycentric. Today, none of the successors of the Imam from Qum could be considered to be the conductor of an Islamic orchestra responding to his solicitations.

---

(1) Idem.

Khomeinism and its theoretician, on the other hand, have exercised and continue to exercise today an indisputable attraction for all the movements. Do certain of them receive more than moral support from Teheran? Since 1979, the Tunisians, Rached Ghannouchi and Habib Mokni, Abdelkrim Mouttii the Moroccan, and the representatives of the quasi-totality of the movements in the Maghreb have indeed all made visits to Teheran. It is very possible that the Iranian embassies in the Maghreb and Europe have played some of the activist role generally attributed to them, and possibly more. But the greatest of Khomeini's gifts to the Islamist movement was his own victory over the Shah. To the movements that were still trying to come to grips with the pain of birth, the Iranian victory provided inestimable support to both their credibility and to their social base. And the real question is not over whether a few Iranian Embassy personnel distributed promises and subsidies here and there: nowhere would this material aid, which the Iranians were suspected of having provided to the movements have been sufficient to give birth to a phenomenon so deeply anchored in the roots of the societies.

The identification of Islamism with the Iranian experience has other limits, which stem directly from the inadaptability of the Khomeini's doctrine and strategy to the context of the Arab world in general, and that of the Maghreb in particular. The demarcation line stems first from the environment in which Khomeinism developed, which is to say Shiism.(1) No equivalent exists with the Sunnis, who form the majority throughout most of the Arab world. The difference, for Arabists like Bertrand Badie, is a striking one. As Badie puts it, "The institutional, official and bureaucratic character of the Iranian religious movement, which rises from a certain traditional legitimacy and hence from a certain point of view, makes it difficult to classify it, even if certain aspects of its action stem from an 'Islamist' logic."(2)

But the differences do not stop there. The first outgrowth of the Islamist ideology, the Iranian regime, and with it the doctrine of its Imam also proved to be the first to suffer the effects of the ever-universal erosion

---

(1) The religion of the partisans of Ali is notably distinguished from that of the Sunnis by the existence of a large clergy which has a long tradition of contesting state power. The tradition has been nurtured by the theory of the hidden Imam (since the death of the eleventh successor of Ali).

(2) Bertrand Badie, *Les Deux Etats: Pouvoir et Société en Occident et en Terre d'Islam,* Paris, Fayard, 1987 (and correspondence with the author).

37

of power. Confronted with the demands of government action, the speech of Khomeini's followers lost its capacity to provide a convincing myth, which up until then had always provided a large part of its mobilizing force. Under pressure of circumstances, the new government in Teheran found itself forced to make choices which could not earn it the unconditional approval of all the elements of Islamist "society," especially in the Maghreb. One example among others, the Party of Islamic Liberation, which calls for the return of the Caliphate abolished by Ataturk in 1924, broke off its relations with Iran after its program for an Islamic constitution was rejected in favor of an alternative proposition deemed too marked by Western influences. For reasons that were sometimes tactical but often also motivated by deep convictions, the leaders of the groups in the Maghreb distanced themselves from certain positions taken by Khomeini, underlining not only the importance of the rupture brought on by Khomeini but also the fact that in their opinion he was no political model. If, on the whole, support remains the rule, Arab Islamists often emphasize the "specificity" of Shia Islam, which they might deny under other circumstances, to expalin certain actions of Khomeini's movement.

Islamism and Integrism (Literalism)

"Integrism" is the term most often used to refer to the Islamists in the media today, and it is hard not to notice that with the possible exception of "fanaticism," it is the name which has the most negative connotation. Right or wrong, it parallels the anxiety that the movement arouses in Western public opinion. For precisely this reason, it is rejected by the Islamists themselves. Scrupulousness has led some observers of the movement to gradually search for a more precise description. The reason is not so much due to the fact (which is often written) that the term "integrism" refers to an internal phenomenon in the Christian religion, but more because its origins attach it to a precise definition which fails to accurately capture the Islamist movement in its current diversity and even less in its essence. Initially, the term was linked not so much to a problem of interpretation of doctrine, but rather to a practical problem: "a refusal to adapt by the church and believers in liturgical, pastoral and social matters."(1) But the term has now begun a second career under a banner that is quite different. Increasingly, it serves to designate the Integrists whose reading of the sacred

---

(1) Olivier Carré, *Mystique et Politique*, page 35.

texts is the most intransigent, the most literal and the most rigid, and as such the most reticent to the innovating demands which constitute the Islamic *ijtihad* (the effort at interpretation). Since then, the term has filled a useful place in the lexicon of terms currently in use. Certainly, there are Islamists who are Integrists, but the term should not be used in a generic sense. Not just because it was intended for a different religion, but also because it only conveys one aspect of the Islamist movement—one which tends to reflect a minority point of view. "Islamism covers the whole body of thought which seeks to invest society with Islam, or rather with an interpretation of Islam, which may be integrist, but can also be traditional-ist, reform minded, or even revolutionary," says Habib Boulares. "The rejection of the term 'integrist' is consequently not just linguistic snobbery."(1)

Islamism and Extremism

After "integrism," the West often resorts to the use of "extremism" or its corollary, "terrorism," to evoke the Islamists, and occasionally Islam in its entirety. "Warriors of Allah" or the "Crazies of God," the metaphors used by the press, are not always divorced from reality. From Rome Airport to the terrorist attack against Goldenberg's Restaurant in the Rue des Rosiers in Paris, the very Catholic Irish Revolutionary Army, the Zionist militants of British-occupied Palestine in the 1940's, or the "resistence" of Nazi-occupied France, terrorism exists. It seems likely that blind violence might make an appearance on the international scene, driven by an Islamist rhetoric seeking its legitimacy in the most radical parts of the complex notion of jihad.(2) The resort to violence in this case is only a question of strategy. For the most part, the vast majority of tendencies in North Africa have, nevertheless, long rejected violence as an institutionalized method of operation.

There are exceptions. The statutes of the Libyan association, the Da'oua Islamiyya, which is used for proselytizing by Colonel Muamar Kadhafi, were modified in 1981. The word "pacific," which qualified and consequently limited the methods to be used by the association for "spreading Islam

---

(1) Interview in *Grand Maghreb,* No. 30, April 30, 1984.

(2) Cf. notably Ahmed Alami in "'Jihad' et Mujahada en Islam" in *Les Cahiers de l'Orient,* No. 5, March, 1987, page 223, and especially Jean-Paul Charnay: *L'islam et la guerre,* Paris, Fayard, 1986.

throughout the world by any means," was eliminated. And there is no question that at the crossroads of the Muslim diaspora, the labyrinths produced by the secret polices and other intelligence services have created individuals who are ready to be convinced that it is necessary to kill in the name of Islam.

The insidious interchange of words and the misleading choice of photographs,(1) is no less inconvenient in homogenizing a phenomenon which ought not to be reduced to the extremist fringes of its expression. Journalistic and academic terminology often conceals more than it reveals. When an Algerian family father praying on a sidewalk in Marseilles because he can't find a mosque is given the same label as a terrorist bomber in Paris or the radical fringe of the Hizbollah in Lebanon, the confusion is complete. There is no question that the intermingling of Muslim religion and political mobilization sometimes expresses itself in violence. There is no question that there have been (as in the case of Teheran) and will very likely be in the future, regimes which will try to use Islam to validate authoritarianism, just as their predecessors did with the ideology of nationalism. But it is dangerous to take the use of a religious vocabulary as a corollary for the emergence of new totalitarian regimes. Just so, it is extremely difficult to demonstrate that political violence in Arab countries is solely linked to Islamist movements. In fact between Christians, Muslims, opposition movements, governments, left and right, violence has been the sole element that has been equally shared. Doubtlessly, the totalizing pretensions of monotheistic religions carry a potential for totalitarianism that is all the stronger in Islam since, at least in principle, it refutes the barriers of secularization. But from the Catholic inquisition to the gulags of Stalin, the history of the world demonstrates the fact that the social conditions under which dogmas of all types are appropriated has always determined the level of political violence to a greater degree than their intrinsic contents. The first lesson of the Gulf crisis was to demonstrate the fragility of the categories forged by the West to establish a hierarchy for political solidarity

---

(1) Cf. notably Jean-François Clément, "Analyse comparative des images médiatiques du terrorisme d'origine proche-orientale dans la presse française." Communication at the colloquium "L'Islam contre le Terrorisme," Paris, Bibliothèque Nationale, March 25, 1988, 172 pages. On the representation of Islam in France, Paris, cf. notably Sadoq Sellam, *L'Islam et les Musulmans en France,* Paris, Tougui, 1987, 253 pages. Bruno Etienne, *La France et l'Islam,* Hachette, 1990; *L'Islam en France,* CNRS, 1991; Gilles Kepel, *Les Banlieux de l'Islam,* Le Seuil, 1990.

in Arab and Muslim countries. The violence of the aggression perpetrated by the "good secular Iraqi ally" of the 1980s has not much to do with Islamic terminology.

A first lesson becomes apparent to a critical reader studying the current political situation in the Arab world: the violence labeled "religious" is increasingly used to conceal that of regimes trying desperately to avoid the verdict of elections and prefering therefore to "satanize" their opponents and to push them towards violence by shutting them out of the legitimate political arena.

Islamism or Islamisms?

The innumerable modalities of behavior and of social and political attitudes linked to religion in Islamic countries justify a certain prudence on the part of anyone attempting to make an inventory. Once the differences in origin and the hierarchy of relationships have been shown and the diversity of different national situations taken into account, nothing prevents arriving at a conclusion that the attempts which have been underway for a half century to bridge the gap that separates society from the State by reintroducing Islam, have in fact taken on forms that are increasingly coherent and more and more homogeneous. It is thus possible to make a first attempt at a systematic outline, and to propose therefore to define Islamism as *the recourse to the vocabulary of Islam, used in the post-colonial period to express within the state, or more often against it, an alternative political program that uses the heritage of the West as a foil, but allows nevertheless the reappropriation of its principal references.* Despite the diversity of their institutional expression, despite their different political situations (clandestine or legal, opposing or as in the case of Iran acting within the state), despite the diversity of their means of action (proselityzing in the mosques, social or political activism or even violence, etc.) and that of their social base, the Islamist movements as a whole can well be attached to the same historical matrix.

It is this matrix that we will now try to demonstrate. Later, the specific attributes (national or otherwise) will be added to the analysis.

CHAPTER 3

FROM NATIONALISM TO ISLAMISM

I think that on the whole it is a healthy phenomenon. It is simply nature which has a horror of vacuums. The Muslim peoples have for the most part been colonized. They were cut off from their cultural roots and it is natural that after winning independence, they would return to those roots. They are searching for the identity national independence did not manage to give them. (Rachid Benaïssa) (1)

In order to make a simple parallel to geology, one may look at North Africa's culture and civilization as being composed of three strata. First, there is the Berber base, named after the first inhabitants of the region;(2) Second is the Arab-Muslim stratum, imposed at the beginning of the seventh Century A.D. (Islamization) and lasting until the end of the eleventh century (linguistic and ethnic Arabization); and, finally, the Western or European stratum imposed during the pre-colonial and colonial period (1830–1962 in Algeria, 1911–1956 in Morocco, etc...). While parts of the Berber foundation have survived ethnically and linguistically, the layer of Christianity has been completely eliminated by its Eastern competitor. The church in North Africa, which produced one of the greatest Christian thinkers in Saint Augustine, vanished before Islam. That is in contrast to the Coptic and other Christian churches which resisted massive Arab-Muslim advances in the eastern Arab world.(3)

These layers have never ceased to "shift" in relation to one another. After its establishment, the position of the Western stratum was constantly challenged by the Arab-Islamic stratum. At the same time the Berber cultural demands, which have developed over the last few years (and were, for instance, partly responsible for the riots at Tizi Ouzou in the spring of 1980), have also challenged the preeminence of the Arabic layer.

---

(1) Interview with the author, cited.

(2) Although it is ethnically Berber, this stratum has nevertheless been shaped by diverse outside influences. The most notable was the early presence of the Carthaginians, then the Romans and finally the partial Christianization which followed.

(3) See notably Christian Decobert, *Le Mendiant et le Combattant*, Le Seuil, 1991.

But, the most dominant movement has unquestionably been the resurgence of the Arab-Muslim stratum at the expense of the most recent Western influences. It would be dangerous to push the geological metaphor too far,(1) but it is nevertheless possible to see in it an essential element of the historical matrix of Islamism. One might make the objection here that the resurgence of the Arab-Muslim base dates from the middle of the twentieth century, with the vast withdrawal of the West and the wave of decolonialization which characterized it. Why then did it take until the end of the 1970s for this "resurgence of Islam" and the "rise of fundamentalism" to capture the attention of the media? In fact, colonialism, which is often hastily considered to belong exclusively to the past, did have something to do with producing these movements. It is indeed necessary to contextualize these phenomena not only in the "contradictions linked to post-independence's rapid socio-economic development" but in the dialectical framework of colonialization/decolonialization. To see the internal logic of this phase, in which different expressions of Western domination are called into question, it is useful in fact to compare it to the period during which Western domination was instituted.

From Military Domination to Dualism

The Western presence was preceded, notably in Tunisia and Morocco, by an earlier economic penetration that was itself the consequence of a growing financial dependence. It was in the transition to the military phase that this penetration took on the dimension of domination. Actually, military action represented only one stage in foreign domination. The traces that the military left were paradoxically less important than those of other presences and forms of domination, made possible by the military presence.

Economic domination, which took various forms (appropriation of lands or simple commercial control) but whose effects were constant, took on an architecture which was no longer that of military camps but of agri-

---

(1) "The (...) distinction between Arabs and Berbers," writes Michel Camau, (...) "corresponds effectively, from the first centuries of the Conquest of Ifriqiya, to an opposition between the new allogenic elements (Arabs) and the earlier populations (Berbers). Nevertheless it offers a representation of the past that is overly simplified and carries only a mythic signification as far as the modern period is concerned." *La Tunisie,* PUF, 1988 (Que sais je?) page 19. But it is precisely this "mythical identification" whose effectiveness is underlined by Laraoui (*Islam and Modernité,* La Découverte, 1987, page 157) that is in question here.

cultural fields (increasingly devoted to export crops) and of roads, ports, and railways implanted to facilitate the draining of mineral and agricultural riches. This opened the well-known cycle, in which the far reaches of the colonial empires were made poorer while the metropolitan centers became richer. Beyond a certain threshold (largely attained in the case of Algeria), economic domination meant social destruction. When the dominant economic logic of a society is disturbed, the social balance is also affected. When the combined effects of laws concerning agricultural land previously held collectively are changed to favor appropriation by individuals, and when, during periods of scarcity, impoverished tribes who have been forced to sell their land are stripped of their economic base, more is accomplished than simply taking a means of livelihood away from its initial owners. The net effect is the destruction of the social substratum of an entire system of production.

It was only when the economic and social structures were profoundly damaged and the group's capacity to resist seriously weakened, that foreign penetration gradually took over the cultural sphere and extended its ability to dominate completely. In the Maghreb the process did not directly affect the practice of religion: attempts to Christianize or re-Christianize the area had little impact, a fact born out by the negligible number of Maghreb Christians practicing today. But even if no wave of conversions materialized and no other religion succeeded in substituting itself for Islam, the religious field of influence narrowed considerably: the values and models—institutional or otherwise—which were linked to it, retreated on all fronts before Western competition. "The inherited order," to use Gilles Kepel's formulation,(1) retreated brutally before the "translated order" or more precisely the "foreign order," since in contrast to the Machreq the dominant values were no longer conveyed by the Arabic language, and French became indispensable to natives wishing to accede to or simply to maintain themselves in the "modern" sectors of their own society.

From Dualism to Domination

It is precisely the domination of one system by another that progressively took over the political, cultural and economic landscape of the colonialized societies, barely masked by the illusion of dualism which long

---

(1) Gilles Kepel, *The Prophet and Pharaon,* cited.

prevailed in Tunisia and Morocco under the double institutions of the protectorate.

"With the establishment of the protectorate," writes Aziz Krichen, concerning Tunisia,

> begins what one may call the era of dualism. Dualism in the economy with the traditional sectors and modern sectors; dualism in the demographic distribution split between French colonists and indigenous populations; dualism of the State with the two-headed structure of the Palace of the Bey and the Residence Generale; dualism of urban spaces with the contrast between the medina and the European-style city; dualism of the military; dualism of the administration, justice, education, religion, press, artistic and sports activities, etc... Even foolishness was affected by this phenomenon with psychiatrists on one side and sorcerers and witch doctors on the other... Nevertheless, it is not a simple juxtaposition on a single territory of two different worlds, each obeying its own logic and maintaining only limited, circumscribed contacts with the other. There were certainly two worlds, two dissimilar universes, but at the same time they were intimately linked, and the principle of their unification was the total subordination of the Tunisian element to the French element.(1)

Through the laws of the colonizer first, and then more efficiently through the laws of their own elites, the societies of the Maghreb saw in this third stage of their meeting/confrontation with Europe, the values of their fathers, their beliefs, their models, their rites, sink one after another into the bottomless chasms of "archaisms" and other "obstacles to progress." Architecture or law, habitats or music, clothes or food, hardly anything escaped the imprint of this "progress" coming from the West. Ways of thinking, value systems, political vocabulary and Western cultural codes were imported bit by bit by the acculturated elites as much as they were imposed. Even if certain dimensions of the process (the linguistic impact, for example) are easier to observe and quantify, the process was slow and the effects less immediately perceptible than those that touched the economy and the military; but their impact was to be felt far longer.

---

(1) Aziz Krichen, "Les problèmes de la langue et de l'intelligentsia" in *La Tunisie au Présent: une modernité au-dessus de tout soupçon*, Michel Camau, (dir), Paris, CNRS Presses, 1987. See also Henry, Jean-Robert, (dir) *Nouveaux enjeux culturels au Maghreb*, Cresm CNRS, Paris, 1986.

From Political Ruptures to a Rereading of the Cultural Legacy

The internal architecture of the period after independence followed a pattern which to a certain extent may look similar to the one followed during the institution of this domination. There was a succession of reactions linked in priority first to the political/military dimension, then to the economy and finally to the culture. Following the stages of European disengagement (direct military occupation up until the moment of "political independence," partial control over economic wealth and persisting linguistic and cultural influence afterwards), nationalism expressed itself in verbal terminology (semantic registers) whose evolution schematically followed the three stages of successive domination. The "nationalism" of the first generation served to express the will of populations, regrouped in more or less completed "nations," who wanted to obtain or recuperate their legal identity on the international scene. The movement was directed first against the dying Ottoman Empire and then against the Western powers (France, Great Britain, essentially, and against Italy in Libya).

Once they had acquired "independence," often limited by the foreign powers holding on to a few military bases (Bizerte in Tunisia, Mers Al Kebir in Algeria, Wheelus Field in Libya, the Canal Zone in Egypt, etc...), there was still the problem of mastering economic resources. In the 1950s and 1960s this was carried out through "nationalizations" of oil fields, agricultural lands (notably in the Maghreb) and diverse infrastructures (the Suez Canal in Egypt). Marxist ideology served in the battle against the interests of the former colonial powers in the beginning, and later against the USA, whose interests in the region soon became vital. With "its conception of the modern world, its universalist sociology offering the same hope to all people, its explanation of the imperialist phenomenon, its practical approach to modernization and development and its recipes for organization, strategy and tactics" etc.,(1) Marxism brought some prestigious additions to the panoply of nationalism. Arab regimes drew a good portion of their legitimacy from exploiting this process of political and economic repositioning vis-à-vis the West. Nevertheless, the first two expressions of this first generation of nationalism were characterized by a formidable paradox: just after supposed independence, the political separation from the colonizer was, in effect, able to express itself only within the Western symbolic and

---

(1) Maxime Rodinson, *Marxisme et Monde Musulman*, Paris, Le Seuil, 1972.

semantic systems, which the architects of modernization continued to develop rather than fight. From the construction of a centralized Jacobin state to the atomizing of the traditional family structures, these "sons of Mendès France or of De Gaulle," who formed the elites after independence, often adopted tactics and strategies that they had fought against only a short while earlier when they had been used by colonial powers. There was no rupture in the colonial dynamic, only the handing over of it to the nationalists and its extension by them. "There we touch on what was certainly the most extraordinary result of colonialist domination," writes Krichen concerning Tunisia.

> The irony of the story is that it was the bilingual and bicultural elite of the cities, which colonialism had wanted to take in, who had taken the lead in the fight for independence; but the real irony is in the second degree: this modern intelligentsia was able to fight victoriously against French domination at the political level, but it turned out to be the best guarantor of the continuing hegemony at the linguistic and cultural level. The bilingual elite presented, and it represented itself, as a successful graft, a harmonious synthesis of opposing civilizing elements; in reality, in the intimacy of its being, it was spiritually submissive to Western values: it interiorized the inferiority of itself and the superiority of the other.(1)

While Mohamed Mzali (2) speaks of "cultural fric-frac (burglary)," Ben Aïssa of "ideological rape,"(3) Krichen evokes the "spiritual earthquake" of

---

(1) *La Tunisie au Présent, une modernité au-dessus de tout soupçon* Paris, CNRS, 1987, page 301.

(2) Former minister of education, then prime minister of Bourguiba (interview with the author, Paris, March, 1988).

(3) "Here in Algeria, it has produced a true cultural distress. After colonialism, we were submitted to a veritable ideological rape. For twenty years, the regime obscured Islam. For 20 years, there was no higher Islamic education. In all the Western universities there were certificates, degrees, doctorates in Islamic theology. And in independent Algeria, there was not one institution of Islamic teaching.   And when one was created, it was an institution for police. With us, the artisans of thought were Marxists.   This was not a de-Islamicized generation... it was a generation that never had been Islamicized, which had never learned anything... In Algeria, there were even people incapable of correctly pronouncing the word, 'Koran.' When they opened their mouths on Islam, it was to say stupidities. They were alienated. Very good French intellectuals, no doubt... but they were not made for the Algerian people. The Minister of Religions? They say that Boumedienne said one day: 'Find me a

the first twenty years of independence and the "infernal dialectic of destruction without construction" that led this dominating group which "lacked an ideology for its domination."(1)

"It is paradoxical," Hichem Djait wrote in 1974,

> to remark today that the national state, which sprang out of the fight against the colonizers, is the first to spread the ideal of modernization and that certain factions of the youth, or of the petite bourgeoisie show themselves more audacious than these supposedly evolved people in welcoming certain ways of thinking and behavior that reflect these times. On the scraps on which this little world subsists, floats the antiquated charm of old Europe, interiorized as a model of civilization around 1920. (2)

Due to massive education in the Maghreb, 20 years after independence, ten times more Francophones are plunging into Western philosophy than during the French colonial period.(3) The prolongation of the cultural dynamic may have seemed even more natural at that time than universalism of Western models—carried by the notion of "progress" and reinforced by a period of strong economic expansion had not yet been called into question in the West or anywhere else. The assumed modernization (at least by the intelligentsia) progressed more quickly than that which the former foreign masters tried to impose. Reinforced with their powerful legitimacy as nationalist liberators, a good number of regimes adopted legislation right after independence that attacked institutions (justice and universities in particular) which colonial powers themselves had not dared to touch. Closing the sleepy but still prestigious religious university, Zitouna, Habib Bourguiba was not afraid to put an end to 12 centuries of university

---

minister for religion....' And someone went to a cafe to look for one of his friends. He said, 'Come. You're a minister.' The minister of religion was at the very bottom of the list." (Interview with the author, Paris, 1988.)

(1) *La Tunisie au Présent,* cited.

(2) Djaït, Hichem, *Le Devenir de la Personnalité Arabo-islamique,* Le Seuil, 1974, page 25.

(3) In the same order of ideas, there was under Nasser an exceptional surge in the production of books that had been translated, etc. Cf. Richard Jacquemond, "L'édition d'ouvrages traduits du français en Egypte: pour un point de vue biculturel," *Egypte Monde Arabe* No. 5, 1991.

tradition. To be sure to accede more quickly to the great technological feast, the South threw away its laws, its customs, its languages, its songs (1) and even its clothing. More than ever, foreign languages, French here, English elsewhere, became obligatory, the point of passage for professional and social advancement. Ataturk had his "rebels of the fez," who refused to give up the emblems of traditional culture, hung, and Nasser had them pursued. The Shah of Iran forcibly cut beards and burned chadors. Those who sought the ultimate refuge for their identity in religious values saw secularism bit by bit become the reference. For several decades nothing troubled this reformist metamorphosis, apart from a few disturbances which the modern state, strengthened by its new efficiency, had little difficulty suppressing. Nevertheless, a winter of "nationalist disillusion" began to appear.

Demographic pressure, the bitter flip side of the development coin, the brutal shock of economic crisis that ruined the first hopes of industrialization, began to tear away the veil of optimism, which masked reality: the promises of modernity began to appear less in the form of triumphant balance sheets than hesitant downturns and stagnant figures, in "bread riots" and other signs of unrest. From Paris May, 1968, to Germany's Red Army Faction, from unemployment to inflation and the National Front and cultural isolationism, the shaky West no longer knows how to play its traditional role. Its long-held position as producer of ideological certainties, whether Marxist or liberal, is severely diminished. It is in this context that the South has begun to feel the need "to speak with a different voice."

Nationalism, Arabness, Islam: the Itineraries of Two Individuals

When in 1980, Tareq al Bishri, in the introduction to the the third edition of his work on *The Political Movement in Egypt*,(2) launched a spectacular rereading of the system of references which up to then had structured his thinking, the echo of this resignation from the universe of secular nationalism hardly spread beyond the limits of the Egyptian intelligentsia. For Tareq al Bishri, now, "the combat is no longer defined between progress and reaction, but between endogenous and exogenous (that which develops from within its own system and that which comes from an external system). The

---

(1) On the process of reforming Arabic music, cf. Philippe Vigreux (dir), *Le Congrès du Caire de 1932*, CNRS-CEDEJ, Cairo, 1992.

(2) Al-harakat al-siyassiya fi misr, Dar al-chourouq, Cairo.

inherited and the imported. The Arabo-Muslim legacy and Western influences."(1) Reread in 1991, the intellectual itinerary during which the Egyptian writer-jurist, vice-president of the Council of State, came to gradually refute his secular culture in order to adhere to that of his former political enemies the Muslim Brothers effectively illustrates the process by which a large number of Arab intellectuals came to adopt Islamist themes in place of the propositions of the secular nationalists.(2)

BISHRI: FROM NATIONALISM TO ISLAMISM

I was born in 1933. My political and cultural conscience was formed towards the end of the second World War, when I was between 12 and 20 years old. My interest in politics took shape when I was a student at university. The question which absorbed all the activity of Egyptians then was national independence, the dream of each was to see his country liberated. What are the elements of independence? Of what is it composed? I believe that from this point of view, the Egyptian national movement passed through several stages. At first it saw independence as something that was purely political. Its desire was to see that no more foreigners remained on Egyptian soil. That is how the Egyptians saw the national movement, and that is how they supported it during the first stages of the 20th century and after the end of the First World War.

To this first vision, they later added the idea of economic independence and they began to demand independent economic development without which there could be no free political decision. It is during this period that the Islamist mobilization began to contradict the nationalist movement. The Islamist mobilization was searching for a legitimate foundation. In the thirties and forties, this con-

---

(1) François Massoulié, in one of the rare studies in French of the work of the Egyptian writer, "Tareq al-Bishri: un intellectuel égyptien et sa problématique." Master's thesis in history under the direction of D. Chevallier, Paris, Sorbonne, 1987, 202 pages, in the process of publication.

(2) Bishri's itinerary, the intellectual rediscovering of the importance of the link between religious thought and national belonging is echoed by the writing of the political militant Adel Hussein, who preceded him on the same path: "to my former Communist friends," Adel Hussein explains today, "I say: how can you call yourselves nationalists, when in the best cases you ignore and in the worst you disdain what constitutes the foundation of your civilization, that which permits your nation to exist? For what built your civilization, what permits you to exist is Islam!" in "F.B. Entretien avec Adel Hussein," CEDEJ, collection Recherches. Cf also "F.B. Entretien avec Adel Hussein," *Egypte Monde Arabe* No. 3.

tradiction expressed itself in the well-known fight between the Muslim Brothers and the Wafd. One could say that the Islamist movement tried to add a third dimension to the independence movement: it called on society to return to values which had previously been dominant and to Islam as a source of legitimacy and of social order. After the appearance of the secular nationalist mobilization, that is what the Islamic movement represented. If the movement of the Muslim Brothers did not appear during the period of Mustapha Kamel before the First World War, it is because the nationalism of Mustapha Kamel expressed itself at that time in the language of Islam and not in the language of secularism. After the war, the liberation movement began to employ references of Western civilization. It represented then the incarnation of the values of modernity, the base of the construction of society, and the ultimate reference in the matter of a manner or model for life.

In the beginning, I belonged for my part to the first of these tendencies. The idea of political and economic independence dominated until the defeat of 1967. It (the defeat) has had an importance that has remained considerable until our time. It is what forced us to reconsider all the foundations of our system of thought, all our presuppositions. After this catastrophe, everything which we call presuppositions or the foundations of our thinking had to be reexamined. In addition to a number of essential questions which the re-examination put on our agenda was that of religion as a central element of the social system and in the development of society, and as a factor in its internal cohesion. My conviction was forged slowly that in fact the Islamist movement prolonged, from the viewpoint of civilizing, the political and economic independence movement. This was not the way I saw it before 1967. It was in 1967 and what followed after that made me see things that way. I evoked this intellectual itinerary in my book, *The Political Movement in Egypt*. The first edition had no preface. The work was the product at that time of a secular and nationalist look at the political forces, the future of the country and its situation at the time. Then in the presentation of the second edition, I took into account my new experience, which is to say the links between religion, the link between Islam and social questions, and the manner in which this vision gradually imposed itself. I realized that Islam was an essential ingredient. That if the future of the country demanded sacrifices, it was Islam which would make us capable of performing them, and that it was in deriving support from it that we would be able to have a future at the expense of the present, no matter what sacrifices that would be required in order to surmount the obstacles to this social and economic renaissance. I don't think that man is capable of responding to the challenges of this historical stage without being able to rely on a psychological foundation which enables him to renounce: to renounce himself for the benefit of the country, to renounce the demands of the present for the benefit of the future. In the 19th century, all the nationalist

51

movements were founded on Islam. I began to understand the language that they used to deal with the realities that they were living. I began to understand how they came to convince people to reduce their materialistic desires in order to construct a better future (...). Little by little, I began to reconsider the vocabulary used in political discourse, and in thought itself in the way it intervened with reality. I began to reconsider the relation between religious thought and reality. I found that there was a link with the question of national belonging and that national belonging had something to do with Muslim religious thinking to which it was associated. Little by little, I became conscious of different social institutions. Society began to appear to me to be composed of institutions which were themselves subdivided into internal sub-units which sheltered individual activity and organized within their breast masses of humanity. I realized that the cement of these different entities, that which composed the institutional fabric of society, was religious thought. One perceived, for example, that the evolution of certain professional groups coincided with that of the Sufi movement and with the social institutions existing in certain popular neighborhoods. This configuration gave society a kind of decentralization and made it possible for the individual to belong to primary micro-societies within the framework of which they live, all the while inscribing themselves in a series of memberships which become larger and larger. When one strikes against the act of belonging to a religion, it is this institutional network which one has struck. Instead of improving it, one has tried to annihilate it. The social fabric is disintegrated. I think it is very difficult to construct a society with isolated individuals. The individual must enter into a network of communities which become larger and larger. Without this interlinking of intermediary social gathering, he cannot in any way maintain a relationship with the State. The loss of these primary group memberships has thus affected all the higher memberships. It has affected the State itself in its capacity to conduct the affairs of everyone as well as the capacity of the individual to join the general entity. I consequently realized that all that had to be reconsidered, and that Muslim thought was that which could permit us to form institutions at every level of activity and human dynamic. There it is. That is what the crisis of 1967 taught me: the defeat pushed us to put everything into question. Result: all through the seventies, the period during which I wrote my book, *Muslims and Copts*, I found serious difficulties in making rapid progress. The period of writing the book began with a series of published studies in *Majalat al Katib* from 1971 to 1974. Initially I had the idea to write three or four studies on the question, but as I continued my reading, the subject took on more importance for me. I made myself finish. Then I stopped writing in 1974. After that I became interested in a series of completely different writings, but the subject remained at the heart of my preoccupations. During the years 1977-79, the idea of returning to the narrow question of Egyptian belonging resurfaced. I had faith in Arabness, and in the discussions that I had outside intellectual circles, the basic argument that linked the Egyptian man to Arabness was Islam. No other evidence was accepted with absolute seriousness. I remember finishing a talk in Beirut by saying: "Coming from Cairo, I can say that there is nothing that protects the Arabness of Egyptians any longer today except Islam." In that moment there, I really felt that this was something very profound, which had a considerable impact and in which one could search for the answers to many questions that people were asking themselves.

The itinerary of Rached Ghannouchi reflects both some specificity and a phase (his transition from Arab secularist nationalism to Islamism) closer to the "universal" process of fabricating modern Islamist intellectuals. The shock born of radical secularization imposed by Habib Bourguiba is indeed comparable to other Arab situations, but it is marked with a certain coefficient of Tunisian specificity linked to the linguistic policy of Bourguiba after independence (cf. infra Chapter 10 on Tunisia).

The mechanism of disconnecting himself from the semantic universe of Arab secularist nationalism is in contrast closer to the almost universal model of transition toward Islamism, at least for those militants (i.e, in the Maghreb for a vast majority) who have previously adhered to another ideology than that of religious thought. Arab secularist nationalism becomes irresistibly associated with Western culture and only religious thought, i.e., Islamic culture appears sufficient to answer the quest for identity.

RACHED AL-GHANNOUCHI: FROM NATIONALISM TO ISLAMISM (1)

It is not easy to put a finger on the precise path from one intellectual and ideological universe to another, and all that that implies in the transformations of human relations. In many respects, this change, especially in its initial phase, was the equivalent for me of passing from one world into another. From one thought, one ideology, one system of relations, one itinerary, to another world, new ideas, new values, and new relations. It was a brutal metamorphosis.

It is not easy for anyone to determine the motivations of such an upheaval with precision. For my part, I can certainly describe the context of the events that took place, but it is not easy for me to reconstruct the exact chain of facts, to distance myself from them so

---

(1) Interview with the author, London, February, 1992.

that I can see them as if they were a film. The essential elements act at the interior of the soul, in a way that may even be subconscious. How did all that happen? How did I come to this change? All I know is that it all happened at a moment that I can situate precisely: the night of June 15, 1966.

During that night, I made my final decision to move from the universe of Arab nationalism and Nasserism to that of Islam. This discovery constituted a kind of seismic shock for me. I realized that I was not a Muslim. That realization seemed like a catastrophe. It was a shock: I discovered that I was a stranger to Islam.

I had nevertheless been raised in an environment that was very religious. My father had learned the Koran. He did all the prayers with the family. And he spread incense throughout the house as very religious people do. But he was not a professional in religion. He was a simple peasant, but he taught the Koran to everyone in the village. Even though he had never been an Imam or a preacher, or anything else, he was known for his good reputation. Afterwards, I received a religious education at Zitouna University. But this education did not help at all in giving my conscience roots in the value of Islam and its capacity to organize existence.

This stage in Tunisia's history was in fact one of considerable changes that followed the return of Bourguiba from exile. Bourguiba's victory, to tell the truth, did not constitute a victory over the French occupiers but rather a victory over Arabic and Islamic civilization in Tunisia. Bourguiba came in as a conqueror, and like the foreign invaders, he took power. Then he began striking religious institutions, the institutions which were the very life of Tunisia. At this period, everything revolved around the University of Zitouna: traditional craftsmanship, Tunisian literature, all thought. Up to a certain point, all of Tunisia was produced at Zitouna. So this brutal blow against these institutions constituted a blow at the social, economic and cultural structure of all of Tunisia. For all those who had been raised in Arab and Muslim culture, that is to say the majority of Tunisian intellectuals who came out of these teaching institutions attached to Zitouna, Arabness and Islam were linked. They gave a great importance to this Arabic language and literature which gave roots to Arab-Islamic belonging in Tunisia, which breathed into it the spirit of resistance to foreign invasion (...) and served as a kind of shield for it against Europe. The attack against religious institutions was one of the first decisions after independence. My generation felt thus that it had been made extraneous, subjected to a very strong alienation, the victim of a kind of banishment. We constituted an Arab-Islamic base and the country was Westernizing; the administration, culture, the university, education, the arts, letters were Westernizing. People began to ask themselves if they were really in their country, in the heart of their country. It was necessary, as Bourguiba used to say, "to do everything to catch up with the march of civilization," to integrate oneself, to melt into the Western environment. They demanded nothing less from this generation, than to cast off its clothes, to rip off its skin in order to integrate into this new world into which Bourguiba was throwing all of Tunisia. Even those who had studied at Zitouna, thinking that there was no longer a future for Arab-Islamic culture, started to send their children to the Lycee Carnot, or to Sadiqi or one of the foreign institutions.

All that produced disorders for the graduates of these institutions, inferiority complexes, a feeling of alienation. There was nothing left for them to do except to withdraw and to huddle together, and to try to control their rancor against this occupation. This was no longer a foreign occupation, but it was still an occupation. Not by the French this time, but by "the Tunisian sons of France." And this occupation was more brutal than that of the French. They were at least openly declared as such in front of us (...) For the generation nourished on Arab-Islamic culture which frequented Zitouna and the traditional institutions, the process of Tunisia's Westernization was experienced as violence. This generation had been repressed. It was the victim of violence. But this generation represented the majority.

At independence, those who attended institutions dependent on Zitouna were about 25 to 27,000. Those who were studying at secondary schools, created under the French occupation, were less than 4,500 to 5,000. So it was the majority which felt that it had been marginalized by the minority. The secularism or Westernization did not anyway represent a popular movement. It was an effective minority, which had been able to marginalize the majority because it could understand the West, and understand foreigners and communicate with the new international order. The majority did not have that knowledge, so it was intellectually marginalized. It was the same for this entire social economic substratum which depended more or less directly on Zitouna, on the traditional crafts sector which surrounded Zitouna for one part, but also on the sector of the Waqfs, the Habous who represented an important part of land property. About a fourth of the agricultural land in Tunisia was attached to the Waqfs, and especially to the Zitouna. It was from these resources that alms were taken to preserve the religious expression of the society. Zitouna was financed by contributions from the people, which amounted to nearly a fourth of its property. So the act of striking at Zitouna, the act of striking the economic institutions which financed it, was the equivalent of destroying the society. It also ended by placing the generation raised in these institutions in the situation of an army that had been vanquished and defeated. All that was left for it was to melt into the new army. But to do that it had to crawl out of its own skin. Either it could withdraw, and close in on itself, or it could resist, or go into exile. A good number of people in my generation were drawn by the East. If the new international order which Bourguiba represented in Tunisia, and its representatives, drew their legitimacy from the West, those who rejected the violence of this forced change turned towards the East, toward the sources of Islamic and Arab thought, where they sought support. Besides, there had just been several upheavals in the East, not the least of which was the coup d'etat, which afterwards became known as the Revolution of Gamal Abdel Nasser. This revolution exalted Arabist ideas, Arab unity and the resistance to the international order. The Zitounians consequently had a special vocation to be Nasserists; they were Nasserists "by nature." They found the moral support they had been looking for in Nasserism. They did not see the secular dimension, or the fact that it was another expression of nationalism: In the Maghreb, the distinction between Islam and Arabness had never been made. Zitouna preached an Arabic Islam or a Muslim Arabness without distinction. In North Africa, Islamization and Arabization were equal. All the foreign aggression in Tunisia attacked Arabness and Islam at the same time, as it did elsewhere in Algeria. The sense of Arab belonging was even more deeply set in religion since there were no religious minorities in the Maghreb, and since the region was not Arab before it became Muslim. North Africa came into contact with Arabness and with Islam at the same time. So Arabness had no other cultural identity except the Muslim one. The regions of the Machreq were Arabized before becoming Muslim. There were Arab tribes who were Christian and remained so, and others who converted to Islam.

In the Machreq, Arabness on the whole was perceived as predating Islam. It was sometimes feared that using the Islamic reference would lead to a kind of segregation. In North Africa, the absence of minorities made it so that the problem never arose.

I already said that in this context, life was weighing on me. I felt a profound alienation. I often went to the gardens outside my village and I passed long hours reading the news and novels. The radio? Yes, I listened to Sawt al Arab, especially the radio stations of the Machreq. I read Naguib Mahfouz, and Tawfik al Hakim. After graduating from Zitouna, I remained a year and a half to work as a teacher. But the life did not suit me. I was filled with this feeling of alienation (*ightirab*) which was that of my generation. We felt a strong nostalgia for the sources of Islam and the Arabness of the Machreq. So I left for Egypt. That was in 1964.

The East, from Arabness to Islam

The discovery of Egypt? My point of view didn't really change. Of course, the dream which nourished my rejection of Bourguibism, Egyptian literature, the songs of Oum Kaltoum, those of Abdelwahab and of Farid Al Atrache, or of Radio Egypt and the speeches of Nasser, this luminous image dissipated when I arrived in Cairo. At first I had enormous difficulties enrolling in the University. We were about 40 in the same situation, having come from North Africa. We were not part of a group that had been sent officially. We only met each other here. We came by land, across Libya. Each one was searching for himself (...). The State of Bourguiba hated to have Tunisian students going to universities in the Machreq. They were afraid that they would be influenced by the Nasserist "madness," or that of the Baathists or

Arabists. A few official groups had nevertheless been sent to Syria. But our group didn't have that luck. It had been chased out. All escapees from Zitouna, we came from the ranks of the army of those defeated by Bourguiba. The survivors had either emigrated, or joined up with the new army. We, we were escapees from the defeated army who were in search of another army to join and to do this had come to the intellectual and spiritual capitals. Strictly speaking, it was not a political decision. It was the result of a confused feeling of alienation, the search for a better life, to insert oneself in the great centers of belonging. It was a sort of return to authenticity (...) The Tunisian University had adopted French. Those who had diplomas from Zitouna had no choice except to enter the faculty of theology in Tunis. I took courses there for awhile, but I wanted to learn science, and (for Arab speakers) that was not possible at the University. So, the rest of the Zitounians went to the Machreq, and especially to Cairo, to Syria and Iraq. Most obtained diplomas in sciences, especially the natural sciences, mathematics, polytechnics, and medicine.

In Egypt, I lived in Agouza, with some friends from my village who were studying here. I lived with them. We spent two or three months trying to enroll in the University of Cairo. The administrative routine, the bureaucracy. We even staged a demonstration in front of the house of Nasser to demand our rights to enroll in Egypt. After intense pressure, we managed to enroll. I enrolled in the faculty of agriculture. I planned to spend my life bettering the conditions of the peasants in my village, since their methods were very backward. (Agriculture was very difficult, especially because of water.) In the village I had been obliged to take part in the work to help my father. I even had to interrupt my studies at Zitouna. But that didn't last. I stayed four months, and I stopped.

Egyptian society, consequently, is very difficult for me to talk about, since to tell the truth I did not integrate myself into it. I did not have a chance to integrate. I passed most of my time trying to install myself, trying to enroll in the university, to take the steps to enter the university. I only visited Alexandria. At this period, I did not find in Egypt what I had dreamed of finding. I thought I would find enthusiastic Egyptians all mobilized behind Nasser. But I found a people who were more involved with their daily life. The mobilization, songs, the speeches one heard on the radio, all that was only a facade of slogans, a media enthusiasm on command which did not correspond to any of the realities in the street. In any case, this stage ended very quickly. Egypt and Tunisia broke off diplomatic relations. Cairo had supported Saleh Ben Youssef in his conflict with Bourguiba. Bourguiba had appealed to the French Army and Ben Youssef to Nasser. That was one of the reasons for Bourguiba's violent bitterness against Nasser and Arab nationalists, and the entire Machreq and Arabness. One of the reasons at least. The important point is that when bilateral relations were restored, the Tunisian Embassy in Egypt began looking for us to tell us that we were no longer allowed to remain in Egypt. And it pressured the Egyptian administration to have us thrown out of the university. After all our efforts at enrolling, we were barred in one stroke. The Embassy asked us to return. One part of our group did. The victorious army of Bourguiba even followed the escapees, those who fled. It managed to get us expelled from Egypt. We had to accept the capture and go back to the country or flee somewhere else. So I left for Syria. I almost went to Albania. How did I take care of my expenses? I had taken some money from Tunisia. I had worked as a teacher and I had saved nearly 500 Tunisian *dinars* which I took with me and which I spent bit by bit. In Egypt, I was satisfied with plates of *foul*, of *ta'miya*, to last as long as possible.

In Syria, on the other hand, the government, the minister of education, gave us scholarships. All the Tunisian students received one. I found a large number of Tunisians there, also the survivors of the Army, who had fled capture.

What was the political climate among the Tunisian students? The Bourguibists (part of the official group) chased us. But in Syria, we still managed to enroll easily in the university. The Syrian university was autonomous with respect to the state. And a short while afterward, we received a scholarship. Not a big one, but enough. And Damascus was not a large city like Cairo. A foreigner could find himself there more easily, and integrate more easily into the environment. Life was very cheap at that time. The liberal period hadn't finished yet. Socialism and Baathism had not destroyed the Syrian society yet. It was in fact the beginning of the Baathist experience and economic liberalism still produced prosperity in the country. Cultural and political freedom still existed at the university. All the political currents were presented and there was still dialogue and political and intellectual debate. We had begun to integrate ourselves into this dialogue and this political struggle. The great debate of the period opposed the Baathists and the Nasserists. The separation between Egypt and Syria had not taken place yet. The principal preoccupation of the Nasserists and their central theme was the restoration of the unitary state. Given the Nasserist background that I had had since Tunisia, I easily integrated myself into this current.

There was no real difference between the Baathists and the Nasserists. That was one of the reasons for my later metamorphosis, the discovery that the Nasserists and Baathists were arguing over things that were really small and futile. That was quickly revealed in the dialogue, and also, at the same time, by the intellectual progress which permitted me to read in philosophy. Philosophy led me to ask questions about everything, including the effective content of the denominations. What did Arabness really mean? What did Unity, Socialism mean? The ambience of permanent political debate pushed us to interject onto slogans more than their content. The dialogue took place at two levels: between Nasserists and Baathists for the one part, but also between members of the Tunisian community. The Tunisian group was divided between those—the minority—who remained

Bourguibist, and the majority which was split between Baathism and Nasserism. The debate was very intense between these two groups. Most of the debates took place in the League of Tunisian Students. There were elections, confrontations, a complete political life. And each made his elections campaign, proposed his program. The Nasserists were in a majority. The Bourguibists had only a marginal role. The Islamists? There weren't any. There were absolutely none. Not one lone Islamist in the League. As far as I can remember, in a group of 150 students, there were only one or perhaps two who did their prayers. That was in 1965. The prayers did not figure in philosophical or general political representations. The struggle concerned one's attitude vis-a-vis the Tunisian regime. Of course there was a consensus, a quasi consensus on the part of the two groups against the Tunisian regime. Everyone was a victim of this war of Bourguiba against Islam and Arabness. A small number of Bourguibists were still in contact with the Embassy. In fact we were divided in two groups: those who had been sent by the ministry of education, received a high scholarship and lived comfortably and the others, the majority who had come by themselves and had no scholarship. When Bourguiba made his famous trip to the Machreq after the reconciliation, we went to meet him in Beirut. The students decided to ask for a scholarship for everyone, which Bourguiba in fact gave each of us. So we all benefited from the good Tunisian scholarship for a certain time. But since, during this famous speech, he had called for the recognition of Israel and for respect for the partition of 1948, Arab public opinion rebelled, and especially in Syria. There was a riot. The Tunisian Embassy was burned. Relations between Syria and Tunisia were broken again and the scholarships were suspended.

The important thing is that the dialogue was not only between the Tunisian groups, but also between the Arab nationalists on one side, with all the tendencies thrown in together, and the Islamists. The Islamists at the Syrian university had a large mosque, a Friday sermon. They counted several famous personalities. At the time, in Syria, they were either Muslim Brothers or members of the Islamic Liberation Party. There were also some famous individuals. The ones who had the strongest power of attraction were of course those who were not official. They were the teachers at the university, the great teachers of the faculty of Sharia. So the dialogue took place between these two currents. What did it deal with? The foundation of the debate was almost always political. We debated the attitude to have concerning different regimes, and the Palestinian question.

The discourse of the Muslim Brothers at the time concentrated essentially on the condemnation of Arab nationalism, based on the fact that it was secular. They blamed secularism for the loss of Palestine, for political corruption, moral corruption and the economy.

In opposition, the discourse of the Nasserists or the Baathists against the Muslim Brothers consisted of saying that they were a reactionary current tied to colonialism, to the Americans. This kind of progressivism was tied to Eastern Europe and so it called the Muslim Brothers Americans, valets of America, supposedly against progress, reactionaries, etc...

Saudi Arabia? It wasn't present at that time. It still hadn't penetrated the religious struggle. It only did that after the oil revolution. It became capable of printing religious books with its point of view. It became present in the Islamic circles and in the circles of the Islamic current with the sort of Islamic books corresponding to its line of thought.

During this period, the great ideological sources were Egypt, Syria, Pakistan, and Abou 'Ala al Mawdudi.

The Liberation Party? It concentrated on the question of the Caliphate. The return of the Caliphate. Did it have a particular social base? First of all, it only represented a minority. It was a "Salafi" current (fundamentalist) which demanded the return to the first sources of religion. They had a sheikh who was the most important, Nasser Eddine al Albani, still considered today in the Muslim world as a great orator. Among the personalities who were emblematic in the field of religious thinking, there was Said Ramadan al Boutii. One debate started during this period in a group of Nasserists: they began to doubt the premises of Arab nationalism. The group accused Arab nationalism of having a content that was not Arab. It accused it of having an Arab form, but a content that was not. I remember that one of the books that was read at this period was a public work entitled *Man, this Unknown*. It was translated from the French, and its author was Alexis Carel. I don't think that it was a book that was very known in France, but it was at the center of the literature of the Islamists at that period. Sayed Qutb used it a great deal to criticize Western civilization and to show the misfortunes of Western man, the degradation of the family and social relationships, or international relations provoked by the Western civilization.

There was also the book of Spengler and of Toynbee, and also the book by an Englishman, *The Fall of Civilization* and a good number whose titles I have forgotten. These books gave credit to the Islamist position. To minimize and to criticize Western civilization was part of the argumentation employed against Arab nationalism.

It's necessary to mention here one of the factors that prepared me to accept the criticism that Arab nationalism as well as its contents was not Islamic but was Western. After having studied one year at Damascus, from January to June 1965, in the first year of philosophy, I left Syria with a group of friends and we went to Europe: Turkey, Bulgaria, Yugoslavia, Austria, Germany, France, Belgium, etc. I would work to earn a little money, and then go somewhere else.

Most of the time, I stayed in youth hostels. That gave me a chance to talk with all sorts of young people. Well, I went back to Syria with the impression that Western youth was living in a sort of confusion. That no doubt prepared me to admit the criticism of Western civilization. This trip, and the attitude of European youth whom I met in the youth hostels made it more acceptable.

What did the Soviet Union represent at that time? The most important contributions of the Islamist discourse, the origin of its force was precisely the very simple resume that it made of the West, and that it put a good number of distinctions which were essential for others into perspective. The debate between capitalism, socialism, the Western camp, the Eastern camp, and all that didn't amount to much. At the bottom, all of it was only the one and the same West. For a young person, the sole fact of breaking the classifications, from an intellectual point of view, constituted a revolutionary act. He discovered that men live in injustice and that they distinguish things which in the last instance were impossible to disassociate. This discourse told the different groups in conflict, the Nasserists, the Baathists, or the liberals: You are all in the same boat. Your references are European and not nationalist, and in the last instance, from an intellectual point of view, you are only the agents of this West. And that was also a revolution. Because the Nasserists at the time considered themselves as the representatives of a grandiose revolution.

The Baathists and the Nasserists fought each other over formal, futile questions. We told them: You, deep down, you are in fact agents of Western civilization. You have no authenticity and that is what explains your failure in all domains. And you will fail in the battle against Israel. You will fail.

And in fact, when the war of 1967 happened (I was in Damascus at the time), the young Baathists in particular considered that they were going to spend the summer on the beaches of Tel Aviv. It was, for these young nationalists, Nasserists or Baathists, an absolute certainty. They believed in Nasserism and they had unshakeable certainties. In contrast, the Islamist discourse broadcast the opposite certainty, that defeat was inevitable for it was not possible for an ideology of this sort to lead to victory. Then the defeat brought an important support to the Islamist discourse.

For my part, the mutation (towards Islam) had already taken place. The most important moment, the most important key for me was a sort of explosion produced in me that made me realize that the Arab nationalism in which we believed was in conflict with Islam. And that for a long time, if I believed that the Arabism, for which I was prepared to die, opposed the Islam which had nourished me and of which I was proud, then I had been duped. This discovery was difficult for me. I returned to a feeling of tension with the Nasserist culture, which I had assumed up until then. I had passed gradually from being a member of a cell which included seven or eight people to being its leader. The cell met secretly in private homes. I began a debate with respect to this cell on the question of the relation between Arbness and religion. Then, at the end, the members of the cell did not manage to convince me. Then they transmitted the question to the leadership of the party. Every time they would send someone to discuss it with me. In the end, I agreed to stay in the party, but on one condition. That faith in God should be considered as a condition of belonging. Even the way the Christians do. They pretended that they had Christians among them, and I told them: Even Christians, they believe in God. Why not make faith one of the elements of membership in the party? Then they told me: We are a party which does not make a relationship between religion and politics, "Religion is for God and country is for everyone" etc. I was convinced, when the discussion began there, that I had been mistaken for too long and that the years of enthusiasm and struggle were founded on an illusion. Like someone who renounced his family, his education, his civilization and who realized that he had been a prisoner for a long time without realizing it, believing that he was free while he lived in a prison in darkness. It was as if my life had been completely turned upside down. I remember that the night of June 15 I did not sleep the entire night. I was very agitated. A little before dawn, I decided to take the step of starting to pray. I made a prayer, whose details I had forgotten for I had forgotten the religious culture of my childhood and my religious culture was a theoretical culture but not one that was practiced, or that had been put into operation, that had performed acts. And I began to give myself a re-apprenticeship in Islamic culture, to read and to make an inventory of the contents of the products of Islam. The available Islamic merchandise, available in the Islamist current, included the books of Sayed Qutb, those of Mohamed Qutb, Abou Ala al Mawdudi, Mohamed Iqbal, Malek Bennabi and several ancient writings by Aboul Hamed al Ghazali and Ibn Taymiyya. After that I began to make the rounds of the religious schools in Damascus. I got to know the school of the Hadiths, of the Fiqh, the different Islamic groups: I listened to everyone. I wanted to know what was in the universe of religion with which I had been communicating from a distance without being integrated into.

CHAPTER 4

THE ISLAMIST RECIPE: LONG LIVE OURSELVES!

ISLAMISM AS THE LANGUAGE OF POLITICAL REACTION TO WESTERN CULTURAL DOMINATION

Our problem is that we had to deal with the West from both a position of psychological and material weakness. Excessively admiring it and paralyzed by our inferiority complex, we tried even harder to ape it and to take whatever it had to offer in every domain. Better, we took what was of little interest to us and we let go what we needed. But, I maintain that this unequal and perverse relationship with the West is not fatal. Japan piously conserves its traditions and culture, its civilization and participates nevertheless in the universal development of modernity. Israel has resuscitated a dead language, given itself a history which goes back to the beginning of time and imposed its place in the world. Europe did not need to renounce its values to grab from the Muslim East. Why should we be the only ones only to taste the good things of modernity through the obligatory trickery of Descartes or Marx. To tell the truth, the only way to accede to modernity is by our own path, that which has been traced for us by our religion, our history and our civilization.

(Rached Ghannouchi)(1)

For the Islamists, independence did not fulfill its political and economic promise, much less its cultural one. The spread of the French language, the permanence of Western institutional and juridical models, exacerbated here and there by the arrogant presence of cohorts of foreign tourists "even more disdainful at times than the colonial expeditions,"(2) are perceived as so

---

(1) Interview with H. Barrada, *Jeune Afrique*, July, 1990.

(2) "Wasted country, prostituted country," wrote Mohsen Toumi. "This is not an anathema, it is an observation. Soon it may be necessary to classify posters 'offering' Al Kantoui (a resort in Tunisia), a cruise on the Nile or Agadir, in the category of posters for X-rated films (pornographic). (...) One has to listen one day to the schizophrenic stories of the inhabitants of Korba in Tunisia: on July 14, 1981, the Club Mediterranee raised the French and Israeli flags simultaneously. The people of the village (martyred by the French foreign Legion in 1952), the mayor (Destourien) at the head, came out to demonstrate. Their government, the same one which had welcomed the headquarters of the Arab League on its soil, sanctioned and imprisoned them, while the foreign press called everyone 'fanatics' and 'anti-semites'." "L'Islamisme," *Les cahiers de la Méditerranée,* No 6, 1984, page 159.

many guilty concessions to the former master and the source of all the evils that have accompanied modernity. "There is nothing strange about a nation trying to take over another," says Salah Eddine Jourchi, one of the founders of the Tunisian movement and a militant in the reformist tendency of the Progressive Islamists. "What is strange," concludes Jourchi, "is that the nation that is invaded accepts and blesses this occupation and puts all its energy into deepening it and helping it take root."(cf infra). What is involved here is the questioning of a cultural relationship established during the colonial period. It is the "third stage of the rocket of decolonization," the third step in the South's distancing itself from the West, which is beginning to express itself on the cultural level, i.e. where the foreign invasion produced its longest lasting effects. The places that have sheltered the incubation of the Islamists all have a common denominator. During this century, they have suffered a brutal eruption of a system of values imposed or imported by the West under colonialism. After politics and its "independences," then economics and the more or less illusory pursuit of autonomy, the ideological and symbolic terrain now provides the framework for seeking a balance of power after decolonialization. Nevertheless, it is now necessary to ask why it is religion, or, more precisely, the *vocabulary* of Islam which plays the central role in this process.

One cannot express the rejection of the West, using its language and its terminology. How better to mark the distance, how better to satisfy the demand for an identity, than to employ a language that is different from its own, along with a system of codes and symbols that seem foreign to it? From Kadhafi and his "Third Universal Theory"(1) to the non-aligned movement, the search for a means of distancing oneself from Western experience, from the East as well as from the West (i.e. this "La chargi-la Gharbi"—neither East nor West—of the Ayatollahs), has indeed existed long before the new Islamist discourse.

But, at a time when the first manifestations of this quest for identity expressed itself through concepts forged by the West (nationalism, socialism or liberalism) and therefore were marked with a deficiency, the specificity of the Islamist discourse and a large part of its effectiveness stemmed from its privileged recourse to a stock of references perceived as untouched by any foreign influences. Without being alien, the vocabulary of Islam, returning from a long absence on the political scene, has the added attraction of novelty. Providing the post-colonial dynamic with a language

---

(1) See infra.

of its own, Islam offers the ideological and symbolic autonomy it had missed vis-à-vis the West, which thirty years after the Arab independences has been able to maintain the preeminence of its language in the post-colonial world.

The recourse to a political vocabulary nourished by categories (less religious than cultural) produced by the local societies, or perceived as such, restores to the references of the parent culture the universal qualities which had been lost to the political language from the North. Consequently, this restoration permits a double reconciliation: It reintroduces in political expression references that colonial expropriation had progressively relegated to "private" culture, and it permits the Arab political individual to renew his relationship with his own living and intuitive culture. In reconciling the individual with his or her ancestral culture, in which a symbolic affiliation becomes once again possible, the historical continuity that the imposition of Western categories had interrupted is restored in the collective imagination. In doing this (and it is here that the secret of its formidable capacity for mobilization resides), the colonial parenthesis is closed at the symbolic level, at precisely the point where the more or less brutal recourse to representations fabricated by other social systems were able to have their most traumatic impact.

For Tareq al Bishri, the reintroduction of religious thought also restores the social fabric that was torn apart by the excess of the Nasserist-like policies of secularisation. In this construction, Islamism helps reconnect the individual with his public environment, i.e. the State, which its secularist discourse had prevented for so long from acquiring its full efficiency, thus maintaining the process of modernization on the fringe of society. If the addition of the word "Islamic" to the word bank thus allows the peasant of Upper Egypt to enter into a relationship with financial institutions of national importance for the first time in his life, we may say that a mere ideological production has reconnected the individual with his or her "public" environment and thus that a major step has been taken toward modernization.

As group therapy, Islamism no doubt also provides a cure for individual "egos" in pain. In effect, it restores the "image of self" damaged by crises of identity. Eventually, as Jean François Clément puts it, it can also become the refuge for "those who no longer exercise superiority over their wife and children at home, playing a role in providing compensation," but it is more likely that it plays the role of creating the sense of "security" which all to-

65

tally encompassing certainties provide, and which the individual in crisis needs to "reconstitute a legitimacy."(1)

For Hassan Hanafi(2), before all, Islamism is an historical conscience.

From a purely historical point of view, the Muslim world, which is to say the Islamic conscience, is in crisis. We are in anguish. This anguish appears in popular demonstrations and in the streets. It appears among intellectuals and Islamic groups. It doesn't matter which groups, or which cleavages and tendencies. We feel now that we have been the victims of a certain number of historical injustices. (...) There is always this sentiment which I can communicate to you in reading history. That explains why the Turath has become a best seller. If you want to make millions and millions: print and reprint all the Tafsir of Al Tabari, of Ghazali, etc. Print and it will sell...in one hour. Why? Because our past image is a glorious image. You know it well. I don't have to give you a speech on the excellence of Islamic culture. The whole world knows it. And if they, the readers, compare us to that reality...the whole world knows where we have fallen. So that creates a sort of lapse within us, an atomic fissure between the past and present.

So we revolt. The form of the revolt does not matter. Me, I rebel intellectually. I don't know what has happened to me. A glorious past and a cruel present. If I use Christian language, I would say that I used to be in paradise. I don't know what error I committed, but there was the fall and the expulsion from paradise. And now I am in this existential and historical anguish.

That is what moves the man in the street. For he reads these books which are called the yellow paper of Al Azhar. He sees an image. And when he sees his reality, he sees another image. It is the conflict between these two images which is really behind what is called the Islamic movement, the Islamic renaissance. It is a certain type of

_____

(1) Jean-François Clément in "Pour une compréhension des mouvements islamistes," *Esprit*, No. 37, January, 1980, page 46, where the author insists equally on the disillusionments of progress (...), and of the destruction of concurrent profane ideologies. Rémi Leveau also insists on the fact that Islamism "offers (equally) a response to all who (...) are challenged in their family and in their work by their daughters or their sisters, or humiliated by the wealth and shocking manners of the Westernized bourgeoisie," "La Réaction de l'Islam officiel au renouveau islamique au Maroc" in *Le Maghreb Musulman en 1979* under the direction of Christiane Souriau, Cresm, CNRS, Paris, 1981, page 206. In the same volume, cf. Abdelkader Zghal, page 41, "Le retour du sacré chez les jeunes Tunisiens," and Yadh Ben Achour," page 65, "Islam perdu Islam retrouvé."

(2) Interview with the author, Heliopolis, Cairo, January, 1988.

historical conscience, which is very clear and very strong, and which asks the question: is it possible to find coherence between the past and the present? Being incapable of addressing the great challenges of modern times, I grab onto the past. It is a kind of defense mechanism, to console myself.

That said, who is responsible for these historical malaises? I cannot say the West. Good, that said, why is there an historical malaise in me? The Islamic world was geographically and historically neighbors to what is called Europe. The drama of the Mediterranean is that when the southern coast is strong it invades the North, and when the northern coast is strong, it invades the South. There is a coming and going.

Our closeness to the West... without going all the way back to the crusades... but all the same... has provided us with an ambiguous relationship to our neighbors...and has created a type of dialectic within us between an inferiority and a superiority complex. In our universities, we have introduced in the last 15 years a subject which we call "history of science among the Arabs." Perhaps we copied the title from some European universities. We were masters in the past. Europeans translated our sciences and were our disciples. Now it is we who are disciples, and the Europeans are the masters. So there is a dialectic between the master and the disciple in the depths of our soul. And that shows, it shows in me when I perform auto-psychoanalysis. An inferiority complex vis-à-vis what may be another complex of superiority. But all the same, if the historical law is that the idea of culture is born, develops, and arrives at a summit and then begins to decline and then fall... If that is the case, then, that would mean that we are at the end of an era.

Toynbee, Spengler, Bergson all presented the history of European philosophy; it is a way of recuperating the past, without having an idea of progress such as during the 17th, the 18th or the 19th century. I am not an advocate of the decline of the West, but it still seems that it is very clear in contemporary writing (...). So we may be living in a time when these complexes will resolve themselves. We are not "less"...not at all!

In the Maghreb, on a path largely swept by linguistic re-Arabization, it is—as in the rest of the Arab world—less a question of renouncing the West than of differentiating oneself from it, and of giving it all the attributes of "otherness." And this process, which requires before all a phase of symbolic rupture, nevertheless, does not in itself prevent further reappropriation. For all that, one must not misunderstand the meaning and the extent of this indispensable moment of rejection.

Return of God, or Return of the South

Even if the Islamists most often sound the death knell of the Western system because of its materialism, and even if their criticisms are strengthened by the fact that they have equipped themselves with an alternative in which morality and spirituality (more than the mere religious dimension) rediscover their place, it is the cultural impact of the recourse to Islam that engages the adherents of its "return." "The Islam of the Muslim Brothers is (significantly) a poor Islam," remarks Michel Chodkiewicz, who, along with others, criticizes the shortcuts occasionally seen with respect to classical thought in the doctrine of the Islamists.(1) Jean-François Clément goes even further:

> They are secular. The Islamists are all byproducts of European thought. They have broken completely with Islam with respect to (...) many questions, which range from politics to the possiblity of men judging the legitimacy of representations of God, and in that they are in complete opposition with the Ulema of Islam.(2)

In forcing the matter, one could go so far as to disassociate Islamism from religion, and see nothing more in this religious vocabulary, which is intended to express an alternative political program, than the ideological logistics of political independence, the cultural prolongation of the ruptures born of decolonization.

At the heart of our difficulty in measuring the tempo of the Islamist mobilization, persists the wide-spread idea that the movement is reducible to a simple mystical itch, and is thus as equally condemnable in the name of the unstoppable "rejection of all fundamentalisms" as it supposedly is equally distributed on the planet. And, indeed, it is true to say that Muslims are not the only ones to turn toward the heavens to find a response which a secular state refuses to provide for them. In a way, Jews seem to do it just as often, Christians too. The phenomenon might be regarded as universal, it is often remarked. It is "the revenge of God."(3)

---

(1) Interview by Zakia Daoud in *Lamalif*, 1986.

(2) Correspondence with the author, November, 1985.

(3) Title of the book by Gilles Kepel, "La revanche de dieu: Chrétiens, Juifs et Musulmans à la reconquete du monde," Le Seuil, 1991, (L'Épreuve des faits).

So Imam Khomeini, Rabbi Kahane and Monseigneur Lefevre fight the same battle? That remains to be seen! It has already been said and will be said again: the forms of political appropriation of a religion are explained less by the essence of its dogma than by the sociology of those who practice it. The analysis of the roles that individuals or groups of the same society demand a religion to play, and even more the prospective evaluation of this relationship, can only be made in close relationship to the internal historical dynamics of their respective environments. In different societies submitted to radically different proselytizations, can one really draw parallels in religious behavior when one realizes that they are inseparably linked to the individual and collective imagination of the actors? For, no matter how stimulating, situating the three monotheistic religions in such a perspective results in obscuring rather than revealing the true nature of the re-Islamization process, the forseeable terms of its evolution and, above all, the reasons for its formidable capacity for mobilization.

More than the return of God, the most perceptible dynamic at the end of the century is probably the return to the forefront of His once-forgotten sons of the South. But if the South is not only Muslim,(1) the North in its overwhelming majority is certainly "Judeo-Christian." It is the vocabulary of its Judeo-Christian culture which has served to express the marginalization from which the "Third World," notably the Muslim, is trying to emerge today.

In the North, whether one is Christian or Jew, the relationship with "the South" constitutes a central element in the formation of cultural and political identity. In the South, the colonial episode and its diverse sequels constitute the hard core of the conscience of each individual, even for those who have not lived it. One can deplore this reality or become annoyed at it. To fail to recognize it or to appear astonished by the fact that most of the Islamist generation has not personally experienced colonization is equal to drawing the conclusion that a society's collective imagination changes completely with each generation. In a country like France, which has just celebrated the bi-centennial of its revolution, or in Spanish "New Andalusia," or in Israel, or anywhere else on earth, who would dare to deny that this long-lasting conscience of the past is an intrinsic component in any sense of national belonging?

The limits of a possible comparison, thus, ought to be clearly enunciated. In the South as in the North, the resurgence of religion in the

_____

(1) For the analysis of the non-Muslim South, liberation theology might profitably be taken into account.

69

systems of representation indeed reflects the difficulties of life in societies that have fallen prey to the questioning of values and categories that have dominated the century. But the analogy stops there. If mosques have had as much success as they have over the last few decades, it is much less because they speak of God than it is because the vocabulary they use to do so comes from the only place that resisted the cultural pressure from the North. In this case, the apparent "return of the religious" is far less concerned with the resurgence of the sacred in a secular universe than with the rehabilitation of local cultural references, political ones among others.

If the European cathedrals are beginning to experience an upsurge in the number of visitors, it is certainly because when one enters a cathedral, one distances oneself from secular values. This is especially true in former Communist nations. But, especially in the capitalist West, these secular values cannot be perceived as "imported" and their rejection signals therefore a value crisis of a different dimension than in the Arab world. If many Europeans are suddenly becoming sensitive to their "Christian" identity again, it is partly because the protection offered by nationalism has stopped working and because some are worried that "French may soon be indistinguishable from Arab." It is tempting, when one's identity is crumbling, to fall back on a religious bastion that is less systematically open to what is seen as an invasion from the South.

The fact that the parental culture in Arab lands is religious makes the language of spirituality more effective in condemning the materialistic North. But this timely convergence of the North and South in the vocabulary they use should not mask the fundamentally different dynamics produced by this apparent "revenge of God." Indeed, the North and South do meet at the crossroads of religion and politics, but that does not stop them from traveling in opposite directions. While the North rejects a secularism created by itself, the South only distances itself from those secular values (which in any case have for the most part been interiorized by only a miniscule acculturated elite) because they are expressed in a vocabulary that it feels is foreign to its culture. This attitude does not deny the relationship that might form in the future with values that might eventually be incorporated into the citadel of Islam, once it no longer feels itself to be under siege from the outside.

Muslim culture is infinitely less receptive than was often said to the idea of some form of distinction between the religious and the secular social life.(1) As much as one wants to shy away from the literal and obscuring fringes of the dynamic of re-Islamization, in fact the secularist tendencies, if they were to be expressed from inside the Muslim symbolic system, would appear to have much more of a chance of anchoring themselves in a popular environment than just in the tiny urban elite acculturated by the colonial presence. If, at the end of the 1970s, the human and sociological substratum of Islam did produce the radical and literalist fringe that often serves today to obscure the true nature of the entire Islamist phenomenon, then the structural tendancy of the Islamic movement in the decades to come will probably be aimed at escaping, at a rhythm determined by its economic and cultural development, these "literalist" bonds that have characterized it up to now. In contrast, the ideological and sociological pressure which Islam exercises on the West and Western religions will tend to encourage the same kind of extremism in the West that Islam has begun to start bringing under control. "Reconquest of identity" for the South where internal doubts are diminishing and a "retreat to identity" for the North where doubts are beginning to grow: there is a significant difference.

SALAH EDDINE JOURCHI

ON THE CINDERS OF CAPITALISM

Capitalism is a human choice (...) which sprang from a Western materialistic representation. The mentality which produced it does not recognize the sovereignty of God on earth, renders religion responsible for the tragedies which humanity has known throughout the course of its history, believes that man is a being separated from heaven whose existence on earth is the product of blind chance, of an evolution which was purely materialistic and biological since it controlled its life alone and without any one else (i.e. without God). The crisis of capitalism is a crisis of civilization. It is a crisis of conceptions and values which have corrupted life, and the economic crisis is only one aspect of this corruption.

One will not resolve the crisis with any depth by searching for a new economic structure and in saving these conceptions. That amounts to going around in a vicious circle. The radical solution consists of rising up against these conceptions, of leading a total revolution against them.

---

(1) Cf. notably, Mohamed Arkoun in "L'Islam dans l'histoire," *Maghreb Machrek,* No. 102, October, 1983, or in *Ouverture sur l'Islam,* Paris, Jacques Grancher, 1989.

AND OF MARXISM

The Marxists advance with trumpets of their propaganda and propose their merchandise to solve the crisis (...) "Our prophet Marx spoke the truth when he foresaw the fall of the capitalist system. The only exit for men is the Communist experience; it is rendered inevitable by the sense of history." We say to them (...) that their remedy can only be temporary. It appeases the pain, but it is not suited to exterminating the roots of the illness (...) for Marxism is nothing more than a byproduct of the (same) Western materialistic mentality (...) Man, with Marxism even more clearly than with capitalism, is nothing more than a materialistic product which has no relationship with heaven; religion is nothing more than a superstition for weak souls. Moral values are nothing more than powder in the eyes of the bourgeoisie for use by the laboring classes. There is no other God by man, no other object of true adoration except Science (...)

The history of the socialist experience has shown us that the distance separating the two camps is small, and that behind the divergences based on interest and position, there is still a common platform (...) the unique mentality which produced the two systems. (...) Marxism is only a violent reaction against the numerous faults of the capitalist economic system (...) a reaction which has taken European man from one extreme to the other: to absolute faith in the individual with capitalism (...) to his smashing and to the rendering sacred of the collectivity in Marxism.

ISLAM AS RESOURCING

Once certain of the failure of the West (...) we discover the comedy in which we have lived and in which we continue to live. We believe that we are developing and civilizing ourselves by marching towards the same failure as the West. It is time (....) that we elaborate a new program. It is time that we open our eyes and realize that we are running after an illusion whose name is "the powerful West," when in reality it is weak and sick.

The first step that we have to take to break the circle of this dependence it to stop galloping after it, and to demolish its culture and to reject it wholesale and retail.

This liberation of our spirits from the hegemony of Western thought is an indispensable condition without which we will not free the land nor the economy and without which we will not manage to reunify our ranks. The paralysis does not hide itself in the lack of money or men, but in the microbe which says "follow the steps of civilization." It is not strange that a nation tries to occupy another (...) What is strange is that the nation which has been invaded, accepts and blesses this occupation and puts all its energy into deepening it and giving it roots. With our goods and machines, we have imported ideas, in believing that we would catch up with the Westerners. But we have won nothing and we have lost our religion. We have rid ourselves of the past with a fever that we suffer from still. (...) Why? Because from the beginning, we have not defined the nature of under development. It is not just an economic reality. It is an entire mentality whose domination paralyzes the movement of the masses. Under-development is in reality the feeling of impotence of a nation confronted with its decomposition. It is also a feeling of confusion in which bathes the Umma, and which made it lose confidence in itself (...)

The underdeveloped nation is the nation which no longer makes its future and is constrained to accept the future that another nation makes for it. It is the nation where one witnesses an hysterical inwardly directed agitation in order to push back the tendencies to rejection which surge with some of its elements. [S.E. Jourchi evokes the example of teaching, of philosophy. Underlining that it is a matter that is obligatory in nearly all the sections and which has a considerable importance in the literary sections which form the leadership elites.] But what does the philosophical program contain if not the ensemble of western representations of man, the universe, of God? In the diverse historical developments of the materialistic mentality of the 170 texts which contain the work of the program, only seven are by Arab thinkers. Nevertheless, the originality of the philosophy in relation to the other scientific and human materials is that it has a vocation to teach us to regard, distinguish, to think, to govern. But it has only been taught so as to deepen the Western conceptions in our life, a natural extension of the cultural invasion and of Western colonialization. The most serious matter in the end is the language in which it is taught—French. For the high school student, this is another obstacle which prevents discussing the ideas which are presented (...) and which gives the professor a free field to vaunt the merits of Western thought, to make the young generations doubt their religion and the values of their nation. Finally, such an education adds to the severing of the nation's roots, building a generation which mocks its patrimony and the works of its ancestors and applauds its enemies (...) Alienation, psychological crisis... that is under development. The only way to get out of this is to refuse all foreign representation. The first step is to destroy in ourselves the idol of the West. We must realize that we are a nation (Umma), and that we have access to a collection of values capable of moving us, of gathering our energies together. (...) We are not birds with broken wings, orphans who need to be taken in by the West to protect ourselves. (...) Our hearts are solid, our ancestors showed us that our Lord will give us help and confidence and our future is full of hope. Jung writes: "The real danger which threatens us violently and directly is the Islamic danger." A French official in the Foreign Ministry writes, "for the Muslims form a world totally independent of ours, they possess their own spiritual patrimony, they enjoy a civilization which is historically original and are apt to throw away the bases of a new world without needing to Westernize it." They fear us, they, the colonizers,.so why should we fear them...we the colonized who have the truth?(...). Free us from fear, from the fear of separation from the West, fear of having to count on ourselves. A little courage, patience, faith, of conscience, of action, and fears and complexes will disappear (...) Then we will regain control. Light will replace the shadows. Wealth will replace poverty. A new dawn will rise over us. The West knows that Islam is strong, and that is why it fights it with so relentlessly.

"(...) The detonating mixture which triggered the invasion by the West," wrote Toynbee, "could finish with a destructive explosion. If such a catastrophe were to take place, Islam would be (...) the catalyst for the violent reaction by the world's proletariat against its Western masters. Certainly, it seems that this destructive possibility of Islam does not necessarily have to take place. Certainly Islamic unity is asleep, but it could wake up (...) its heroic history is seen during the period of the Rachidin caliphs and during the period of Saladin. (...) If the international situation should provoke a racial war, Islam could well go into action and play its historic role once again. I hope that that will not happen."

The return of Islam as a culture and as a model for life is our unique chance to come out from under-development, while all other doors are closed to us. Any other way will bring us only decline and decadence. One can feel why the West feels threatened by this return, but we do not understand why it manages to frighten and traumatize (...) those who speak the same language as us. There is no other solution than our liberation from the inside. It is the role of the new generation, of these Islamist avant-gardes everywhere, to free the Umma from the inside, to rid it of any trace of adoration of the West, and to make it feel its force, its power, its responsibility and its role in past history and history to come.

(*Al-Maarifa*, No. 5, Tunis, 1976.)

AND GOD?

Nevertheless, it is not surprising that very few in the Islamist camp agree with this interpretation. Abdessalam Yassine, one of the most "religious" of the actors on the Islamist scene in the Maghreb, is a case in point:

> You observers from the outside, in reading the writings of the Islamists... in analyzing their speeches, you only see the tip of the iceberg which is emerging. The common element which one can see directly... is... the denunciation of Western culture... the denunciation of the bad management, the existence of social injustice. This you see. The rest, the 'unspoken' or better the 'unperceived', which is this spirituality, the return to God, whose spirituality for us is not completely obliterated...that exists. And that is what unites us.
>
> I notice that you persist... with stubborness on the materialistic level (...) You are affected more than the others by this materialistic dialectic which the West has assimilated... whether it admits it or not.

You do not call yourself a Marxist, but you persist in relativizing everything in relation to this absolute which for you is the social dialectic, the dialectic between the West and the Orient... and Islam. Islam as a religion comes up as a complementary factor which is not at the heart of the question. I tell you that what ties me to these people who are before you... It is not so much the ideological mobilization in the name of Islam to fight against those who deny our personality, our authenticity, to fight our historical adversary... It is not so much that as it is our attachment to God.

In your articles, I read the analysis of a pure Westerner who sympathizes with Islamism. That... yes...you find Islam sympathetic. But for you, this spiritual region remains voluntarily opaque. You do not want to see it. You do not want to look at it. I find that the fault of these intellectuals who make things look good from their point of view is that they do not take into account the way others see it. That is what makes them adopt this interpretation, which I find a little facile and superficial; it consists of explaining the Islamic phenomenon through economic and political determinism. I remember a phrase by Jean-Francois Clément that you quote and which states that to be an Islamist, "It is necessary to lose hope for the economic situation, to have no possibilities, to have no openings...." to be in a certain way in despair. I find that this explanation is a little too easy and that it does not take into account the internal subjective factor. People do not come to Islam as an alternative for their social misfortunes. People come to Islam in response to a call, a call which goes very far and deep in the human soul. I do not know by which accident of history or by what misfortune "Homo Occidentalus," as you say, has lost this organ which permits the perception of things that are spiritual... All that he has left are elements of economic, political and social analysis... things that are earthbound in some way (....)

For you all is Western action, reactions by under-developed countries in search of a language for combat, of an ideology, and they find everything ready in this Islamic doctrine which is a solid construction, isn't it, which has roots in the people. So it is a thing that has been found which the Islamists have appropriated to combat the West with an intention of passing it, of denying it, all the better to get what the (West) has as material products. You have a nice expression... you say the technological "loot."

F.B.: No, the feast. But I use the expression in a different context... which should also be close to your analysis. In any case, in the book, the restrictive dimension of my approach... will be attenuated by your comments! They will be in their full force.

A.Y. So much the better... your work will only be better for it... if you can manage to place the West and Islam face to face on a cosmic plane... not in a given historical period but in the long march of human history. The West has lost its religion. It has renounced its religion which now remains not much more than a memory. The Vatican is still there. The Protestants are still lively, but this secular and materialistic culture dominates you, while with us what is everything for us is this fundamental question... Does God exist or not...?

F.B.: But you have existed as Muslims for 14 centuries. How do you explain the extreme variety of forms of mobilization for a dogma which has by definition not changed? Why do the conditions for appropriating a unique message have so much variety in time and space? Under the same banner of Islam, we have seen an entire range of political and economic systems which have been born and then died.

A.Y.: You limit yourself as an outside observer... (...) It is your right... But, it is not a question of knowing... it is a question of feeling also. And then on the plane where you situate yourself...you do not invent anything at all... you only repeat in a fashion that is more extended and modern what others have tried to say concerning the appearance of Islam. The Marxists have gone to great lengths to say that Islam appeared in the seventh century in a peninsula where all the conditions were found ready for a new ideology to save the situation. When a man wants absolutely to blind himself to reality, when he is absolutely determined to attribute to himself the prerogative of the absolute, then he explains everything in relation to himself. He is egotistical...individualistic...he turns every subject back on himself. If it is a culture or civilization which is in question, it attempts to focus everything on itself and its own existence in the world and and. If Islam appeared in the past centuries...Why did it not start in 1969 in Libya...why did it appear on the agenda in Tunisia in 1981? Well, I will tell you, in considering things as they are...that it is God who is running the game. (...)

F.B.: All the same, this Islamist resurgence corresponds to a particular moment in the relationship between East and West?

A.Y.: Yes. Yes, certainly, because the challenge of the West became unsupportable. One cannot reject the historical framework. One would be near-sighted or even blind. In your training and your Western culture, divinity was cast aside for the solely human dialectic; you forget that this dialectic was part of the divine plan. God says so expressly in the Koran. If there were not this mutual opposition, the humanity itself would be lost. So it is part of the divine plan.

We spoke of Marx. What did Marx say? What gives his doctrine force? He said, "In the world there have always been classes who have oppressed other classes." No one with sense can deny that. His historical analysis, socialism—that is something else—but the essential mark of what he said was that basic truth which gave Marxism its effectiveness, its force, its elan; its call to the oppressed of the earth.(...) To say on the other hand that Islamism is in the end a secular movement, I would not buy that. I would tell you rather that this long march of Muslims, which started 30 years after the death of the Prophet.(...) It has made Muslims of today forget that Islam is a message for combat, the Jihad. It is a call to God before all else, but God demands that we oppose anything that prevents the message of

God from reaching the people for whom it is intended...There were, let's say, a hundred years from Al Afghani to Mohamed Abduh afterwards, and then to Rachid Redha and the Muslim Brothers movement. People wanted to begin to face the West, because the West represented the most menacing challenge. It was something which threatened the essence of Islam. It was then people began to speak a political language. Little by little there has been an avoidance... or more accurately a stripping away of such language in the speech of the Islamists.

Take Hassan Al Banna: his language definitely cannot be called secular. He is a man of God who speaks for God, who showed in all his activities, such as the education of his troops, a spiritual unrest. His successors were a bit more secular, if you want—I put "secular" between quotation marks. It's true that you find less spirituality with Mawdudi, for example (...) but the politicians are not the only ones who have adopted Islamic language, religion and doctrine to serve their (political) ideology, absolutely not (...).

(Interview with the author, Rabat Salé, October, 1987.)

Allah Akbar! Down with the Prince!

The functions of the Islamic discourse are not limited to the logic of a cultural "regrounding." It is equally a language of challenge. Partly appropriated by the State, Islamic discourse is also and above all a means of resisting the State. The critical rereading of the legacy of the West reunited even more followers once it began defying rulers. The "Allah Akbar" that emanates from the mosques, therefore, usually has a double message of rejecting both the West and the secular government accused of being its servant, allowing challenges to the methods of the prince to be clothed in the protection of religious demands.

On the economic level, Islamic discourse gives coherence to the expression of frustrations of all types (from the student looking for a job to the consumer with nothing to buy), and it facilitates their articulation in political demands. On the political level, it aids the expression of civil society's democratic demands. Its impact on the local scene is therefore proportional to the authoritarianism of the Arab regimes at present, none of whom has so far dared to follow the path of democracy to its natural conclusion. For, he who initiates an opening up of the political scene would be obligated to step down from power.

This is the essential Islamist theme (simplistic, perhaps, but as such very effective), and the basis of its formidable capacity for mobilization. However, like every reactionary process, Islamism is far from exempt from contradictions, and its capacities for mobilization are not without limits.

The Temptation for Reaction

The limits of the movement stem first of all from the fact that the reactionary dimension of the Islamic resurgence provides only a current and temporary quality to the advantages gained by those who exploit the movement politically. This diminishing of resources, which may to a certain extent be perceptible in the case of Iran, is nevertheless far from being the rule in the Arab world. It is more in the dimension of its own logic that the real limits of the Islamists' approach are to be seen; not in the analysis, which proceeds from the effects of Western cultural domination, since in this area most historians agree to take into account the social and political effects of the colonial "deculturation." It is in the nature of the responses which it seeks to bring to this cultural schizophrenia that Islamist logic most probably finds its true limits. Thus, the denunciation of "cultural dependence" is part of the logic of a claim of an "alternative model" that pretends to satisfy the impossible criteria for "authenticity" (more or less precisely designated by references to the Sharia or to the Tourath/patrimony or heritage) and to give such references the dominant position which they lost in our dependence on Western sources. But the very fact that Islamic references need rehabilitation is enough to demonstrate that those references (perceived as divine although they are for most part the product of a human mediation between dogma and its juridical expression) have lost the vital contact which any system of standards needs to maintain with the society it pretends to govern. Thus, the recourse to the culture, notably juridical, of a mythical golden age, for a would-be totality of practical situations only leads to the willful imposition on modern societies of standards created in a different historical context and therefore just as disconnected from the societies they are intended for as the standards they are intended to replace. To cure the imputed cultural "schizophrenia" of the victims of colonization, the Islamist doctor thus runs the risk of innoculating his patients with the germs of a new schizophrenia. In the place of a culture perceived as having been imported from the West, they take the risk of substituting another culture which is just as far removed: not across the Mediterranean this time but across centuries. It is doubtless on this terrain that Islamist literalist attitudes are the most fragile, and—logically—that anti-Islamist critics are the most effective. For Fouad Zacharia, among others,(1) the weak leg of

---

(1) Cf. notably, *Islamisme et Laïcité, les Arabes à l'Heure du Choix,* La Découverte-Dar Al-Fikr, Cairo, 1990. In Egypt, Nasr Abou Zayd also identifies with finesse the eccentricities of the religious discourse. Cf. notably, "Le

Islamist mobilization basically results from the incapacity of its militants to establish a dispassionate and consequently constructive relationship with their past glory. Zacharia tells us that rather than falling into passionate and indiscriminate rejection of their patrimony on the grounds that it is archaic, which can be just as alienating, the Islamists need to renew a connection with their past creativity while disassociating themselves from its more archaic manifestations. To bring back the glory of their fathers, they ought to accept the idea of burying them. For, excessive mythification of an historical patrimony is the cruelest way to strip it of its value. No matter how perfect it is, the stone that a mason is afraid to plaster over in the belief that he is honoring it by leaving it exposed to the open air, will halt all progress on the building's construction. Zacharia goes on to point out (in substance) that just as the stone plays its role only in providing (by being buried) support for the next stone, so the Arab Tourath, and most notably its normative expression, serves its inheritors only when it has been demystified and "integrated" into the construction, when it has been situated at an objective distance and criticized, the way the artisans of Europe's Renaissance dared to do with their Greek heritage. No matter how luminous the past might be, pleads Zacharia, it is important not to insist on extracting more from it than it can provide, and above all one must not expect to obtain the innovations from it that the present impatiently demands, and that (except for confounding dogma [*ibadates*] and standards for social life [*mu'amalate*]) no religious rule has ever forbidden. A necessary corollary, continues Zacharia, is not to use the battle against all forms of dependency as a pretext for taking secularism as an institution over which the West should have a monopoly. The amalgam (secularism = Western = atheism) distorts the debate. It is a cruel paradox that this "fundamentalism" that insists on its attachment to Islamic civilization sometimes constitutes indeed its most formidable adversary.

---

discours religieux contemporain: mécanismes et fondements intellectuels," *Egypte Monde Arabe,* No. 3, 1990, page 73, where the author emphasizes the absence of historicity as a sign of weakness in the Islamist themes. Farag Fodha, "Qabla al-souqout," Cairo, 1985, and Al-Haqîqa al-gh'iba, *La Vérité Absente,* Dar al-Fikr, Cairo, 1986, 149 pages. Ashmawi (Al) Muhammad Saad, *L'Islamisme contre l'Islam,* preface and translation by Richard Jacquemond, La Découverte/ Dar al-fikr, Paris, Cairo, December, 1989.

The Itinerary for Reappropriation

It nevertheless remains to be seen whether the political expression of the Islamist dynamic can be reduced to that somewhat caricatured essence (present in the fringes of the movement, and evolving in a symbiotic relationship with traditionalist elements in the society), in which its adversaries, who sometimes confuse themselves with its analysts, are naturally pleased to enclose it.(1) The temptation of absolutism takes aim at the least demanding of the ideologues in the literalist fringe of the movement, and produces unconditional and inflammatory demands from leaders ranging from Ali Belhaj to the leaders of the Egyptian *Gemaat Islamiyya* for the "immediate," "exclusive" and "literalist" implementation of an antiquated Sharia law. It nourishes the very legitimate fears of all those who cannot accommodate themselves to such a strictly reactionary logic. And in fact such a "step backwards" could not operate without the support of a dictatorial structure. That is one of the first lessons from the Iranian experience, whose most radical phase has ended with the death of its principal architect. Without measuring the ambiguities and insurmountable limits of such a position, the "literalist" component of the Islamist tendency may well see its capacity for mobilization diminish rapidly,(2) and the bastions

---

(1) Cf. among others Fouad Zacharia, op. cit., who insists on the "formalist derivation" which the Islamists demonstrate in their call for a literal observance of religious rites and has a tendency to ignore too systematically the political dimension of their discourse. That does not stop the ensemble of his ideas from presenting the most remarkable product of the ideological counter-offensive among the secular Arab intelligentsia. See also Alain Roussillon in (notably): "Islam, islamisme et démocratie: recomposition du champ politique," in *Egypte Recompositions, Peuples Méditerranéens*, No. 41-42, October, 1987, March 1988, Page 303. "Entre Al-Jihad et Al-Riyan, phénoménologie de l'Islamisme égyptien," *Maghreb Machrek,* No.127. Leca Jean, "A propos de l'Europe et de l'Orient," *Maghreb Machrek-Monde Arabe,* No. 126. On the articulation of the Islamist currents on the political scene, cf. Rémi Leveau, "La Tunisie du président Ben Ali, équilibre interne et environnement arabe," *Maghreb Machrek,* 124, April June, 1989, page 4. Ghalioun Bourhane, *Ad-Dawla wal-dîn*, Al-Mouassassa al-arabia lil-dirassate wal-nachr, Beirut, 1991, 560 pages.

(2) And in this hypothesis, but only in this hypothesis, finds itself enclosed within the limits of the "tribunician" functions, (comparable to those of the Communist parties in post World War II Europe) evoked in the eightees by Rémi Leveau as a possible future for the Islamist tendencies (in *Les Trajectoires du Politique*, Colloque Fondation Nationale des Sciences politiques, Bordeaux, September, 1988).

where the secular ideologues have anchored themselves today while waiting for a second wind could retake the initiative. But the reactionary quality of the first doctrinal expressions of the Islamist trend as a whole seems today to be indeed a long way from being its only future.

The fact that the "integrist" core appears condemned to evolve does not permit prejudging the future of the tendency in its entirety. Far from being monolithic, the movement is composed of components who are already conscious of the limits of the "integrist" approach and determined to overtake it. Because it contradicts the predominant perception of the phenomenon, this "progressive," or "reformist," "liberal Islam"(1) is systematically underestimated or obscured. It can be identified by (among others) Rached Ghannouchi in Tunisia; Mahfoudh Nahnah but also to a certain extent Abbassi Madani in Algeria; Hassan Hanafi, Adel Hussein, Tareq al Bishri and many others in Egypt; Leith Chbeilat in Jordan; Hassan Tourabi in the Sudan etc. The internal doctrinal dynamics of the Islamist formations, which ought to be considered as essential parameters for analysis, are also often ignored or obscured for the same reason. Because of the tactical demands of politics in the Middle East, the official Arab media, which Westerners are overly prone to rely on for their information, are often more attentive to the violent clashes of partisan confrontations than they are to the internal doctrinal evolution of the movements. But the fact that the Islamist discourse needs to use the heritage of Western culture as a springboard it can react against and that it tends to function in a privileged manner with those elements that express mistrust and defiance of the West, should not mask the reality that its deeper logic is closer to one of selective appropriation than of rejection.

The true paradox of the Islamist "cultural protest" is that it may succeed precisely where colonial violence and nationalist counter-violence have both failed: the nineteenth-century conditions under which the invasion of Western references took place, in the full wave of colonial expansion, made such references impossible to absorb by societies whose cultural codes were brutally marginalized. The reintroduction of the parental culture could paradoxically succeed in reconciling the cultural codes of formerly dominated societies with values, which neither the colonialist invasion nor later ac-

---

(1) From the the title of Leonard Binder's approach to Islamism: *Islamic Liberalism, a Critique of Development Ideologies,* Chicago, 1988. In the United States, John Esposito is also among the few who have efficiciently overcome the "devil" syndrome in the approach of Islamism: see *The Islamist Threat, Myth or Reality,* Oxford, 1992.

tions by the acculturated elite that fought for independence were able to succeed in assuring.

An examination of the internal dynamics of the Islamist movements, so often absent from contemporary analyses, leads in all cases to the conclusion that sensible corrections are beginning to be applied to the first credos. Their dominant logic is to reduce the distance between the two different universes of reference (between classical Muslim thinking and the supposedly Western universe of political modernity), whose contradictions were too hastily considered as impossible to overcome. The ideological itinerary followed by the Tunisian ITM (Harakat Ittijah al Islami) from 1975 to 1990 was such that the group has fully adopted today a number of proposals (on democracy, women, and all the major issues which the media concentrates on today) that only a short while earlier had been so strongly rejected that their original promoters had ultimately quit the movement.(1) In Algeria, where the potential for mobilization is in proportion to the depth of colonialist deculturation, the reformist process has been seemingly approached with more timidity, notably by Abbassi Madani or Mahfoudh Nahnah(2), and the expressions that are the most literal (like those of Ali Belhaj) seem to still satisfy the expectations of a large part of the powerful Islamic Salvation Front (FIS). But behind the fog of the regime's counteroffensive, these "sensible corrections," almost everywhere in the region, are clearly perceptible. After the Tunisian En Nahda (previously ITM), the first group to have (in 1981) explicity adopted democratic principles and all their institutional implications, all leaders of the legalistic movements have unreservedly begun demanding the very pluralistic rules that some of them had once denounced.

If the origin of the political resources of the Islamist mobilization are now clear, the way in which this capital will be exploited and the more or less authoritarian or democratic nature of the regimes it might produce remains highly unpredictable. In any case, it escapes the sole recourse of resorting to a religious vocabulary, and instead depends on the more numerous and complex parameters which permit the characterization of the forms of

---

(1) To express itself since then in the review *15/21* of the Progressive Islamists (cf infra).

(2) Founder of a supposedly apolitical association, Jam'iat al-Irchad, created outside the FIS in 1989, he is unquestionably in Algeria the closest to the Egyptian Muslim Brothers.

political development in the Arab world, in the social and economic environments in which each of the different Islamist parties are evolving.

Beyond just quantifying the spellbinding chant of the "Islamist menace," which too often limits the field of interrogation, it is this socio-historical environment, different from one country to the next, on which the analysis must concentrate more effectively.

An element of unpredictability in the future of the Islamists also lies with the secular intelligentsia. Its attitude with respect to the Islamist credos, in spite of the hardening of its tactical positions, is less clearly entrenched than it might once have seemed. From Cairo to Tunis (1) the "leftists" and Islamists have been for a few years now sending signals that effectively openned the door to approaches that are quite different from the open warfare that has existed up to recently. In Tunisia, the magazine, *15-21*, and especially a majority faction in the Movement for Renewal (En Nadha), has been following the same trend. Here and there, throughout the Arab world, part of the secular intelligentsia has already begun to reposition itself in a way that brings it much closer to the cultural preoccupations of the Islamist approach. The reluctance to mix religion and politics remains intact, but the left in the Arab world, as elsewhere, is now confronted with the hemorrhaging that has affected the credibility of Marxist themes from the USSR to Peking, and even Cuba. The brutal collapse of the Soviet Union's political satellites, the ideological "hara kari" of the leading

---

(1) The terms of the Tunisian debate (which led to a variety of petitions) were presented by Mohamed Al Ahnaf in "Religion et Etat en Tunisie," *Maghreb Machrek Monde Arabe*, December, 1989. Among other examples, the effort at self-criticism by the Islamist current manifests itself notably in *Al-Harakat al-islamiyya: rou'iat mustaqbaliya*, Cairo, Madbouli, 1989, a collective work (edited by Abdallah Fahd al-Nafissi) which brings together the contributions of authors covering the quasi totality of the Arab world (Tunisians, Sudanese, Syrians, Egyptians, etc...). The authors wanted to reflect on what Abdallah Nafissi (a Kuwaiti political scientist) had qualified as "breaches" in the Islamists' thought, namely, the absence of methodical reflection in the long term, an unfamiliarity with the means of mass communications, the underestimation of ideologies that are still strong (leading to the erroneous belief that the Islamist movement was evolving in an "ideological vacuum" which they alone were to fill), the absence of an official historiography, the relative inflexibility of the Islamists' discourse to mutations in its environment, the necessity of getting beyond tribal and clan thinking, the necessity for its approach to evolve from confrontation with authority to opposing authority, and organizational reform (greater transparence, separation of organizational questions from religious ones, a greater respect for the rights of members).

Communist regime, the rise within the ex-Communist camp itself of religious demands, and especially in the South of the "empire" of demands that are specifically Islamic, has considerably accelerated the disintegration of the leftists' environment.(1) Last, but not least, is the dramatic change of heart of the leader of Baghdad, who was considered to be the last great representative of secular Arabism, and who at the beginning of the Gulf war spectacularly attached himself to the very vocabulary that he had previously derided when he was fighting Khomeini's Iran.

It has also become difficult for the Arab left not to disassociate itself with the repressive practices of the regimes in power without taking the risk (the case of the left in Tunisia since 1991) of losing its political identity. In the same sense it is difficult for the left not to admit that there have been evolutions in the doctrine of the movements concerning demands for democracy. Since 1989, a noticeable process of relative "Islamization" of the secularist oppositions has begun to take place. Small parties, admittedly without much future, compete with the Islamists on their terrain for mobilization.

In Egypt, more spectacularly than in the Maghreb (since Egypt has an older multiparty tradition), the old liberal formations feel constrained to make more and more ideological concessions. The Egyptian Neo-Wafd Party consequently decided in 1987 to ally itself with the Muslim Brothers and helped them make their first electoral penetration.(2) In 1989, the inheritors of Hassan Al Banna worked their way around the laws preventing their electoral participation by joining forces with the Socialist Labour Party (an Islamist faction had just taken over control of the party). The Wafd, in an attempt to acquire something of the Islamic aura, tried to convince Sheik Omar Abderrahman, the ideologist of the Jihad organization, to run under its colors. That a party that founded its credibility on the promotion of secular values and on "national unity," (often meaning the defense of the Coptic Community) should solicit the collaboration of a spiritual or-

(1) The Tunisian Communist Party, which was one of the first to draw the explicit consequences from these events, decided in December, 1989, to "refound its identity," which is to say end its existence as a Communist party.

(2) See the most useful series of annual surveys by the Al-Ahram Center for Strategic Studies (Cairo). Also Hala Mostepha, *Al-Islam al-siyyassi fi misr, min harakat al-islah ila jemaat al'unf* (Polical islam in Egypt: from the reformist to the violent groups), Cairo, Markaz al-dirassate al-siyassiya wal-strategia, 1992, 214 pages. On the history of neo-Islamist Socialist Labour Party, see Hanaa Fikry Singer, "The socialist labour party: a case study in contemporary Egyptian opposition party," MA Thesis, A.U.Cairo, 1990.

ganization blamed for the assassination of Sadat, says more than anything else about the difficulty that non-Islamist parties are having in conserving their ideological identity in the face of their omnipresent challengers.

In the same way that the Islamists were forced to treat problems of social justice in order not to let the left monopolize the issue, the left is now being forced to deal with tradition so that the Islamists do not monopolize it completely. Even if the language used by each is still quite different, it is on the question of local culture that the Islamists and the nationalists are beginning to approach one another. The final outcome of this process, which is still taking place, is difficult to predict in the abstract. Under powerful dynamics for transformation, the thrust from the Islamist does not come from the emergence or resurgence of a political ideology that is complete. Its contours are not just as intangible and the political comportment of its actors not just as timeless as the verses of Koranic dogma. Following the nature of the social terrain and the economic landscape that it crosses, according to the nature of the political forces which appropriate it, according to the capacity of the regimes to turn a part of it to their advantage, Islam can express itself in ways that are remarkably diverse. It is, therefore, in socio-political situations, which are very different in each national terrain, that one must watch it take shape.

CHAPTER 5

FROM SERMONS TO THE VOTING BOOTHS

Milestones on the Route.

In the Maghreb, the Islamist mobilization went through a period of gestation in the 1970s during the period following the defeat of Nasserism. But it was really in the 1980s that the movement came out of its adolescence, and at the same time left the obscurity of the mosques in the suburbs and began via the universities to come into public view.

International circumstances had illuminated the rise in power of the different national currents. The rapid increase in mobilization coincided in fact with a dizzying acceleration in the number of events affecting Arab Muslim history. From 1978 to 1982, it became nearly impossible to keep track of the symbolic ruptures that cascaded one after another. They included in rapid succession, the Khomeini revolution (the Imam returned to Teheran on February 1, 1979), the Camp David Accords (March 1979), the attack against the Great Mosque in Mecca (November 20, 1979), the entry of the Soviets into Afghanistan (December, 1979), then the Israelis' entry into Beirut (June, 1982), the assassination of Sadat (October 6, 1981), the conflict between Iran and Iraq (September, 1980), the crystallization of the division of the Arab states into two camps after Egypt's eviction from the Arab League and the transfer of its headquarters to Tunis. Taboos and certitudes crumbled at a rate not seen since the upheavals at independence. After the crisis of Arab socialism, it was, in the words of Abdallah Laroui, the Arab crisis which burst onto the scene in 1978 under the brutal calling-into-question of "the givens and principles which had seemed evident to everyone until then (...): Marxist Communists and fundamentalist Muslims (...) had been forced up until then to espouse the Arab nationalist ideology so closely had it corresponded to the sentiments of the masses. When President Sadat decided to follow a strictly Egyptian policy and encouraged a press campaign intended to justify his new orientation, the non-Arabists in Egypt and elsewhere raised their heads; the events of Lebanon and Iran only accelerated the movement."[1] In the Maghreb, the bloody repression of the Neo-Destour against Tunisian rioters (January, 1978); the physical and political death of Houari Boumediene (November, 1978), whose economic

---

(1) *Islam et Modernité*, Paris, La Découverte, 1987.

and Third World policies were both abandoned; the riots in Casablanca (January, 1981); and the military rapprochement of Morocco with the United States completed the landscape of these regional turbulences. The great mobilization coincided finally with another symbol: the death of the fourteenth century of the Hegira, and the birth of this fifteenth century of which Rached Ghannouchi wrote that "it would be Muslim, or would not be." The mounting cries in the Arab theater occasionally sounded like so many cannons saluting its birth.

The Space of the Mosque

Ibn al Khachab, in 1111, entered a mosque in Bagdad. He broke the pulpit to make the believers understand that prayer was not enough at a time when the empire was in a physical danger.(1)

From Tripoli to Marrakech, 850 years later, it was again the mosque which constituted the first framework for the gestation of the Islamist discourse and its very first receptacle. It played first of all the role as protector, a shelter where the first militant trajectories could be elaborated. The governments everywhere assessed little by little the danger which existed in tolerating a liberty of association and freedom of speech which was all the more subversive since it contrasted with a civil environment that was still tightly controlled. Very quickly, the mosques' highly symbolic space became one of the principal places for confrontation between Islamism and the government. The creation of the mosques—or simply the affectation of a place reserved for prayer on the grounds where one worked—became one of the first places where (especially in Algeria) the Islamists began to judge their margin for maneuver with respect to the regime. The arsenal of law was consequently progressively solicited to establish and then reinforce the controls: control of spaces themselves by the attempt to limit the number of new constructions, control of men charged with operating these spaces and of running them, and finally direct control over their discourse. A space

---

(1) "They forced the preacher to descend from the pulpit, which they broke, and then began to cry, to weep about the misfortunes which Islam had suffered because of the Francs (...) As they prevented the believers from praying, the people in charge made promises to appease them in the name of the Sultan; they would send armies to defend Islam from the Francs and all the infidels," Ibn al Qalinissi, cited by Amin Maalouf in *The Crusades Seen by the Arabs,* French edition, J. C. Lattes, (J'ai Lu), page 104. For his statistics on the development of the mosques in eastern Algeria (more than for the explanation that he gives) read Ahmed Rouadjia, *Les Frères et la Mosquée*, Paris, Karthala, 1990.

for confrontation, the mosque also became that of the higher rivalry between "state fundamentalism" (which today disputes the emblem of the greatest mosque in Africa, the advantage having just passed into the camp of the Moroccans) and that of its opponent. The restructuring of the university apparatus, of religious training in general and of that of the Imams in particular—modernized and centralized; the construction of new "official" mosques; the attempt to take control, or failing that, to discredit the others; as well of course as the remobilization of the apparatus of the civil service clerics, would become the axes of the government's redeployment in the field of religion. Everywhere, the first arrests would attest to the importance of the role of these free Friday preachers capable of remaining independent from the state-created credos. Desperately needing to express themselves, they had served as an outlet to escape the monotony and the redundance of the State's discourse and that of its official clerics. In Morocco, first of all, and then in Algeria, the Friday sermon was submitted to a strict centralized control, edited by collaborators with the Ministry of Religion. It became obligatory in all the mosques accredited by the state, to diffuse sermons without changes.

In Algeria, the five-year plan called in 1980 for the creation of two universities of Islamic Sciences (in Algiers and Oran), three institutes of the same type (at Tlemco, Mascara and Medea), a mosque and a Koranic school in each of the 160 *dairate* of the territory, an Islamic cultural center in each *wilayate* that did not already have one, and the financing of 5,000 posts in religious education.

On November 17, 1981, an inter-ministerial decree drafted a list of 45 mosques considered to have "a national character" and on December 1, of the same year, new regulations were drafted setting the conditions for recruitment of imams and masters of Koranic education. On August 6, 1983, the school for training the cadres of the Meftah cult, created in September, 1971, was entirely reorganized. And on August 4, 1984, the Emir Abdelkader University of Islamic Sciences of Constantine was created in the sumptuous building erected facing the "secular" university built ten years earlier by Oscar Niemeyer. It was given the responsibility for graduate and post-graduate teaching consecrated to the Sharia, to the Sources of Law (*Oussoul al Fiqh*) and Religion (*Oussoul al din*), and the science of the propagation of the Islamic faith (*Da'wa Islamiya*).

The number of imams, more or less uncontrolled, increased at a rate that was no less spectacular, i.e. about as rapidly as the minarets. From 3,283 in 1968, the number of mosques increased to 5,000 in 1980, of which more than 2,000 had no officially authorized imam. The state remunerated, according to the nomenclature of the ministry of religion, 159 imams outside the hierarchy, 592 preaching imams, and 2,130 imams classed as "prayers."(1)

Since 1980, under the impulse of multiple associative structures, legal or not, the rhythm of construction has accelerated even faster. In November, 1986, the then-president Chadli Benjedid alerted his prefects to the dangers of such a situation. "In constructing a mosque," he said,"we must guarantee all the conditions necessary so see that it can fulfill the important role for which it was built. We cannot leave it to the mercy of certain pernicious elements who would use it for destructive ends. It is thus necessary to plan and to program in function of our needs and our capacities (...) The demagogic policy which leads the wilayas and the communes to give authorizations to those who construct alone and without any planning must disappear. I insist again on the fact that you must not let yourselves be influenced by narrow-minded elements whose erroneous conceptions interfere with Islam." (2)

A few months earlier, it was the authority of the Egyptian Imam, Mohamed Ghazali, Director of the Scientific Council of the Emir Abdelkader University, who had been solicited to discredit the "uncontrolled" clerics: "There are not enough religious scholars to equip the (new) mosques. Those who preach are often volunteers. Some of them are competent and others are not. But it is not possible to stop a person who leads the Friday prayer from preaching. For there have been no provisions for competent replacements. There is no complete religious apparatus which can satisfy all these mosques. The mosques that follow the State effectively exist, and there one can find imams who are capable. These are the imams which the State pays. While those who have no capacity nor qualification, the state does not pay them." (3)

---

(1) Fatiha Akeb in *Algérie-Actualité*, May 8, 1986. On the place of the mosque in the development of the Islamist mobilization in Algeria, read also Mohamed Tozy in *Les Nouveaux Intellectuels Musulmans* (under the direction of Gilles Kepel and Yann Richard), Le Seuil, 1990. In 1990, the number of mosques was as high as 11,221 (including 1,790 "prayer's rooms" and 952 mosques under construction). *Le Nouvel Hebdo*, No. 32, January 30, 1991, page 15.

(2) *El Moujahid*, November 12, 1986, cited by Hanafi Chabbi, *Islam et Socialisme dans l'Algérie Contemporaine*, thèse de 3ème cycle, Aix-en-Provence, March, 1987.

(3) Interview in *Algérie-Actualité*, No. 1057, January 16, 1986.

The authority of the Egyptian Sheikh, which was solid in a certain sector of public opinion, but was already being called into question by the Islamist movement, whose representatives openly boycotted his courses, had little impact on the multiplication of minarets. For Abbassi Madani, the leader of Algeria's FIS, it was not a question of denying that the function of the mosque was clearly political.

> If the mosques are not there for that, what purpose do they serve? (...) The mission of the mosque is not the same as that of a church. It is the place for all the acts of good, in which all the affairs of the Umma are treated. It is in the mosque that the Caliph was designated and pronounced his political discourses. It is from there that the armies left to confront the enemy. The mosque is a place of consultation. The appeals to separate the mosques from political activities date already back to the colonial period.(1)

In June, 1991, then in January, 1992, the regime, nevertheless, attempted to perfect its control over the apparatus of the mosques in adopting laws increasing the control of the administration over the buildings and men. Such a measure, notes Arun Kapil,(2) is not without danger. In the fashion of the electoral law of June, 1991, which was designed to lay the foundation for an FLN (National Liberation Front) victory, but had the effect of amplifying that of the FIS (Islamic Salvation Front), this heavy-handedness by the State, which aimed at working to the detriment of the diverse Muslim currents, would take a fundamentally different direction.

In certain contexts the control took a more radical form. A few Libyan mosques were leveled to the ground (cf infra) and their clergy were imprisoned, i.e. eliminated. But almost everywhere in the Maghreb, there was a movement by governments in question to limit and often, pure and simply, to ban access to the mosques outside prayer times. Merely frequenting the mosque at Sidi Bou Said Tunis at the wrong time was enough to earn a police interrogation. The tactic risked turning visitors to the mosques, who might be in search of a bit of isolation, into Islamist militants.

From Msaken in Tunisia (on July 17, 1981) to Laghouat (cf infra), the nomination of the imams, the contents of sermons and in general all of the State's taking control of the space of the mosques led to confrontations: on

---

(1) Interview in *Algérie-Actualité*, No. 1264, January 4–10, 1990, pages 8 and 9.

(2) "The Algerian Elections of June 1990," *Merip Report*, 1990.

January 17, 1961, the Tunisian administration, which had imprudently given authorization to a team of Western film makers to shoot a remake of the "Thief of Baghdad" in the walls of the great mosque of Kairouan unleashed one of the first religious riots in the country. (1)

From the Mosque to the University

Between 1978 and 1981, the period of great mobilization, it was through contacts with the student left and the discovery of the virtues of dialectics and organization that the Islamist current really took off. "In 78, there was only one Islamist at the university in Rabat...in 82, there were 500."(2)

From Rabat to Tunis, if the first protests had come from the mosques by professionals of religion, it is in the universities that the first battalions of militants were deployed. Even among the militants themselves, the students constituted the spearhead of the current, and outside the university, the teacher furnished the greatest number of its cadres. At the interior of the student movement, the faculties of sciences most often provided the largest numbers of troops. A number of hypotheses explain this particular propensity of scientists. The acculturation doubtlessly functioned in a manner that was more effective in legal and literary matters than in the abstract universe of the exact sciences, where the cultural vacuum was undoubtedly felt more quickly. The fact that the faculties of science remained French-speaking longer than the others may also have played an amplifying role. Contrary to an idea that was widely spread at the time, the first mobilizations more often took place in the ranks of the French-speaking students than the Arab speakers. That is the thesis concerning the situation in Algeria maintained by Rachid Benaissa,(3) and there is no reason not to hold the same for the situation in Tunisia. The movement of re-Islamization would crystallize itself during the arrival at the universities of the first beneficiaries of the democratization of higher education, that is to say the sons of the rural peasants. For R. Benaissa (cf infra):

---

(1) L'Imam of the Grand mosque, imprisoned following a demonstration, would significantly, 28 years later, be the candidate of Rached Ghannouchi's Islamic Tendency Movement in the elections of April 2, 1989.

(2) Cited by Mireille Duteil in "L'intégrisme islamique au Maghreb: la pause," *Grand Maghreb*, No. 27, December, 1983.

(3) Interview with the author, Paris, April, 1988.

The re-Islamization of the university was done by the accession of these modest people to the University. These were the modest, the peasants, the sons of peasants who, arriving at the University by the penchant for democratization of education, had conquered this liberty to express in discourse the culture they had lived. While during the first ten years, the university had only received the sons of the fathers of the intellectual bourgeoisie, or those who had been influenced by France.

The ideological gestation of the student cadres sometimes borrowed from the itinerary of Marxism, or from one of the nuances of Baathism, then of Nasserism, in which the quasi-majority of the Arab intellectuals, Rached Ghannouchi included,(1) recognized themselves at one time or another. "For my part," says Benaissa,

> I was a "Muslim Marxist." I had read a great deal of the *Wretched of the Earth*,(2) Garaudy or Lefebvre. At the level of the structure of my reflective thought, it was Marxism. I was never a primary anti-Marxist. I did not hesitate at accepting all that was acceptable in Marxism. I was even a little Maoist while ours were not. When around 1968, we initiated a counter-campaign of posters at the university, we adopted a Marxist, pro-Chinese language. The clique was accused of being revisionist... Social imperialist... In brief, we took all the language of *Peking Information*. But I had also read the Christian theologians who helped me to disengage from the scientism of the Arab speakers

"In Tunisia equally" confirms Enneifer,

> this competition with the ideology of the university left was decisive in the ideological and political structuring of the current: It is this direct confrontation between traditional Islamic thought positioned in the opposition, of course, but very unfocused, and the thought and modes of action of the leftist groups, who were at the time regularly standing trial, which was to lead to a process of radicalization. I believe that it was at that moment then that the true political profile of the Islamist current was forged. At the university, it was necessary to militate, to militate politically and on foundations that were clear. The Islamist students could not escape the university customs. Meetings, wall newspapers, political "analyses," or supposed so... Imperialism,

(1) Cf. supra.

(2) Of the Algerian nationalist militant, Frantz Fanon, who was of Antillaise origin.

for example, we never spoke of imperialism. It was in the contact with this left that we discovered that there had been a certain interference from the outside in the life of the underdeveloped countries. The university played a role that was central. (1)

After the sermon of protest (relayed by cassettes and leaflets) and the mobilization of the student community (by attentively taking charge of its interests as a body and the organization of protest), before finding access to the legal political scene or by necessity of having to disengage itself from it, the movement spread was deployed—in a register that was much less explicitly political—to the heart of civil society. It most often developed there with methods of social and educational action that took advantage of the weaknesses of state policy. Free medicine, distribution of school equipment; legal and administrative advice; the organization of youth in scouting and militant outings; the taking charge of civil and religious festivals,(2) permitted the students to go out from the territory of the university and to win sympathy, if not adhesion, from the popular sectors of society who had not yet been affected by the first mobilizations.

To respond to each of the limits or each of the obstructions of the modernization "from above," the Islamist militants began to weave the fabric of a veritable "counter-society." In pretending to ignore the State and inculcating in the society the means to bypass it, they managed to be much more efficient at discrediting the regimes (if not the states themselves) than when they had engaged in simple confrontation. The authorities understood very well, and especially in Egypt they used all the means at their disposal to try to discredit the Islamist initiatives in the economic field.

These itineraries were never the result of the sole will of the Islamist strategists (who were treated roughly by circumstances they were almost never able to master) but were as much an adaptation to their national environment. They depended on the rapidity with which the regimes were able to judge the seriousness of the phenomenon and the effectiveness with which they undertook to reconquer the terrain lost to their new challengers in the mosques, social policies, democratization or symbolic level.

---

(1) Interview with the author, cited.

(2) Notably, circumcisions accompanied by Koranic recitation. Expensive marriages, feared by a great number of young couples, were forbidden, along with the fashion of any pagan form of festivities, such as dancing.

The Role of the Written Word...

In the lycees we distribute little books.
(Enneifer, Tunis)

After a meeting of nearly all the members of the Islamic Youth in Rabat, I was offered the book of Sayyid Qutb, *Alam fi tariq*. I read practically the whole book that night, and it overwhelmed me. Thanks to him, I began to understand things. He completely changed my life. I decided to give myself to...I don't like the word to militate, I prefer the word *Da'wa* or Jihad, one of the two, or the two.
(Abdallah Benkirane, Morocco).

After the direct contact with words, public or private, accidental or researched, heard or understood, direct or recorded on a cassette, writing in the form of tracts, brochures, newspapers, reviews or books were inscribed very naturally into the chain of media used by the Islamist mobilization. While words lend themselves to passive listening, a book demands that its reader make a conscious effort. If it appears to reveal certain vocations, it is more often the instrument of their consolidation, serving to structure the argument of a neo-militant and the foundations of his doctrine. At a time when contacts had not yet been established with Egypt, and when it was still physically difficult to travel there, Egyptian brochures came unquestionably along with the teachers who were imported, the first vectors of the export of the doctrine of the "Brothers."

Very quickly, the relay was taken up by the local production which initially consisted most often of articles accepted by the national press (such as the collaboration of Rached Ghannouchi on the daily newspaper, *Al Sabah*). This was followed by the creation of proper magazines and newspapers. Their inventory, which remains to be carried out in greater detail, constitutes a good indicator of the "religion" of each of the states in Islamist matters. At the same time. it reflects the specificity of the national currents, and the opposite, their areas of convergence. Diversified in the Morocco of the Commander of the Faithful, more tightly limited in Tunisia until 1990, strictly state-controlled in Algeria until 1989 and in Libya, clandestine and imported everywhere, in the Maghreb the Islamist press must of course be read in the light of its environment and the conditions of its production. Tolerated during the gestation period of the fundamentalists, it was subjected to a wave of interdictions in the Maghreb, which sometimes even affected whole publishing houses (Bouslama in Tunisia) when its political dimension became clearer.

The Islamist press then plunged most into expatriation and clandestinity. It reappeared at times with the imprimature of the State (such as the review *15/21* in Tunisia, or *Al Forkan* in Morocco) as an expression of the state's tolerance or an instrument of its counter-offensive. The authors had to circumscribe the territory of their protest, on the one hand to the springboard of reaction to the West and on the other hand to certain of the West's supposed avatars—especially the nationalist Arab left, provided that they were not themselves too close allies of the regime. The incitation to concentrate attention on the West, did not constitute, it is true, a violence for authors who were more or less familiar with this register. The inventory of the social and individual pathologies of the West was a recurrent theme of the Islamist press. It stretched the lengths of the pages and showed a method and minutia that were not without relation to the quality of its sources (a major reference being *Le Monde Diplomatique*).

In this discourse, the appreciation of the national environment, especially its political dimension, was turned because of restrictions from the censors into one of the major unspoken subjects. Readers were invited to find the references to their own situations in the extrapolation of generalities, which became even more allusive as the subject approached the throne or the presidency of the place. The clarification of the passage into politics of the authors of these reviews through the increase in the frequency of articles was clearly related to politics. The Tunisian example of the review *Al Maarifa* (between 1972 and 1979, date of its interdiction), studied by Saida Nelouti and Mohamed Baki Hermassi, helps clarify the chronology of the passage to the future Mouvement de la Tendence Islamique of Rached Ghannouchi.

THEMES OF THE REVIEW *AL MAARIFA* (1972-1979)

Themes	Number of Articles	Percentage
Spiritual and cultural subjects	299	53.5%
Ethical and doctrinal subjects	177	31.7%
Social questions	51	9.1%
Political questions	31	5.5%

(**Source**: *Al-Harakat al-Islamia fi Tunis* - Abdellatif al-Hermassi, Baïtam lil nachr, Tunis, 1985, page 105.)

The Way to the Urns (Elections)

The Islamist mobilization has little by little gained a legitimate if not quite legal access to the political scene first in Tunisia, and then much later in Algeria. Formed primarily by the techniques of proseletyzing in the mosques, the militants needed some time to familiarize themselves with modern political action. From press conferences to communiques, they learned in Tunisia first, and afterwards in Algeria, the difficulties in trying to confront the professionals of the political class on an equal footing, and the potential dangers in becoming relatively commonplace. The obligation to elaborate a political program often unleashed the dynamics of diversification, with the militant discourse logically suffering from the demands of public action. This adhesion to the logic of the pluralist system often implied a rupture in theory, with the literal reading of the Sharia contradicting democratic principles (cf infra). This rupture took place in an explicit manner in 1981 for the ITM (Islamic Tendency Movement) of Rached Ghannouchi (cf infra) following the Muslim Brothers, who had also clarified their adhesion to democratic principles. In Algeria, the authorized spokesmen of the FIS all subscribed to the principles of pluralism. Except in the case of the FIS (at least until the wave of repression of June, 1991), these recognitions of pluralism were far from reciprocal. From Morocco to Cairo, the same legislation, which proscribed the use of religion in the references

96

of a political party, has served until now to keep most of the Islamist formations on the periphery of the legal political scene.

For the candidates seeking power, this side-tracking of the institutional logic of the political system to which they were still asked to integrate themselves led to numerous strategies of adaptation. They sketched out the itineraries of a "poor man's policy," a kind of antechamber of the legitimate political scene, whose pathways (the world of labor unions, humanitarian associations, and socio-educational groups, etc.) all include a coefficient of Islamist presence. Its importance varies from one place to another, but the overall tendency is a constant increase.

The Social Anchorage

Because not many studies have been performed, our knowledge of the social anchorage of the Islamist current remains uneven. The dominant vision in the social sciences at the moment is that fertile ground for Islamist recruitment exists within the middle classes who are suffering from the "sickness of modernity"; with those who have paid a heavy price for the process of accelerated modernization, with the "sickness of urbanization"; with those whom urban living has projected into a universe which is brutally different from the social forms that existed before; with those who have tried to keep a sheep in the bathtub to soften the absence of a genuine system of social protection; with those to whom a television was given before they were provided with a means of accessing at least a part of the lifestyle they were likely to see on it. Indeed, the frustrations over identity might have been expressed more rapidly in this particularly destructive universe suffering from the sickness of modernization. The first available evaluations, even though they are only partial, indicate that rather than being recruited from pockets of archaism that had been excluded from the dynamic of modernization, the vast majority of militants appear, in reality, to come from the modernist stratum of society (university teachers, low-level civil servants, etc.) and from the young.(1)

---

(1) The average age of the 72 who were sentenced in the trial of September 1987 in Tunisia was (at the date of the trial) 32-and-a-half years old.

97

PROFESSIONS OF THOSE SENTENCED IN TUNISIA IN SEPTEMBER 1987

Teachers	14 (of which 2 at the university and two in religious educations.)
Engineers	07
Administrative employees	07
Students	05
Technicians	02 (computer programmers and technical instructors)
Small businessmen	03
Doctors	03
Artisans	02
Lawyers	02
Paramedical	01 (laboratory worker)
Farm worker	01
Primary school teacher	01
Military	01 (national guard)
Unemployed	03
Not declared 26	26 (of which 4 had Ph.D.'s)

(**Source:** *La Presse* [Tunisian daily])

The cadres of the movements, notably in Tunisia, tend to be urban professionals. They are high school teachers, but also accountants, or civil servants as well as small businessmen, and artisans in the private sector. They themselves have only recently integrated with the system. They often come, it is true, from these newly urbanized sectors which especially suffered economically and culturally from their transplantation. Their family background, that is to say the socio-economic category, appears from available studies to be mostly from poorer levels of society, small salaried workers, or the sub-proletariat.

Forty-eight percent of the fathers of militants who were questioned in a survey conducted by Abdellatif and M.B. Hermassi, were illiterate. Twenty-seven percent were at a primary level. Nineteen percent were "modest white collar workers." Forty-six percent were urban workers or farm workers. Finally, forty-nine percent belonged to what the authors described as families that had suffered a loss, that is that the father had died, or become an invalid, or retired or was "at the limit of survival."(1)

In welcoming a foreign visitor, Abdessalam Yassine comments on the diversity of the militants who have come to listen to the master debate. The doctor (unemployed) rubs shoulders with the post office employee, or that of the ministry of planning, the computer operator with the bookseller, the cousins from the countryside and the whole range of students. Of course it is possible that the selection was put together to impress the visitor and such a gathering cannot be taken as a scientific sampling.

If one judges by observing the large riots of Tunis (1978 and 1984), Casablanca (1984), or later Constantine (1986), it appears that the urban sub-proletariat had not yet been significantly mobilized. The mass mobilizations of the ITM throughout the repressive wave of 1987, which never took in the populations of the shanty towns (who descended on the residential quarters in the "bread riots" of 1984), did nothing to contradict this evaluation. The upsurge of the Algerian FIS marked a first deviation from this point of view and showed the current's capacity to mobilize large fringes of the urban sub-proletariat. At the end of 1991, a study by CENEAP (Algeria) confirmed the Islamist presence among laborers and workers, 44 percent of the (young) members of this category having declared that they voted for the FIS.(2) In Egypt, if the Muslim Brothers especially concentrated their ef-

(1) Al-Baki Hermassi, *Maghreb Machrek,* op. cit.

(2) The study of the CENEAP (cited by *Liberation* of February 10, 1992), which concerned the young aged from 18 to 29 years who had already left the educational system, showed that of 65% of the youths who declared themselves

forts on the urbanized middle classes, the Gemaat Islamiyya, which was far less present in the large cities, mobilized apart from the student groups the rural and semi-urban proletariat in Upper Egypt.

But rather than deal with estimates that are only partial, it might be better to express the hypothesis that the Islamist phenomenon appears less and less to be limited to specific social territories. Its social geography cannot be considered as being limited to economic victims of modernization. Otherwise, how can one take in all the victims of these identity crises who in the farthest reaches of society make very authentic militants? The doctor in Constantine who ejects the symbols of Westernism from his lifestyle? The highly placed Tunisian public official covered with honors who, at the end of a successful administrative career, renews with traditional culture and all the codes that that implies, including the clothing, which he had once renounced? The high-ranking Moroccan administrator who verbalizes with a disturbing lucidity the failure of his career "in the service of importing Western technologies in a social framework unable to benefit from them"? Or all those again who, before the breeze turns into a tempest, prefer to follow the analyses which they once rejected, and to place themselves in the moral comfort of the growing majorities? If Islamism manifests the displacing of the entire range of political ideologies towards the "religious terrain" more than it does the simple emergence of a political current, the process might well accelerate even more noticeably during the course of the next few years.

The Role of Women

> *The first is a party (FIS). The second is a piece of fabric, the Hijjab. Both are used to weave the same material: a shroud.*
> *(Martine Gozlan)* (1)

---

to be interested in politics, 41% supported the FIS. (25% FLN and 10.5% FFS). The Islamist party seemed also to have the favor of bachelors (38% against 25% for the FLN) and of the unemployed (46% against 20% for the FLN). Finally only 50% of the partisans of FIS declared themselves favorable to the installation of an Islamic Republic.

(1) "The victory of the Islamists in the first round of the Algerian election? It was entirely in the Hijjab. (...) Even if those who were silent voted on January 16, Algiera has already chosen the shroud." *L'Évènement du Jeudi*, January 2, 1992, No. 374, page 57.

The fact that the relationship between Islamism and "women's rights" is often presented in an unusually heated environment does not help in arriving at a clear understanding of the relationship—especially in the absence of good sociological studies on the subject. The "feminist" awakening in the West has further complicated matters. For "homo occidentalus," the masculine adhesion to the Islamist credo is irritating because of its rejection of Western symbols; the presence of women in the Islamist movement generates reactions that are even more passionate. Such imitations gently reinforce the Western propensity to take short cuts in analysis. The first shortcut consists of reducing the essence of Islamism to an "anti-women" campaign, in this way closing the entire dynamic of the ideological repositioning of the South into the analytical ghetto of a "misogyny," or with even less nuance, an "apartheid"(1) which is erected as a central and absolute principle "explaining" the phenomenon. In ridiculing "bearded villains forcing the Hijjab on fragile young girls in tears," talented caricaturists have not run into much opposition when it comes to anchoring a simplistic, unreal image in Western public opinion. Instead of the "stumbling block in the Islamist movement" that the most automatic detractors see it to be,(2) might not the "question of women" really be one

---

(1) This includes Michel Camau, who usually demonstrates more nuance, but for whom "... it was impossible to hide (...) the fact that a compromise between the regimes and the Islamist movements would run a strong risk of taking place at a high cost to women. Would one be right in speaking of democratization in relation to a process of apartheid founded on sexual discrimination?" in "Democratisation et changement des régimes au Maghreb," *Elecciones, participacion y transiciones politicas en el norte de africa,* Madrid Institut de cooperacion con el mundo arabe, 1991, page 67(May, 1990), page 77.

(2) Cf. Al-Ahnaf, Botiveau and Frank Fregosi, *L'Algérie par ses Islamistes,* op. cit. page 239. "The question of women," they note in reference to Algeria, "is no doubt the stumbling block which the Islamist current will come up against in Algeria and elsewhere."
This peremptory statement does not prevent them from approaching a more complex reality a few lines further down, once their ardor for denunciation has been brought under control. They note that "Hassan Al-Banna, founder of the Association of the Muslim Brothers and a contemporary of the first Egyptian women's association, had nothing to say that we know, concerning this movement." And that, "If the defense of the closing in of women and the control of their conduct was the specialty of the old turbans of the Azhar and the Zitouna, all those who considered social change to be a vital necessity for the Arab world, and who felt that it was worth more to participate in it than to be the victim of it, saw the evolution of the condition of women as a thing to be desired and as something that was inevitable."

of the set ways in which Westerners see Islamism? Let's take a hypothetical look at the terrain of the debate.

In nearly all human societies, without diminishing the importance of their function it is safe to say that women have usually constituted the "weaker link" in the social chain. They feel the tensions crossing the corpus of the society more directly than others, and more systematically than others, they end up paying the price of these tensions. In the turbulence of mutations generated by violent transformations of the systems of references induced by cultural invasion from the North, the feminine segment of Arab societies throughout the century has had a special propensity to pay the price for change. Each time the two models of socialization, one based on the Western model and the other more directly adapted from traditional Muslim society, have entered into competition with each other, the violence directed against individuals in the conflict between the two competing systems has more naturally affected women, who were less autonomous with respect to the dominant normative system. In the present phase of reinterpretation of the models perceived as inherent in Western culture, the "weak link" in the societies of the Maghreb is indisputably being targeted again in a privileged manner. Yet, to articulate the undeniable existence of such "constraints" on the growth in power of the Muslim current, it is necessary to reconcile givens which at least have the appearance of being contradictory. On the one hand there is a long-standing reputation, notable, but not exclusively found in the West, of an Islam (*a fortiori* of Islamism) as a great oppressor of women's rights; and on the other hand there is the fact that Islamist mobilization has affected as many women as men. Contrary to a wide-spread impression, it has done this without systematically or seriously calling women's freedom of action into question.

Who are the many thousands of women who swell the ranks of the Islamist formations? Their numbers at least suggest that on the two coasts of the Mediterranean there are different ideas about the freedom of women in general, and the wearing of the veil in particular.

We must not underestimate the importance of the polysemic dimension of the language of the veil (1) and the extreme diversity of ways it expresses

---

(1) Concerning Iran, even if the situation is only partially comparable to that which prevails in an Arab context where the Islamist currents are not in power, "Logique étatique et pratiques populaires: la polysémie du Hejab chez les femmes islamiques en Iran," CEMOTI, No. 10, 1990, *Une approche anthropologique de l'Iran post révolutionnaire: le cas des femmes islamiques*, Paris, EHESS, 1990, published in 1992 by Karthala under the title, *Révolution sous le voile*. For an

the attitudes of women with respect to the Islamist mobilization. "The Hijjab is certainly a symbol of the rejection of an imported and imposed modernity, but its significance is richer in other ways," emphasizes Fariba Adelkhah, who scornfully points to "the inanity of the Western discourse when it sees in the imposition of the Hijjab, a simple sign of the repressive character of the Islamic regime." (...) "The Hijjab is the material expression of a continuity between human nature and the Koranic revelation and it structures the relationship between the private and public spheres, between the family and social spaces."(1) In a society whose physical infrastructure (notably transportation) imposes a mixture of the sexes that is difficult for them to accept, the veil offers an undeniable protection that the system of cultural norms is no longer able to impose. "When a girl takes the Hijjab and renounces 'mixing'," says Mohamed Tozy,(2)

> she certainly appropriates a cultural identity. But this identity is ef-
> fective to the extent to which it is in response to a concrete obstacle.
> In a university restaurant with endless lines, or on an overcrowded bus
> where promiscuity often threatens physical integrity, the Hijjab
> becomes a vital requirement (...)

There is no question that the pressures from the family, or from peers, as well as the response to a diffuse social movement cannot be left out of the analysis. These pressures can lead to the anticipation of the supposed tastes of a potential husband who has emigrated to the Gulf, or to the satisfaction of the tastes of a professor, brothers or cousins. No doubt economic circumstances (the rise in prices at the hairdressers or the cost of imported blue jeans) also need to be introduced into the analysis.

On a larger scale, adherance to the Islamist cause also reasonably functions to set the latest fashion for socialization on the part of Arab women. It permits women who ask to wear the Hijjab to go out of the family home with an assurance of morality. In doing so, these women enter into a circle

---

equally contrasted vision, cf. Chahla Chafiq, *La femme et le retour de l'Islam, l'expérience iranienne,* Editions du Félin, July, 1991, 146 pages. Mireille Paris, *Femmes et sociétés dans le monde arabo-musulman, État bibliographique,* Travaux et documents of IREMAM, No. 9, Aix-en-Provence, 1989.

(1) Op. cit.

(2) *Lamalif,* Interview with the author, 1988, page 5–30.

that seems more worthy than the non-existent "youth centers" or the forbidden discotheques.

But, the unfortunate paradox in the vision of Western "feminists" is that they are all too ready to refuse these Muslim women the very thing that they have been trying to protect them from by defending them against the abuses of male domination—namely, the right to decide the course of their own lives, outside all dictates of feminine specificity as "thinking individuals." However, everything leads one to believe, in fact, that the leading factors motivating "the entry into Islamism" of women are very simply the same as those that affect men. The greatest number of female adherents feel they have joined up for exactly the same reasons as their brothers or husbands, without necessarily attaching any significance especially linked to the female condition. With what result?

Once again, it is not a question of deliberately replacing the "black reality of the feminine condition in the Arab world" with another over-simplification that is just as ideological and far from reality. Certainly, the social status of women constitutes one of the terrains on which the invasion of Western references has disturbed the dynamic of the internal normative evolution of the universe of Islam. Certainly the literalist and authoritarian reintroduction of the normative apparatus of the pre-colonial culture is eventually bound to call into question some important and recent modernizations in the domain concerning women, the sole error of such changes being that they happened during the "imperialist" phase of the West and were phrased in Western language.

No one will deny that women are often the target for specific forms of violence. But it remains to be shown, if there is violence, whether this is specifically due to re-Islamization or is simply part of the underlying cultural situation. First of all, it is worth noting that the machismo of Mediterranean culture has most often functionned without the "ideological cover" obtained from a literalist reading of certain Islamic references. Neither has it so far been shown that "sexist" violence has disappeared toward women who satisfy the new Islamic codes, from the inside of the Islamist movement. It remains to be asked whether the discriminatory practices which are related to the Islamists are not more often attributable to sociohistorical circumstances during the growth of Muslim culture than to the "essence" of that culture. It seems more reasonable that the impact of the dynamic of re-Islamization in this domain, as in others, is ambivalent and pluralistic: exacerbations of discordances between two models of reference and thus creating new tensions, but at the same time resulting in a progressive reabsorption of this formal dualism and of the tensions that result from it.

The Western perception often deforms the nature of the debate between these references and tries to see a symbolic confrontation between two opposed cultures when in fact the differences are often more a question of form than of substance. "The essence of the debate concerning the emblematic question of the veil," pleads Tareq al-Bishri,

> is not concerned with the question of the length of clothes or whether or not the hair is covered, but with the necessity for the woman to have access to education and work. The concentration on the symbolic meaning of the veil most tends to turn the debate into a confrontation between two systems of references which are not as antagonistic to one another as they might sometimes seem. Where is the point of divergence between the followers of the veil and its detractors? The Western mentality prefers to place the difference on the terrain of progress and backwardness. The hijjab would thus be the expression of bad treatment reserved for women at the same time as it is the corollary for underdevelopment. It would be both the origin and the expression of women's inferiority. The fact of not wearing it becomes, to the contrary, a sign of progress, of equality, of recognized liberty. Since one speaks of liberty, would the Western reader believe me if I told him that no one obliged the women of this generation (the 1970s and 1980s) to wear the veil and all those who decided to wear it did so in a manner that was completely deliberate. (...) This insistence on presenting the problem in terms of wearing the veil or not in terms of education and of work corresponds in fact to a desire to approach the question from the angle of different frames of reference instead of seeing a simple social problem that warrants discussion. For some, this insistence signifies a will to dethrone one system of reference in order to impose another. For others, it expresses a concern to safeguard their frame of reference from destruction by the other system. Within Islamic thought, the disagreement with Western thought is not profound: both admit the "particular" nature of women and argue that this specificity justifies giving women certain kinds of work and not others. The difference in thought is only quantitative: it concerns the list of approved and disapproved kinds of work (...) But instead of being presented in the terms of a controversy, a subject of discussion, in terms of the access of women to education for herself and so that the society can profit, the question is presented to Muslims by Westerners in terms which attack their essential beliefs. In contrast, in the secular West, it is presented as a model of behavior, a reference of life, of judgments of value. (1)

---

(1) Interview with the author, Cairo, April, 1991.

At the interior of the new symbolic space, nothing prevents the reformist dynamic from following or resuming its natural course. The critical construction which might forbid polygamy from the interior of Islam has already been verbalized numerous times.(1) "This double function (of the Hijjab) leads Islamist women to demand (...) elements of a modernity already put in place in the last decades: the right, without any restriction, to a modern education and to work, recognition outside the family scene, outcomes from participation in all the debates led in Iranian society," says Fariba Adelkhah.(2) "On the individual scale," adds Fatiha Hakiki Talahite.

> the wearing of the Hijjab does not necessarily signify regression, as one might believe at first. One could make the hypothesis that through the Hijjab, a woman affirms that her submission to God outweighs her submission to man. Here, the submission to man signifies submission to a social order in which man has a preponderant role (...) Of course she will not go as far as contesting her submission to man, since religion orders it. But to demand direct submission to God, without using the mediation of a man, can be interpreted as an affirmation of self, a beginning to the emergence of woman as an individual, in a society in which the individual itself is only in its early stammerings.(3)

"The greatest contribution by Iranian Islamic women," says Fariba Adelkhah, "was not so much their numerical weight, as it was the critical dimension of their support to the revolution and, in the phase afterwards, their essential participation from inside the Islamist movement to the resumption of the process of reform, the fact that each text is discussed today, contested and, if the occasion arises, amended under the pressure of their interventions, by a 'feminist' movement whose activism never had an equal before the revolution."(4)

---

(1) Cf. Ahmida Enneifer, *La Tunisie*, infra.

(2) Op. cit.

(3) Fatiha Hakiki Talahite, "Sous le voile, les femmes," *Les Cahiers de l'Orient*, No. 23, September, 1991, page 123.

(4) Fariba Adelkhah, interview with the author, CEDEJ, Cairo, April 1992. For an illustration, one can recall that the first woman elected to the Sudanese parliament was on an Islamist list, and even more recently (April 1992), the first woman to be elected to the governing bureau of the powerful Egyptian Medical Union was also on an Islamist list.

Nevertheless, for the reformist process to resume its course, it is necessary, as Tareq Al Bishri explains, that the "Citadel of Islam" not feel itself under siege. "One does not advance, when one is on the defensive," says Bishri. "One doesn't move forward when one is defending one's positions." On the question of women as with so many other questions, the reformist process which had made its appearance earlier was interrupted by the invasion of Western values and has only imperceptibly resumed since then. Under the threat of an invasion by foreign references, the tendency to criticize and reform Islamic practice was often silent and the reaction to the question of women here as elsewhere was of one absolute conservatism.

"Contemporary Islamic thought feels itself threatened." says Tareq Al Bishri.

There is the sentiment that its philosophy, its spiritual roots are in danger. When Islam shows its dogmatism, it is often from the dread of becoming rootless. It is an attitude of self defense. Who can move forwards, when all his energy is mobilized for the sole defense of the status quo and the maintenance of positions. If one considers the history of Muslim thought from the point of view of its aptitude to reform, and if one compares the position of the reformist movement between 1750-1850 and 1850-1920, one notices that the first period was marked by an important withdrawal from sectarianism and dogmatism which had prevailed for a certain time and by the return to the first fundamentals of Islamic thought, to its first sources which are the Koran and the Sunna, a return which had an innovating effect. The first of the stages of renovation in contemporary Islamic thinking operated with materials, principles, references and methods which had come out of Islamic thought itself. No other adverse attitudes had any positive social impact or interfered with the process then.

During the second stage, in contrast, which is to say after around 1850 (and afterwards), the military and cultural threat from the West was in full development and would increase even more over the following decades. It was in this context that the conservatism of Islamic thinking began to manifest and reinforce itself: under the double effect of the attitude of self defense and of resistance, the fear of losing one's roots and the determination to preserve the universe of beliefs, the fear of losing these frames of reference and the sources of their civilization. Bit by bit, this conservatism began to have a social impact. Little by little, it found a large, popular clientele and received support that attested to the existence of a true social demand in this domain. At the beginning of the 20th century it was among the intellectual elite, rather than with the people, that the calls for renovation found an echo. The nationalist movements had taken a position concerning Islam that was infinitely more conservative. One can verify that perfectly if one looks at the place which the National Party enjoyed at that moment when it played the Islamic conservative card. Any movement of thought, regardless of which one it is, ought to be evaluated with constant criteria, that is to say, criteria that are drawn from its environment and its intellectual and historic context, taking into account the practical function that it fills in society. Thought renews itself from the interior, with the help of its own material or with intellectual material extracted from its fundamental components in a process of interaction with social reality. When we evaluate a structure of thought outside its intellectual context and outside its socio-historical frame of reference, when we apply ideas from another environment (as is the case when we read Islamic thought with the instruments of Western thinking) we run the risk that it will not have the same meaning that it did in its original context.

That takes nothing away from the force of the thinking or its effectiveness in its original environment. But it is a question of interaction between one thought, the global intellectual context and the assigning of distinct social functions. This is what I hope that we will notice when we speak of the conditions of dialogue between our two systems of references. If one underestimates this dimension, one reduces the chances for a fruitful dialogue between Western and Muslim rationalities. Western thought presents itself as a model and an example. Islamic thought goes on the defensive and ignores from then on what can prove profitable to it. A good number of Muslim thinkers are reformists until they feel the existence of a danger threatening the foundations of their thought. They then swing towards conservatism.(1)

When it comes to "women" as with the other levels of articulation between Islamism and modernization, everything leads one to search for the most significant traces of evolution within the internal dynamics of the movement—certainly looking for more than what is in the dialogue of the deaf between the "feminists" and "Islamists" on the two shores of the Mediterranean. From this point on, these dynamics most probably will lead to attitudes that are infinitely more sophisticated than the anathemas, which have too often taken over analyses in this domain, might have led one to think.

---

(1) Interview, cited.

CHAPTER 6

GOD OR THE PEOPLE?
ISLAMISTS BETWEEN THEOCRATIC VIOLENCE AND
DEMOCRACY

Islamist Violence?

Even if for the most part acts of blind terrorism and political assassination have long been the exception in the Maghreb even more so than they were in Egypt, a certain segment of the Islamist movement has shown itself to be more than capable of violence.

It requires an objective evaluation of this dimension of the movement to avoid falling into a double trap, one that leads some to disregard the violent aspects of the movement completely and others to overemphasize what is after all only one expression of the phenomenon. Both errors run the risk of seriously distorting the understanding of the movement in its entirety.

Combating the "Infidel Prince"

In the inventory of violent attitudes, real or supposed, that "come from Islam," the strategies for the conquest of power occupy a prominent position. First of all, violence vis-à-vis others challenging the powers that be: the archetype of these confrontations is the war waged between the Marxists and the Islamists in the universities at the beginning of the 1970s. In these skirmishes neither group showed signs of being more effective or imaginative than the other.

The second confrontation is violence against the state and it evidently surpasses mere university activity. Up until the formal recognition of the rules of the electoral game, the principle formations of the Islamist movement definitely considered the recourse to violence as a legitimate method of operation against the state and its representative whenever the "prince" was considered "infidel," i.e. perceived as disrespectful towards divine law. A fringe of the Islamist current—immortalized by the assassination of Sadat—continues without any doubt in its ambitions to overthrow the prince by force. Small armed groups periodically constitute themselves on the edges of the "Return to Islam." Their influence, internal organization, and durability varies greatly. They often call themselves after the Jihad (in Egypt, but also in Libya, Tunisia, and Algeria). Dissatisfied with the limited confrontations between students and authorities, they have chosen to try to give themselves the means of fighting against the State with more equal force.(1)

"Command the Good, Interdict the Evil"

In the name of the "Commandment of good and the interdiction of evil," or more exactly, in the name of a literalist reading of this Koranic principle,(2) at least one component of the Islamist movement refuses to

---

(1) In Egypt especially, the mental universe of these small groups, often exploited by the media, is less and less misunderstood, since the work of Gilles Kepel, of course (*The Prophet and Pharaon,* La Découverte, 1984, and in English, *The Prophet and the Pharaoh,* Al-Saqi Books, London, 1985). More recently, also, since the remarkable documentary efforts of Sid Ahmed Rifaat in *Al-Nabi al-Musalah: Al-Rafidoune* (The armed Prophet: those who refuse) (263 pages) and *Al-Nabih al-Musalah: al -Tha'iroune* (361 pages) Riad-al-Rayyes Books, London, 1991, *Al-Islambouli, Rou'ya jedida litanzîm al jihad* (Al-Islambouli: new reading of Jihad's organisation) Madbouli, Cairo, 1987, 166 pages, *Li medha qatalou al-sadate: qisat tanthîm al-Jihad* (Why did they kill Sadat: history of Jihad organisation), Dar al-charqia, 157 pages, Cairo, 1989.

For one of the few insider analyses on the Gemaa Islamiya see (although the author is closer to the Muslim brothers than to the Gemaa) Badr (Muhammad Badr), *Al Gemaa al-islamiya fil gemi'ate al-misriya: haqa'iq wa watha'iq* (The Islamic group in the Egyptian universities: facts and documents), Cairo, 1989, 140 pages. See also the *Bitaqat al-ta'rif: men nahnou, medha nourid,* (Identity card: who are we, what do we want?) as well as the *Mithaq al-amal al islami* (Charter of Islamic action) written in 1985 by Najih Ibrahim, 'Assim 'Abdelmajid, 'Assim Eddin Darbal, under the direction of Omar Abderrahmane.

See finally "Genina No'mat Allah, Tanthîm al-Jihad" (The Jihad's organisation), *Kitab al-houria,* No. 18, Dar al-Houria, Cairo 1988, 329 pages, preface by Saad Eddin Ibrahim (summerized in English: *The Jihad, an Islamic Alternative in Egypt,* Cairo Papers in Social Science, Vol 9 Mono 2, A.U.C.. Summer, 1986, 108 pages). Mourou Mohamed, *Tanzim al-jihad: jouzourouhou wa asrarouhou* (The Jihad's organisation: its roots and its secrets), Madbouli, 1991, 193 pages. Hamouda Adel, *Qanabil wa massahif: qissa tanzim al-Jihad* (Bombs and Korans: the History of Al-Jihad Organization), Sina lil nachr, January, Cairo, 1989, 279 pages. Events of the confrontation with the state are recalled in Ouardani Salah al, *Al Harakat al-islamiyya fi misr: ouaqi'at-thamaninate*) (The Islamist Movement in Egypt: Facts of the Eighties), Markaz al-hadhara al-arabia lil i'lame wal nachr, Cairo, 1989, 179 pages.

(2) "Al-Amr bil maarouf wal-Nahi 'an al-Munkar," whose reading evidently varies from one militant to another. An essential controversy opposed Adel Hussein, editor in chief of the weekly *Chaab* and Ala Mohieddine, spokesman in Cairo of the Gemaat Islamiyya (assassinated since then in September, 1989, in Cairo), who reproached the members of the PST for neglecting this essential

renounce the dangerous idea of reforming individuals as well as the State "with the hand," that is to say by constraint. The violence that flowed from that concept ranges from the immoderate use of decibels in the adjusting of amplifiers on minarets to assassinations—which remain exceptional—as well as various forms of proselytizing under pressure.

Very often, the weak links in the social chain, cultural or religious minorities (in the Machreq, more often than in the Maghreb) and women to a certain extent constitute a privileged target for this kind of violence. To strike the weak allows one to step around the obstacle of an unequal comparison of force with the regime. The attacks against these minority segments often play the role of an outlet for a desire for confrontation with the state. "To take after the Christians," notes Alain Roussillon, "is to metaphorically designate the illegitimacy of the authorities without being obliged to attack directly against them. The Copts and also the Jews, the Franc Masons, the Rotarians, ...play here the symbolic incarnation of impious power."(1) The most natural targets of this strategy are the wine shops or their customers, those who break the fast of Ramadan in public, the distributors of video cassettes or publications judged immoral, women accused of not following the canons of Islamic morality,(2) and more exceptionally churches and synagogues.(3)

The small group of "Moujahidines Maroccains," which was guilty in 1978 of a political assassination, no doubt was in the Maghreb the first ex-

---

principle. The co-leader of the PST, claiming for his part that it is illegitimate for anyone to resort to force to make it respected. Cf. *Chaab,* first week of January, 1989.

(1) The Christians are accused of intruding on the territory of Islam and of wanting to dictate their law to the Muslims (...), Alain Roussillon in "Entre al-Jihad et al-Rayyan: phénoménologie de l'Islamisme égyptien," *Maghreb Machrek Monde Arabe,* 127, March, 1990, page 23. "In fact," also suggests Roussillon, "the violence appeared more visible and central in the practices of the Islamist groups since in most of the cases, given the suspicion which journalistic or sociological investigations inspire in the Islamists, the only 'terrain' and the only 'populations' accessible to investigations were furnished by the militants who were imprisoned or the transcripts of the trials made against them for 'subversion' or attempts to overthrow the regime."

(2) In Algeria, this moralizing violence eventually degenerated into assassination. The child of a woman, living alone and accused for this reason of being a woman of loose character, died when her house was set on fire.

(3) Attack on the synagogue of Jerba in Tunisia in 1989.

pression of this extreme Islamist violence.(1) In Libya, equally, a "Party of God," was responsible for at least one assassination, that of a representative of the regime, who was himself directly implicated in the repression.(2) The Algerian Islamist movement of Mustapha Bouyali (cf infra) and Tunisia's Islamic Jihad are responsible for the deaths of men, but only in the context of confrontations with the police. The Bouyali group had, it seems, planned the assassination of a Prime Minister, the kidnapping of a Western ambassador, and the bombing of various monuments in the capital.(3) In Egypt, several political assassinations have failed,(4) but in October, 1990, the president of the parliament and five of his companions were shot to death, and on June 8, 1992, Farag Foda, a writer known for his anti-fundamentalist mockeries and his demands for new juridical measures against what he indiscriminately called "terrorism" was also assassinated, supposedly by the members of the same Jihad organization. In Tunisia, to procure arms and funds, the Islamic Jihad of the old nationalist militant Habib Dhaoui (cf. infra) was guilty of two armed attacks against a police station and a post office, one of which led to the death of a policeman. The Islamist Jihad had broken away from the Islamic Tendency Movement (ITM), accused of compromising with the government of Mohamed Mzali, who had appeared in November, 1985, to have been reconciled with the leaders of the movement.(5) On several occasions, acid was thrown in the face of magistrates (in Algeria and Tunisia) or (in Tunisia) at members of

---

(1) History will probably acknowledge that this action was not totally foreign to the effectiveness of the political police in the Moroccan kingdom.

(2) Judged before a videocamera, he was executed at the end of a show trial (cf. infra Chapter 8 on Libya).

(3) His program supposedly included the implantation in the back country near Nice of a center where militants received military training before going to perfect that training in Syria. Only a police intervention, which was more preventative than repressive, made Bouyali and his disciples enter into clandestinity (cf infra).

(4) Against three ministers or former ministers of the interior, particularly implicated in the anti-Islamist represion (Nabawi Isma'il, Hasan Abou Basha in 1987 and Zaki Badr in 1989). On political violence in Egypt's history, see Talatt Kheir Eddine, *Al-ightiyalat wal-ounf al-siyassi fi misr* (The assassinations and the political violence in Egypt), 1991, Dar al-Hara (Miniah).

(5) See infra, Chapter 10 on Tunisia.

the militias of the government party implicated in the repression against members of the ITM. The period of repressive agony under Bourguiba also saw the crossing of a decisive line with the placing of four homemade bombs in hotels of the president's home region. In the very last wave of Bourguiba's repression against the party of Rached Ghannouchi, the riposte organized or tolerated by the latter movement led to the death of a watchman in the local Rassemblement Constitutionnel Démocratique (RCD) party offices when the building at Bab Souika was set on fire.(1)

The temptation of the Islamist current to get around the obstacle of dictators and, when the case arises, that of elections by resorting to the armed forces, also needs to be mentioned. For several years, the filter provided by the entrance examinations of the military academies have let a good many more students in than merely those qualified in mathematics. In September, 1987, the aborted attempt to overthrow Bourguiba came from members of the army who were following the thesis of the ITM, highlighting the Islamist presence in the state apparatus. The army, police and customs service had all been penetrated. Three year later, however, the intervention of the Algerian army in the repression against the FIS showed that the regimes still possessed a certain margin for maneuver.(2)

Islamist Violence or Social Violence?

In the writing of Islamist militants, to deny that Islamist themes can feed an interpretation of dogma supporting fascist or totalitarian conduct is nothing but a politician's fragile argument. First, a good number of Islamist theoreticians had expressed their conviction that only armed action against the State had a chance of succeeding, having integrated the limits of this approach to the institutional clamping down by military dictatorships born after independence. And second, because even before having taken in the fringes of the urban proletariat (as is the case in Algeria), the diverse social substratum of the Islamist movement already contained adherents of the "legitimate" use of violence. Although completely reprehensible, alarming

---

(1) Cf. infra, Chapter 10 on Tunisia.

(2) Nevertheless, the massive recourse of the army to repress the Islamist surge incites one to ask about the limits of loyalty on the part of the troops which will be too actively and durably mobilized in such operations. In Algeria, the chief of staff takes particular precautions, since he recruits only 10% of the possible conscripts, who are picked after a selection which is much more "ideological" than technical or scientific.

details of their conduct decorated with portraits of bearded sinister figures, or armed *putchists* still are not a sufficient basis for us to construct a realistic appraisal of the situation, and even less so of the possible future of the meeting between Islam and politics. Why?

One first has to ask whether the violence against the state is representative or not of the movement in its entirety, or if it is only representative of a part of the movement on the fringes. If, as we have already said, most analysts can happily distinguish between the Italian Red Brigades (who are terrorists) and the Italian Communist Party (which is leftist but far from being terrorist), or between the Ku Klux Klan and the right wing of the American Republican Party etc., they still often forget to make the same basic distinction between the assassins of Sadat and the totality of the Islamist phenomenon.

It is, therefore, essential to ask ourselves if Islamist violence is a permanent component in the essential references of the actors, or simply a passing part of their economic and social profile. No historian worthy of the name has taken the risk of attempting to show that Islam has produced significantly more political violence than any other secular or materialistic dogma. Recent examples do nothing to alter this assessment. At the origin of a particularly frequent mistake in methodology is the artificial separation within the socio-political phenomenon of the political actors from their social and educational characteristics, whether collective or individual. The fact that the references in the Islamist discourse in question are self proclaimed (from the interior) or too quickly considered (from the exterior) as intangible and timeless, obscures the situation even more and increases the misunderstanding. In reality, it is Islamist individualities which "make" Islamism, more than the reverse. Much more than the slogans which serve it today, it is its social substratum which conditions the political expression of Islamism. The course of a river varies according to the terrain it crosses, as does the sound it makes and its impact on the environment. The same can be said for Islamist mobilization, whose methods of expression vary according to the social landscape it crosses, and which has here and there a totally different impact on the environment.

Peremptory conclusions related to the violent "nature" of water, expressed by the observer standing where the river is running down a mountain, would be approximately as "scientific" as the one commonly made about "Islamist violence" by those who concentrate their analyses on the more violent fringes of the social base of the movement. In fact, the human substratum of Islamism happens to be extremely diversified, and it is, furthermore, crossed (along with the policies for development) with

114

dynamics of constant transformation. The view from the outside, lacking the means for determining origins, too often has the tendency to integrate into the inventory of "Islamist violence" virtually any form of social violence. In not measuring it within the context of its environment, one misses seeing that, rather than being the product of a specific part of the society, this violence is in fact a characteristic of the entire social system at a certain moment in its historical development. In the universe of the Gemaate of Fayoum or in that of the Algerian Mustapha Bouyali, daily examples demonstrate that, political references not withstanding, men still settle today their financial, family or electoral differences with a gun rather than in front of an administrator or judge. Therefore, it is dangerous for us to transplant such practices from Upper Egypt or the Fayoum into the salons of Cairo, or those of Batna into the salons of Hydra, and *a fortiori* into those of Paris or New York. One cannot forget that a relativistic evaluation of social practices, cannot be undertaken outside the terrain of which it is part. Nevertheless, outside observers too often plug in their microphones in rural upper Egypt and open their loudspeakers in Zamalek(1) or Paris, not measuring that the distance which separates them from the sound they hear is more social or cultural than it is merely political. Neither is the reactionary dimension of some of the recourse to political violence taken into consideration.

Violence or Counter-violence?

The strictly reactionary dimension of the supposed "Islamist violence"—a response to the violence of the social system, or more specifically, a defense against the preventative repression of the states—is too often simply excluded from the analysis. "We always forget to make an essential distinction," says Hassan Hanafi,

> about what separates violence from counter-violence. Which side is the primary violence? On which is the secondary violence? Someone in the street or at the university has a knife; why this violence? Do you know the oppression in which the students live? Their status, the exploitation by the professor who sells courses, the absence of the freedom to congregate... The student is frustrated, so he is violent. For me, the most violent of the two is not the student, it is the oppression. Then the student rebels. He rebels because there is no dialogue. If there were a dialogue, if one asked him for his opinion, if one listened to

_____

(1) Upper class residential area of Cairo.

115

him... perhaps the discourse would be the means for expelling all this frustrated energy. But their status is oppressive. There is no dialogue... then, it explodes. That is the situation everywhere.... (1)

In the North, but not only there, the "informations" relative to the Islamist deployment have an annoying tendency to resemble the communiques that come from Arab ministers of the interior. The fact that one by one the principal Islamist formations have clarified their adhesion to the requirements for free elections has not changed the fact that only information which contradicts this tendency, regardless of how old it might be, comes to the attention of the larger public. Well outside the circles of the opponents to the Islamists, less illegitimate than others to make "an arrow out of any kind of wood," it is in fact the arguments of regimes threatened by the newly rich of Mediterranean politics who too often control the terrain of analysis.

In fact, it is the State, more often than the rest of the social system, whose violence amasses the highest number of victims. Even when it does not act directly, the State can give orders, for example, of violence as it wishes.

From Libya, where the executions in the 1980s were counted in the dozens, to Algeria, where the violence of the State showed itself first in the methods of its police, and later by the secret services and its military, and in Egypt, Morocco, and Tunisia,(2) the Arab regimes without exception have allowed themselves to be seduced into operating a "preventive" repression. "Mustapha Bouyali" (cf. infra), "only went into hiding after his brother was killed and his sister-in-law was raped by policemen," today explains his brother-in-law, who is an Imam in a mosque in Marseilles.(3) "The ITM had 25 deaths, of which nearly a dozen happened during police interrogations, before it decided to move," Salah Karkar, the successor to Rached Ghannouchi at the head of ITM, pleaded in 1988.(4)

---

(1) Interview with the author, cited.

(2) And where, it seems, the security services try today to identify those officers who had prohibited the serving of alchohol during their marriages.

(3) Interview, cited, with the author.

(4) Interview with the author, Paris, March 1988. The Tunisian Human Rights Defense League acknowledges ("only") 12 deaths for this period.

Even the very official strategic report from the studies center at Al Ahram, admits that in Egypt, the violence between the State and the Islamists is not always as reciprocal as the communiques issued by the ministry of interior would like to lead one to think, when they speak of difficult arrests which inevitably terminate in the death of the suspects.(1) The American orientalist, Emanuel Sivan, believed for his part that he could affirm (by way of congratulating them!) that the Egyptian regime "even employed the sharp shooters in order to sow terror."(2) The assassination on September 11, 1989, in Cairo of Ala Mohieddine, the spokesman for the Gemaate Islamiyya, attributed by the Gemaate to the State security services, is believed to have constituted one of these warnings by the authorities to the most determined of their challengers. Moreover, the discourse of the regime tends in Egypt to exaggerate the "anti-Christian" dimension of the strategies of Islamists groups, thus trying and apparently succeeding beyond all limits, to generate inside the country and in the Western world a full and blind support for its own repressive stand against the "terrorists."

In fact, even if each ideological current inevitably has its own fringe which is susceptible to the ease of taking "direct action," even if the temptation to resort to force was part of certain strategies at a certain time, violence has more generally come at the end of a peaceful proselytizing which began in the mosques, and the regimes have most often resorted to a repression that was largely disproportionate to the initial acts. From Tripoli to Casablanca and Tunis, the first sentences were pronounced on the basis of dossiers of accusations that were astonishingly light, and in fact often frankly empty. In many cases the simple supposition of belonging to a forbidden association has been justification enough for extremely heavy prison sentences.

The repression under Bourguiba finished by crossing the frontiers of all legality. The repression which his successor, Ben Ali, and his emulators in Algeria instituted is hardly less massive, but more "scientific." The methods employed in Tunisia throughout 1987 ought to have been analyzed at the time with the same meticulousness as the armed preparations engaged in by the ITM and revealed shortly after the bloodless deposing of Bourguiba. And

(1) "La violence politique en Egypte, Rapport stratégique d'Al-Ahram," *Egypte Monde Arabe,* No. 4, 1990.

(2) "Thus some 70 fundamentalist agitators of the first plan were eliminated for good in Upper Egypt, and in the rural provinces the most affected..." (*Le Nouvel Observateur,* February 7-13, 1991).

the fires (in 1991) at the headquarters of the militias of the RCD ought just as well to have been analyzed with the same care as the 6,000 arrests carried out "on the spur of the moment" in the spring of 1991. Arguably, this was done because President Ben Ali realized after the results of the elections in April, 1989, that he had no other way of saving his throne. One should keep in mind the rapid increase in repression that he deliberately chose two years later, just after the Gulf crisis, and all the violence initiated in Algeria in 1991 after refusal of the Algerian regime to come to terms with the election verdict without trickery, and the resulting massive use of the army. The violence which these practices may unleash one day (1) will need to be analyzed in the light of this very same violence that was carried out against the militants of the movement of Rached Ghannouchi or those of Algeria's FIS in 1991, carried out against a background of obliging silence on the part of both Arab regimes and Westerners.

Bloody though they might be, the methods used by the states in the Maghreb cannot be compared to those of Syria's Hafez al Assad, although in his case he was confronted with a veritable armed movement. The long destruction of the city of Hamma, in which a full-fledged military assault with air-force jets and tanks took nearly three weeks to hunt down and kill anywhere from 5,000 to 25,000 people (most of whom were cold-bloodedly sealed off from escape) is unequalled in the modern Middle East to this day. It is questionable whether the thousands who died anonymously at Hamma ever carried quite the same weight in the world's media as did the few dozen victims of Islamic "terrorism" that the good "secular" Hafez Al Assad claimed he was trying to avenge on the day he ordered the slaughter.

God or the People?

> When preparing for the legislative elections in 1989, the Socialist Labor Party opened its doors to candidates from the Muslim Brothers, and there was a debate within the party ranks, which were not yet dominated by the Islamists, over which slogan to pick. The secular leftist tendency within the party finally put its weight behind the motto: "God and the People," thinking that in doing so, it had managed to make a point by including the two symbols held most important by both wings of the party. A story made the rounds to the effect

---

(1) And, in the case of Algeria, has started (at the end of February, 1992) with a campaign of assassination of security forces and army personnal that has created over one hundred victims in a period of less than six months.

*that the Islamists went along with the choice, remembering that they
still had their own motto: "Allah Akhbar—God is the Greatest!"*

Is democracy condemned to die in Arab lands the moment it sees the
light of day? In the event of an election victory, would the Islamists refer
solely to the principles of the Shura, which limits consultation to the interior of the Islamic community, and decide to deny the identity and the rights
of those who had lost the election? And more to the point, would they respect the rights of other minorities, and especially those of a different religion? Once installed in power, would the emulators of the Imam of Qom
respect the verdict of the urns if it turned out that one day it consecrated
their defeat? How can a system founded on the "sovereignty of God" and
consequently on the primacy of divine standards accommodate itself to a
universe which opposes it with the primacy of human will?

Among the Arab elites near power, this analysis (1) is being used more
and more frequently as an argument for slowing the process of democratization. Behind the screen of the ban on founding a political party based on religion,(2) it is Islamism's presumed opposition to democratic values, which
from Egypt to Morocco and Tunisia, serves as a pretext for excluding the
Islamist parties from the legal political scene. In Algeria,(3) it is the
supposed recourse by the FIS to violence in order to "interrupt the democratic process which threatened it," which served as the reading guide for the
media (4) on both sides of the Mediterranean, in order to explain and sanction the return of the Army as an institutional player in the spring of 1991.

---

(1) Which goes so far as to evoke here and there the unstoppable principle of
"no liberty for the enemies of liberty." "It is the (argument) without appeal!"
says Alain Griotteray in one of the rare protests raised in France after the forced
resignation of Chadli Benjedid: "But that reduces democracy to a club of people
of good company who, under some outside divergences, think and act in the
same way. It is true that such a formula of government exists, but it is mistaken
to call it a 'democracy'. It is better to say 'oligarchy', 'patriciat', 'feudalism',"
in "La démocratie sauvée?" *Le Figaro Magazine*, January 18, 1992, p.28.

(2) Either a language or a particular region, the theoretical foundation of this
legislation being to protect the State against all forms of religious or ethnic
separatism.

(3) Cf. infra Chapter 11.

(4) See for example *Financial Times* (Francis Ghiles, June, 6, 1991) whose
analysis—entitled "A bloody path to the ballot"—was roughly that of the main
Western media: "(...) In the space of a violent 24 hours, the fundamentalist
Islamic Salvation Front (FIS) has succeeded in derailing President Chadli

Essentially, the reasoning behind the hesitation to give the Islamists an opportunity to enter into the democratic process is based on the supposed absence in Muslim classical thinking (and especially in the Shura) of a tolerance for the modern notion of opposition.(1) More significantly, it also stems from the fact that the founders of "modern" Islamism, Abou 'Ala al Mawdudi and Hassan Al Banna, especially,(2) seemed always careful to separate themselves more or less explicitly from the idea of democracy. Certain leaders continue to do the same today. A quick look at the Iranian experience, during which Khomeini's camp used force to eliminate its leftist opposition, is usually enough to close any discussion on the subject.

It would be indeed impossible to neglect or underestimate either of these parameters. Each leads to a certain perspective. Certainly, it is not easy to superimpose classical Muslim thought and its institutions on the European and American constitutional institutions created during the eighteenth century. There is no question that the first doctrinal expressions of the modern Islamists were based on a more or less explicit rejection of the principle of pluralism. But for all that, the hypothesis of the incompatibility between the Islamist mobilization and the values of democracy should not be employed, as is too often the case these days, as a unique standard according to which one equates the chances for the survival of Arab democracy with the talent of the regimes in power to suppress their Islamist movements. First of all, since it is presented as a unique case, it tends to lose its status as a hypothesis and to slip into that of a postulate, to play, therefore, in the landscape of the cognitive process, the same role that the single party plays in the fragile universe of pluralism. But beyond this first defect, we will see that this postulate of absolute incompatibility between the Islamist forces and the values of liberal political thought is not immune to numerous other fundamental criticisms.

Benjedid's plan to hold the country's first multi-party general election in three weeks."

(1) At least with observers outside the Arab world, the Arab regimes who all claim more or less Islam (and democracy!) cannot adopt this lone thematic.

(2) For a very rigorous documentary inventory of the positions of orthodox Islam with respect to the notion of pluralism and of democracy, and the revelation of the relative rupture which Rached Ghannouchi (notably) brought to this landscape, cf. notably Gudrun Kramer in *Islam et Pluralisme, Démocratie et Démocratisation au Proche-orient*, Cahiers du CEDEJ, Cairo, 1992.

Let's first of all set the limits of the search for an absolute correspondence between the Western and Islamist themes. The principle of the functionality of the Islamist discourse is, as we have said, to make at least a symbolic rupture with the universe of Western culture. Therefore, one should not expect the presence in this discourse of the entire Western political terminology, a terminology with which we have become so familiar that we tend to see it as universal. When he recalls that "The Arab world still lives, to a large extent, in reaction to the democratic model (which was) strongly associated with the dominating powers who inspired it," and that "the usage of one and the other of these terms (Islam and democracy) still raises the cultural and political conflict of forces that are definite and partisan," Ghassan Salame,(1) in this sense, goes straight to the heart of the question.

The comparison, it follows, should go beyond vocabulary and the symbolic rites of Western democracy, and concentrate instead on its values and its essential nature (the space given to politics, the institutionalization of political opposition, the modes of renewing power, etc.). It must finally integrate the idea that no juridical institution, even if it is essentially religious, is in the end totally sheltered from transformation. Israel is a religious state, but the balance of power between State and Rabbinate remains in question.

"The Islamists," are they "democrats?" One is finally tempted to respond "And the Christians?" to underline the dangers that constantly stalk generalizations made from the exterior. Instead of attempting the impossible, we won't waste time trying to answer the question in this form. On the other hand, we will suggest that the relationship between democracy and the universe of *values* (which we will take care to disassociate from the *vocabulary* of democracy), which prevails among the different components of the vast Islamist movement on different political scenes at the end of the twentieth century, depends on multiple interrogations which, if we cannot

(1) Ghassan Salame, "On the causality of a deficiency: why isn't the Arab world democratic?" *Revue Francaise de Sciences Politiques*,1991, page 307. (Also in *Egypte, Monde Arabe,* No. 8, 1992). "The terms seem to us better presented," adds Salame, "when the Islamists began to broach the democratic question having extirpated the charge of culturalist polemics (Tareq al-Bishri, Adel Hussein among others) in making a demand that is disconnected from mimicry and its condemnation (...) It is equally interesting to see that the Islamic Republic of Iran was founded, among other precepts, on the legitimacy born of elections, even if it often appears that the duality between religious legitimacy and that which comes from the urns is not harmoniously linked."

answer completely, we can at least try to inventory. And we will try to take a more realistic look at whether contemporary Arab societies—that is to say the different concrete "Muslim" communities—which have all been produced by different historical itineraries, have reached a level of political development yet in which pluralism, including respect for the rights of minorities, has a chance of existing in significant proportions. The answer is, no doubt, mitigated. But it cannot be simply a question of dismissing the issue with a mere reference to the "Islamist menace," and that is the essential point.

What Islam? What Islamists? What democracy?

In these limits, what is "Islam" and what is "Democracy?" Do precepts exist in the dogmatic references of the Muslim community which explicitly and definitively forbid the expression of democratic values? "Is Islam," Leonard Binder asks, "capable of admitting liberal thinking without losing its own essence?"(1) Because the institutionalization of the representation of pluralist political currents is a recent product of Western thinking, there is a great temptation to conclude that classical Muslim thinking is intrinsically foreign to the idea of a political opposition that has a legitimate task of limiting power. It is also a temptation to conclude that the "doctrine of Islam" (of which the Islamists are supposed here to be the natural inheritors and the vigilant guardians) prevents the Islamists from incorporating the categories that are indispensable to the construction of the institutional universe of democracy. Can the concern with maintaining the unity of the community at any price accommodate itself to pluralism in political expression? Can the primacy of divine law reconcile itself with parliamentary law?

In law, even if the regulation of the power of the Prince by an institutionalized pluralist body seems indeed to have remained foreign to Muslim classical system, the power of the Muslim Prince, which was always quasi-contractual since it was based on a *Ba'ya* that took the form of mutual recognition with the community, was never considered unlimited. The Caliph, unlike the Pope, never claimed to have infallibility. The idea of a possible sanction, and more often revocation and death, was, indeed, represented in the Islamic institutional universe. Yet, it was expressed within the dominant political culture, which was then a religious culture. The legality

(1) And "if it exists, what does it consist of?" Leonard Binder in *Islamic Liberalism, a Critique of Development Ideologies,* Chicago-London, 1988, cited by Gudrun Kramer, op cit.

of the Prince's actions, were judged not on the basis of the advice from a majority of his subjects, but on the Prince's capacity not to transgress a norm that was said to be divine. Nevertheless, the interpretation of this "divine" legality was indeed confined to intermediaries who were perfectly human, and to whom political theory accorded the right, if they succeeded in convincing the majority of the "political class" of the period, to decide to put an end to the excesses of power.

More ambiguous is the classical attitude with respect to pluralism that was often taken to mean the division of the community, which was considered a supreme evil that the Prince had to be fight at any cost. This line of research, which has already largely been explored, is far from irrelevant, even if eminent specialists of historical comparatism show that the conclusions to which it leads can in many respects be relativized. For comparisons between concepts produced in different historical environments have limits.(1) Does the conceptual universe of the Shura cut across the notion

---

(1) Cf. the illuminating remarks of Jean Leca in F.B. and Jean Leca "Les Élections algériennes et la mobilisation islamiste," *Maghreb Machrek Monde Arabe*, September, 1990. "One finds oneself confronted here with a familiar problem in the history of ideas (...) that of the sense that an institution or an idea, developed in another historical context, can take in another context and its translation in another system of ideas (here the notion of 'opposition') that one does not find in the original context. Technically, the ba'ya is not the choice of the government (that it follows) nor the term of allegiance (which it precedes and conditions in law). It is a commercial exchange between two parties: the ruler and the small group of notables at the center of power (including the religious authorities (Bernard Lewis, *The Political Language of Islam,* Chicago University Press, 1988, page 58). Without this exchange of ruling principle ruler—ruled the first has no legitimacy. According to certain expressions, however, a ruler who imposes a contract by violence on a people keeps his right to be obeyed, to maintain the unity of Muslims and preserve the accord among them. (Lewis, op. cit., page 102; Ann Lambton, *State and Government in Medieval Islam,* Oxford University Press, 1981, pages 110-111). It remains to be seen if this vertical exchange can really be transposed into a "horizontal" exchange of law between a government and one or more oppositions eventually incarnated by the parties who would not receive the traditional pejorative sense of "factions" in classical Islam (and elsewhere) (...) See also Jean Leca in "Democratization in the Arab world: uncertainty, vulnerability and legitimacy. A tentative conceptualization and some hypotheses," "Democratization and social tensions in the third world," University of Madras and Indian political science association, January 27, 1992; Jean-Claude Vatin in "Les partis pris démocratiques. Perceptions occidentales de la démocratisation dans le monde arabe," CEDEJ, 1992.

of democracy? Do they share elements in common? No doubt, not completely.

But the heart of the debate is not only there. Important as it might be, this first interrogation is far from being the only one. In the case of a partially negative response, which is reasonable enough, the interrogation tends, by in effect overestimating the impact of the past, to deprive the Muslim community of precisely the ability that, in its time, provided its force in other civilizations: the capacity to evolve and to adapt its normative universe. Far more than the appreciation of the political practices of Muslim societies of the classical age, or even those of the founders of the new Islamist ideologies, it is the reaffirmation of the capacity of the Muslim community, including the Islamists, to evolve its normative system which needs to be reintroduced into the analysis. Was Muslim civilization democratic? No more, one is tempted to respond, than was the Christian one, before it became so.

Islam and Democracy: From Rejection to Reappropriation

Certainly the first expressions of "modern" Islamism were based on the denunciation of the principle of pluralism, and reservations about the principles of democracy have not disappeared from some of the Islamist themes. From Ali Belhadj to the Gemaat Islamiyya in Egypt and the Hizb Tahrir in Jordan or elsewhere, a significant number of Islamist leaders(1) refute the universe of democracy. Just as significantly, there are many examples of individual and collective conduct that show that some of the new "converts" to democracy are a long way from understanding the real meaning of the vocabulary they employ. Some of these verbal adhesions are therefore not worth much more than talk. Why? Because the recognition of the primacy of the people's will in their minds amounts to calling into question the omnipotence of the Ulema-guides, and of substituting the law of numbers for divine law, and because it implies the constitution of the community in parts, and thus flies in the face of the sacrosanct principle of unity (on

(1) Of which the inventory is scrupulously kept up to date by the press and occasionally by researchers. For Algeria, Cf. notably *L'Algérie par ses Islamistes*, M.Al-Ahnaf, B. Botiveau et F. Fregozi, Paris, Karthala, 1991. In Morocco, Ben Kirane (cf. infra Morocco chapter) expresses also a rejection of the principle (cf. interview by James J. Coyle in "Islamic Movements in the Maghreb," Middle East Studies Association, 1991, Annual Conference Washington DC). The Party of Islamic Liberation (cf. infra) also holds to the principle of "incompatibility of democracy with the principles of Islam."

which the search for the *Ijmaa* is based), and may end in a dangerous *Fitna* (division). Also, the idea of legislation determined by humans, the basis for the recognition of political autonomy, contradicts the literalist reading of the principle of primacy of the divine norm and the role of the Koran and the Sunna in satisfying the totality of the normative needs of the community. Even if a question has been raised by some, the idea that the democratic formula compromises the primacy of the religious norm remains very present in the arguments of at least one component of the Algerian FIS. It was in the rejection of the principle of majority rule that Ali Belhadj, in a dossier published by the FIS, lashed out at what he called "the democratic poison":(1) "Among all the reasons for which we refuse the democratic dogma" said Belhadj,

> there is the fact that democracy relies on the opinion of the majority. The criteria for what is just and reasonable is understood as being the opinion of the majority. Starting from this principle, one sees the heads of the democratic parties trying to win over the greatest possible number of people, even if it is to the detriment of their faith, of their dignity, religion and honor, in the sole objective of winning their votes in an electoral battle. (...) As for us, the people of the Sunna, we believe that justice (*haq*) only comes from the decisive proofs of the Sharia and not from a multitude of demagogic actors and voices. Those who followed the Prophet were a very small number, while those who followed idols were a multitude.

Said Belhadj also, "...The ruler is not qualified to modify the law (...) That right belongs neither to the ruler nor to the people, but to scholars who know the rules of the Ijtihad at the same time as the temporal conditions existing in the societies to which they belong."(2)

More circumstantially in the end, the democratic vocabulary has long been identified with the heritage of the West and its regimes from which the Islamist theme has tried carefully to demarcate itself. "It is a victory for Islam and not democracy," gloated the same Belhadj after his party's election victory in June 1991.

The image of the very selective use of democratic references by Arab regimes hasn't added to their credibility. The idea that nothing in these ex-

---

(1) *Al-Mounquid*, No. 23 and 24 (excerpts reproduced in *M. Al-Ahnaf*, op. cit., pages 94 and following).

(2) *L'Algérie par ses Islamistes*, op. cit.

pressions, considered "foreign" to the parental culture, has ever brought anything that is good is even more naturally argued by those Islamist leaders who have lived through the repression of those regimes who call themselves "democratic," "popular," and are concerned with "human rights." Thus, Abbassi Madani describing the need to determine which political model Algeria should use for its government: "Which is the political model that can constitute an alternative to the present regime? Otherwise, why are we opposed to this regime? Now, this regime calls itself democratic. It calls itself the Democratic and Popular Republic of Algeria. That makes us think that the slogan 'democracy' preached by some is nothing more than clowning around (...)"(1)

In Tunisia, Rached Ghannouchi, although explicitly converted to a democratic vocabulary for a long time, also pointed to the blatant contradictions in the discourse of the regimes concerning their Islamist challengers. Ghannouchi's assessment has points in common with the arguments used by most candidates asking for legal recognition. "The annoying thing," he says,

> is that when it comes to democracy and human rights, the record of most of the accusers plausibly leaves one skeptical... They have not stopped persecuting liberties, falsiying elections, and monopolizing information. We are bathed in absurdity... The truth is simple. Our adversaries have always had difficulty in accommodating democracy and a multiparty system. For a long time they have openly rejected them in a way that was explicit, and today they do it shamefully, in a way that is disguised. They only accept the game of democracy on the condition that they are in every instance the winners. I will go further: suppose that we are inveterate anti-democrats, and that our adversaries are irreproachable democrats. They could, if they were sincere, constrain us to play the game of democracy. In France, the democratic sentiments of the extreme right (as those of the extreme left) are not evident, but no

---

(1) "For certain ones, the democracy constitutes a model and a finality. Historically, democracy is not there. It is necessary to come back to the first Greek philosophers according to which democracy signifies a love of the people. For my part, I believe that democracy is a means, not an end. It is a place of debate and not a model for reform which puts an end to the economic, political, cultural and social crisis... This regime hides behind this concept because it does not dare to admit that it is Communist. Communism is not seeing its best days. Our understanding of democracy is to permit the people to give its point of view. Our country lives today in a situation of political crisis. The dialogue is thus for us the best means of bringing it to an end." (Interview with *Algérie-Actualité*, April, 1991.)

one thinks about excluding them from French democracy. The same for Israeli democracy or for democracy in America, Britain, Germany, etc... It is thanks to the game of democracy that all the political parties nourished on authoritarian ideologies have been, in all countries, integrated, even if marginalized. So, if only to re-educate us, one should find a place for us in "democracy." There is (in Tunisia) a Communist party. No one asked them to renounce Marxism, or defend Marxism as a democratic ideology in order to be recognized. In fact, only against us do they brandish this requirement, because they want to get rid of a party that is strong and powerful.(1)

It remains the case, nevertheless, that most of the Islamist leaders have one by one surmounted this reactionary phase and one after another have adhered in an explicit manner to the principles of democratic pluralism. Among some of them, particularly but not only Rached Ghannouchi, the democratic line is now being argued in more than simple tactical terms and with a constancy which cannot fail to be recognized.(2) Ghannouchi's Islamic Tendency Movement was one of the first parties to declare itself clearly in favor of pluralism in 1981. "Even if it is Communist," announced the ITM, "we will be ready to respect any majority that legally comes out of the urns." "Stop saying that the concept of democracy is foreign to our culture. Stop saying that it belongs only to the West. You are wrong. Democracy is Islam," the leader-in-exile of the ITM (which has since become En-Nahda) pleads regularly in front of his Arab listeners.

What should one think of those of the Islamists who say that democracy is a *kufr* concept? If it is a simple linguistic difference, the problem is one of formal order... Democracy is simply a method of peacefully organizing political and intellectual battles... Liberties are not a danger for Islam since it represents their essence... Those who consider democracy as kufr are thus in error. This question has already been decided by eminent specialists of the Ijtihad. To assimilate democracy to the kufr is an erroneous Ijtihad.(3)

---

(1) Interview with H. Barrada for *Jeune Afrique Plus*, July 1990.

(2) But equally by at least one component of the Egyptian current, the Socialist Labor Party of Ibrahim Choukri, notably, in which the members of the Islamist tendency have held the majority since the Congress of March 1989, and which takes a line comparable to that of Tunisia's Ghannouchi. Cf. the positions of Adel Hussein, editor in chief of the weekly *Chaab* organ of the PST, in "Nationalism, Communism, Islamism: Itinerary of an Egyptian Intellectual," cited.

(3) Interview with *Horizons*, August 22, 1991, page 1 and 12.

With Abbassi Madani also, explicit declarations have multiplied.

> ...(In case of electoral defeat) our position will be to accept and to respect the will of the people... there exists in this country some people who demand Islam, and others who do not. As a consequence to avoid "Lebanization," we understand each other on a minimum, that is to say the will of the people.(1)

For all that, the view from the outside still refuses to take into account the explicit winning over of these new adherents to democracy. For many outside observers, Arab as well as Western, this proclaimed adhesion to pluralist values has most often been dismissed as nothing more than "stratagems" and other "tactics" of a facade.

"At first view, 'democrats' show themselves among the Islamists," writes Mohsen Toumi, who captures well the state of mind of a part of the Arab political class, and in any case represents the heights of the anti-Islamist argument.

> It is possible that they are sincere. They could also be Trojan horses, to which a division of work at the heart of the "integrist" movement has assigned a mission: to participate in public life, show oneself in the street, put suspicions to sleep, reduce hostilities and benefit other groups who can thus remain clandestine beneficiaries of the possibilities offered by the democratic institutions until the propitious day when they all launch an assault against the apparatus of the State. This strategy rests on a postulate: to know that the democracies are fragile and lend themselves, more than any other regime, to conquest. ...As the law on political parties defines it now, (democracy) is de facto selective in terms of participation. It is possible to regret that in the absolute. But it is necessary that a democratic society be able to resist terrorism, and to frustrate totalitarian enterprises without having to resort to the same methods as its assailants.(2)

If an Islamist leader announces clearly his adhesion to the demands of democracy, it is not taken as a sign of evolution, but only an empty speech, or the *positive* side of a "double language." This duality is not even consid-

---

(1) Interview with *Algérie Actualité,* April, 1990.

(2) Mohsen Toumi, *La Tunisie de Bourguiba et Ben Ali,* Presses Universitaires de France, 1988, page 38.

ered to show ambivalence since it is held to be implicit in this kind of "demonstration" that only the *negative* side of the supposed double langage has a chance to prevail.

Failing to give the "hard" response his interlocutors expected from him, Abdelfatah Mourou (ex-secretary general of the ITM) was regularly dismissed as "Mr. Valium."(1) Abbassi Madani, who has made countless nuanced and moderate declarations, even if they received far less attention in the media than those of his colleague Ali Belhadj, is only presented as "the positive flip side" of the latter, with whom he supposedly shares roles, etc... When Belhadj feels the need to demarcate himself from democratic terminology, his statements cease to be mere double talk and suddenly qualify as "proof." The prudence so abundantly employed earlier, and which ought to be used here to decode the need from which the speaker might feel to distance himself, has disappeared from the observers' methodology. And the conviction is thus reinforced that a structural and irreversible antinomy exists between the forces gestating in the Islamist movement and the emergence of democratic systems. Nevertheless, this position is just as "ideological" and arbitrary as is the opposite position of attempting to see a sudden upsurge in democracy in the speech of a part of these Islamist forces.

Sharia and Secularism: the Frontiers of Reappropriation

Just how far can the reappropriation of the secular universe of Western democratic thought be taken by those whose thinking is based on religion? Is the popular sovereignty which founded democratic thought compatible with divine sovereignty? If one wants to consider that the essence of democracy resides in the principle of primacy of human will in normative matters, it seems clear that an insurmountable barrier exists between the "secular West" and "religious Arabia." Does one really exist, though? To show that the supposed antinomy of the two systems is less than sometimes believed, it is first necessary to emphasize at what point the symbolic image which identifies Islam and "sovereignty of God"—principles that seem a priori to exclude any kind of autonomy in politics—should be put into perspective. But it is useful to determine, in the opposite direction, to what extent secularism has been raised by the democratic West as an absolute principle and,

---

(1) Cf. Philippe Aziz, *Le Point*, February 18, 1991, No. 961, page 53, "In Tunis he is called 'Mr. Valium'. The Islamist who reassures and puts to sleep through his moderate statements and his attachment to legality... What he says is surprising and not very orthodox on the part of an Islamist leader."

notably, if the primacy of human will really constitutes an absolute principle in Western liberal thought. It seems that with rare exceptions, this vision has to be nuanced. First because secularism is a principle which is very unequally distributed in the west. The force with which it is applied also varies greatly. Not to mention the case of Israel. It is easy to forget that the "Israeli democracy," often cited as a positive example in the West, was constructed in a state whose foundations are explicitly religious. With the exception of France, few countries in the West have built democracies based solely on the primacy of human will. The United States, although stressing the "separation of Church and state," still uses "In God We Trust" and "One Nation Under God" as its mottoes. Great Britain, Germany, and others have always admitted, in effect, the existence of divine principles that were superior to human will, regardless of the majority. No doubt that, in France notably, the absence of explicit reference to the divine origin of the normative corpus marks a difference. But this difference itself should be put into perspective: It is the result of the form and context of its formulation—in France, the emancipation from ecclesiastical tutelage—as much as from a desire to affirm an essential principle. Undoubtedly, the formal precision of the Koranic text might seem to be constraining, and very different fundamental principles of natural law. But this is once again to underestimate the extent of the autonomy recognized by Muslim jurists and the capacity of the techniques of the Ijtihad to adapt the letter of the sacred text. There is no shortage of examples today of this production of interpretation (Ijtihad), which only requires the support of a political majority to become the norm.(1)

Isn't there a danger that "religious" law will make minorities who refuse to follow it victims of its absolutism? A fair number of nuances are expressed between the lines of the Islamist discourse which establish the difficulty in admitting the complete legitimacy of the political rights for declared opponents of Islam. The effect is to see in this difficulty additional proof of the irreductible anti-democratic "difference" of the Islamist theme in this domain. Thus, Mahfoud Nahna: "The moment that democracy does not touch the foundation of the Islamic faith, it becomes a quest for the be-

---

(1) For example, cf. infra (Chapter 10 on Tunisia) how, at the interior of the Islamist trend, Ahmida Enneifer argues the possible prohibition of polygamy. For an example of reconnecting pluralism and Islam, see Amara Mohamed, "Mafahim islamiyya: al-islam wa ta'adudiya alhizbiya" (Islamic Concepts: Islam and Pluralism), *Al-Arabi*, June, 1992, page 97. Or Rifaat Sid Ahmed, *Al-Islam wal taadudiya, Minbar al charq*, Cairo, No. 1, March, 1992, etc.

liever."(1) Or more again from Abbassi Madani, whose words often illustrate what the view from the outside considers to be an insurmountable contradiction. "We say," states Madani,

> that the elections are determinant for everyone. No matter what the results are, we will respect the majority even if it is only made up of one lone vote. We consider, in effect, that he who has been elected by the people reflects the will of the people. In contrast, what we will not accept is this elected person not acting in the interests of the people. He must not be in contradiction with the Sharia, its doctrine, its values. He cannot make war on Islam. He who is the enemy of Islam is the enemy of the people.

Once again the extent of "contradiction" should not inhibit an attentive look by ourselves at the reference (Western democracy) which implicitly serves us as the criterion of appreciation.

To progress in the effective measurement of the limits of this apparent antinomy in the two universes of reference, it is important to put in evidence the compartments of normative Muslim thought which determine the status of non-Muslim minorities outside the system. But at the same time, it is also necessary to underline the limits that Western liberal thought brings to the liberties of these same "foreigners" inside its own system. We can ascertain in doing this that the techniques for protecting the system of references have existed a little bit everywhere in the history and time of the Western democratic experience, which also shows some remarkable trends outside the general principles credited with founding it. The Western liberal experiences have always posed limits to the freedom of expression of followers of systems perceived as antagonistic to it. One needs only to recall one example among others: that the United States has forbidden access to its territory by Communists, or those reputed to be such. Or that the German constitution denies all political rights to those who do not adhere to its principles, etc.

---

(1) Interview with *Horizons*, November 18, 1990. "In each Muslim," says Nahnah, "it is demanded to search wisdom where he can find it, as long as it does not go against the faith. If this point of view intersects with the democrats in our country or elsewhere, we are the first to be obliged to call for democracy, not according to the Greek conception, which has torn apart society, nor according to the Roman conception which imposed a military regime, but following the Islamic vision which gives the right to the most humble to express himself."

There again, the historicizing of systems of reference inevitably leads to relativizing the amplitude of the apparent fracture between the two universes. What constitutes a "divine law" in Islam may appear to distinguish it from the "natural law" or the "general principles" of Western thought. And, yet, when it is presented as an ultimate reference for the production of norms which are originated by human beings, it appears infinitely less distant from those principles, which, in the secular universe of democracy, appear to us to have legitimate claim to universality. The rest is mere...politics, that is to say, the individual and collective will which may (or may not) express itself at a given moment in "Muslim" history, in a given socio-political context. It is this essential idea that often emanates from the thinking of Mohamed Arkoun, when he expresses his conviction that to think of the separation of the spiritual from the temporal and of the religious from the political in Islam is "more a political impasse than a psychological or even cultural obstacle" (more a bolt on the door of politics than a psychological or even cultural obstacle).(1)

Islamism and Minorities

Adel Hussein attempts to address this political impasse when he argues that while the Islamic references should not be monopolized by a single formation, it is necessary to have a common reference that responds to all the sensibilities, including Christians, present in the political field. His proposal thus contains the basic elements for an ideological construction which would permit the articulation of Christian communities with the cultural dimension of the Islamist surge. "Every nation has a general framework, a constitution or general principles which coordinates the efforts and regulates politics," says Adel Hussein, whose party (the SLP) was the only

---

(1) "If one favors (on the terrain) a certain form of culture and intellectual activity" he continues, "the question of politics and religion in Islam finds the fertile problematic (as that of the Koran created-uncreated)." In Mohamed Arkoun, interview by Thierry Fabre, *Al-Qantara*, No. 2, January, 1992. In the same spirit, cf. Mohamed Al-Cherif Ferjani, "La laïcité et les pièges du culturalisme," *Passerelles*, No.3, page 107: "The political and juridical status is not more fundamental (in Islam) than elsewhere. (...) It is enough to remark on the evolutions — and occasionally involutions — of Muslim political and juridical systems, and to pay a minimum attention to the disparities between these systems. There is only the ignorance of the specialists which could confound them and conclude that there is unity of Islam, its faith and its Umma cited, or its incapacity for evolution."

one to put a Christian(1) on top of its electoral list for the elections of 1987 in Assiout.

The rules, the general principles which govern the political game are clear, and from that the game proceeds peacefully and in a constructive manner. That is what we need here. We need a general ideology, which is to say general principles which would regulate the game in all its parts and would direct the different constituents, the condition needed for the game to proceed peacefully. Well, these general rules, these general principles, I think for this country they are Islam.

It is not a question of creating a single party. The Muslim Brothers should be there, the Nasserites as well, etc... But all of that should be propelled under the emblem of Islam. Because our identity is there. We must not make Islam the monopoly of the Muslim Brothers. The Muslim Brothers represent a certain tendency in Islamic society, but they are not and ought not to be the only one. We must all work from the same base, compete on this same base. Certainly, we have differences when it comes to details, even divergences in points of view that are even more fundamental, but all that would remain in the frame of Islam. The Copts? The same goes for the Copts. Islam, as I said, is our heritage, our identity, our soul, but that goes as much for the Copts as for the Muslims. They are the sons and daughters of the same history. Whatever the circumstances, the Copts have always been part of the society (...) It is only very recently that one has been able to see Muslim women in the cities, in Cairo, wear certain clothes, while the Christians are still dressed in Western styles like many other Muslim women. (...) but if you leave Cairo, if you go to Upper Egypt, you will see that Muslim women and Coptic women all wear the same clothes, and that represents a common culture, a common tradition. Islam with its values, its life style is the heritage of all those who live in Egypt, Muslims as well as Christians. You know the famous formula of Makram Abeid(2): *"Islam is my country, Christianity is my religion."* Some of us have the habit of saying that "the Copts are Muslims who go to church on Sundays." In the Coptic language the word *Rab* is always used to say God, and not Allah. *Incha Rab* and not Incha Allah. In practice, most Copts say *Inch cha Allah* like the Muslims. It is very

---

(1) Jamel Ass'ad. Read his reaction to the invitation by Adel Hussein to open the dialogue between Islam and Christians (right after the riots of Dairout in June, 1992) in *Chaab,* June 28, page 2 (and notably his fear that Adel Hussein's understanding of Islam would not be well enough represented in the Egyptian street).

(2) Former leader of the Wafd party, cf. Ebeid Makram Mona, *Ebeid Makram: Kalimat wa mawaqif* (Speeches and positions), Hay'at al-masriyya lil kitab, Cairo, 463 pages; ann. 42 pages, photos.

rare to hear anything else. It's possible to multiply the examples. That is why we say we face the future armed with a unique culture, whether we are Muslims or Copts and why under this unique "umbrella" the different political tendencies ought to be able to compete peacefully.

In Amman, a part of the Christian community seems to have given their votes to help make Leith Chbeilat, a member of the moderate fringe of the Islamist current, into an influential deputy in parliament.

"Yes, it's true," pleads Chbeilat, "I received Christian votes, and I kept them. I have a growing number of supporters in the 'grass roots' of this country, among the Christians, but also in the left, with all sorts of people." (...)

Why? "Because," he explains in substance,

I have known how to do what the West has failed so completely to do today: to apply my values, that is to say those of Islam, without distinction to mine and to others. Why is the West in the process of failing? It has values that are very worthwhile. The problem is that when it applies them, it is in a racist manner. It reserves them entirely for itself (...) If the West were human, we would all have become Westerners! With the formidable cultural offensive that we have been subjected to, we would not have had the strength to resist... We should all be passionate about the West. But it is difficult to be passionate about someone who does not act like a human being. How can a current pass between us? (...) the Christians and the Jews have benefited from the history of justice in Islam. It is this Islamic justice which protected their churches. They have even recognized that they were better treated than before the Christians came to the Near East. Victor Saad, the Lebanese Christian writer recognized it: "You were never persecuted before the Western Christians arrived here...!" he told the Christians of today.

The Christians of this region of the world, in Muslim nations who respect their religion, should identify with this Muslim nation: they "are Muslims by nationality"... and "Christians by faith." That is what the great Makram Abdeid, said. It is what Faris al Ghoui also said. But also read Michel Aflaq. I believe that I misjudged Michel Aflaq and his Baath. It is he who said to the Christians: "As Arabs you can only be part of this Muslim society. You are Muslims. Arab Christians are Muslims, by civilization. It is their culture and their civilization. It is necessary that they fight for it. They must." Why wouldn't you fight for a civilization which gave you all this liberty and did not exercise any constraint on you?(1)

---

(1) Interview with the author, Amman, October, 1991.

It follows that the forces exploiting the Islamist themes cannot simply be judged by a static, unique criterion, in which the rest of the political contestants are miraculously absolved from decades of authoritarianism to find themselves suddenly ipso facto carriers of the flame of individual liberties simply because they demarcate themselves from the Islamists. Because their presence is one of the main components in the Arab world, the participation of the Islamists appears now as one of the conditions sine qua non, of a democratic transition which would lose all significance in their absence.

CHAPTER 7

GHANNOUCHI, YASSINE AND THE OTHERS:
THE LOGIC OF DIFFERENTIATION

Even if the origins of the Islamist phenomenon trace their roots to the reaction to the colonialist invasion, the actual environment in which it takes place varies from country to country.

Although claiming common intangible references based on the holy writings, the men and women who create its setting are in no way indifferent from their national environment, even though national characteristics are often considered foreign to the original Islam. At the same time these divisive centrifugal forces have been operating, the Islamist movement has also experienced factors of homogenization and integration, which lead to a certain attenuation of national differences and feed a dynamic of regional integration.

To take the measure of the phenomenon after having attempted to clarify its historical matrix, it is necessary to identify the specific national characteristics and the evolutions which affect them. One can then try to systematize them.

The diversity of the paths that have been followed stems first of all from the historical modalities of the encounter with the West. These have varied depending on the intrinsic characteristic of the different societies affected. Without having instituted the extreme form of the nation state, precolonial history had already traced quasi-national differences throughout the Maghreb.

The duration and the form of the foreign presence accentuated these first differences. The national expressions of Islamism consequently followed the paths charted by the gestation of the post-colonial states.

As much as with the colonial policies, the terms of the cultural relationship with the West largely depended on the policies conducted by nationalist elites following independence. In the cultural domain, the attitude toward Arabic language first, then toward cultural Arabness, and after that the Muslim religion, constituted the principal parameters. In the institutional domain also, the choice of the political formula, the political culture of the elites in power, and their attitude towards traditional institutions inherited from the pre-colonial period were also determining factors.

The modalities of inscription of Islamism on the political landscape varied finally in the capacity of the regime's policies to maintain beyond independence the consensus earned during national struggles. The amount of democratic and economic frustration which Islamism helped to express varied in proportion to the capacity of these regimes to satisfy the expectations of the mounting wave of consumers, and those of the citizens.

The Historical Modalities of the Cultural Relationship with the West.

If each of these societies experienced a direct foreign presence, the juridical setting of this presence, its duration and its effects in leaving were noticeably varied in time and space.

Direct Western Presence in the Maghreb and in the Arab World
(19th to 20th Centuries)

Algeria: 1830–1962	132 Years (French colony)
Tunisia: 1881–1956	75 years (French protectorate)
Libya: 1911–1951	40 years (Italian colony)
Morocco: 1912–1956	44 years (French protectorate)
Mauritania: 1907–1960	53 years (French colony until 1946)
Egypt: 1882–1922	40 years (Great Britain and France)
Syria: 1920–1946	26 years (French mandate)

Lebanon: 1920–1946	26 years (French mandate)
Iraq: 1920–1932	12 years (Great Britain)
Sudan: 1898–1956	58 years (Great Britain)
Emirates: 1992/1916–1971	55-79 years (Great Britain)
Yemen (Aden): 1839–1967	128 years (Great Britain)

This presence was framed by societies which were themselves very different, and which were more or less armed politically, socially, economically and culturally to resist. The 132 years of French presence in the regency of Algiers, cannot be compared to the 45 years of the protectorate in Morocco or in Tunisia, for instance. In the future Algerian colony where centralized authority was "highly concentrated in a weak faction and very diffused and atomized in the rest" (...) (1), the territory conquered during 17 years of war was transformed into departments (provinces) of metropolitan France. Elites and institutions were nearly totally eradicated there at the same time as a policy of financial appropriation and then a long war of liberation provoked an impressive social mixing. In the protectorates, in contrast, the principal national institutions survived, even if greatly weakened, a French presence that was two to three times more brief without the same major trauma.

Imposed in Algeria, modernity was imported into Egypt and to a certain extent Tunisia, by regimes that had already taken steps towards Westernization albeit limited to certain social groups even before a foreign military presence was felt. In the continuation of the reform campaign undertaken by Bey Ahmed (1837-1855), Tunisia adopted a fundamental pact (1857) which, even if it served foreign interests as well as national ones, by establishing

---

(1) Vatin, Jean-Claude, *L'Algérie Politique: Histoire et Société*, FNSP, 2nd. revised edition, Paris, 1983.

the legal equality of taxes, liberty of conscience and religion and freedom of commerce and industry, "stated a certain number of principles raising (...) the image of the modern State."(1) But even in this case and in that of Morocco, the disturbances to the symbolic universe of traditional societies were still felt. "Driven by an external dynamism," this first wave of government reform which is today the target for criticism by the Islamists (2) as much as the post independence elites are, was in effect most often "stripped of a social foundation and of any support from local society."(3) It even created certain significant reactions of rejection, such as the Tunisian insurrection of 1864, which ended in the abandoning of the first constitution, seen by some as having been imposed by foreigners.

It is essentially after independence that the effects of this confrontation of cultural models manifested itself. The process was fed first by the choices made in the cultural domain (and notably in the regime's position concerning religious values), and then by economic and institutional choices. Without hindering a certain process of secularization and the extension of Western cultural codes, the North African elites did not draw political references from one or another traditional reservoir or Western modernity with the same rhythm: the traumatizing effects of the rupture caused by the colonizers were thus managed through differentiated styles. By differences in the use of Arabism, which is to say not only the identification with linguistic values, but also the Arab ideology of unitarianism,(4) and by a selective

---

(1) Camau, Michel, *La Tunisie au Présent,* PUF, 1988, p. 44. On the spirit of Tunisian reformers towards the end of the XIXth century, cf. Kheireddine, *Essay on necessary reforms for Muslim states,* presented by Magaly Morsy, Edisud, (Archives Maghrébines), 1987; Noureddine Sraieb, "Elite et société: l'invention de la Tunisie, de l'Etat-dynastie à la nation moderne," in *La Tunisie au Présent,* Op. cit., page 65-116.

(2) "If they tell you that Ahmed Bey is dead, say that you don't believe it," writes Jourchi in a paper in which he stigmatizes the attitude of the Bourguiba regime in comparing it to the one which Bey Ahmed would have had when during his visit to France, according to his chronicler, he punctuated his delight at each new industrial achievement by exclaiming, "I wish to heaven that we had that in Tunisia."(*Al-Maarifa,* 1977.)

(3) Camau, Michel, *La Tunisie au Présent* , Op. cit., page 45.

(4) Djaït, Hichem, *La Personnalité et le Devenir Arabo-Islamiques,* Le Seuil, (Esprit), 1974; Saaf, Abdallah, in "L'unité arabe dans le discours maghrébin," *Annuaire de l'Afrique du Nord,* 1985, Editions du CNRS, Paris, 1987.

reference also and above all, to the religious values. Central in the language of Mohamed V in Morocco, religious values in Algeria and in Tunisia were considered more or less as factors of social immobility and consequently pushed to a peripheral position in the political discourse. And, finally, the apparatus of the legal and religious institutions (consultative, juridical or teaching), deftly recuperated here, i.e. they were reinforced and integrated into the political system, whereas elsewhere they were suspect, marginalized or simply suppressed.

When the diffused aspirations of a part of civil society, reinforced by the cultural implications of modernization and then eventually exacerbated by growing economic disillusionment and political frustration, manifested itself in the Maghreb, it was with rhythms and intensities that took into account these differences.

In nearly every case, the themes of mobilization in the Islamist discourse have had to be adapted to the specific nature of their time and place, taking advantage of the failings of state policies, of mutations in the discourse of the regimes or in their alliances, and thus developing numerous national specificities in the institutional expressions of the phenomenon in the Maghreb.

The Price of Modernity.

More than anyone else, it was Bourguiba, the modernist, who in order to "pull Tunisia away from the winds from the east,"(1) readily worked to diminish some of the local religious and cultural values which he considered to threaten his projects for national development or to be potentially limiting to his national leadership. Only able to tolerate "Tunisianity" and, fearing that his personal power would "dilute in a larger Arab (and *a fortiori* Islamic) entity,"(2) he did not hesitate at nationalizing to the extreme, and at secularizing the field of his references. An admirer of Auguste Comte, and impregnated with the Third Republic's secular and cultural positivism, he even allowed a few references to be made in public concerning his doubts about a religion certain dimensions of which he judged to be anachronistic or contradictory to his project for development.

In that vein, Bourguiba declared in a speech on March 17, 1960,

---

(1) Camau, Michel, *La Tunisie au Présent, O*p. cit.

(2) Djaït, Hichem, op. cit., page 26.

There are those who prefer to fast, and they make the necessary effort to see to it that the fast does not affect the output of their work. We see no objection in that... Nevertheless, the extra effort is undeniable. And there are others, who have followed my reasoning and who have grasped my thoughts more accurately. They too have wanted to make an extra effort, but in the sense of increased productivity, and without depriving themselves of eating.(1)

The inventory of symbolic violence of Bourguiba's reforms (2) recalls Turkish nationalism of the 1920s and the "White Revolution" of the Shah of Iran. They ranged from the public daytime consumption of a glass of orange juice during Ramadan to the closing of the Zitouna University and included the absorption of the Sharia courts (charged with applying Islamic law in matters dealing with civil statutes) into the jurisdiction of common law, the promulgation of a civil code notable for forbidding polygamy (and making the woman's consent to marriage obligatory).

In contrast, considerations stemming from the very nature of the regimes such as the maintenance of traditional legitimacy in the case of the King of Morocco, or structural considerations such as the pan-Arabism of Kadhafi, led other leaders in the Maghreb to preserve their symbolic supports more systematically when it came to traditional and religious values. In doing so they left less to the discourse of their opponents. The "fundamentalism of protest" here and there had to accommodate itself to the competition from the "fundamentalism of the state" and to respect its frontiers. In the Morocco of the Commander of the Faithful and in Libya also,

---

(1) Two months later, Habib Bourguiba explained his thoughts: "The bodily disciplines were only prescribed by the Koran in assuming a powerful Islamic state," he declared. "If this state were in danger, political necessities would take precedence over religious necessities. The State first.... for without the state, religion would be in danger. It is for the state to assure the security of the man who prays in the mosque and of him who wishes to safeguard his dignity, which was ridiculed during the protectorate."

Even more spectacularly, 13 years later he called into question the coherence of the Koranic text during a conference on "Culture and the National Conscience." In a speech, which was not repeated by the press, he pointed out verses which appeared contradictory ("God changes nothing in a people before they change what is in them" and "You cannot wish what God wants, because he is knowing and wise.") For a well-researched study of the personality of Bourguiba, cf. Bernard Cohen, *Bourguiba, le pouvoir d'un seul*, Paris, Flammarion, 1986.

(2) Cf. notably Aziz Krichen in *La Tunisie au Présent*, op. cit.

where under the green flag of Islam, banners and bumper stickers proclaimed the sovereignty of the Koran as the "law of society" (Sharia al Mujtamaa); in the Algeria of Chadli, where finally, according to the formula of Kateb Yacine, great propounder of the Arabo-muslim myth, "when one erected a mosque, the other built two,"(1) official Islam and Islam of protest both had to adapt their strategies, the "discourse of sedition" to struggle against the "discourse of seduction."(2)

In Morocco, the subjects of a monarch who had inherited the title of "Commander of the Faithful" did not receive the same calls for political modernity as the citizens of Bourguiba's republic, which found itself obliged to construct its political network *ex nihilo* above the ruins of the Beylical system.

The Libya of the 1970s, in which revolutionary Arabo-Islamism constituted the pivot for the regime's policy of *cultural de-colonization* with a multiplication of symbolic repudiations of Western culture (language, clothing, music) has long represented the archetype of a strategy in which Islamist demands were seemingly met by the regime. The question of Arabization, the spearhead of the Algerian movement, could not possibly have the same mobilizing force in a setting such as Libya.

Since it was harder to use a reaction against state secularism as a rallying point in Libya or Morocco, the Islamists were forced to look for other footholds in the social and economic terrain. Social demands occupied more space in the challenges against Tunisian liberal Hedi Nouira (Prime Minister from 1970 to 1981) or Hassan II of Morocco, than in that of Boumediene's socialism or Kadhafi's self-government. The denunciation of military rapprochements with Washington were more prevalent among the opponents of Bourguiba (honored with one of the highest American medals a few weeks before President Reagan's approval of the Israeli raid on Tunis) or Hassan II (who gave the U.S. the use of several military air bases in exchange for support during the war for the Western Sahara) than they were in Libya, whose leader lashed out at the "enraged dog of Israel" (i.e., Reagan).

---

(1) "We are in a situation in which the government and its opposition on the right rival the Islamic demagogy. (...) It is increasing continuously at our expense, and we are being clubbed daily and from all sides with Islam, Islam, Islam..."(in Luc Barbulesco and Philippe Cardinal, *L'Islam en Questions,* Paris, Grasset, 1986).

(2) Vatin, Jean-Claude, "Seduction and Sedition: Islamic polemical discourses in the Maghreb," in William R. Roff, *Islam and the Political Economy of Meaning,* London, Sydney, Croomheld, 1987.

Attacks on Communism carried more weight in Algiers or Tripoli than in Rabat. The "degradation of the value of women" carried more weight in Tripoli, Tunis or Algiers than in the shadow of the Alawite Throne.

As with cultural policies themselves, the cultural implications of economic policies accentuated national differences. At independence, the partisans of modernization were equipped with liberal or Marxist models whose credibility had not been challenged by the economic crisis. Their preeminence was not even questioned by the religious fundamentalists who did not direct their moral demands to economic and political questions. In the Maghreb as in Egypt, the policies of development were, thus, at first imprinted with an unqualified belief in one or another Western economic credo of the moment. The "foreign" character of economic models was only denounced when doubts grew about their effectiveness. The need to break with "imported" development plans was imposed first when their Western promoters began to show hesitation, and then when their local advocates performed an about-face, and finally when oil prices and other sources of revenue fell (from the Suez Canal, closed in 1967, to the drop off in tourism and the drop in remittances from emigrants). Thus, the genesis of the Tunisian pattern is linked to the May, 1968, riots in France, which apparently shook as many Arab certainties as they did Parisian ones. In pointing to major flaws in the universalist pretensions of the Western model, these crises, which hit nearly all the consumer society nations in the 1960s, were successful everywhere in reinforcing the credibility of alternatives coming from the Orient.

But, not all countries in the region followed the same calendar when it came to remedying the drawbacks of their early strategies. This tearing apart that represented the Western-inspired infitah, which sometimes took place under cover of changes in personnel renouncing previous credos (as in the case of Tunisia, with the creation of the post of Prime Minister), only became generalized in stages.

In Tunisia, the socializing experience of the team backing Ben Salah (a partisan of the generalization of cooperatives in agriculture) was brutally interrupted, and its promoter thrown in prison, which brought out in the open the disarray of a regime that was forced without a transition to adopt a liberalism that had only recently been stigmatized. In Egypt after the death of Nasser, Sadat renounced the Soviets and their project for centralized state control, and without any transition launched into economic and political cooperation with the absolute enemy of the country's former allies. Ten years later, Algeria also called into question 20 years of state socialism, dismantling stone by stone the heritage of Houari Boumediene, who had died in

December, 1978, and burying him politically less than two years later. Bit by bit, the credo of twenty years, which gave primacy to the public sector, was renounced, starting with the private sector. This allowed private investors to return to Tunisia after December, 1981. After this came the law of August, 1983, on private land holdings, which completely overthrew the principles of the sacrosanct agrarian revolution of 1971 and launched the privatization of the public sector. Finally, there was the "enrichment" in 1986 of the National Charter of 1976, which completed the return to private capitalism. Each development helped spell the ruin of the universalist pretensions of the government's economic discourse. The political and economic liberalization of 1988 accelerated the collapse of this symbolic heritage of the FLN. A decade after Algeria, it was finally Libya's turn. When revenues from oil were no longer sufficient to protect its ideological certainties, it also began to adjust itself to the new liberalism prevailing throughout the region.

Morocco also began turning more and more towards privatization. But while the issue took a prominent place in the national political debate,(1) the King, who had been the only leader not to be tempted by Marxism, was not obliged to make any spectacular renunciations. And, paradox of paradoxes, Moroccan Marxism, which (except for a brief experiment during the cabinet of Ibrahim at the end of the 1950's) had never had a place in government policy, was able to remain longer than elsewhere capable of mobilizing troops at the expense of Islam, at a time when the disappointed Marxist movements in Algeria, Egypt and Libya had long since lost their credibility.

The Islamists' discourse, as we have said, goes further than simply providing an ideological replenishment. It serves more and more as a vector for expressing frustrations not only over identity, but also on a larger scale over the economic, social and democratic frustrations of a middle class affected as much by the authority of their leaders as by the relative failures of their economic policies. In providing the coherence which their previously inarticulate demands lacked, Islamic discourse enables those left by the wayside during rapid expansion to develop an effectiveness in their political demands. In this respect, its mobilizing force is different according to economic circumstances and the capacity of the regimes to exert control over them.

---

(1) Habib al-Malki, *Lamalif*, October, 1987, and in *Grande Encyclopédie du Maroc*, Casablanca, 1986, page 222.

Economic Determinations.

In the 1970s, Islamism did not encounter the same social frustrations in Algeria and Libya—both rich from oil—that it did in Tunisia and Morocco. But the end of the oil boom arrived earlier than expected. "Anesthetized" by the vapors of oil and the first steps towards the promises of industrialization, social protest was awakened during the cold wind of the third oil shock.

For, the disenchantment with development models was in proportion to the hopes which the models had aroused. The recession resulting from the oil counter-shock in the 1980s, amplified by the fall of the dollar in 1985, threatened in Libya and Algeria to make up for the time lag more brutally than anywhere else. The disillusion was that much stronger for the citizens of the Jamahiriya al ozma,(1) who had tasted the fruits of opulence provided by oil or, as in Algeria, had come close enough to them to believe that they might be accessible, before demographic expansion devoured the benefits promised by industrialization.

Everywhere the rapidity and intensity of the process of disengaging the State from its role as benefactor, simultaneously to or after the infitah, set the pace of disillusion. The dependence on the IMF (International Monetary Fund) constituted one of the parameters of this evolution. Strong in Egypt, in Tunisia and in Morocco, such dependency was initially less in Algeria, which did not yet have to ask for an official rescheduling of its debt, and was next to nothing in Libya, which although indebted had not yet presented itself to international financial markets. Although adapted to the structures of national economies, the policies of adjustment,(2) which were intended to compensate for the fall in oil prices in Libya and Algeria (where oil represents the sole export) and for the drop in revenues from tourism and remittances from overseas workers in Tunisia and Morocco, spared no one. The social effects of adjustment policies hastened a certain harmonization of the economic background of the Islamist current, which was favorable to

---

(1) After the American bombardment on April 17, 1986, the official title of the Libyan Jamahiriya, which until then had been "Socialist and Popular," took on the qualification "al ozma," "Very Great."

(2) Which everywhere consisted expecially in establishing a greater "truth "in pricing, which is to say a modification of the government efforts at subsidizing essential food stuffs, and a consequent price increase for these goods. The measures led to major riots in Tunisia and Morocco.

their development—even if the population expansion did not have quite the same impact in Libya, which was short of man power.

Political Determinations

As an ideology of opposition, Islamist discourse also profited from the incapacity of the regimes to respond to the growing demands for democracy. Subsequently, this discourse was influenced by the response of the governments when faced with its emergence on the political scene.

Thus, the rigidity of the monocratic Algerian system, which was total up until 1989, and of Libya, which was equally monocratic once the institutional mystifications had been stripped away, served as a powerful stimulant. Algeria and Libya represented the only regimes not to have undertaken the process of ideological replenishment that was inescapably imposed on them. The wind of liberalism which blew on the Algerian economy took, in fact, nearly ten years to affect the political system. During that time it nourished formidable frustrations in the hearts of an excluded generation. In Libya, the timid questioning of the Jamahiriyan ideology was completed with the liberation of nearly all political prisoners. But this gesture (cf. infra) did not succeed in restoring confidence. The overly unpredictable character of Libya's "Guide" had already discredited the regime in the eyes of a large part of its vital forces.

In Tunisia, the pluralism whose existence had been entrusted to the good will of its legislature by Article 8 of the Constitution of June 6, 1959, vanished from the political scene four months later. The right of free association was consigned by the law of November 7, 1959, to the vigilant guard of the Ministry of Interior. The result was to keep democracy under the strict control of a single party for 25 years, only barely softened by the tolerated existence of a strong central labor union, which itself had to function between two waves of repression. In 1981, pluralism reappeared in principle. It remained very theoretical in practice and did not allow the potential opposition to express itself in any real terms. By the end of 1992, Bourguiba's political opening had still not succeeded in costing the party in power even one of its seats in the parliament. And the legislation concerning parties adopted by Bourguiba's successor (cf. infra), which in principle excluded political groups claiming to be Islamic, did not improve this situation at all.

In twenty years, Morocco has had three constitutions, each one assigning room for institutional expression to political opponents. But the first constitution, which was only promulgated six years after independence, was suspended after functioning effectively for less than two years. The second, adopted in July 1970, was abrogated 18 months later, and the third only had its provisions governing the legislature put into operation five years after its adoption in March, 1972.(1)

If the Islamist message did not find as many echoes among the opulent, revolutionary and populist Libya of Kadhafi's beginnings as it did among Tunisians disappointed with Bensalhism, it is safe to say that ten years later opposition to the "Guide of the Jamahiriya" is more noticeable than the demands for democracy expressed by Tunisia's middle classes, who were not ignored as completely. Morocco and Tunisia also allowed the voices of the preachers of protest to confront other discourses in the opposition. Those included the unions (UGTT, Union Generale des Travailleurs Tunisiens), associations (the League for the Rights of Man in Tunisia) and, in spite of the limits on pluralism, other partisan voices.

The only regime in the region which did not receive the poisoned gift of legitimacy's monopoly at independence, the "Party of the King" showed itself to be more politically adept than any of its neighbors. Without being the direct heir of a national movement like Kadhafi, King Hassan, nevertheless, shared the advantage with the Libyan leader of having had a long reign (30 years by 1992 compared to 23 for Kadhafi), which has provided a source of charisma not available to the young successors of Boumediene and Bourguiba. In the Maghreb as elsewhere, the time of great popular movements has given way to a more pedestrian administration in the style of France's Pompidou rather than that of DeGaulle. From Egypt's Mubarak to Algeria's Chadli Benjedid to Tunisia's Ben Ali, legitimacy now depends on balancing accounts, a task which is far more difficult than delivering fiery speeches.

From the guarded tolerance of Tunisia and Algeria and of Morocco up until 1980, to the blind repression in Libya after 1978 and everywhere else after 1980, the diversity of government reactions to the Islamist challenge accentuated latent national characteristics. The Algerian Mustapha Bouyali, who no longer believed in legalistic action, died under a hail of police gunfire only shortly after the Tunisian, Rached Ghannouchi, had listened to

---

(1) Michel Camau, *Pouvoirs et Institutions au Maghreb*, Tunis, Ceres production, 1978; cf. also Michel Rousset, especially "Le retour aux urnes: consultation alibi ou consultation démocratique?" *Grand Maghreb*, No. 28, June, 1984. A revision of the Constitution was made public in August, 1992: the main liberalization is that the King, when he nominates the ministers, has to do so "following the proposals of the Prime Minister," whom he has chosen.

his prime minister praise his "moderate and reasonable" attitude. Shortly afterwards, Ghannouchi was back in prison.

It is true that from Tunis to Algiers and Casablanca, the "princes" for a certain time disdained the nature of the protest coming from the mosques. Where a reaction to the excesses of modernization was taking place, they saw nothing more than the aftermath of an archaic world destined to vanish beneath the rising tide of modernity. They were also frequently tempted to treat the Islamists as potential allies against their Marxist opponents. When they heard the formidable echo of Khomeini's revolution, for the most part the Maghreb's political leaders gave in to the temptation for repression. After realizing its limits, they concocted a more subtle cocktail of repression, concessions, intimidation and state fundamentalism.

Certainly, the reaction of the Maghrebi regimes to the Islamist surge was not always an attempt to convert the movements. Even if he was alone, Bourguiba, whose cultural policy was the favorite target of the Islamist critics, did not shrink back from reasserting some of his policies with an obstinacy (or serenity) that sometimes seemed suicidal. Whether it was his relations with the Jewish community, where Islamist rhetoric often crossed the line between anti-Zionism and anti-semitism or his position on the burning question of language when he raised the number of school hours taught in French in primary schools in 1986, Bourguiba never hesitated to go on the offensive against anything which he felt to oppose the deeper logic of his political program.

The summer move in August, 1986, of Hassan II in the direction of Israel's Prime Minister Shimon Perez (who was received in the Palace of Ifrane) also showed that the monarch had the capacity of ignoring the reactions of part of his public, or that he was not afraid of provoking them (just as Bourguiba demonstrated when he called for a dialogue with Israel in 1965).

The behavior of the Maghrebi governments was equally diversified according to the terrain on which Islamist opposition movements mobilized themselves in their attitude towards Khomeini's revolution. The Iranian experiment was severely condemned by Morocco and Tunisia (especially the latter after Iran's implication in 1986 in a terrorist network which had manipulated several Tunisians in France). In Algeria it was supported with some reserve, and in Libya it received nearly unconditional support. The Afghan situation also highlighted a number of differences. Because of their alliances, Algeria and Libya uttered the weakest condemnations of the Soviet intervention on Islamic territory. The Palestinian dossier was another theme in which each regime's concerns affected the capacity for Islamist mobilization. Bourguiba gave no reaction to the Israeli air raid on Tunis, in contrast to Algeria which hosted the Palestinian National Council and Morocco, in which Hassan II presided over the "Al Quds committee" for the defense of Palestinians' interests.

The attitude of the North African governments had consequences not only on the impact but also on the internal evolution of the different Islamic currents, and on the crystallization of their doctrinal foundations. In Tunisia, as in Algeria, the momentary arrival of the Islamists on the legitimate political scene considerably accelerated the evolution of their doctrinal base, and the development of their relative autonomy on a national footing. Inversely, in those two cases, the return to massive repression facilitated an increase in the number of partisans of violent action on the edges of the movement.

The Factors of Integration

The factors leading to increasing autonomy should not obscure the presence of factors operating in the opposite direction to create the homogenization of the Islamist currents with respect to one another. Even if it is difficult to actually prove the existence of institutionalized international relationships between the movements, it is nevertheless clear that the currents in the Maghreb were not cut off either from each other or from the rest of the world. The emigration towards Europe, and especially but not exclusively to France, was undoubtedly the first driving force for the confrontation between different national movements.

Members of the Algerian Bouyali group (cf. infra) attended some very cosmopolitan Islamic conferences in Paris. The complete palette of nuances from the different Islamist currents were represented, if not already implanted between Paris and Marseille. Student associations came into contact with a prevailing internationalism that was a long way from the tense nationalism of the regimes. This encouraged a certain doctrinal homogenization, even if the process of confrontation occasionally led to the same kinds of ruptures and splits found at home. Neither France nor Europe held a monopoly on the circulation of ideas and of men. The American Muslim associations, especially the student ones, were also numerous and vigorous. Moroccan "Brothers" and Saudis, Libyans and Tunisians confronted doctrines and strategies there and were often in contact with representatives of opposition groups in exile.

Another window on the Arab world, the pilgrimage to Mecca, has always facilitated the circulation of men and ideas, and often of money. At least one of the predecessors of Bouyali (Belkacem Boukasmia, who had created one of the first small groups at Sidi bel Abbes) participated in the occupation of Mecca's Great Mosque in 1979, where he was killed. The Moroccan, Abdelkrim Moutti, was also reported to have been present at Mecca. Ahmed Lazreq, an ex-member of Tunisia's ITM, and a former writer for the review, *Al Maarifa*, whose activism led to his execution in August 1986, had installed himself in 1982 in Saudi Arabia where he imported Tunisian dates and...represented the Afghan resistance movements at the Organization of the Islamic Conference (this earned him a para-diplomatic status, which nevertheless failed to protect him from extradition back to Tunisia).

The policy of Arabization which, especially in Algeria, succeeded in exporting students towards the Arab East and importing from these primary and high school teachers and university professors to the Maghreb, evidently accelerated the penetration of the ideas of Hassan Al Banna and the methods of Sayyid Qutb. Two founders of the Tunisian ITM, Ahmida Enneifer and Rached Ghannouchi, studied in Syria, where they discovered the first Muslim Brothers. A large number of teachers imported from the Near East to work in Algerian universities at the start of the 1970s began to replace their French-speaking counterparts. The release by Sadat in 1971 of Muslim Brothers imprisoned by Nasser made a major contribution to this transfer of ideology. The role played by external factors in the diffusion of Islamism should not be exaggerated though. From Egypt where the "evil" was supposed to have come from Saudi Arabia with returning immigrant workers, to Lebanon which complained that it was too near to Khomeini's Iran, and in the Maghreb, which denounced its Egyptian teachers, etc... the anti-Islamist arguments had a natural tendency to "blame the neighbors" for a phenomenon that in any case would not have had a chance to develop if it had not responded to a need that was already felt in the local socio-political terrain.

The connections were often superimposed, the trip to the Middle East completing a stay in Paris. Educated in Egypt, one of the founders of the Bouyali group fled Algeria before the group entered its phase of armed struggle, to look in France for the security and freedom of action which his native country had denied him. Henceforth, trips and meetings no longer needed the pretext of immigration or pilgrimage: Iran, of course, but also the Sudan of Hassan Tourabi received numerous visitors from the Maghreb.

The last years have witnessed an acceleration of this trend towards internationalism of the Islamic movement. The passport of Rached Ghannouchi which is filled with visas from all over the world testifies to "globalization" of Islamist travels.(1) The Gulf crisis and the cracks which it initiated in certain intellectual circles briefly slowed the process (especially among Kuwaitis and Saudis). Regularly visited by Ghannouchi, the Sudan of Hassan Tourabi, founder of an Arab and Islamic Popular Congress, who works on mobilizing the "Iraqi camp" of the Gulf War, has lately been accused of becoming the "new headquarters of the Islamist international."(2) For many militants reluctant to visit the Gulf because of the

---

(1) Rached Ghannouchi sketched out for Hamid Barrada (in *Jeune Afrique*, cited) the main highpoints after his departure from Tunis, which gives an idea of the effectiveness of his role as itinerant ambassador. In May 1989, he arrived in Paris, where a group of the movement's leaders in exile were living, and where he had kept numerous friendships. From there, he left for Cologne (at the invitation of an association of Palestinian students), then to Hamburg (for an association of Turkish workers), London, Vienna (Congress on the condition of Muslims in Eastern Europe), Istanbul (commemoration of the Islamic conquest of Constantinople organized by the Islamist party, Rafah), Jeddah and Riyadh (pilgrimage and World Islamic Conference), Kuwait, Abu Dhabi, Dubai (Emirates), Tripoli, Benghazi (Libyan Islamic Conference), Cairo (Conference on the nationalist Islamic dialogue), Algiers, Lahore (Conference and meeting in Afghanistan with the leaders of the resistance), Malta, Lagos, Abuja, Paris (interview cited). Since then, Rached Ghannouchi has visited the U.S., where he attended a round of conferences, but also where the U.S. State Department refused to see him except at a very subordinate level. After that, forbidden from returning to French territory (a concession from Paris to the repeated demands from Tunis), he split his time between Sudan, which accorded him a diplomatic passport, Algiers and mainly London, where the demands from Tunis have not yet managed to secure his expulsion as was the case in Cairo in September 1989, just after the above mentioned Conference (al-Hiwar al-Qawmi al-dini) on the nationalist-Islamic dialogue.

(2) On the Arab and Islamic popular congress see Chapter II (Arabism) footnote No.1, page 24. On the Islamist trend in the Sudan, the best source would be the insider's look of Mekki Hassan: *Tarikh al-ikhouane al-musulmine fil Sudan* (History of the Muslim Brothers in the Sudan), Institute for African and Asian Studies Khartoum and *Al-Harakat alislamiyya fil sudan 1969-1985* (The islamic movement in Sudan), Dar al-maarifa lil intaj al-thaqafi, Khartoum, 1991. Hassan Tourabi has himself published *Al-Harakat al-Islamiyya fil Soudan*, al-Qara' al-arabi, 301 pages Cairo, 1991, aimed at exposing the methods of the Islamic movement more than its history. Under the same title of *Al-Harakat al-Islamiyya fil Soudan*, has also been published the speech Tourabi gave in front of the second congress of the Sudanese Popular Islamic front as well as a comprehensive interview with Mohamed Al-Hachemi Al-Hamdi (Cairo, 1991). Opponents to the Islamist trend have published numerous critical readings of the experience started in June, 1989, by the "inqadh (salvation) revolution" of General Al-Bechir. Among them: Hassan Ahmed Al-Hassan, *Ightiâl al dimocretayya fil soudane* (Assassination of democracy in the Sudan), Cairo,

151

proximity to American military forces and American policies, it has indeed become, in spite of its peripheral situation and its limited financial resources, some sort of a "meeting point."

1991; Hiber Ibrahim Ali, *'Azmat al-islam al-siyassi, al-jebhat al-islamiyya al-qawmia fil soudane namoudhijan,* (Crisis of Political Islam: the Model of the National Islamic Front in the Sudan), ed. Markaz al-dirassate al-soudania; Markaz al-bouhouth al-arabia, Cairo, 1991, 274 pages. See also Prunier, Gérard, in *Le Soudan contemporain,* Marc Lavergne (ed) Paris, Karthala, 1990.

CHAPTER 8

LIBYA: PETROLEUM, THE GREEN BOOK AND THE SUNNA

In Libya, the opulence of oil and a policy of "cultural decolonization" conducted by Colonel Kadhafi with an unequalled radicalism have combined their effects for a long time to defer the growth of the Islamist movement.

With the establishment of an intransigent Arabization, the introduction in the penal code of Koranic punishments, the adoption of the green flag of Islam, the massive financing of a missionary association (Da'wa Islamiyya, created in 1972),(1) the broadcasting of television spots which equated wearing a tie with the emblem of the cross, and the public destruction of Western musical instruments, the practices of Kadhafi's regime have, in many respects, anticipated the demands that were likely to be made by the Islamists. The "fundamentalism of the state" has thus occupied virtually the terrain that might otherwise have been taken by a "fundamentalism of protest." Throughout the first decade of the Revolution of September, the religious establishment remained on good terms with the regime. The Libyan juridical and legislative landscape was in 1969 very close to that of Egypt or Syria, which is to say marked by the progression of legislation directly inspired by European models, to the detriment of the Sharia which at the time only covered certain areas of personal status. On October 28, 1971, a commission was created to reexamine the laws vigorously with the goal of expurgating any provisions that were contrary to religious law.(2) Even if the real results were limited in practice to a minor retouching of the penal code, the symbolic impact was noticable. Libya became the first Arab state with the exception of Saudi Arabia to systematize this kind of reference to a religious source. The effects of this cultural policy were added to by the favorable economic situation created by petroleum, which was not likely at the time to feed social frustrations. Even when the regime launched itself into an economic revolution fairly late in the game (with the publishing of

---

(1) Cf. Hans Peter Mattes, *Die innere und aussere islamische mission Libyens*, Kaiser-Grunewald, 1986; T. Monastiri et F. Burgat, "Chronique Libye," *Annuaire de l'Afrique du Nord*, 1982, Paris, Ed. CNRS, 1984.

(2) Cf. Ann Elisabeth Meyer, "Le droit musulman à l'âge du Livre Vert," *Maghreb Machrek*, No. 93, July, 1981, page 197. Borham Attallah in "Le droit pénal musulman ressuscité," *Annuaire de l'Afrique du Nord*, 1975, page 227.

the second part of the Green Book in 1978) and began to limit private ownership of land and private commerce, it still had the financial resources to avoid having to pay a political price. In a country of three million inhabitants, whose principal source of foreign currency had for a long time been the fees paid by Western powers for the use of Libyan military bases and the resale to Italian scrap dealers of the carcasses of military equipment abandoned by multiple occupying powers, the massive injection of petro-dollars (which the Libyans believed to be inexhaustible) had a decisive impact for a long time. Against the backdrop of opulence provided by the impressive revenues from oil (nearly $20 billion in 1980; $6 billion in 1986) the Libyan "political laboratory" functioned at first with an apparent consensus. Many foreign observers, sensitive to the impressive results of the first industrial investments, thought for a time that, in the spreading network of existing institutional systems, the "committees" (*lajane*) and other "Popular Congresses" (*mu'atamarate chaabia*) of the Jamahiriyya, had managed to open genuinely new perspectives. The Islamist current was also a "victim" of this economic and political prosperity.

In the second decade of the "Revolution of September" (*thawra fatih*), the economic crisis coming just after the rapid fall in petroleum resources would brutally bring to the surface both the limits of the development experience (too largely dependent on oil and foreign labor) and the relative fragility of the social base of the regime. And it is in this context that the first confrontation between the defenders of the Koran and those of the little Green Book would take place.

FROM IDEOLOGICAL RUPTURE....

The rupture with the Islamist movement revealed itself when the regime adopted an initiative at the end of the 1970s that was aimed at circumventing the resistance by the Ulema to certain social aspects of the Jamahiriyan program. Into this breach moved a growing number of people who were disappointed with the country's development. They included small businessmen whose commerce had been closed in 1979 and others who, with the fall in oil revenues, felt that their social footing had more or less brutally been called into question. In gestation since 1973, the principles contained in the third part of the little Green Book, which included the "Social Foundations of the Third Universal Theory," were not made public until the end of 1978. The publication followed in the tracks of the speech of Zouara, which started the process of abolishing administrative and classical political institutions in favor of "people's committees."

It is in the current of the same year, when the economic implications of this new policy began to enter into contradiction with certain sectors of the traditional society, that Kadhafi took the risk of rendering official his desire, which had already been expressed many times, to simultaneously abandon part of the Tradition of the Prophet (the Hadiths) as a source of religion, and the Sharia (in fact the Fiqh) as intangible juridical reference. The declaration of "returning power to the people," solemnly adopted at Sebha on March 2, 1977, had already stated in Article 2 that henceforth the Koran would provide the "law of the society" to the exclusion of all other sources. But this spectacular promotion of the revealed text to the rank of positive legislation had primed public opinion on the implicit restriction with respect to the Sunna. On February 19, the argument (already developed in fact during an Islamo-Christian seminar on February 1, 1976), was clarified before a specifically Libyan public. On July 3, the reformist "Rubicon" was crossed. The walls of the Mosque Moulay Mohamed echoed with a passionate debate(1) between Kadhafi and an angry swarm of Libyan and Arab Ulema, who spent several hours trying to force the Libyan guide into the ways of orthodoxy. But, for Kadhafi, the proof lay that in the supposed acts and gestures of the Prophet, many additions forged during the great internal quarrels (and especially the birth of Shiism) had been slipped in to authorize the practices of such and such a party. Without doubt, hadn't Boukhari and Muslims registered 200 years later the Hadiths whose genealogy had been scrupulously verified thanks to a technique in which Muslims today want to see one of the first scientific approaches to history? But this selection between the "healthy" (*sahih*) and apocryphal (*makdoub*) represented for Kadhafi no more than a human maneuver, imprinted with too many approximations (certain Hadiths contradict each other, and even the text of the Koran) for the Sunna in its entirety not to be affected. Thus, the Koran imposes the principle that there should be no constraints in religion while a Hadith condemns apostates to death. Kadhafi was not the only one to stress the need for a prudent reexamination, or failing that, a selective examination

(1) The text of which is reproduced in the *Sijl al-qawmi* (Official record of kadhafi's discourses), 1978, and translated in French in the annex of the long interview accorded to Hamid Barrada and which appeared in French and Arabic under the title "Je suis un opposant à l'échelon mondial" (I am an opponent at the world level), H. Barrada, Marc Kravetz, Marc Whitaker. On the attitude of the regime before 1978, cf. Lisa Anderson, "Kadhafi's Islam" in Esposito, John, Ed. *Voices of Resurgent Islam,* New York, Oxford Univ. Press, 1983, and "Qadhdhafi and his Opposition," *The Middle East Journal*, Vol 40, No. 2, Spring, 1986, page 225.

of the body of the Sunna. Without speaking of Fatima Mernissi and her remarkable "investigation of the misogynic Hadith and its author, Abou Bakra,"(1) certain fringes of the Islamist current itself are not very far from Kadhafi's assessment.

Salah Eddine Jourchi, founder of the progressive current, does not hesitate also to preach the principle of a reflective and prudent utilization of the Hadith. He suggests distinguishing those who touch on religious practice and are consequently less susceptible to alteration, from those who deal with values of the society, and have been collected in a historical-political-economic context, which may have influenced those who transmitted them, and which should today be submitted to a rigorous ijtihad.

> They (i.e. the ITM) reproach us for being against the Sunna. Why? Because they say that the Koran is the first source, that it is there where the fundamental realities of Islam are found. The Sunna only comes in second place. It only developed historically two or three centuries after the death of the Prophet. Now, these three centuries saw the birth of many political problems. The choice of the hadith are not the same between Shiites and Sunnites, etc. So this period should be considered attentively. One should not recognize just any hadith on which (the ITM) to rely. We think that it is necessary to make a serious historical analysis. But for them (the ITM and especially Rached Ghannouchi) this attitude is very dangerous.(2)

For Kadhafi, such a circumspection is de rigeur both with respect to the Sunna itself, as well as the Fiqh, which is to say the juridical construction of the theologians which he feels is even more dated and stained by its human origins.

> What one calls today Muslim legislation (Sharia) cannot be attributed to religion.... These are speculations. Today, I declared for example that the continental plateau between the Jamahiriya and Malta is located at the 35th degree of the North latitude. These are affairs which concern men. They have been the object of reflection on my part, which has been dictated by scientific, material and temporal considerations. Well, it is the same for the juridical schools.

---

(1) *Le Harem Politique*, Paris, Albin Michel, 1987.

(2) Interview with the author, Tunis, August, 1984.

I hold the Sharia for a positive law in the same way that I hold Roman law, the Code Napoleon, and all the laws elaborated by lawyers in France, Italy, England and Muslim countries.(1)

Doing that, the ideologue of the Jamahirization aims from the evidence as much at pushing forward with indispensable reexamination of the Fiqh as at abstracting from it those religious prescriptions which enter the most directly into contradiction with his own political philosophy, the ultimate implications of which had just been made apparent by the publication of the third part of the Green Book. With the Sunna, would also depart the rules and their guardians, the troublesome corpus of the Ulema, theoretically entrusted with the mission of guarding over the religious orthodoxy of the Prince and capable of limiting his reformist autonomy, especially in questions related to personal status.

TO REPRESSION

Even if Kadhafi defends himself today as having acted as a head of state who had to impose his view ("I spoke and acted as a simple Muslim and I did not force anyone to adopt my point of view")(2) and even though that point of view, as we have seen, was shared by certain components of the Islamist current, the denunciation of the Sunna would mark the end of the peaceful coexistence of the regime and the Ulema and the start of a muscled effort to domesticate the latter, whose position would degrade rapidly. Coming just after the attacks against private property and the Waqfs, which directly threatened the Ulema economic base, the position taken by Kadhafi was unanimously denounced by the body of the Ulema as pure heresy. Those who refused this attempt to scuttle their institution were severely repressed. The population was invited by the revolutionary committees to "take by assault" the mosques of the most recalcitrant. On May 16, 1978, Tripoli radio announced that the Libyan masses were in the process proceeding "to the purification of certain mosques in putting an end to the activity of certain preachers who led in these places of worship a campaign of atheism and propaganda in favor of the exploitation and oppression of man by man."(3)

---

(1) Cited by Barrada, Kravetz, Whitaker, op. cit.

(2) Interviews with the author, Tripoli, Bab Azizia, December 6 and 10, 1987.

(3) Cited by H. Bleuchot, *Chroniques et Documents Libyens,* CNRS, 1984.

On November 21, 1980, the Sheikh Mohamed al Bishti, who had publicly denounced in a sermon the accusations made against him that he was "an agent of Saudi Arabia" was imprisoned. He was said to have later died under torture. Other arrests followed and several mosques, including that of Jaghboub, the historic seat of the Senousia, 500 kilometers to the southeast of Benghazi, as well as the Islamic university of Al Baida, were closed, which is to say destroyed. The tiny mosque of Sidi Hammouda, was blown up with mines placed at 3 a.m. to symbolically permit the enlarging of the "Green Plaza" at Tripoli. The antique mosque of Sidi Abdussalam in Zliten(1) was also demolished for reasons that had little to do with urbanism. Since then Kadhafi has reconciled with Saudi Arabia, whose Ulema had "excommunicated" him in 1983, declaring him to be the "enemy of Islam."(2) He has established good relations with the Iran of Khomeini, which was prepared for the price of several thousand tons of arms to forget the disappearance of the Lebanese Shiite Imam, Moussa Sadr, on Libyan territory in 1978, undoubtedly assassinated but possibly...by mistake.(3) But in spite of these international overtures, the internal climate continued to degenerate.

The opponents of the regime were systematically qualified as "Muslim Brothers," a group against which Kadhafi had maintained a reticence that was completely Nasserian. This was the case of the authors of the aborted attack of Bab Aziziya compound on May 8, 1984, but also of several other victims of the repression who came from varying backgrounds ranging from the military to small businessmen, militant Berberists, or students, executed by hanging during the course of the last six years. One of the caricatures of the star Libyan cartoonist, Al Zwawi, which was duplicated in official posters, represented a bearded man (in the role of the Islamist); a slap deliv-

---

(1) Reconstructed since at great cost.

(2) Which led the Grand Mufti Zaoui, co-founder in 1972 of the Association Da'wa Islamiyya—deceased in 1986 and not replaced since then, to take distance himself from the regime, and Kadhafi to have a book written to defend his positions (*Al-Kadhafi wal-mutaqawilun alahi,* Tripoli, Muncha 'amma, 1984.)

(3) To the number of interpretations which circulated, the least unreasonable one is that at the end of a meeting that was particularly stormy, the members of Kadhafi's body guard misunderstood an ambiguous order given by Kadhafi "to take care" of the Lebanese guest.

ered by the masses makes a mask fall away and reveals the face of Ronald Reagan.(1)

From Reticence to Resistance

More than anywhere else in the Maghreb, the Islamist current experienced difficulties in constituting itself into a force of opposition in Libya, given the political and ideological radicalism of the regime. "We are a non-organized organization" (*munadhama ghir munadhama*) living "in a country were one finds 'books' which are not worth the price of the paper used to print them" declared some of those who dared to express their distaste for the regime to a foreign visitor.

The national Front for the Safeguard of Libya (Jebhat al watani li inqadh libya) created in September, 1981, at Khartoum by Mohamed Youssef al Muqarief, former ambassador in India, and co-directed by El Haj Abd al Majid Seif al Nar, one of the participants in the first serious plot against Kadhafi in 1975, would not be considered as a completely Islamist movement. Based in Sudan until the fall of Nimeiry, in the United States and Great Britain afterwards, the Front regroups, as its name indicates, several of the composants of the opposition in exile, including the Islamists. Its influence in the interior of the country remained difficult to determine, at least until its expulsion from Chad, with the help of both the CIA and the French troups,(2) after the fall of Hissene Habre in 1991. Most of those who rallied to it, such as 17 officers who were detained in Chad in February, 1988, had come from the large Libyan Diaspora. From outside Libya, the movement has published a review in Arabic, *Al Inqadh*, for a long time, and a bulletin in English, the NFSL's *New Bulletin*. It has also published several brochures such as "How Kadhafi ruined Libya's Economy," "How Kadhafi ruined the Libyan Treasury," "Kadhafi's Action in Light of the Principles of Islam," etc. At the interior of the country, small groups of activists, rapidly dismantled by a particularly radical repression, still sporadically follow a strategy based on harassing the symbols of the regime.

---

(1) Zwawi has published two volumes of his drawings under the title of *Ijtimaiyate,* and Hans Peter Mattes has analysed some of them in *Muhammad al-Zwawi libysche Karikaturen,* Hans Peter Mattes Verlag edition Wuquf, Scheessel, 1984.

(2) Which undoubtedly removed some of the credibility from the militants at the Front.

In the spring of 1982, twenty-one presumed members of the Party of Islamic Liberation were indicted for plotting, and eight of them are believed to have been executed a year later. In April, 1984, two students were publicly hung in Benghazi for having tried to set fire to the great amphitheater where Kadhafi had made some of his more important speeches. At least one of the masters of ceremony at this rally where students and teachers of Gar Younis had been taken by force, was found himself hung in the toilets of the amphitheater in question. The episode bears testimony to the violence of the confrontations and of a certain crystallization of the currents present.

In the month of July, 1986, the members of the previously unknown Party of God tried several times to poison the water of a hotel in Tobruk, where several important Soviet military advisers were staying. The group, whose relations with Pakistan surfaced later, also "executed" an important member of the revolutionary committees, charged with enforcing the restrictions on private agricultural commerce. His death followed a long interrogation in front of a video camera, during a mock show trial. The six alleged kidnappers (to whom was added, with no apparent reason, the son of a former prime minister who was alleged to have set fire to his father's house to protest against its transformation into a dispensary) were also submitted to a televised self-criticism. An old man wearing a beard was presented as the author of a small book on "the permitted and the illicit" and as the doyen of the Libyan fundamentalist group. He was reproached for his "hairy beard" and mocked and ridiculed for his finicky precepts.

A few weeks earlier, the 48 Koranic schools in the country had been closed and the surveillance of the revolutionary committees on the frequentation of mosques was reinforced. On February 17, 1987, Tripoli television rebroadcast the spectacle of the hanging of all six members of the small Party of God in a gymnasium, before three rows of the public noisily demonstrating its approval.

The Liberal Redeployment.

Starting in the month of March, 1987, Kadhafi gave the impression of searching in the double redeployment of his economic policy and his exterior alliances, for the keys for the survival of his regime which appeared to most observers as having lost the essential part of social base that it had had in the 1970s. Since then, he has held to this reformist line, at least in his foreign policy. On March 27, the Guide delivered, in one of the long speeches he favors so much, the signal that a re-examination of his Third

Theory was about to begin with less of an eye towards centralized state control.(1)

Two major shocks had shaken the regime during the preceding months. First of all was the American bombardment, which contrary to earlier skirmishes with the Sixth Fleet had very clearly revealed the limits of the effectiveness of the revolutionary committees and of their loyalty to the regime.(2) The second shock was the conflict in Chad, in which Kadhafi, from the defection of his allies to the military reverses of his elite troops on the ground, had encountered a resistance that was totally unexpected and two bloody defeats at Aouzou and Matten Es Sahra.

It is in this context that the Theoretician of the Third Universal Theory seems to have taken the decision to resort himself to the political recipes of the infitah. After having seriously changed the principle of forbidding the return to the use of manual labor, he authorized the taking in charge of the "quasi-totality of the industries of the current state sector" by "the individuals who work there." Tacharukiats, supple cooperative structures regrouping a small number of partners on the basis of voluntary adhesion, became the juridical instrument for this reform. On the political plan, this infitah received a first prolongation a few months later.(3) After having

---

(1) See Dirk Vandewalle, "Qadhafi's 'perestroika': economic and political liberalization in Libya," *Middle East Journal*, Volume 45, No. 2, Spring, 1991, and "Kadhafi's revolution," to be published early 1993.

(2) During the night of the bombardment, when rumors of an uprising at a military camp in Misrata arose, and that on the faith of alarmist rumors it was possible to believe that Colonel Kadhafi had died in the rubble of his villa at Bab Azizia, about 50 members of the revolutionary commitees are believed to have not only taken flight, but for certain, according to the NFSL's news bulletin, burned dossiers attesting to their engagement in the service of the regime. Less than six months later, the revolutionary committees (created in 1977 to facilitate the passage to direct democracy of the Green Book, and progressively converted to guard dogs of the regime) were completely restructured. Cf. F.B, "La montée des oppositions en Libye," *Maghreb Machreq Monde Arabe*, No. 116, June, 1987, page 101.

(3) If one believes the speech given on October 26, 1991, before the committee of the municipality of Syrte, the enterprises — which is not totally new — but also the banks, the schools, universities and hospitals were able from then on to transform themselves into "tacharukiat" and acquire a private title. "The first 20 years of the Revolution were only an initial phase during which the citizens did not manage to convince themselves that they were really proprietors of the national economy. It was useful then," the Colonel declared in substance, "to pass to a more direct form of property."

renewed the contact, without great success it is true, with certain of his opponents, Kadhafi delivered a spectacular amnesty by personally destroying the walls of their prison and releasing the quasi-totality of the political and common law prisoner. Among the beneficiaries of this measure which was destined to boost the prestige of the regime were the first Islamist victims, and notably several members of the Islamic Liberation Party, arrested in 1973.

The frontiers with Tunisa, closed down after the crisis of 1985 that had led to the expulsion of 30,000 Tunisian immigrant workers (as many Egyptians and a few thousand Syrians, Pakistanis, etc.), were reopened without restriction, unleashing a sudden influx of Tunisian and Arab workers (between 20,000 and 30,000) and a temporary exodus that was even more massive (70,000) of Libyans looking for goods on the Tunisian market, which the rigor of Kadhafi's import controls had stripped from the local shops. The following year, the normalization with Egypt, which had resisted the tempests of the Gulf War, also gave a new reality to the discourse on unity. But 1989 provided an opportunity to see the limits on the regime's capacity for political reform.

1989: Falling Back on Old Ways

The armed skirmishes that took place in the east of the country (Benghazi, Jdavia and Misrata) in January and through the first quarter of 1989,(1) gave the signal for a new wave of repression which went farther than the small groups of activists to touch a full sector of Libyan public opinion. Spectacularly emptied in April, 1988, of hundreds of prisoners, the prisons were refilled with several thousand Islamist activists and sympathizers, arrested during the first four months of 1989 in Cyrenaica and transferred by plane to Tripoli. The Colonel for the first time at the end of September of this same year explicitly evoked this upsurge of protest by reading a text (which was later pinned to the door of Libyan mosques) calling for the physical elimination of "atheists." Just a year earlier Kadhafi had

---

The regime nevertheless continues to suffer from a near total lack of credibility in the eyes of local and international investors. This new symbolic rupture on the way to privatization has little chance of profoundly affecting the economic landscape of the Jamahiriya.

(1) Including perhaps an assassination attempt against the Guide which only failed, thanks to the vigilance of the bodyguards of President Hafez al-Assad of Syria who was on an official visit.

asked the same assembly to vote for a "Green Charter on Human Rights" that was supposed to warn of any possible excesses by the executive.

The regime's counter offensives did not limit itself to simple repression. The unprecedented deployment of the Sufi brotherhoods seemed to indicate that the associations that were considered less dangerous had benefited from discrete support. More effectively, Kadhafi succeeded in attracting several dozen world religious personalities to a meeting in Benghazi on September 26, 1989, whom he tried to constitute into a "Leadership of the World Islamic Revolution." Among the participants was Rached Ghannouchi (who had just been expelled by the Egyptians at the request of Ben Ali) who, while enlarging his own influence, nevertheless provided an estimable support to the Libyan leader. The boxing in of the mosques continued to be reinforced by the recruitment of a hundred Egyptian imams and the reopening of a carefully controlled institute for the training of religion teachers, which had imprudently been closed down at the end of the 1980s. After that the regime managed to get through the difficult Gulf crisis without major shocks. Supreme paradox — Muammar Kadhafi, always for union, has without doubt been the Maghreb leader who has provided the least support for Saddam Hussein.(1) Kadhafi even took the risk of damaging his popularity on the terrain where he had the most chance of encountering demands from the street.(2)

On October 15, 1991, the tone of the regime reached a new level of violence towards the Islamist opposition. The subject had begun to seem an obsession in his recent speeches, leading one to fear the worst for the fate of the 2-3,000 opposition members held in prison. "They will not benefit in any way from the legal guarantees now in force," Kadhafi told a gathering of magistrates at a ceremony to open the judicial year. "When an animal is sick, the veterinarian kills it to avoid contaminating the others...We cannot let this epidemic annihilate the society. We must be cruel... Anyone touched should be considered infected by a serious and incurable disease and he must disappear."

---

(1) With whom his relations had been, it is true, particularly difficult since the pro-Iranian position of Tripoli during the first Gulf War, and the supplying of Iran with arms.

(2) On February 18, shortly after the air war had begun, a crowd demonstrated in front of the embassy of Saudi Arabia, shouting slogans ("Saddam, come liberate Libya"). It was the first time in recent history that slogans had been turned against Kadhafi. The press tried awkwardly to recuperate the next day by assuring that "Colonel Kadhafi guided the demonstrators himself."

Prospects

For a long time, the Libyan leader succeeded in successfully managing three institutions, the army, the people's congresses and the revolutionary committees, which have constituted the foundation of his power for more than ten years. The network is crisscrossed by horizontal solidarities (the revolutionary committees have cells in the army and the people's congress, but tribal solidarities also affect the revolutionary committees and the people's congress) which pervert the internal logic of each of the institutions, attenuating the risks of corporatism and reinforcing the powers of Kadhafi, who controls the summit of the pyramid.

This system, reinforced by exceptional police precautions, was certainly not enough to prevent more than a dozen attempts at a coup d'etat over the past decade. But it was enough to see to it that they all failed. No crystallization of general dissatisfaction has yet permitted the disorganized and silent critics to transform themselves into organized oppositions and even less to constitute themselves into an internal political alternative that is credible. From reticence to resistance, from suspicion to opposition, the step is particularly difficult to take in Tripoli. Social movements, strikes or urban riots that have occurred in all the other countries of the Maghreb from Casablanca to Tunis, have simply not materialized in Libya, which lacks the "demographic logistics" of the overcrowded capitals of the rest of the region.

The hypothesis of the pursuit of a reformist process sufficiently serious to be politically and economically effective nevertheless remains unlikely because of the structural characteristics of the regime. The physical disappearance of the figure who created and incarnates the Jamahiriyan experience seems to provide the only real expectation for the kind of profound change in the internal political situation needed to allow the start of a transition towards democracy comparable to that which the other states in the region have begun to engage in, albeit with extreme prudence.

Even abandoned by the quasi-totality of the political landscape,(1) Kadhafi still manages to hold onto the unconditional support of the revolutionary committees and of his own tribe, whose members do know that beyond their privileges, it is their own physical survival which is linked to

---

(1) Like the Lokerby affair has once again shown. The Libyan point of view has been exposed in several books, among them *Al-Tariq ila libya* (The road to Libya), Rifaat Sid Ahmed, Markaz al-qada lil kitab wal-nachr, Cairo, 252 pages, 1992.

that of the regime. The violence of the accumulated rancor makes that apparent. Until now, in a country with a very feeble density of population, this support has been sufficient.

In contrast, in the event of a disappearance of Kadhafi it is most likely that his ideological heritage will not be claimed by any segment of the political class.(1) Even if the benefit from his departure is recuperated by one of his close collaborators, the succession of the Guide is more likely to end in rupture than continuity.

The Islamists, who, given the amplification of the repression directed against them are the most likely to recruit the human element needed for an attack, do not seem capable of mobilizing the organizational resources to organize a political alternative without the support of the army — especially in a regional environment that is hostile to them. But here, as in the other states in the region, the time is favorable to them.

---

(1) This is to say, the institutionnal doctrine of the Green Book. Nothing indicates, on the other hand, that the major lines of action of Libyan diplomacy, apart from a few readjustments touching more on style than on substance, would be called into question.

CHAPTER 9

MOROCCO
OR
THE WEIGHT OF STATE FUNDAMENTALISM

My letter is unlike any other you have received up until now. It renders an answer obligatory, and even your silence will be an eloquent response. (...) No matter what your answer, my dear nephew of the Prophet, you will not be able to forbid the word of truth and justice which I proclaim. No matter which man rises before me, the king or his authority, or the faithful slave of God who accepts the counsel, know that God the glorious cannot be vanquished. It is your right and that of Muslims to know who dares to write to you (...) I am the slave of God, sinner, son of peasants, raised in poverty with few material goods. I learned the Koran. It is and will be the reading that I prefer. But early on, I learned to search for a knowledge that is larger than that which characterizes our religious institutions.

I add a necessary clarification: the son of the Berber peasant is a poor Idrissid of Sharifian origins, which, like that which I am going to write on the nationalism of the Arabs, will reveal its true meaning.

The duty of giving you advice is an obligation which God has imposed on the Ulema of the Umma. (...) God has warned you twice, (1) when you despaired of living, and this letter is a third warning. (...) Two kings and a president have affronted two men of God. The former were cursed and quickly vanquished. The latter are blessed martyrs.(2) I am the fourth this century. Abd el Hafid the Alaouite, you must choose your camp.

It was Abdessalam Yassine's impertinent letter to the sovereign, "forgetful of his obligations to Islam," which, while failing to cross the threshhold of media recognition, nevertheless, constituted the first expression of the Islamist current and one of the first formalizations of its doctrine.

---

(1) Allusion to the double attempt at a coup d'état of Skhrirat and to the air attack against the plane carrying the King (July 1971 and August 1972).

(2) Allusion to the hanging of Al-Banna and of Sayyed Qutb. The Moroccan Sultan, Abd al-Hafid, opposed Mohamed al-Kattani, founder of the powerful brotherhood Ahmedia Kattani, which was responsible for the creation of a hundred Zaouias.

It will be "Islam or the deluge,"(1) this studious civil servant in public education wanted to explain to his king in 1974. "I told myself, there it is," Yassine has since explained. "The first thing to do is to say something to the Prince. I found two friends who approved of my project. I wrote the letter. We printed it. We distributed it and we sent two copies to the governor of Marrakech so that he could give it to the King. What happened after that, you know."(2) Instead of the death which he expected (he had prepared the linen which is used to wrap the bodies of the deceased), the letter earned Abdessalam Yassine a three-year internment in a psychiatric hospital, and then on December 27, 1983, a new sentence to two more years in prison. He was incarcerated along with two of his disciples. The sovereign showed that he understood the gesture's true subversive nature, which was not unlike that of Hassan Al Banna when he faced King Farouk or Sayyid Qutb when he faced Nasser.

But, in a very traditionalist society, the Sharifian monarch was alone among his fellow heads-of-state in the region, having renewed his links to a political system that predated the protectorate. He was unique in that the Constitution committed to, among other things, (3) a double leadership that included temporal and spiritual powers. He knew better than anyone else how to preserve his support in the field of religion.

The Bastion of State Islam

"From the force of its opposition," underscores Remi Leveau, "Islam in fact became the principal force of legitimizing government power just after independence."(4) This privileged relationship, however, did not manage to halt a deep process of secularization of Moroccan society. But it did explain

---

(1) Title of the letter of Yassine.

(2) Interview with the author, cited.

(3) The term "Amir al Mou'minine," which does not figure in the initial text of the Constitution of 1962 has paradoxically been added with the accord of the parties and the personal support of Allal al-Fassi. "It is striking to see that at the moment in which the King was concerned with giving the monarchy a legitimacy through suffrage," underscores Rémi Leveau, "it was the representatives of the parties who reintroduced divine right among the instruments of power." "Islam et contrôle politique au Maroc" in *Islam et Politique au Maghreb*, Paris, CRESM-CNRS, 1981, page 273.

(4) Op. cit.

the natural reticence of the sovereign to allow the religion's place to be reduced in the field of politics and, thus, his ability to prevent any detraction from his religious legitimacy.

"As you know, I am the Commander of the Faithful," the successor of Mohammed V can, in effect, assert himself.

> I received this title at birth, without asking for it, without wanting it. That means that I am one of the descendants of the Prophet, which is not exactly common, and which means that as deeply rooted as I am in Morocco for generations, my original tribe is that of Mecca. This title, "Commander of the Faithful," for some, including the Iranians who have accorded such an importance to the question of the descent of the Prophet, does not meet with indifference. It is a title that imposes a great deal of humility and, all the same at certain times, great responsibilities.(1)

Consequently, the "spring board" (the bounce-back effect) of secularism functioned less well in Morocco than in the country of a Boumediene or a Bourguiba, or even the modernist Kadhafi. The old structures for religious mobilization, the brotherhoods and the marabouts, also were both more numerous and more lively than elsewhere, and the transition with the plan of Islamist mobilization evidently operated with much greater difficulty. Like Kadhafi, although in a very different language, Hassan II knew how to anchor the fundamentalist discourse within the heart of the state, reducing the territory left to the fundamentalism of protest. Fundamentalist-inspired measures largely counterbalanced the few secular, modernist or ecumenical "provocations" made by the regime (First Congress on Birth Control, the welcoming of the Shah of Iran, contacts with the Jewish community and then the State of Israel and a more general reticence to align itself with the more anti-Western positions of the other Arab regimes).

Contrary to the Tunisian legislation adopted at the same date, the code of civil status promulgated in 1957 was in strict conformity with Koranic prescriptions. Prayer in schools was made obligatory by the King, who in 1968 reintroduced the institution of Koranic schools. He repressed those who did not fast during Ramadan (800 imprisoned in 1965) and created a High Council of Ulemas (in 1980, seven years before Bourguiba thought of a similar measure), whose approval he took the precaution of obtaining for all the major decisions of his reign, even if nothing obliged him to do so.

---

(1) Interview with the *Nouvel Observateur*, reproduced in *Le Matin du Sahara*, Saturday, October 3, 1987.

The monarch, whom certain of his own cadets felt was far too Westernized (in 1971, they destroyed his palace and tried to do the same to him), was thus alerted at the start of the 1970s, and, far sooner than any of his peers, he went on the counter-offensive. Faced with the mounting current of popular Islamism, which little by little began to take on the "look of a shrewd political protest" (...) the monarchy's reaction consisted of effectively "pushing official Islam's control as far as possible over the signs of vitality of popular Islam."(1) Thus, the rural structures of traditional Islam were mobilized, reinforced, and in some cases completely revived, in order to be given new means to watch over and control all the suspect forms of religious mobilization. Here, as in Algiers, the centralization of the demonstrations of official Islam, and, notably, the control of the *khotbas* was set up within the system.

Favored by the structural fragility of the economy (the GNP in 1983 was only $760 per inhabitant compared to $1,290 in Tunisia and $2,320 in Algeria and $8,460 in Libya) and the frustrations which it carried with it,(2) the Islamist current was, by contrast, "deprived" of the monopoly of protest. It always had to contend with a political opposition and a labor movement endowed with a certain margin for maneuver and with the manipulation of a leftist discourse that remained more credible than in Algeria or in Libya (cf. supra).

Along with the other opposition tendencies, the Islamist current finally had to pay solid dividends to the exceptionally able management by the King of the conflict in the Western Sahara. Forced to recognize the validity of the policy of "recuperating the Sahara provinces" or more often constrained to awkwardly distancing itself from the nationalistic project, the Islamist movement doubtlessly lost a significant portion of its capacity for mobilization. Since then, Abdessalam Yassine as well as Abdelkrim Moutil (cf. infra) have explained their attitude (cf. infra).

---

(1) Leveau, op cit., page 206.

(2) In 1989, it increased to $950 in Morocco and to $1,315 in Tunisia. It fell to $4,962 and $2,270 in Libya and Algeria. *L'État du Maghreb*, Camille and Yves Lacoste dir., Paris, La Découverte, 1991.

Diversity of Disintegration

At the beginning of the 1980s, Mohamed Tozy counted 23 religious associations which were more or less explicitly politicized:(1) From the local chapter of the Hizb Tahrir al Islami (cf infra) to the small regional convert associations,(2) this diversity attested as much to the echoes of the new Da'wa as to the effectiveness of the government in dividing their ranks in order to control their political impact.

Parallel to Yassine's group, the Jam'iyat ach Chabiba al Islamiya (literally, Association of Islamic Youth) emerged from this mosaic, mostly due to media coverage of the government repression directed against it. The movement was founded in 1970 by a former inspector of primary education, Abdelkrim Moutii, and a teacher, Kamal Ibrahim. As elsewhere it was able to build itself ideologically in opposition and thanks to the discourse of the Marxist left, from which it borrowed a part of its platform. As with the Tunisian "Islamic Group" (cf. infra), this discourse presented itself above everything else as a champion against "subversive doctrines" inspired by the

---

(1) or Jama'at al-Wa'd wal-Irchad (Derb la'fou, Casablanca) whose activity was then concentrated on the formation of preachers; Jam'iyat ad-da'wa al-islamiya (Chaouen) who limited itself to the religious animation of its members, for the most part teachers of Arabic, Ansar al-Islam (Casablanca); Ad-Da'wa ila al-khair wa at-tasuh (Oujda), Ad-Da'wa ila-al-haq (Casablanca); Allihaaq (Tangiers); Ansaral-islam (Casablanca); Jam'iyat ad-dawa ila-al-khair ahl as-sunna (Casablanca); Jam'iyat al-ba'th al-islami (Oujda); Dar al-qor'an, Ahl al-lioua (Nador); Ikhwane as-safa (Casablanca et Ouazzane); Al-harakat al-qadyaniya (Casablanca); Jam'iyat al-tabligh wa ad-da'wa (Casablanca, Rabat, Nador, Tiznit, Tangiers, Ksar al-Kebir; Jam'iyat ach-chebiba al-islamiyya (Casablanca and especially Rabat); Jam'iyat ad-da'wa ila-allah (Casablanca); Jam'iyat ad-da'wa al-muhamadiya (Casablanca); Jam'iyat tala'i al-islam (Casablanca) created in 1975 and close to the Muslim Brothers, led then by the former members of the USFP; Jam'iyat inqadh al-Jahil (Casablanca); Hizb at-tahrir al-islami (Tanger); Jam'iyat chabab an-nahda al-islamiya (Rabat); Jam'iyat al-ba'th al-islami (Tetuan); Jam'iyat jama'at ad-da'wa al-islamiya (Fez), Mohamed Tozy, *Champ et contre champ politico-religieux au Maroc*, Mémoire de Sciences Politiques, Aix-en-Provence: U3 1984, 437 pages. Th. d'Etat Sciences Politiques of which several elements are analyzed by Munson in *Middle East Journal*, Vol 40, No. 2, spring, 1986.

(2) Of which the most important is perhaps the Jama'at ad-da'wa al-islamiyya (Islamic call society), implanted especially in the region of Fez, directed by Dr. Abdessalam Harras (professor of Arabic at the University) and who publishes the periodical *Al Hoda*.

West (Marxism, Maoism, the hippy movement, etc.) which were allegedly threatening Moroccan youth.(1)

One of its founders, Abdelkrim Moutii, was a former leftist activist, an ex-member of the National Union of Popular Forces (UNFP). Until the end of 1975, the Chabiba movement was virtually unknown to the media. It had recruited its members almost exclusively from student and high school movements, the professional universe of its two founders. Acts of violence directed against two personalities of the secular left finally enabled it to break out of its anonymity. On October 27, 1975, Meniaoui Abderrahim, a teacher at the Lycee Moulay Abdallah, and a member of the secretariat of the Party of Progress and Socialism (PPS) was assaulted and wounded in front of his high school. Less than two months later, Omar Benjelloun was attacked in front of his house with knives and steel bars, and mortally wounded. Benjelloun was director of the leftist newspaper, *Al Muharrir*, and a member of the political bureau of the USFP (Socialist Union of the Popular Forces, formerly the National Union of Popular Forces), the party in which Moutii had been active during the 1960s. The aggressors, one of whom, Saad Ben Driss, was arrested on the spot, said that they belonged to a small group calling itself "Al Mujahidoune al Mughariba." The group, they said, was run by a law student at the Faculty of Rabat, whose name was Abdelaziz Naamani. The prosecution attempted to prove that the group was an armed branch of the movement led by Moutii. Since then, Moutii's followers have tried to prove that the Naamani group had a very special relationship with the police.(2) They have based their arguments largely on

(1) Cf. *La Révolution Islamique*, (major articles related to the creation of MJIM), 1984.

(2) Cf. notably the long Communiqué éclairant la vérité sur ce qu'a publié l'hebdomadaire *Jeune Afrique* , March 13,*1985* (No. 1262), as well as the work published by the MJIM under the title "Complot contre la Jeunesse Islamique Marocaine" (The Plot against the Moroccan Islamic Youth), (October, 1984, 15O pages) which reproduced large extracts of documents presented as the transcripts of the interrogations of the authors of the agression against Mr. Menaoui and the assassination of Omar Benjelloun. It provides the information that Ennou'mani maintained relations with the police that pushed him to form a small group called "Al-Moujahidoune al-Maghariba" which to discredit the Islamist current allegedly ordered the assassination of Benjelloun. According to the MJIM, Ennou'mani resided in a farm in the suburbs of Azemour after the assassination before returning to Casablanca and being named student instructor at the regional Pedagogical Center in Meknes until December 1976. Denounced by some students, he is believed to have left Morocco by the Spanish frontier, and to have returned to Europe after being mistakenly arrested and immediately

documents presented as transcripts of interrogations with the eight members of the group. Less credible are the protests by Moutii's organization that it had no relations at all with Naamani. Naamani was sentenced in absentia to life in prison. Taking in account that he is still presumed at-large (since no one knows where he is), his detractors in the MJIM are convinced that the sentence was nothing more than a last-minute maneuver by the government intended to give Naamani credibility *a posteriori* as a member of the opposition. In May, 1991, the French review *Arabies* published a document presented as a written avowal by the authors of the assassination of O. Benjelloun. The contents of this document were supposed to be extremely damaging to Mouttii, who was presented as the sole initiator of the affair. But the facts that the authors had been in prison since the events, and that the avowal itself radically contradicted all their previous testimony, cast extreme doubts on its credibility.

THE THESIS OF ABDELKRIM MOUTII

The Moroccan security services do not accuse me personally of the murder, but of the incitement to murder the activist Ben Jelloun. His murderer is, in effect, in the hands of the Moroccan government. And to be precise, he is imprisoned at Kenitra. At every stage of the police and judicial investigation, he declared that he did not know me, that he had never met me, that he did not know the Islamic Youth, and that he did not belong to it. That raises several questions:

1. Why didn't I present my self to the judicial authorities instead of being judged in my absence?

2. What is the regime aiming at in trying to implicate me in this affair?

3. Has anyone clarified our attitude and the changes in that of the Moroccan regime in this affair?

The answer to the first question is that no rational being would willingly place himself in the hands of an oppressive regime and a judicial structure completely stripped of competence and independence. As for the second question, the Moroccan regime considers itself personally to be the representative of God on earth and the only one to speak officially in the name of Islam. The accusation against us that we

---

released. Since then, he is believed to have tried to pass himself off as a member of the "armed wing" of the MJIM, a group whose existence is denied by the MJIM. Cf argumentation of the MJIM in "Le complot contre la Jeunesse Islamique Marocaine."

propagated Islam puts it in contradiction with itself, with its slogans and with the position which it occupies, and it is because of that, that it has decided to accuse us of a fictitious crime.

In the same way the government decided in 1974 and 1975 to give democracy a formal space in order to reform the domestic front to launch the war in the Sahara, but it feared the internal opposition represented by Omar Ben Jelloun's movement and by that of Abdelkrim Moutii. These were friends and colleagues as much of the UMT (Moroccan Labor Union) as of the regional secretariat of the UNFP (Union Nationale des Forces Populaires) in Casablanca. (...)

The Moroccan regime decided to kill two victims with one stone, and to get rid of both together, the first by direct murder, the second by legal murder as with a death sentence.

The intelligence which planned the assassination of the activist Ben Jelloun is the same one that planned and executed the kidnapping of Mehdi Ben Barka and his assassination in the heart of Paris, where he was supposed to meet the president of the French Republic. And if one says that Chebiba Islamiyya in the person of Abdelkrim Moutii has incited the murder of Omar Ben Jelloun, it is a little as if one said that it was the French government which incited the kidnapping of Mehdi Ben Barka and his assassination, even though any sensible person would reject that logic.

There is a good deal of similarity in the methods used for the liquidation of these two men. The Moroccan apparatus used the French in the Ben Barka Affair and some Moroccans, whom it managed to collect in the mosques, in the Ben Jelloun affair. The regime attempted to disengage itself from any responsibility in the Ben Barka affair and to implicate the French security services. It delivered no judgments against Moroccans, while it took very heavy sanctions against French citizens (...) In the same way, the regime has tried to disengage itself from responsibility in the Ben Jelloun affair and to blame the Chebiba Islamiyya.

The regime eliminated all its agents implicated in the Ben Barka affair in order to erase the traces of the crime. In the same way, it assassinated in prison one of the men accused of the murder of Ben Jelloun, Abdelmajid Khachane, who declared before the court that he himself and his associates had no relationship with Chebiba Islamiyya nor with Abdelkrim Moutii and that he himself and his associates maintained surveillance over Omar Ben Jelloun's neighborhood, while hidden inside the commissariat of the second arrondissement, on which the home of Ben Jelloun depended, and in front of which he was killed.

ON THE WESTERN SAHARA:
YASSINE AND MOUTII

Moutii: In 1975, we did not agree with the official presentation of this affair, but considering that it was all very sensitive and (...) we undertook the engagement to remain silent. We neither approved nor criticized it. We did not participate in the march and we decided to let the regime have the time to discover its error. But the regime did not respect our silence and the fact that we refrained from any provocations. It persisted in trying to obtain our support and I was personally invited to participate in the Green March. I politely refused. The sanction was my forced implication in the Ben Jelloun affair and the pursuit using that pretext of all the members of the Jemaa. (...) The question of the Sahara was not posed in terms of Islamic doctrine (...) or in terms of the common interests and objectives of the Saharans and of ourselves, nor from the point of view of our common origins (...) It was not asked in terms of attachment to the Alaouite throne. In this sense, the official thesis is triply erroneous: historically, religiously, and politically.

Historically, for the Saharans existed well before the Alaouite throne, and they will exist after its disappearance. And their link to the throne, the symbol of their being Moroccan, is thus the proof that they were not Moroccan before the Alaouites and that they will not be so after the disappearance of the Alaouites....this completely destroys the official thesis. This thesis also lacks any religious foundation for the legal allegiance which has been used as a pretext is no more than a forced allegiance whether it was in the past, an act by the ancestors of the Saharans, or now. The Malekite doctrine to which the regime refers forbids it, and makes the *bai'a* an individual act, which does not tolerate the representation of one person by another. Consequently, it is not transferable. And that supposes that the ancestors of the Saharans had actually pledged allegiance to the King....

Politically, this thesis is erroneous, for civilized people do not in our day engage themselves for individuals but for principles, interests or doctrines which they share. This thesis makes us appear in the end as expansionists in the eyes of world opinion for if one accepts this point of view, it is not the West of Algeria which we should be demanding but all of Algeria, Tunisia, Libya, Senegal, Mali, Niger, Spain, Portugal and the south of France, under the pretext that the inhabitants of these regions had pledged at one time or another under one circumstance or another their allegiance to the King of Morocco.(1)

------

(1) Source: written interview addressed in 1987 to Bernard Cohen for *Liberation* and not published. Translated from the Arabic by F.B.

Yassine: I was in prison during the Green March.... I did not have to take a position on it. Today...? You really want an answer to that question...! Oh well, lets say that... I would contradict myself, if I demanded the Sahara in a nationalistic manner. I would not contradict myself, on the other hand, if I tell you that the Sahara belongs to Muslims. These Muslims have been called. God has ordered them to unite. You, the nation-states, Algeria, Tunisia, Morocco, Libya, Mauritania, you have spoken of unity, you have spoken of the will for unity for decades, you have done nothing but that. Now work concretely for that unity, look for a process by which these frontiers between nation-states will disappear little by little and by which the Western Sahara will play a bit role of being the foreign body which one introduces in order to accelerate a chemical reaction. Let it be the catalyst of this chemistry of unity. (...) Nationalism can be the support for something superior or we will get smaller and smaller. Already these states of North Africa are not economically or technologically viable. Already they are unable to industrialize with one against another, in competition with one against another. So if these contingent demands call for unity, the obligations of Islam call for it too. And if the Sahara, a road accident or a drama, comes quite simply across our path...let's profit from it. Let's consider that it is an occasion to unite, to advance this project for unification. I don't say that we should be hasty, for all acts of hastiness lead to an abyss, but we should prepare for this unity.(1)

From 1975, Chebiba Islamiyya found itself deprived of two of its principle leaders. Ibrahim Kamal was imprisoned and condemned to 20 years in prison. Moutii, exiled, circulated between Europe and the Middle East where he attempted to gather material subsidies and political support. But the Moroccan secret services, which even tried to kidnap him in Brussels in 1984, tracked him constantly. His movement maintained a certain following for several years, thanks to the support from outside elements where expatriated students in Europe formed the majority of the troops. Moutii continued to direct the doctrine of his group through a newspaper, *Al Moujahid,* published from Belgium. He published diverse booklets, including "The Islamic Revolution," in which he pleaded the inevitability of an Islamic revolution in Morocco, given the failure of the secular opposition. On the inside, most of the militant activity had long ago turned toward the goal of obtaining the liberation of Ibrahim Kamal and the amnesty of Moutii, condemned to life in prison in 1980. But the distancing of its leader increased

(1) Interview with the author, cited.

the difficulties of the internal administration of the movement little by little, and the tensions multiplied between the collegial leadership in Morocco and Moutii, described by some of those who knew him as a person who wanted to exercise the responsibilities of power alone. The teams of leaders were renewed in any case at an accelerated rate which seemed to testify to the degradation of a consensus and led to numerous defections at the end of the 1970s.

At the beginning of the 1980s, the MJIM also experienced the corrosive effects of the regime's attempts to recuperate the religious sector of its political opposition. A large portion of its members who were increasingly tired of their exiled leader's personality and of the very provocative line being followed by the newspaper published from Europe (*Al Moujahid*), decided to give up their clandestine existence and to form a new group, which, in homage to the Pakistani, Mawdudi, was named "Jemaa Islamiyya." Many of the members who left the MJIM were marked by repression, but also convinced little by little of the foolishness of maintaining an action that was strictly against the throne, in a "fundamentalist" environment that did not lend itself to doing so. The formation of the new movement was with the implicit agreement of the authorities. Without yet having full official recognition, the new group had the possibility of publishing a newspaper, *Al Islah*, in the name of one of its leaders (Abdallah Benkirane, a former member of the youths of the Istiqlal, and then an active member of the MJIM until his rupture with Moutti in 1982.(1)

"When we decided to leave Abdelkrim Mouti," explains Abdallah Benkirane, who in 1987 still complained that he had not achieved full judicial recognition for his movement, and had written to the King about it,

> we entered into discussion on the opportunity and means of leaving clandestinity. There were different points of view. Me, I knew that many of us were known to the police and so there was no question of remaining clandestine. The dialogue went on for a long time, and there was a danger that things would deteriorate. At that moment, Mr. Abdelkrim Moutii understood that he had lost his footing inside the country and he started sending tracts slanted in favor of a few activists who had remained faithful to him, or slanted for Mr. Naamani, it is not very clear... and these tracts attacked the regime in a way that was very direct and provocative. I understood that it was a question there of causing us problems. And in effect, these tracts did not take long to arouse the police concerning us, and we were all put in prison. All those who were known at that time. First a dozen and then it was... the

(1) Today he directs a primary school in Rabat.

deluge. We were nearly 60 gathered in camps... illegals as they say, or for certain of us, assigned to different police stations in the country. But it happened that the regime understood that we had really cut our links with Moutii. And they let us leave and kept practically no one. Me, at first, I stayed for 15 days in the police station in Rabat, before being imprisoned again in Casablanca for two months. In the interval between the two imprisonments, I announced to the press, in an article which appeared on January 12, that we were members of the Islamic youth who had decided to create an association for us alone. Of course, at the start, we were convinced that the regime was responsible for everything... which is to say that it was for the regime to apply or not to apply Islam in its entire field of action. Islam was a matter of regime. And since Islam was not being applied, the responsibility went back to the regime. From the moment that we left for prison, many things happened. There was the episode of the Syrian Muslim Brothers, who with Hafez al Assad, ended very badly. In Egypt, the Ulema began to clarify the fact that the problem of Islam was not a problem of regimes. We began ourselves to admit that Islam was not only a story of regimes (...) that even if the King or a head of state wanted things to go in a good direction, it would practically not be possible. That the elite which had taken power after the protectorate was an elite which had essentially been formed in Europe and which saw things in an even more Western manner (...) So one could exhaust oneself by fighting against a political regime and afterwards one would find oneself in the same situation or perhaps even worse than before. Perhaps worse... If one fought against a political regime and this political regime, weakened by us, fell by the action of another, then the comportment of those who would follow would be without doubt even more in the direction of the de-Islamization of the masses... At that moment, we understood that our duty was first of all to make those with whom we were in contact, and in priority the elite of the country understand that Islam is indispensable.(1)

Two other groups linked to this current legally publish two magazines today: *Al Forqan* and (in Fez) *Al Houdah*. The "Islamic Youth" did not completely disappear, but is more clandestine today than ever. Mouttii took refuge for a time in Libya, but then fell victim to the rapprochement between countries in the Maghreb. Today, he seems to have disappeared from the front ranks of the Islamist scene in Morocco.

Divided or partially recuperated by a government that was expert on the subject, the Moroccan current seemed for a long time to have difficulty in moving out from the university and high school movements, and in crystallizing itself against the "soft belly" of Hassan's adeptness and its particular

---

(1) Interview with the author, cited.

capacity for mobilizing the totality of the field of symbolism. If the movement has managed at least partly to assume the leadership of the opposition today, it has taken much longer to do so than its fellow Islamist movements, notably in Tunisia. At the time, the review published by Yassine barely exceeded 3,000 copies, while *Al Maarifa*, the magazine of the ITM in Tunisia, distributed 28,000. Solidly encamped on the positions of institutional Islam, the king was faster and more effective than his fellow leaders in the Maghreb at anticipating the dimension of protest of the Islamists and in shifting the center of gravity of his discourse. In the last ten years, there have been numerous examples of this turn-around, which he has been partially successful at carrying out. Thus, the long reminder during the throne speech of 1985 of these "principles which founded the authenticity of Morocco, meaning Islam and the constant usage of the Arabic language, which is that of the Koran." Or his adeptness at appearing in front of Westerners as if he himself were a true "fundamentalist." Or, finally, when he can offer himself the ultimate luxury of appearing providentially as the most Khomeini-like actor on the political scene just after his own official press has finished a long campaign disparaging the Iranian experience.

During the Gulf crisis, Hassan II, who had prematurely engaged himself on the politically dangerous path of armed assistance to Saudi Arabia, managed to survive a particularly dangerous obstacle in tolerating the expression of anti-American discontent and brutally suppressing the excesses of popular defiance. Hastily called into session at the end of August, a "Summer University of Islamic Awakening" allowed the regime's newspapers to publish a headline to the effect that "Six hundred Ulemas of Islam" had chosen to meet in Morocco to examine the Arab world's situation.

In the long term, the Machiavellianism (or political sense) inexorably reveals itself to be double-edged. The exceptional hold that the King exercised over politics, his consummate art of dividing his opposition and repressing its remnants undoubtedly increased its duration, but was unable to stop the erosion of its public support. This erosion is evident today in every sector of public opinion. It is in this cumulative weakness of the regime and the ideological fragility of the left that the Islamists find their greatest opportunity.

Abdessalam Yassine, who left prison at the end of 1986, began to receive his pension as an academic inspector, and seemed for a time to have some freedom of action at the head of his new group. If his review (*Al Jemaa*) is still banned from publishing, he has, nevertheless, begun to receive followers who have come to take counsel from their Morchid al Am (Guide). They come from the four corners of Morocco, and apparently from diverse socio-professional backgrounds. At the end of 1987, he published in France a work on Marxist-Leninism.(1) More than the spiritual danger inherent in Marx's doctrine, he emphasizes its effectiveness in mobilization, and denounces the error of leaving social justice completely in the hands of the left. In this sense, he gets closer to the strategy adopted several years before him by Tunisia's ITM, and completes in a certain manner his passage to Islamism. Without renouncing his Sufi roots, but clearly distancing himself from the methodological limits of his former *tariqa*, he advocates an activist political action that is closer to the social needs of the candidates for Islamism: the change in the name of his Jemaa "Ousrat al adl wal Ihsane" (in 1987) is a witness of this evolution. To the Sufi notion of the Ihsane is joined a consideration for social justice that is intended to deprive the left of a future monopoly over the terrain. The timeliness of this development is guaranteed by the adjustment programs of the IMF and the disengagement of the welfare state.(2)

---

(1) In 1989, he published *Al-Islam wa al-qououiya al-'ilmaniya*, 175 pages. In 1973, he had published *Demain l'Islam* and in 1980 *La Révolution à l'Heure de l'Islam* (op. cit.).

(2) The type of organisation of Adl wal-Ihsane has been exposed in Yassine's Al-Jemaa as a model for building an Islamic institutionnal system:

At the head of the Group (Al-Jemaa) is, according to a terminology in fact taken from the Muslim Brothers, the Amir or Morchid al-Am, (i.e. the guide, he who shows the way, the leader or the grand master). He is assisted by a leadership council (Majlis al-Irchad al-'am) composed of seven members, and a national executive council (Majliss Tanfidhi al-Ouatani) composed of 40 members who are elected for three years and who are presided over by a Naqib (chief, or in the army, a captain, whose role is close to that of a secretary vis-à-vis the assembly; as far as possible, he should also be the Katib, or preacher of the mosque at that place). An identical assembly meets once a month under the presidency of a Naqib at each of the territorial levels: — the province (*aqlim*) — the region (*jiha al aqlim*) (a large city can be divided into several *jihate*) — the cell or branch (*chuba*) which on the average gathers together about ten families.

The family, the last level in the structure, is on the average composed of ten members and also functions as an assembly under the direction of a Naqib al-Ousra. The Nuqaba of these assemblies elect the members of a National Executive Council. The activist at the base is called al-Nasir. At the very base of the hierarchy of representation is the emigrant, absent but nevertheless represented. The emir has the right to enter into the choice of the Nuqaba and a right to veto all the decisions of the councils. He can dissolve the general leadership council (Majlis Irchad al-Am), revoke a Naqib or a member of the National Executive Council (Majliss Tanfidhi al-Tangidhi). He manages the budget in collaboration with the CGD and the CEN Majliss al Irchad al-Am and the Majlis Tanfidhi al Ouatani.

At the end of 1989, hoping to put an end to the slowly increasing power of Yassine's association, the regime decided to break the status quo. After several trials of his activists, the leader of the movement, henceforth considered to be the hard core of the Islamist opposition, was again put under house arrest. The entire leadership of the movement was imprisoned a few days later.(1) The student component of the movement has nevertheless managed since then to occupy the forefront of the protest scene. In February 1990, elections at the UNEM, a former breeding place for leftist opposition, were won by Najib Abderrahim, a member of the Adl wal Ihsane. The year 1990 saw the multiplication of forceful demonstrations by members of Yassine's group (sit-ins at the heart of Casablanca during various trials of members of the group), and Yassine's control over the university movement became clearer. An example among others, at the beginning of the month of August in Casablanca tens of thousands of demonstrators organized an imposing sit-in at the center of the city to show solidarity with their colleagues who had been tried after clashes at the Faculty of Medicine. They succeeded in bypassing all the security precautions taken by the police and creating a monstrous traffic jam which paralyzed the city. On October 25 of the same year, Islamists and "leftists" clashed in a fight for control over the campus of Fez. In April 1991, the quasi-totality of the faculty of Casablanca went on strike and the troubles which followed (April 18) left one dead and ten wounded.

In the springtime of 1991, the regime offered the possibility of normalization to Abdessalam Yassine for the first time. In exchange for a certain number of concessions, it proposed changing his association into a party. But since the only concession Yassine would agree to was to "work in respect of the laws in force," the initiative has so far not had any effect.(2) "For two years," comments Yassine,

---

The Emir, who is replaced in the event that he dies by the oldest member of the General Leadership Council can be removed from office by a vote of two-thirds of the National Executive Council called together at the request of the leadership council.

(1) Or January 10. They included Mohamed Abadi, Fathallah Arsalane (36 years old), Mohamed Bachiri (teacher, 43), Mohamed Alaoui (60) and Abdelwahab al-Moutawakil (English teacher, 36).

(2) Correspondence with the author, September 28, 1991. "The personage who agitated the symbols of an Islam that was completely new," commented Yassine concerning the crisis in the Gulf, "was only providing the support for a collective phantasm in search of dignity. The Islamists, hypnotised (*omnubilés*)

our organization has been the object of judicial actions and continual harassment. Circumstances have pushed us into marching in the streets and into openly defying public force. Our implantation, especially in the universities, has the system very worried. The heavy cost of the Western Sahara has led the King to free Abraham Serfaty and to liquidate the somber Tazmamart affair. Official contacts have been made with us with a view to recognizing us as a political party in exchange for concessions, of which we have only accepted the one calling for us to work while respecting the current laws. This has been going on for three months and our activists continue to sample the delights of royal hospitality.

Questioned on his vision of the evolution of the rest of the Maghreb, Yassine concluded: "Well, we say that the *tergiversations* (evasions) of the Algerian ruling party and the improvidences of the general in Tunis announce days to come which will not sing for the false democrats."

In Morocco, as elsewhere, in spite of the specific character so often emphasized by the King in the "religious field," the Islamists appear undiminished as the most popular of its challengers.

---

by the cloud, happily returned to the evidence. The terrible tragedy of the Muslim people in Iraq remains a virulent wound in the side of every believer and the new gendarmes of the world, the modern Genghis Khans and Atilas, have destroyed many illusions at the same time that they revealed the perversity of the West which for eight years played the secular Baathists off against Khomeini's Islam, which was a little too noisy."

CHAPTER 10

TUNISIA
THE MAGHREB REFERENCE

In Tunisia the circumstances of the formation and subsequent insertion of the Islamist current into the field of politics quickly became more apparent than elsewhere in the Maghreb.

The importance of the current and its strong structure first of all, then the legalistic strategy of its principal component, and finally the size and effectiveness of the police repression directed against it, all worked together to give it a relative transparence, which had not existed in Algeria or in Libya.

The Tunisian Islamic movement was the first to be created in the Maghreb. At the Arab level, the Egyptian movement was the first. At the Maghrebian level it is, therefore, possible to say that the Tunisians have had the same situation of anticedence as the Egyptian current had in relation to its young descendents in the Maghreb. This pre-existence conferred a certain exemplary quality on it in the eyes of outside observers as well as those of the political actors in the region. It passed through stages and also triggered mutations that are still not fully known among corresponding movements. The personality of Ghannouchi, unequalled in the region, had also contributed to giving him the image of a founder (even if in the media, the emergence of his counterpart in Algeria stole some of the spotlight).

The specific character of the movement in Tunisia was reinforced by the type of acculturation that produced Islamism in the Maghreb, which was more intense in the linguistic domain than it was in the Machreq. Offshoots of French culture, the Tunisian Islamists were the first to add a new tone to the Eastern current that had been formed primarily in Egypt and the Sudan as a reaction against the influence of Anglo-Saxon culture.

In the fertile environment of Bourghiba's secularism, the gestation period of the Islamists took place during a time of general disenchantment, which, once the inebriation of independence had passed, marked the end of the 1960s. The historical framework in Tunisia more than elsewhere was one of "an end to certainties." The brutal abandonment of the socializing experiments of the regime in 1963 amplified the ideological disarray of intellectuals, which had been spawned as much by the defeat of Nasserism as by the increasing problems of the West itself (whose facade of certainty also appeared to be cracking in May 1968). The political entry of the Islamists did not at first imply that they would become a force in the opposition. The growing political awareness was directed as much against the Marxist left, which was fighting the regime, as it was against the regime itself. The Islamists even shared several points in common with the regime, including a common animosity towards the union and university leftist movements, and later on several facets of the educational policies of Mohamed Mzali. That continued throughout the 1970s.

It was the experience of Khomeini and the increasing power of the movement in the universities that finally altered the initial equilibrium: by the start of the 1980s the Islamists and the Bourguibists started identifying themselves as politically opposed forces on the national scene.

From Political Entry to Protest.

"In Tunisia," explains Ahmida Enneifer,(1)

it is the departure of Bensalah's team which came first. The rupture of that experiment was very brutal. The minister was put on trial. But the most important result was the fact that a certain number of young people saw that the same government could be on the left and then abruptly change to a tendency that was manifestly on the right and to economic options that were resolutely liberal (i.e. favoring a free market). Many of them were completely disoriented. They no longer understood the direction of the government's plan. How could a state be on the left and then on the right, just like that...? (...) And this choice rebounded on the Tunisian government, for the party in power had insisted strongly on the fact that it had a definite program for building a modern state, etc. We realized that what had happened was not just a change in government but the proof that there was no plan. The uneasiness was not just political, but much larger than that. We did not know any longer where we were going. Those who joined the ranks of the Islamists were those who realized that they did not know what to hang on to, that they were neither on the right nor the left, that they were rootless. All those who came from the countryside into the cities, and for whom there was no plan to anchor them. They did not know what to identify themselves with. But to this national shock, one must also add what happened in France in 1968 (...) The question was raised of where the West was headed... When I arrived in Paris, I thought that I would find a country in which the problems had been stated clearly... and I discovered the same intellectual disarray that we had at home... It was not just a Tunisian problem... or Arab or Muslim. The West, itself, was passing through a dangerous period of general reflection on its style of life....

And then the third thing that can help in the understanding of the birth of the movement in Tunisia is the defeat in 1967 in what is called the

(1) Interview with the author, Tunis-Beni Khiar, July, 1985.

"Six-day War." It was at that moment then that a certain number of intellectuals, including Ghannouchi and myself, began to meet one another. Very quickly, the problem of religion began to be raised insistently. We couldn't see how to escape it. Neither the theses of the Arabs, nor the thesis of the Tunisian nationalists with a tendency towards the socialists could provide an answer; nor could the West which for a long time had appeared to us to possess certain solutions.

[It is in the shadow of the institutions of Islam that the gestation of the current began to operate in 1970.]

At that period there was an association, calling itself the Association for the Safeguard of the Koran, which had been created by the ministry of religions, and in which some elderly men gathered together. That is where we began to meet. We wanted to find a framework for action. At the beginning the religious side was essential, on the other hand the political side was very vague... We didn't really know what we wanted. We were not in a general fashion in agreement with the government, but we did not have a line of action that was well determined.

Starting in 1972, the doctrinal crystallization accelerated with the launching of a review entitled *Al Maarifa*, which until its banning in 1979 contributed to clarifying the ideological foundations of the current. Its analysis (cf. infra), confirmed by the themes developed by Ghannouchi in his religious lessons, makes it possible today to follow with some precision the "entry into politics" of the Tunisian Islamists, since under the influence of the Egyptian Muslim Brothers their preoccupations moved from the terrain of the strictly spiritual to that of culture, then to social considerations, and finally to the field of politics.

At that moment [explains Enneifer] two new givens intervened. First of all we entered into contact with a Mr. Benslama, who had been given the right to publish a magazine—it was a sort of reward which the Administration attributed, a bit like patronage. This gentleman had received an education from Zitouna (...) We easily reached an agreement to launch the review, *Al Maarifa*, or more to the point, to relaunch it, since an issue had already appeared in 1962. The Sheikh Salah Enneifer had written a small article concerning the Arab calendar, and on a subject which was taboo at the period, the method of judging the changes in the moon. It was this article, it seems, which provoked the closing of the review. But its reappearance remained possible. So we decided to relaunch it. At the beginning it reflected our groping. We were moved to tell people what was licit and what was illicit, etc. the type of preaching which is very down to earth. And at the same time we were attracted by something that was also much more radical. It was in 1972. The second element which strongly influenced Tunisia was the liberation by Sadat of the Muslim Brothers that Nasser had imprisoned. The Brothers had started to publish books again (and in 1973, the First Tunisian Book Fair greatly facilitated their distribution). (...) And it is this current which was to influence us and push us to engage more directly in political action, as well as in a certain underground formation. We began at that time to form secret groups to give them training, but always with a spiritual dimension that specified it.

For Ghannouchi, I believe it was in Syria that he had his first contacts with the Muslim Brothers. In Syria at the end of the 1960s, it was certainly possible to meet the Muslim Brothers, but it was a minority tendency. It was the Arab nationalist currents which dominated then. Not the left...let's say Nasserian and Baathists. The Islamic tendency was very weak. At that time we were 150 Tunisian students in Damascus. Well, of the 150, there were perhaps two Islamists, about 20 Destouriens, which is to say sympathizers with the Tunisian regime, about 30 who were apolit-ical, and all the rest, the vast majority, were Arab nationalists, either of the Nasser tendency or the Baathist tendency. Returning from Damascus, our education was rather sketchy. We had managed to grasp the problems of the Arab world on the whole, but not in an ideological manner. It was more political. There had not been any really consistent ideological formation. It was more with the Muslim Brothers that we were to find that. We read everything concerning the formation of a brotherhood, how the Egyptian Brothers had conceived their first cells, etc. (...) At that period, there were no problems with the government.

It was the contact with the student left, a privileged springboard on the doctrinal as well as strategic level, where the lack of structure of the Islamic group made itself felt progressively and that the vocation of the group as an opposition movement, which had been in a larval stage at the beginning of the 1970s, began to manifest itself. There was a context in which the Marxist labor and university movements had become the principal political interlocutors of the regime.

In 1979, a few months after the brutal repression against a union head-quarters that had been considered responsible for the riots which followed a general strike order in January, the revolution of Khomeini breathed life into Islamist movements everywhere. From religious outlet to the absence of a channel of expression for society, the status of the Islamist current passed irreversibly to the ranks of political alternatives. Paradoxically, the leadership of the Islamic Group welcomed the Khomeini explosion with prudence, having grasped the Shiite dimension more than anything else. Nevertheless, the Iranian Revolution, little by little became a point of refer-ence for the entire Islamist current. It was the Iranian Revolution that would justify, in fact, the first genuinely repressive reaction by the government. On

December 19, 1979, Ghannouchi and Abdelfatah Mourou were arrested after Hedi Nouira denounced the "troublemakers who drape themselves in the Islamic garb in order to enter politics by burglary." The charges against Ghannouchi were distributing false news, defamation and a call to subversion. The charges were based on Ghannouchi's role as the director of the review, *Al Mujtamaa*, the most explicitly political organ of the movement, which had been launched in August and had just been suspended. The magazine's editor in chief, Abdelmajid Attia, was also indicted.

"At the time, Ghannouchi was still afraid of the revolution," says Enneifer.

> He thought that it was above all an Iranian Shiite revolution, and not Islamic. And he was right. At the beginning he remained at a distance. But taking into account the magnitude of the revolution, the integration of the Iranian population, it was impossible to remain like that, neither for nor against. So they put themselves deeply on the side of the Iranian Revolution. Especially with the appearance of *Al Habib* and *Al Mujtamaa*. The last issue of Al Mujtamaa, before its banning, published the photograph of Khomeini on its cover, and it was at that moment that the authorities decided that it was necessary to make a decision. And at the end of 1979, they arrested Ghannouchi for a few days. I saw him three or four months before his arrest. He thought that the movement was sufficiently implanted in the country, that the government might arrest them but that it would not take the risk of a major trial. When I told him that now he was involved in a political affair and that it was difficult to step back, he told me that even if the government took the risk of having a trial, it would be difficult to pronounce sentences of more than six months in prison. For them, that was more a victory than a defeat.

In the month of October, six months after the return of Khomeini to Teheran, 60 delegates met for a constitutive congress at La Manouba, near Tunis. They gave the movement a structure that remained nearly unchanged until the great wave of repression in 1987. The informal circles spread throughout the mosques of the capital, and certain cities in the provinces were from then on integrated into a rigorous structure that covered the entire national territory with a tight network of cells at the base, with regional councils and executive committees whose methods of operation were formalized to the smallest details.

The supreme executive authority was left in the hands of a congress that met every three years. In the meantime, a national consultative council (Majlis Shura) met four times a year to approve of the orientations set by an executive bureau, which was itself composed of nine commissions. The congress designated the regional officials charged with developing the movement and relied themselves on regional consultative councils. The regions were divided into *jihate* (districts) supervised by *wukala* (agents). At the base were diverse circles (or families, or cells) which might be open or not to non-Members, and might or might not have a territorial footing. These served as cadre first of all in the work of mobilizing, and then in the structuring of doctrine for potential recruits and for manpower. The university and, from 1984 onwards, the secondary schools, constituted two autonomous structures.

It was not surprising that Ghannouchi was elected to the head of the movement (with the title of Emir, which would soon be abandoned for the more modern title of President). Ghannouchi was born in 1941 in the village of Hamma, 30 kilometers to the west of Gabes, an oasis in the extreme southern part of the country, into a family of ten children of which he was the youngest. When he became head of the ITM, he was 40 years old, the father of five children (three daughters and two sons), and lived in a villa in the small town of Ben Arous, in the southern suburbs of Tunis. After finishing his secondary studies at Gabes, he left for the capital where he obtained a baccalaureate in Arabic in 1962. He was subsequently assigned as a teacher to the village of Ksar Gafsa, in the south where he stayed for two years before leaving in 1964, with a "head full of dreams" for Cairo.(1) He enrolled in the faculty of agronomy. But the degradation of relations between Tunisia and Egypt following the Six-Day War forced him to leave Egypt. Out of an attraction for the Communist world, he opted for Albania, which he appreciated for "the originality of its insults against the West"(2) in radio broadcasts which he listened to attentively, and which eventually led him to start a correspondence. In spite of the support from the embassy of Tirana in Cairo, he yielded to the advice of his close friends who suggested that he go to Syria instead, since it had a large Tunisian student community. He obtained a degree in Philosophy and Social Sciences in Damascus in 1969 and joined the Arab Socialist Union. He took a break during his stay in Syria to make a trip to Europe, traveling via Istanbul, Sofia and Dusseldorf, where he worked two months as a stevedore and warehouse worker. In France where he worked for several weeks on farms and for construction companies, he had hopes of preparing a doctorate in Islamic Philosophy at the Sorbonne. He made a trip to Belgium and

---

(1) Interview with the author, cited.

(2) Interview by Hamid Barrada, *Jeune Afrique Plus*, July, 1989.

Amsterdam. But family circumstances forced him to return to Tunis to work. He taught philosophy in a lycée in the capital for ten years, publishing articles in the daily *As Sabah*, and then becoming chief editor of the review *Al Maarifa*. On January 5, 1980, he was jailed for a few days for the first time, then sent (as a teacher) to the little town of Makthar. During this period of time, he traveled to Saudi Arabia, Sudan (where he met Hassan Tourabi), the Gulf and (in 1979) Iran.

In April, 1981, a second extraordinary congress was held in the region of Sousse. Mohamed Mzali, the "good" minister of education, had just been appointed. The shock of Gafsa unnerved the regime and pushed it to try to enlarge its political base. The delegates of the ITM meeting, on exactly the same days as the PSD, followed the progress of the latter on the radio and were thus able to incorporate into their own discussions on April 10, the recommendations made to Bourguiba by his followers for the creation of opposition parties. Ghannouchi, re-elected, pleaded for a double strategy. On the one hand, he wanted the reinforcing of the clandestine base. For security reasons the delegates to the congress were not suposed to know each other, and faces were masked during certain speeches; no contact between sections was to take place; and finally an oath of loyalty to the Muslim Brothers was taken, of which Ghannouchi was probably the Tunisian representative. On the other hand, he wanted the development of contacts with the Tunisian political class and foreign Islamic movements, especially the Sudanese. On April 30, the future ITM joined the Movement for Popular Unity (MUP) of Ahmed Ben Salah in the first press conference held by opposition groups. The Communist party and Ahmed Mestri's Movement of Social Democrats also took part. The discovery at the house of Benaissa Demni, who was in charge of centralizing doctrine for the movement, of a certain number of working papers likely to alert the government to the movement's size and structure, hastened the decision which was then already under discussion by the 25-member executive committee meeting at Bardo to turn the Islamic Group into the Islamic Tendency Movement. President Bourguiba had just taken into account the vow of the PSD delegates, and evoked the possibility of opening a breach in the monopoly that his party had exercised since independence. On June 6, during a press conference held at Tunis, Ghannouchi, Benaissa Demni, Habib Mokni and Abdelfatah Mourou announced the creation of the Islamic Tendency Movement and its intention to be recognized as a party. Sixty days later, this demand was rejected, and the attitude of the regime after a long period of ambivalence took a hard turn towards repression.

INTERNAL STRUCTURE OF THE ISLAMIC TENDENCY
MOVEMENT (a)

NATIONAL COUNCIL
The supreme body. Meets every three years. Includes the Emir, the Shura Majlis, and the central executive bureau.

SHURA MAJLIS
Legislative body, meeting
every three months

CENTRAL EXECUTIVE BUREAU
(includes nine committees)

- Political Action (Hamadi Jabali)
- Follow Up and Training(MedChemam)
- Propaganda (Ziad Doulatli)
- Organization and Management (Med Trabelsi and Ali Zrouri)
- Cultural Action (Jamal and Aoui)
- UnionAction (Mohamed Kalaoui)
- Social and Financial Sectors, Women's Sector (Mohammed Akrout)
- Education (Mohamed Oum)
- Priorities (Ali Laaridh)

A'AMEL
The a'amel is named by the Emir in conjunction with the central executive bureau.
REGIONAL EXECUTIVE BUREAU
REGIONAL SHURA MAJLIS

DISTRICTS
(District Chiefs)
CIRCLES (CLUBS) (KHALAIA)
Closed or open
THE UNIVERSITY/ SECONDARY SCHOOLS

Source: *The Press*, October 10, 1987, and Walid al Mansouri, *The Islamic Tendency and Bourguiba: the trial of who by whom?*, s.e. 1988 (in Arabic)

a) The national territory was divided into 14 regions: 1) Tunis, itself, was cut into four sub-regions: North, West, City, and South + Zaghouan; 2) Bizerte; 3) Nabeul; 4) Beja-Jendouba; 5) Kef-Siliana; 6) Sahel (Sousse, Monastir, Tozeur); 11) Gabes-Kebili; 12) Medenine-Tatouine; 13) a region endowed with a university structure; 14) the secondary schools. The assignments were from the beginning of 1987.

189

The PSD: from Connivance to Repression

"Until the end of 1979, apart from a few secondary problems, relations between the Islamist current and the regime was one of peaceful coexistence" says Abdellatif Hermassi.(1) In 1974, the review *Al Maarifa* was banned for the first time after having criticized the merger concluded with Kadhafi in a few hours at Jerba.

For Mohamed Mzali, it was this signature written (after only a few hours discussion) on a piece of paper with a letterhead from the Hotel Ulysses that marked the beginning of the period during which it became legitimate for a Prime Minister to resort to article 57 of the constitution, which permits deposing a president on the basis of "absolute impossibility of governing." "But one does not kill one's father easily," he says today. "It had to be done, but I didn't dare." (interview with the author)

The Association for the Safeguard of the Koran was purged of these "Young Turks of Islam," which an article in *Le Monde* denounced in 1974, to the great surprise, it seems, of part of the PSD's political apparatus. A group of militants who had left Tunis and were heading towards the Mosque of Sousse made the police nervous, and they forced them to turn back to the capital. But the principle of publishing *Al Maarifa* was not called into question, and throughout this period, signs of tolerance of the authorities were far more in evidence than defiance.

Without actually having been encouraged—a thesis which certain concerned parties dispute with virulence,(2) the disciples of Ghannounchi and Abdelfatah Mourou were underestimated, if not frankly ignored, by the regime.

Entirely mobilized by its traditional opposition on the left, the Neo-Destourien party was hesitant about seeing rivals in the ranks of those who critized Marxism with a conviction that equalled their own. The policy of

(1) *The Islamist Movement in Tunisia*, Birm lil nachr, 1985, op cit.

(2) Notably Sadoq Mahdi in *History of the Muslim Brothers in Tunisia*, Oriente Moderno, 1979, and Mohsen Toumi, who wrote in this context at the beginning of the 1970s, "Fearing the corrosive ideas of the left more than those of 'cultural' Islam, (the authorities) encouraged among other things the emergence of the Islamist movement and literally installed it in the universities, and gave it the material means necessary for its development ... the government line made more and more references to the Koran, to the Hadith and to the Suna. A climate of returning to the sacred reigned in the country, and notably in the areas where the socialism of Ben Salah had destroyed authority." (In *L'Islamisme au Maghreb*, op cit., p. 160.)

Arabization undertaken by Mohamed Mzali after becoming Minister of Education (who thanks to this would be the only Tunisian political figure to have his photograph published by *Al Maarifa*) constituted another area of convergence.

This very relative proximity of Mzali with certain cultural demands of the review would reinforce charges later on that Mzali had been too accommodating to the Islamists ("Bourguiba chose a man of the Islamists," the London-based review *Ad Destour* remarked when he was chosen to be prime minister). This would eventually contribute to his political disgrace.

For the time being, though, in the fashion of Bourguiba, the political class as a whole saw nothing more in Islamism than a form of traditionalism condemned to give way before the irresistable force of modernization. As such, it seemed to present little danger to the regime. The episode of Hind Chelbi (1) illustrates the incapacity of political men, little given to doubt, to accept the idea that these Egyptian seeds, whose produce were already visible in the East, would take root in the soil of the Maghreb. A first press campaign certainly took place towards the end of 1977. But the riots of January, 1978, (in which it played no significant role) would eclipse its effect. The authorities nevertheless gave the Islamist group the possibility of publishing in *Al Maarifa* its first truly political communique: far more than the regime, it was the left which was denounced in it.

BEFORE THE IRON CURTAIN FALLS
(*Al Maarifa*, No. 5, January, 1978, 4th year)

The National scene has witnessed two dangerous events in Tunis lately which will have the worst effects on the future of this country if one does not stop to analyze them and to find a corresponding remedy.

The first: in the domain of teaching. During the meeting of the national group for teaching (*jemaa qumia lil ta'lim*), several representatives made propositions, which included: the refusal to consider Tunisia as an Arab country, the suppression of religious education from the program for teaching in order to get rid of the "hidden obscurantist teaching" which it disseminates, the suppression of the faculty of theology, the establishment of teaching shocking literature, and the abstention from teaching anything about Islamic history.

We did not think that such impudence or such cynicism could be carried out by a son of this country, more than a quarter century after independence, that he could demonstrate such disrespect for himself and

---

(1) See Chapter 1, Islamism and Traditionalism.

for his country even though he claimed to belong to a group of "progressives."

The second event touches student life. We know that the representation of the students at Tunisian universities has continually been dominated by groups brandishing the banner of "progressivism," whether it be Russian or Chinese. These groups have been able, with their organizations and their methods of "revolutionary violence" to impose their will on the ensemble of the students. Such was the situation, until in the course of the last few years a nationalist Arab-Muslim current invited them to break the Communist monopoly, to eliminate the terrorist methods and to give freedom of expression to all the movements. After a long combat against the terrorist Marxist forces, this current managed to make its voice heard by the student base, which joined with it in heaving a sigh of relief. And for the first time this year, the possibility was offered to students to choose their representatives and to express their point of view. When these groups saw that the power was slipping from their hands and that the iron collar in which had been placed around their necks was beginning to loosen, they resorted as they usually do to "revolutionary violence" to terrorize the students, and to smother the new born voice of liberty and to eradicate the current of national belief. They drowned the faculty of science of Tunis and Sfax in blood, as well as the faculty of law. They occupied the mosques, they profaned Korans and set them on fire. And they left behind them in certain mosques traces which will remain a wound in the heart of every Muslim. They struck some of those who were praying, to force them to blaspheme, then they turned towards Sfax, to the university dormitories, and they burned 20 rooms of religious students.

What does all that mean?

1) It is a call to rob this nation of its Arabness, its Islamicness, and its history.

2) It is not just an invitation or a call. They went directly to a plan of execution and this formidable plan, in eliminating the nationalist Muslim elements and in making false descriptions of them in order to fool public opinion by qualifying them as Khoanjia (a popular name for the Muslim Brothers) and opportunists.

The objective is clear, and that is to fasten this nation to the wheel of the Communist camp in Russia or China, after the nation has thrown off the domination of the Western camp, at the end of a long combat, whose traces it still carries...

"That does not go very far ... and they are prudent enough ... there is no reason for that to take hold ..." the prime minister, Hedi Nouira, still thought in 1979, as he commented on the activity of certain preachers in the mosques of the capital. It would take the thunder of Khomeinist revolution —perhaps—the repeated warnings of certain ministers (but "not to Bourguiba" protested Mohamed Mzali; "He did not have a character that would let him be influenced by foreigners, whoever they were"), by the

American CIA, who were still moved by the episode of the hostages of Iran, for the regime to grasp the size of the problem.

During the course of 1980, a second press campaign was begun, and then interrupted by the attack on the city of Gafsa, which caught the government's attention for a time. The campaign started up again in the summer of 1981, and it was paradoxically Mohamed Mzali to whom it fell to put it into operation (the same Mzali accused by his colleagues of "making his bed with the fundamentalists" when he launched his progrma of Arabization, while minister of education). The repression, which fell on Ghannouchi and his disciples, was decided by Bourguiba whose intrasigeance with respect to the Islamists had gradually sharpened. It was without precedent in the history of the regime. Mr. Driss Guiga, his minister of the interior (who was dismissed in January, 1984, after Mzali accused him of being responsible for the size of the "bread riots") recognized the disproportion with the menace which the movement actually represented ("We overreacted, as the Americans say."). With a certain credibility, Mohamed Mzali, from his exile in Paris, now defends his role in supporting his political "father." "I was absent from Tunis; I was getting some dental care in Lausanne and the decision to arrest the leaders of the movement was taken entirely behind my back and against my will. Everything I did was to try to limit the damage..."

From the beginning of 1981, a series of occasionally violent incidents implicating the Islamists provided the desired pretexts for a crackdown. The Movement first tried to publish a review, *Al-Habib*, whose first and only issue was deemed inacceptable and was immediately seized. On February 20, some particularly violent clashes took place on the university campus. The doyen of the faculty of sciences was held prisoner and threatened with death. During the month of Ramadan, powerful acts of intimidation were directed at those who broke the fast in public. In June, after a fire broke out on a Soviet ship that was being repaired, demonstrations were directed at the police and Islamic slogans were shouted. On July 15, the buildings of one of the two resorts operated by the Club Mediterranee in Tunisia (at Korba) were partially sacked because one of the organizers had played an Israeli song for the summer clients. Finally on July 17, several clashes broke out in Msaken between police and demonstrators over the choice of a new iman. After that day, nearly 150 student militants and sympathizers of the ITM were arrested, including all the members of the leadership bureau with the exception of Habib Mokni, who reached France along with some student militants. A violent repression was launched against the entire movement, with some 25 trials in three years. From the month of

September, the leaders were condemned on the basis of often fragile evidence to prison sentences, which were confirmed after being appealed, of from two to twelve years. On July 25, the Majlis Shura, meeting in a suburb of Tunis, entrusted the leadership of the Movement to Fadhel Beldi (born in Bousalem in 1952), who assumed the role for three months before leaving the country and turning his duties over to Jabali Hamadi (an engineer and an expert on solar energy, who was born in Sousse in 1949). Hamadi retained his functions throughout the entire period of incarceration of the leadership.

The idea of eventually collaborating with these banned individuals is still totally excluded. It is the entire political class, from the Socialist Democratic Movement to the Tunisian Communist Party, (both of which having just received recognition as parties), that the regime has tried to close ranks to in order to "bar the way to these messiahs of terror and darkness," as Mohamed Sayah, director of the PSD, qualified them while showing a particular zeal in following the presidential orders concerning anti-Islamist repression.

1984: The Legalist Hypothesis

Less than three years later, the regime would nevertheless change its aim once again. In the prison of Borj ar Roumi, the leaders of the Movement received a visit from a lawyer who was close to Mzali, and negotiations began. A political platform was submitted to the prime minister. "I found nothing to change in it," he says today. "I would even have been able to use it as an editorial in my review, *Al Fikr*." Abdelfatah Mourou, who was received at length in his house, and who was subsequently released for health reasons, presented the attitude of the Movement in terms that the prime minister agreed to try to have the president accept. The president, however, at first only agreed to free Mourou, whom he judged to be more moderate than Ghannouchi. But Mohamed Mzali attempted to demonstrate to the Supreme Combatant that such selectivity would consecrate the intransigeant wing of the current and would not lead to the possibility of rapprochement. On August 3, 1984, on the occasion of the 82nd anniversary of the Chief of State, the majority of those sentenced in September, 1981, were granted amnesty.

The ITM then entered into a period of semi-liberty, an unpredictable mixture of openess and repression that was not too dissimilar from what the other opposition groups were experiencing followed. This situation would allow it to confirm its legalistic profile, but it would also accelerate within itself a process of doctrinal mutation. In November, 1984, a few months after the amnesty, a third congress was convoked at Soliman. Ghannouchi, clearly worn by his long imprisonment ("It is a physical test," he declared after leaving the civilian prison in Tunis where he had been transferred since leaving Borj al Roumi), resumed the presidency of the movement. In the context of relaxation following the amnesty, the ITM began preparing its internal structure in order to prevent another wave of repression. At the same time it resumed more than ever its offers of legal participation. "It is a unique occasion which has been offered to Tunisia," he pleaded in the platform he issued on the 3rd anniversary of the Movement's creation.

For the first time in its history, the Movement explicitly expresses its adhesion without reserve to democratic principles. "When even it might be Communist," it promised to recognize "any government that came out of a regular election."

A UNIQUE OCCASION IS OFFERED TO TUNISIA

In spite of the objective difficulties which presented an obstacle to any serious dialogue between a large component of the political and intellectual class on the one hand and fundamentalist Islam (Ousouli) and its standard bearers on the other, relationships between the two camps still managed to develop. Apart from the black pages which only profited the imperialists and their lackeys in the country, there were a number of positive developments which have no other equivalents in the Muslim world.

Certain actions that we have seen in Tunis have contributed to the amelioration of the relations between the Islamist currents and the rest of the nationalist forces. They have had an impact on the reality of the Tunisian Islamist scene which is very different from the ready-made theories which lead one to believe that religion is the opiate of the masses, that it is by nature at the service of absolutism, of feudalism, of capitalism and of reaction, and that it is impossible for it to play a positive role in the movement of national liberation (...) At the very moment when certain people try to persuade the others in the Muslim nation that only the Islamists are free (...) and that, as General Zia al Haq (the late president of Pakistan) declared recently, "there is no place for opposition in an Islamic system which searches for unity and stability." (*La Presse*, November 29, 1983).

Of course, what else remains after that except the cold war and preparations to "warm" it again? What remains for the secular intellectuals afraid of the specter of an Islamic power—as it has been known during the period of decadence or as it is applied today in certain countries—except to try to protect oneself in running to local despots or to strangers, and to ally themselves with them in order to conjure the specter of this fear?

195

And what remains for the Islamists except to be deprived of their civil rights, the rights to expression, to association and to propagate their ideas so that others can benefit from them? What remains once they have been impregnated with the doctrine of Holy War and martyrdom, if it is not to abandon themselves to violence, to call for a Holy War against those who fight them and repress them or to fall back on themselves and to fall into exaggeration and extremism, preparation and the wait for an occasion to pounce on their adversaries?

A unique occasion is presenting itself in Tunisia to break out of this impasse which presents the face of fatality in the relations between the Islamists and the other political forces, and in which many Islamist groups have fallen. The political forces have plunged into bloody battles from which it is impossible that the regimes and their allies can come out as definite victors. They have entered into incessant wars which exhaust the forces of the nation (Arab) and have relegated the fights against under-development or the Zionist and imperialist enemies to the second rank in relation to the battle against the principal enemy, which is to say the Islamists. (...) So, is it Tunisia, which a journalist described as "a country that is small in size, but great in civilization (*Al Sabah*, December 18, 1983), which cannot come out from this impasse and create a unique experiment, which would serve as a valuable model for others in avoiding the waste of its energy in battles whose sole beneficiaries are imperialism and its valets?

Doesn't it have a special reason for doing so, since—for the first time in our knowledge—in the Arab world, the repressed Islamic movements and the forces of political opposition have adopted a common position? Faced with a repressive regime which calls for a union against "the terrorism which threatens democracy" (that is to say the Islamists), the opposition has taken a clear position of support for the Islamists and it has held to it.

For the first time in our knowledge, in the Arab world the Islamists are taking for their part a clear position in favor of democracy, which they demand, in defending despite their ideological differences the rights of expression and organization for all the parties in presence, even when they represent on the ideological level—as is the case with the Communists—an opposite extreme. And they even let it be known that they would be ready to consider their power as legal if that were to be the result of the choice of the majority of the people consulted democratically. (Cf. the press conference of the founding of the movement, June 6, 1986).

Tunisia ("This country that is small in size, and great in its civilization"), cannot it make it so that its children succeed in establishing a dialogue among themselves and in putting all its energy and all its development to the service of the battle against the principal enemies which are dependence, exploitation, tyranny, Zionism and colonialism?

Such is the challenge whose success conditions the future of democracy and progress in Tunisia, and we do not exaggerate in evoking the future of Tunisia and the region. How great is its responsibility? What more important gift could Tunisia give to Arabness and to Islam?

All the same we find ourselves constrained to affirm to a few thinking elites who occupy an important place on the national scene and in the political and cultural orientation and persist in refusing to consider the Islamist phenomenon as an authentic given and not as a pathological manifestation born of accidental circumstances which would be possible to exorcise and to bypass. We affirm to those who by the Grace of God are not very numerous, that one of the reasons for our existence is your incapacity to understand the Islamic reality and to resolve its problems. Our country will only be saved from their incapacity and their dependence if you want to get out of our way and stop making obstacles for us and finally consider that we are an authentic given, profoundly rooted in the history of this nation and its masses.

(SOURCE: *Third anniversary of the Mouvement de la Tendance Islamique* (in Arabic), Tunis, 1984, pages 7 to 9.)

In August, 1984, the relative optimism of this declaration seemed justified. The ITM had just passed two years in which an eventual legalization of the party did not seem to be completely excluded. The process culminated in November, 1985, when Mohamed Mzali received the Islamist leaders along with two other opposition parties. This new level of relations appeared to be the result of a double evolution.

First, there was the evolution of the regime that had begun to realize the remarkable capacity for resistance of the movement and of the undeniable reality of its existence. What Hedi Nouira saw in 1979 as nothing more than the "froth of social agitation" had in spite of all repression become a political movement in Tunisia, whose existence could no longer be considered purely circumstantial. Once over the initial surprise and with the realization that repression was not working, the card of rapprochement seemed to Mzali, if not to Bourguiba, to provide the best means for drawing the Islamists from a clandestinity that was increasingly worrisome, since it was pushing the harassed activists towards radicalism.

Above all, an amnesty would, in the government's thinking, put an end to the Movement's uncontrolled development. Without according official recognition and without completely abandoning the repressive option, the regime still hoped to give itself increased means to follow the Movement's evolution more closely and to better judge the implications of an eventual legalization.

By receiving Mourou and Ghannouchi, Mohamed Mzali entered a second phase in 1985, in which he confirmed his desire to follow the process of normalization begun by the amnesty. "If they do not pretend to have the monopoly on Islam and if they renounce certain of their demands, (their legalization) is possible," Mzali declared to the press.(1)

> When I received them, they denied ever having asked for a referendum on the personal statute. In that case, there are no problems. I found them comprehensive, moderate, reasonable. They are valuable people. There is no reason to exclude them. I want the next elections to take place as I had wanted the ones of 1981 to take place. At the time, I was trapped myself. I am sorry that there is no opposition in the assembly. I want the opposition to be serious, patriotic, and to play the game with me.

The context in which this reopening of the dialogue was made is not without significance. It was at the very moment when, after several months of unceasing warfare, Mzali had just succeeded in beating down Habib Achour, his eternal adversary in the labor unions who had had the imprudence to declare to the press that "he would have the head of Mzali, as he had had the head of Nouira." His defeated opponent was accused of having broken the national consensus while Tunisia faced "aggression" from Libya. The aggression consisted of the expulsion of 30,000 Tunisian workers from Libya during the summer of 1985. Habib Achour was put under house arrest and accused of a variety of offenses. Mzali seemed to be delivering a stick to the left and a carrot to the right. Was the designated successor to the Supreme Combatant attempting to increase the Destourien Party's legitimacy by enlarging its political base before the inevitable departure of its chief? That is what he maintained several years later, insisting on the role that he had played in making the decision for an opening in 1981.

The terms of the eventual contract with the Islamists were on the other hand extremely restrictive. Pluralism did not mean alternation. The prime minister explicitly reminded everyone of that in evoking the possible role that the Islamists and more generally all the opposition had to play. "There is one party which has a history and a legitimacy (...) If they want to participate, there are ways of arriving at that... (...)If they want to replace it, that will not happen tomorrow."(2)

The government positions were not the only ones to have evolved. Even if it is more difficult to determine the Islamists' internal evolution, there was clearly a quantitative change. There is no question that the new arrivals, inspired by politics, began to fill out the ranks. As elsewhere in the

---

(1) Interview, "Le Quotidien de Paris," in *La Presse*, November 15, 1985.

(2) Interview in *Le Matin de Paris*, cited.

Maghreb, the movement took root in the urban universities and high schools. It also implanted itself in the outlying towns, including the Sahel, as well as with the lower-ranking civil service, technical agents and small businessmen. The army, police, customs and national guard were also affected.

But in each case this development was matched by internal tactical and doctrinal mutations. The media, concentrating on the reactionary dimensions, anachronistic thinking, or the occasional acts of violence, tended to miss the fact that the nature of the current was becoming more complex.

At the origin of the mutations was first of all the increase in the Movement's audience and the number of its activists. From the small group of critical reflection at the beginning of the 1970s to the relatively well-structured movement of several hundred members who requested official recognition as a party in 1981, there was a path strewn with victories, but also with errors, disillusionment and self-doubts. The test of a long imprisonment and the forced reflection that it imposes had marked bodies and spirits, as well as changing individual itineraries. Prison had produced relatively few defections, but it had accelerated the hardening of the activism of some of the last to have hesitated.

Even more than these classic stages, it was also the relative liberty, unique in the Maghreb, which led the Tunisian current to confront its doctrinal presuppositions with the reality of its environment. The effect was to unleash a process of transformation. The increase in the Movement's power had taken place during a period of clandestinity. Starting in 1981, the nascent ITM found itself, in contrast, confronted with a legalistic strategy that it was ill-equipped to deal with. This emergence on the public scene, therefore, accelerated the crystallization of a certain number of its internal contradictions which had remained latent since the beginning of the 1970s. After a period of growth accompanied by self confidence, the ITM had to face the hour of reckoning.

The Price of Legalism

The first consequence of the movement's being granted semi-official status was that the political scene proved less tolerant of doctrinal approximations than clandestine action. The shadowy zones of the Islamist project dropped away one after another, and with them the fragile compromises which had maintained unity within the movement. Anchored from its beginnings more in the rejection of Bourguiba's "secularism," than in any alternative for society and government, the Movement found itself forced to move progressively from the stage of rejection to that of elaborating a global political project that would make its partisan pretensions credible. The transition was not without difficulty. First, because in choosing this path the Movement paradoxically lost the pretension to universality which had until that point constituted part of its force. "In pronouncing itself for pluralism and its constitution as a political party," notes Camau, "the ITM reassured a part of the public, but at the price of its own declassification to the rank of a 'tendency' among others and a weakening of its expression as a counter legitimacy."(1) Each clarification of the Islamist credo, reducing the haziness that was characteristic in the beginning, served to accelerate the structuration of its clientele. The frontal layer of original founders was no better at resisting the changes than the Algerian movement would prove to be several years later. Every time tensions inherent in the process of clarifying doctrine were unable to be absorbed by negotiations, resignations followed, and in certain cases there were important divisions.

Thus, two important offshoots gradually developed from the main current. First, there was a radical tendency which was disappointed in the lack of effectiveness of the legalistic approach, and upset at seeing some of the first doctrinal formulations being diluted. This tendency was prepared, regardless of the price, to take more direct pathways to power.

In the opposite camp, the Islamic group gave birth to a tendency that was considered progressive. At the end of the 1980s, it would occupy a position in the range of Islamist organizations which was far more important than the number of its activists led the world to believe at first.

The Radical Temptation

Several far less important groups began to recruit from the radical fringes of the movement. Their role could not be ignored, first of all because they participated in the global reality of the Movement, but also because the violent image—occasionally justified, and at other times exaggerated—which was attached to them was regularly used to justify the intensification and generalization of repression against the Movement as a whole. According to the more or less repressive periods which the ITM and

---

(1) *La Tunisie*, op. cit.

its successor, En Nahda, passed through, these groups played a role in the Movement which was far from negligible.

The Party of Islamic Liberation (PLI)

The Tunisian section of the Party of Islamic Liberation (PLI-Hizb Tahrir al islami) was a case in point. Led since 1977 by Sheikh Abd Qadim Zalloum, an *a'lim* of Kurdish origins, the PLI was founded in Jordan in 1952 by its principal theoretician, Sheikh Taqi Eddine Nabhani, a Palestinian judge who believed in the reestablishment of the Caliphate.(1) Like Yassine and Ghannouchi, Nabhani reproached the reformists of the nineteenth century for having attacked dogma in order to make Islam yield to the rules of modern society, instead of forcing modern society to conform to the rules of Islam.

Nabhani's strategy, laid out in three works which highlighted his thought, foresaw three major phases for the party, which he considered to be the privileged political instrument at that time. The phases, whose chronology was inspired by that of the Prophet's actions,(2) consisted of:

a) a phase of preparation and study destined to formulate the culture of the party itself.

b) a phase of interaction with society which would gradually be won over to the party's principles. This is the phase which the party feels itself to be going through right now.

---

(1) Taqi Eddine Ibrahim Youssef al-Nabhani was born in 1910 in the village of Ajzem near Haifa, where he attended primary and secondary schools before leaving for university in Cairo (Dar al Ouloum). He received a diploma at the beginning of the 1940s. His political teaching is entirely built around the idea of the necessity of giving an institutional foundation back to the Muslim nation. Deceased in 1952, he was buried in Beirut, where his family lives today. Cf. Mahmoud Salem 'Oubediat, *Athar al-gemaat al-islamiyaa al-maïdani khilal al-qarn al-acherin*, Amman, Maktabat al-rissalat al-haditha, 1990, 464 pages, as well as Kilani al-Moussa Zied (Dir.), *Al-Harakat al-islamiyya fi al-Urdun*, Amman, Dar al-Bachir, 1990, 203 pages.

(2) Review *Sou'al*, Paris, No. 5, op. cit., page 21. On the PLI, cf. especially Kilani Al Moussa Zied, op. cit., as well as 'Oubediat, op. cit., pages 16–23. The very first political position taken by the PLI was a reaction, published in 1955, against the Anglo-Israeli project, Johnson.

c) a phase of total conquest of power once the resistance of civilian society had been lifted.

From 1982 (the probable implantation of the movement in Tunisia) until 1988, members of the group were the object of a series of court trials and sentences. Some of the followers had been recruited from within the Army, and that fact constituted an unknown factor in the Islamist equation. One of the last trials took place in 1985, a year in which several arrests of militants in the PLI had taken place in Egypt following similar arrests in 1983 in Tunisia and Libya. Thirty-four members of the Tunisian branch of the Party, of which 19 were military soldiers, were given sentences in March and August, 1985, ranging from two to eight years in prison (the civilians received two-year terms; the military received eight-year terms). The charge was "membership in an illegal association with a political character." The principal accused was a physical education teacher named Mohamed Jerbi, who was alleged to have belonged to the PLI during the 1970s and to have been in charge of its Tunisian branch. Composed mostly of lower ranking civil servants who were not very inclined to philosophical reflection, the PLI enjoyed the tranquil force in Tunisia of ideological certainty: "We are the only Islamist movement, today, to have a complete alternative (*badil*)," proclaimed an activist waiting for an appeal to his sentence, "The class of 1985," they joked with their visitor, "is going to rejoin the class of 1983."(1)

And in fact, the work of the Palestinian judge Nabhani, notably "The Islamic State" and the trilogy, "Organization (social, political, and economic) in Islam" is teeming with technical "solutions" as detailed as they are peremptory. They reassure uneasy activists and permit a seductive economy of reflection. Except for a few tracts, the PLI hardly wrote any analysis concerning Tunisia. The concrete implications of putting the political program into operation needed nothing more than the analyses of the founding Sheikh and nothing in the contemporary reality of Tunisia appeared to justify changing that. In any case, the activists sent anyone who contradicted them as well as the followers who were being trained, back to the intangible generalities of the sole Taqi Eddine Nabhani. After a period of relative calm, the government's interest in the PLI increased and during 1990 and 1991 the repressive measures directed against it were similar to those used against the Party of the Renaissance, En Nahda.

---

(1) Interview with the author, Tunis Le Bardo, August, 1985.

Two Tracts from the Tunisian Branch of the
Party of Islamic Liberation
In the name of God, the clement and merciful

PARTY OF LIBERATION

And they ill treated them
For no other reason than
That they believed in God
Exalted in power
Worthy of all praise.(1)

At the moment when the power in place in Tunisia pretends to be Muslim and the youth of the Party of Liberation is continuing to stagnate away in prison, the police apparatus has launched a vast campaign of arrests in the ranks of the young members of the Party which has affected 37 youths who will be judged on March 9, 1985. This apparatus has subjected them to all sorts of tortures for the unique reason that they believe in God and work sincerely to put into place an Islamic State under the banner of the Party of Liberation. This party is a political party whose principle is Islam, which works to begin again an Islamic life by putting in place an Islamic State which is the Caliphal state. Its way of arriving at that is politics. Its action is purely political, a politics reposing on the precepts of Islam considered as the directing principle of all conduct. The Party of Liberation has taken on itself to liberate the Islamic Umma from all forms of colonization, political, cultural, economic, social and others. In saying that, we do not want to attract sympathy. We want, on the contrary, to show the failure of all politics today that are founded on rules other than those revealed by God.

We call on the sons of the grand Islamic *umma* to rise with us and to work to reestablish the Caliphate which the impious colonizers have suppressed and to reestablish Islam in the Islamic territories.

O ye who believe! Give your response to God and His apostle, when he
calleth you to that which will give you life. (2)

March 8, 1985

---

(1) The Koran, Sura 85, verse 8, translation by Yusuf Ali.

(2) The Koran, Sura 8, verse 24, translation by Yusuf Ali

PARTY OF ISLAMIC LIBERATION.

In the name of God, the clement, the merciful.

Among the believers are men who have been true to their covenant with God: of them some have completed their vow (to the extreme) and some (still) wait: but they have never changed (their determination) in the least.(1)

The Party of Liberation is a political party. Its principle is Islam, its finality the restarting of Islamic life which puts into application the precepts of Islam and carries its appeal throughout the world. It is a party which invites all men to Islam, to adopt its conceptions and its rules. It relies on interaction with the umma to reach its ends. It combats colonialism in all its forms and under all its names in order to liberate the umma from its domination and to eradicate its cultural, political, economic and other roots from the soil of Islamic countries.

Those who work to cement these authentically Islamic ideas in real life with sincerity and piety, looking by doing this for the satisfaction of God, the very high, have just been judged: 48 young people of the Party of Liberation were sentenced to imprisonment on March 16, 1985 for the sole reason that they tried to save the Islamic umma from the claws of the regimes (illegible).

The Islamic State, which is to say the State of the Caliphate which draws its legitimacy from that which God has imposed in his divine law on Muslims so that the umma can shelter under the banner of Islam and enjoy the security, justice and confidence.

O sons of the grand Islamic umma: the rulers of Tunisia who oppress Islamic youth in prisons celebrate what they call the festival of independence. What they celebrate, is in reality the concentration of the forces of impiety and of colonialism on the country. The impious colonizer (*kafir*) when it appeared clear to him that it was impossible for him to remain openly on our soil, with his army and the other colonial powers, changed his manner, withdrawing his material forces and installing in their place his culture, his standards, and his conceptions of life. He has made the rulers, children of this country, the guardians of this culture, of these standards and of these conceptions, the guardian of the interests of colonialism in the exploitation of its riches and its goods. And he has given to the umma the illusion of these so called independences, in Tunisa as much as in the other countries of Islam.

For that the Party of Liberation has risen and taken in charge the mission of saving the Islamic umma and of taking it out of the shadows and deviation towards the light of the guided way and the happiness of life.

---

(1) The Koran, Sura 33, verse 23, translation by Yusuf Ali.

O sons of the grand Islamic umma! Rise up (...) to crush the regimes which adopt the culture of the West and apply openly the rules of disbelief. Act to bring back the lands of Islam to the rule of Islam, to rebuild the State of the Caliphate.

O ye who believe! Give your response to God and His apostle, when he calleth you to that which will give you life.(1)

March 22, 1985

THE ISLAMIC JIHAD

The radical temptation also won over a small group of former members of the ITM who called themselves the "Islamic Jihad," and who the Tunisian press began to refer to in 1986 as the "Band from Sfax." Having opted for the radicalization of Islamic action after the amnesty of 1984 and the confirmation by the ITM in the Congress of November, 1984, of the legalistic option, the group carried out several weak attacks, including assaults on a post office and a police station. Several members of the group were arrested during the summer of 1986, condemned to death and executed at the end of August after president Bourguiba rejected their appeals for clemency. They included Kilami Ouachachi, a lieutenant in the Tunisian Army; Habib Dhaoui, a preacher who was known in the region of Sfax; and A. Lazreq, a previous activist in the nationalist movement, who was an ex-member of the ITM and had worked on the review *Al-Maarifa*, before escaping to Saudi Arabia where he was eventually extradited. "Lazreq was our brother. But he did not accept it. He left. He is free," says Salah Karkar,(2) successor to Ghannouchi at the head of the ITM from March to November 1987. "Neither Dhaoui nor Lazreq were active members. They had no responsibilities and they were never national members, nor even

---

(1) The Koran, Sura 8, verse 24, translation by Yusuf Ali.

(2) Karkar was born on October 22, 1948, in Boudher, a village of the Tunisian Sahel. His family had modest means. He received his secondary education at Sousse (Baccalaureat in June 1968) and then obtained a degree in Economics at Tunis (1972). Afterwards, he worked at the Economics Institute of the Ministry of Planning. In 1976, he took a one-year course and obtained a diploma as an engineer in communications. He participated in diverse financial studies concerning the problems of debt and helped create a data base. He obtained a DEA in Economic Sciences in 1978 and a second DEA in 1981. He is currently working on a thesis in Economic Science. (Cf. notably Mohamed Al-Hachemi, *Achraqq al-Houria: qissa al-hourria al-islamiyya fi tunis*, Tunis, 1989, 243 pages.)

regional ones. Like everywhere else in the world, there are people who are not happy about being in the minority. They let go of the majority totally. They left."(1) It was the members of the same group who—evoking vengeance for the hanging of Ali Dhaoui almost exactly one year before— claimed responsibility for the most violent action in the history of the Tunisian Movement: the placing of homemade bombs on Sunday, August 2, 1987, in four hotels of Sousse and Monastir, the region in which Bourguiba had been born. Although responsibility for the bombs was explicitly claimed by the Jihad twice, (notably in a letter to the newspaper *Liberation*, signed by the "Islamic Jihad") the attacks which wounded more than ten people (one of whom had to have a foot amputated) were used to justify the intensification of the repression against the ITM. Less than ten days after the attacks, during a police investigation that was particularly violent, one of the members of the group, Mehrez Boudegga, was arrested. Sentenced to death during a major trial in September, 1987, he was executed on October 8 at the same time as Boulbaba Dekhil, the perpetrator of an attack with acid on a member of the PSD who had denounced him to the police on several occasions. Several of the members of the Jihad are still at liberty, including those who had placed the bombs themselves (Boudegga had only manufactured them, and was consequently not legally liable to the death penalty). The group could very reasonably have continued to constitute the radical wing of the ITM. In 1991, their presence was still attested to, and they regularly sent communiques to the press on major regional and national political developments.

Without crediting it with significant political weight, members of En Nahda also qualified the small, self-styled "Islamic Front" as a "resurgence of the Egyptian Muslim Brothers—first version." While on the fringes, it has, nevertheless, succeeded in drawing a militant clientele.

In 1991, the representatives of En Nahda did not contradict the fact that the PLI had assumed a relatively important following among the ranks of the core of activists. But they downplayed any notion that the PLI had the capacity to win over voters from the edges of the electorate that En Nahda, itself, had succeeded in attracting. Without them any political progress could only be by chance and unpredictable.

> Yes, certainly the PLI exists. It was born at about the same time that we were, as a small group. Now, it is true, it is beginning to have some weight. Especially at the university. But it is necessary to know which

---

(1) Interview with author, cited.

point of view one is taking. Taking its ideology and mode of operating into account, the PLI cannot become a popular movement. Who are its clients? That depends on circumstances. When the situation here is blocked, or in times of "peace," the tendency will be for those who dream of fighting with the authorities to go to the Hizb Tahrir, or to the Jihad. During the 1989 elections, those who did not agree with this legalistic approach may have been tempted by the PLI. Today, Tahrir has been hit almost harder than Nahda, so perhaps it is time for the young who are looking for action to turn towards the Tablighi. If one day Nahda is tolerated—we saw that in 1989 with those who opposed the democratic process—well, they will find refuge with Tahrir. Those who are in a hurry, those who find us too legalistic. But that can't last because the Hizb Tahrir has no solid ideological and intellectual base. I don't see what fundamental ideas specify Hizb Tahrir and what can attract people who have passed through these groups. At an intellectual and ideological level, Jemaat ad D'awa or Hizb at Tharir or al Iassar al Islami (the Islamic Left), even if they have come from very distant families—from one extreme to the other—do not belong to the most current Islamic school, the one that is accepted everywhere in the Muslim world as well by intellectuals as by the masses. They are marginal. But it is necessary that these little groups exist. Their existence keeps up the vigilance of the principal movement. That helps to make its ideas go more deeply and to correct it. But ideologically, these groups cannot have much success.(1)

The Iranian Connection

Within the ITM a few individuals have also been implicated in actions which were undoubtedly ordered by Teheran, even though formal proof is still missing today. Fouad Ali Saleh, arrested in March, 1987, by French police and implicated in the Paris bombings of September, 1986, (he is accused of having stored some of the bombs), had spent a certain amount of time in the "Islamic Group" movement. Current representatives of the ITM try to minimize the effect of this bothersome connection in emphasizing that Fouad Ali Saleh "frequented Islamist meetings, but exercised no responsibilities." Born in Paris on May 10, 1958, he spent his childhood in Tunis, where his family had established themselves after returning from six years spent in France. In 1982, he left Tunis definitively for Iran, where he spent several months before leaving Teheran for Paris. It is probably during that period that he joined up with the Iranian Vahid Gorgi and the Franco-Lebanese Mohamed Mohajer. In 1983, he received a scholarship to study at

---

(1) Salah Karkar, in the presence of Habib Mokni and Abderraouf Boulaabi, interview with the author, Paris, June 28 and July 29, 1991.

the University of Qom and left again for Iran where he followed a program in religious training. But the stay in Iran was for reasons which Véronique Brocard, who patiently reconstructed the itinerary of the young militant, never managed to elucidate.(1) He was imprisoned for several weeks and then expelled towards Paris, where a few months later, in company of one of his friends, a restaurant owner, Mohamed Araoua, also of Tunisian origins, he was arrested in flagrante delitto while transporting explosives.

The Islamic Left and the Dynamic for Reform

At the opposite of the radical offshoots, the internal debate of the Islamic Group over a four-year period led, after the resignation of several members of the leadership circle, to the crystallization of a tendency called the "progressive Islamists" (*al-islamiyoune at-taqadoumiyoune*). It expressed itself from 1982 onwards in a review entitled *15/21*, a reference to the Hegirian and Gregorian calendars. The magazine demonstrated the ambitions for reform of its organizers, especially Ahmida Enneifer and Salah Eddine Jourchi. The aim was to "reconcile two epochs," to ask oneself, as Enneifer puts it, "how one can be a Muslim and live in the twentieth century—how to be a Muslim today."

Founding members of the Islamic Group, Ahmida Enneifer and Salah Eddine Jourchi both, were successively editors-in-chief of *Al-Maarifa*, before separating themselves at intervals of a year from Ghannouchi and Abdelfatah Mourou. Ahmida Enneifer, although he was not educated at Zitouna, is the descendant of a prestigious line of Zitounian Ulama, and the respectability of his name served as a guarantee for the movement. Salah Eddine Jourchi, who comes from a more modest background, managed to impose himself by his intellectual presence alone. Both played roles as intermediaries with the hard core of ITM, where Jourchi had long maintained a certain credibility. The political itinerary of Enneifer, in contrast, accelerated towards the end of 1990. He preferred to leave the Islamist opposition and accepted a post as counselor to Mr. Charfi, ex-militant of the League of Human Rights and a brilliant minister of culture but identified equally with the authors of the plan to eradicate the Islamist movement launched in 1991 just after the Gulf War (cf. infra). Well before that, Enneifer, like Jourchi, had come into conflict with the increasing authority of Ghannouchi, and the relative rigidity of his doctrinal positions.

(1) Véronique Brocard, *Libération* , March 17, 1988.

Abdelfatah Mourou, the Tunisian lawyer (eight years younger) who had long served as secretary general of the movement, and who "could have become another Barzagan,"(1) as Jourchi said of him, in other words "a religious man, but all the same a liberal," had demonstrated a sensitivity to the interrogations that had circulated among the more thoughtful thinkers of the current for the latter half of the decade. In contrast, Ghannouchi, who might seem cordial and even warmer than Mourou in the first contacts, had long had the only partially justifiable reputation of being more intractable and more *harfi*, which is to say more literalist than his colleagues of the Majlis Shura.

While Enneifer left the current as much from fear of suffering the consequences of its radicalization as from ideological divergences, the departure of Jourchi, and progressively of several intellectuals of the group including Abdelaziz Temimi and Kamel Younes, who would found an ephemeral movement of independents, confirmed that a malaise had installed itself within the "mother" current, and that a process of diversification was underway. Several documents, which confirm the accounts of Jourchi and Enneifer and do not deny Ghannouchi attest to the depth of the differences which developed and which would give the Progressive tendency its specific character in 1982.(2)

While it contained heterogeneous currents itself, the Islamic left little by little set itself apart from the rest of the movement by refusing to constitute itself as an alternative to the government, the accent being placed instead on renewing the doctrine of the current. This approach was natural, since in Tunisia as elsewhere the Islamic left never had a capacity for mobilization to match its political ambitions. It does not appear to this day to be capable of mobilizing a base of militants who can seriously compete with the ITM. But the importance of this part of the Movement is elsewhere. It has unquestionably contributed more than the rest to defining the axes of evolution, and in that sense its impact surpasses its limited membership. It constitutes, in effect, the Tunisian echo of a reformist tendency that one can observe—at different stages of development—in the totality of the Islamist currents, and that, despite the fact that they begin on the periphery, tends to affect the itinerary at the center of the current. It generally develops a more

---

(1) Allusion to the Iranian Prime Minister of the first period under Khomeini.

(2) Comments of Ghannouchi in "Hiwar maa al-cheikh Rached Al-Ghannouchi," *Qira'ate siyassiya*, No. 4, Spring, 1991, pages 5-40, World and Islam Studies Enterprise, P.O. Box 16648, Tampa, Florida.

realistic relationship with its political environment, gaining ground with a road that is less difficult to follow, but, nevertheless, is sterile in confrontations with authority. It is especially at the heart of the argument for an historicized and less formalist reading of the normative expression of dogma. It is this approach that prepares the terrain for the adaptation of normative references to the exigencies of social modernization, which can ultimately require the distancing from certain elements in the Sunna of the Prophet. The inventory of the doors opened by the reformist dynamic demonstrates in doing this that none of these "juridical windows" of Islamism (notably polygamy and the rights of women) on which the outside world tends to focus, is totally sheltered from exegesis (*Ijtihad*). As long as it is supported by a sociological majority, "a quarter of an hour of Ijtihad" can be enough to reintroduce the reforming dynamic of a time that has disappeared into the contemporary scene in Islamic thinking.

On the doctrinal plane, one of the theoreticians of the attitude who has most influenced the Tunisian "progressives" is undoubtedly the Egyptian Hassan Hanafi. He has campaigned, in his own words "to reconcile the revolutionary legitimacy of the left, to that, which is historic, of the people and of Islam."

"In 1952," he explains,

I was inflamed for the Revolution. There was in me, as in everyone, two demands for legitimacy that were completely authentic: Islam, political and militant Islam, and the Revolution. In me, there has always been a conflict between the two legitimacies: the revolution and the revelation. The present and my history. I cannot sacrifice one for the other. Well, the movement of the Islamic left is perhaps the only hope of filling the gap between these two legitimacies...between the secular and the fundamentalists. In Cairo, in one class of a hundred students, there are five who are fundamentalists, perhaps ten. There are five who are liberals, Nasserites or Marxists. Now there are a few less, let's say three. But the eighty-five others, they are waiting. They are not content with the discourse of the fundamentalists. They are not content with the secular discourse either. It does not matter whether they are socialists, Marxists, liberals or nationalists... They feel that the Islamist discourse has a "de jure" right, but not a "de facto" right. They have the feeling that the secular progressive current has a right on the "de facto" but not on the "de jure." And me, that is where I would like to intervene. It is there that I want to bring the identity between the "de jure" and the "de facto."

In my class, one finds beards and Marxists, socialists and nationalists. They do not exclude each other. They do not slander each other. Each one respects the other. From time to time, I am called an opportunist, and I am asked which camp I belong to. I answer that it is not a question of which

210

camp (...) They do not know what a synthesis is... the glory of the synthesis. Islam is reason and nature... Plato and Aristotle, deep down, only represented two faces of the same reality: reason and nature, the ideal and the real, the beyond and the here and now, the spirit and the body, God and the world... Anyone who classifies me in one alone, is someone who still lives in the psychology of warfare, and that is not mine.(1)

While keeping its vocation to intervene in the field of politics,(2) the progressive tendency introduces a first rupture in the Islamist scenery. The necessity of that is argued by Hassan Hanafi whose observations in reality oscillate between the recognition of the ineffectiveness of action against the State and its impossibility, at least under the circumstances, given the balance of forces at present.

Whether you are a free young officer or a Muslim Brother at the bottom, you participate in the same mentality which is the following: one cannot change society without changing the political power. As if, without the State, without reigning, that is to say by ideas, speeches, preaching, one cannot do anything (and that it is necessary to have) the power, the decrees (...) which is not the Islamic way, for Islam did not have a State... The State is ulterior.... (there were) what one calls politically the mobilization of cadres, then the mobilization of the people... The State did not come until after, as "the Mekki" before "the Madani" in the suras of the Koran.

There is only one power and several pretenders. The conflict is inevitable. And who is the strongest: the State, the Army, the police or the opposition of the Muslim Brothers? That is why for me the battle against the State and the political power is a dead end. Lets say that I feel like a Muslim Brother who, instead of starting at the top, starts with the civil society. (...) No, I do not exclude politics. But for me, politics is the political culture. That is the idea; for the idea is not an empty one. It is an idea that contains the real. Politics is the political culture and the political culture is the challenge of the other. Can one establish a dialogue with you? Have we a common perception of reality? There is a beautiful woman and two suitors. Then, are we going to fight or establish a dialogue?

---

(1) Interview with the author, Heliopolis, January, 1988. Cf. equally "What Does Islamic Life Mean?" in *Al Iassar al-islami, kitabate fil-nahda al islamiya*, Cairo, January, 1981, which is the unique issue of Hassan Hanafi's journal, and the two series of essays *Al-din wal-thawra fi misr* (Religion and revolution in Egypt) and *Min al-din ilal-thawra* (From the religion to the revolution), Madbouli, 1989-1990.

(2) "It is we ourselves," insists Jourchi,"who have theorized on the necessity to come to politics: look at all the written texts, and it will be seen."

The opposition against the political power, that is a schema which leads nowhere. And the secret opposition with the hopes of power, perhaps to take power one day, that is again a schema which leads no where. For the eyes of the State are everywhere. Even if I am completely silent...it will be heard! So why put oneself at an impasse... If I am historically legitimate and I am not a suitor of power?

Me, I would like the Revolution not to be betrayed, that it lasts, that it has a permanence. In my head, I have the experience of Nasser and of Mohamed Ali. Was there anything more glorious that the state of Mohamed Ali? The army was strong. The State was strong. There was the expansion in Syria, in Saudi Arabia, in Sudan, the uprising against the Western powers... What was more glorious than Nasserism...? Agrarian reform, the Third World, industrialization, free education. Arab unity, socialism. Why are we so out of breath? Why haven't our rockets been able to pierce the atmosphere? Because we want to engage in politics but we conceive of it (only) as a change of government. Me, I do not want to engage in politics in that sense. I want to prepare the mentalities, what I call the culture of the masses. To be susceptible to receive the Revolution without being betrayed. One can change the political power, one can change the social structures, but the culture of the masses remains conservative. I understand by that that they remain open to accept dictatorship, whether it is from free officers or the clergy. For me the French Revolution was not on July 14, 1789, but before. It was Voltaire who carried it out, the encyclopedists... the Enlightened... If one makes a revolution without enlightenment... what guarantee is there for this revolution? The avant garde... But the avant garde will die... it will be overthrown by a strong power.... (1)

For the new arrivals on the Tunisian scene, the solution was not to be found, at least at the time, neither in confrontation with the authorities nor even in participation in the pluralist game. "It is something essential," affirms Jourchi (2) who theorized on the Tunisian scene about this return to action outside of politics to which the ITM, itself, could not remain completely insensitive:

Up until today, we did not want to constitute a party. We did not aim at a direct participation in the political life. We didn't think that it would be there that the beginning would be found. We think that it will first be necessary to carry out the reconstruction of civil society. We think that the true revolutionary movement, it is that which will transform the civil

---

(1) Interview, cited, with the author.

(2) Interview with the author, July, 1984, and July and November, 1985.

society. The problem of the ITM is that it entered into political action without having a real doctrinal base. The last example which it provided was perhaps that of the Code of the Personal Statute. The ITM declared itself opposed to the Personal Statute and demanded a referendum on the question. But despite that, when it asked the question and had to face a violent reaction from most circles, it withdrew. Why did it withdraw? Because it had taken a position without having placed it in an ideological framework that would allow it to justify it and to defend it.

We want first of all to review all that. We want to review all these questions, to go into them more deeply and only after, when we will have a theoretical base, will it be possible to pass to the next step and to apply these question to direct political and civil action.

"The political question remains important but it is no longer a priority. It is the problem of rereading the religious thought which has taken first place," adds Enneifer.

That is the first point. The second, this is where we may have posed a problem for the first time at the interior of Islamic thought. The problem is the following: "Which comes first, the State or society?" One observes that the State, in the history of Islam, is the result of social, economic and geographic conditions, and that its influence was limited. Its competence is limited to the Army, public order, sovereignty. But numerous domains were free of any State intervention: education, the economy. As a result, notably of the Industrial Revolution, the State developed. In the West, there still existed institutions which permitted a fight against this invading presence of the State. With us, these institutions did not exist. Society found itself alone facing a State that was particularly strong, which as it controlled communication, the economy, education, planning, etc. had become in a way, the base for society...its dependence. In Tunisia, when the president of the Republic expresses himself, he speaks as if he had created society himself. It is his society. I think that the intellectuals, in their different tendencies, have become tangled up in this problem. They defended this State, each in their turn, the modern State. For them, it is the modern state which can create a modern society. Most of the intellectuals have disagreements with the PSD, but they agree on one point, that the State is the prerequisite for the creation of a modern society, and for the total transformation of society. We think that that is both an error and dangerous. An error because the true changes do not come from the State. When the State carries out changes, changes from above, these changes are temporary, circumstantial. They do not have a historical continuity. Historical changes are those which are embedded in the society, which result from a choice, a conviction of the society. Let's take a simple example: the Code of Personal Statute. We believe that it is a very important objective. At the present time, thirty years after its promulgation and its application, ask the Tunisian population (...) there are many who are not satisfied with this statute and consider that a part of the problems of Tunisian society are attached to it.

Why? Because a political decision was taken from above... Bourguiba, in all his speeches, when he spoke of the Code of the Personal Statute, evoked it as a gift, as if it was a debt of society with respect to the State and its force. We, we believe that the real change is that which goes in the sense of the reconstitution of the civil society. So that it can be capable of fighting against any State, be it Islamic.

It is for that that one campaigns first for a cultural revolution. It is the essential element for the reconstruction of the conscience of the society, and second, the restructuring of this society. In the past, society had cadres; tribes, Zaouias, extended families. The mosques played an important role in providing a framework. Today there is nothing left.

The dynamic initiated by the "progressives" would become clarified much more rapidly with them than in the rest of the current. Eventually the entire ITM, which had its own questions on these issues, would subscribe to it. It was not limited only to this option of cultural action, but even more essentially, it paved the way for the historicization of the relationship with dogma, or at least with its normative expression, which was the condition sine qua non necessary for relaunching the reformist dynamic.

"I think there is one other point which distinguishes us from the ITM," adds Enneifer.

It is this notion of the historical continuity that the ITM refuses to take into account. It is because of that we diverge on an essential point: there were things that were acquired (before the birth of the Islamic movements) which one cannot ignore and which it refuses to take into account. It uses a term that is very significant. It says often, and perhaps it wrote that "everything happened—*fi ghaflatin min az-zamane.*" That means that time "fell asleep." These gentlemen, the colonialism and its valets, as they say, arrived and it is "as if time fell asleep." It is ridiculous, this way of seeing the world and its evolution. When in guise of history, one evokes *ghaflat min az zamane*, "the sleep of time," one can no longer analyze, one can no longer see the stages. (...) But there are things that were acquired during that period which we cannot ignore... that we consider as acquired and which they ignore... For example, the problem of the Personal Statute. There are points really where it is aberrant to say that it does not concern things that were acquired. When one teaches girls and boys... it is normal that the girl, the next day, cannot accept the superiority of men over her... And the same goes for the freedom to change religion, which we have just been debating at the League for Human Rights. It is difficult to say that because my father was a Muslim, I should be one. That comes from this same way of looking at things. Even on the religious level it is not just.

214

When the Prophet arrived in Medina, he found certain families who had converted to Judaism. Their fathers asked Mohamed if they should force their children to renounce Judaism to rejoin the Muslim camp. The Prophet said no, that it had nothing to do with it. If you, the fathers, have become Muslims, it is your business, your faith. They have chosen Judaism before my arrival in Medina. If they discover one day that they must change, they will change, but you have no right to force them.

The question poses itself in the same terms for polygamy. If one places oneself at the level of the Islamic religion, polygamy was tolerated by the Prophet. But we have to step back a bit. Before the arrival of the Prophet, a man in Saudi Arabia had the right to as many wives as he wanted. Ten or more. It wasn't important. In a society which had always needed children to defend itself, or to make war, they needed several wives to have many children. That is easy to understand. When it arrived, Islam said: we will not leave things like that. It couldn't make a radical total change. It said: "Listen, from now on it is only possible to have four." And even concerning these four... it is necessary to consider equality in treatment. If one reads the religious text, one sees this change in direction very clearly. A woman is not a sexual object. She is the equal of man on the human plane. That is fundamental. And then, afterwards, it said, we will proceed by stages. It expressed a general view; then came the realization of that view. That is something that the ITM will not admit. For them "There is the text that permits you to marry," that is all. It is the *harfi* (literalist) spirit.(1)

THE CRITIQUE OF THE MUSLIM BROTHERS and the "Nationalization" of Doctrine.

While remaining the most important formation in terms of mobilization, the ITM, *volens nolens*, was not untouched by the dynamic expressed by the emergence of the "progressive" voices. The debate clarified by the departures of Enneifer, Jourchi, Krichen, etc. as well as other intellectuals of the ITM was also to be found at the heart of the "mother" core.

The points of rupture of the "progressive" tendency with the founding current were situated at the periphery of the doctrine of the central current, but they still established the limits of the terrain on which an essential part of the internal debate, and especially the intellectual component, took place

---

(1) Interview with the author, cited.

for virtually the entire movement towards the end of the 1970s. In the first formulation of this work, the hypothesis was developed that it was credible, in a political context that was less propitious to radicalization and to the retrenchment of the 1980s, that the positions of the "progressives" could be considered as reasonable points of passage, in the medium term, for the current as a whole. Four years later, there is no reason to revise this position.

With the 1980s and the relative loss of its monopoly, the ITM had to assume the fallout from the doctrinal divergences of which the birth of the "progressive" current had been the extreme expression. Confronted with the exigencies of official action, its strategies would to a certain extent show the distance which separated their capacity for clandestine mobilization from their talent in politics, in the full sense of the term.

Each time that they attempted to extract concrete responses from their ideological background, they quickly discovered the limits of the doctrinal foundation of their movement. Without truly renouncing their initial choices, they would thus little by little learn to reconcile them with the constraints of their political and cultural environment, in a progression in which the preoccupations of the progressives were far from absent. Ghannouchi persisted in marking his distance from the discourse of the progressives, remarking that its "importance is considerably exaggerated."(1) Nevertheless, the leader of the ITM admitted himself in 1985 that his first ten years of experience had led him to introduce (in the absence of water in the wine that he doesn't drink) *chai min al nisbii*—a little "relativity"—in his first convictions. Certain historical shortcuts, and especially the negation of the colonial period and the irreversible character of some of its effects, were progressively abandoned. The relationship to the West had already become the object of a new, more nuanced formalization in which, if only to set itself off more effectively from the others, "the positive aspects of Western philosophy" were more explicitly recognized. But more fundamentally, it was on the terrain of rejection of political confrontation and the recognition of democratic principles that the transformation would become the most perceptible.

The teachings of Hassan Al Banna, Sayid Qutb and Abou 'Ala al Mawdudi, which situated in their time and space were sufficient when it came to criticizing the secularism of Bourguiba, would gradually show themselves to be insufficient when it came to creating a foundation for a credible political program for the Tunisia of the 1980s. The development of

---

(1) Interview with the author, Tunis-Ben Arous, July, 1985.

216

doctrine on a more profound level, which was felt as a necessity, carried the implication that the Tunisian current needed to equip itself with a certain coefficient of ideological autonomy. This doctrinal "independence" could only be achieved by a rereading of the relationship with the rest of the Islamist current and especially with the "cumbersome" Egyptian founding fathers. Behind this distancing with the "dogma" of the Muslim Brothers there was a gradual taking into account of the national experience of the last half of the 1970s. For Ahmida Enneifer (whose account was never disproven by other actors and witnesses of the period,(1) it was the question of the identity of Islam which pushed him into separating from Mourou and Ghannouchi. His personal itinerary aside, his point of view attests to the manner in which the debate was put to the members of the current. A trip to Egypt, where he met several Muslim Brothers freed by Sadat, led, after a brief phase of enthusiasm, to demystification. It was this disappointment which led him to pose the problem of "nationalization," if not of Islam as a dogma, at least of the Da'wa as a method susceptible to returning Islam to its rank in society:

> After 1975, I began to travel. I had met a certain number of religious personalities, especially the Muslim Brothers: Omar Talmasani, Nechi Chibi, Abdelhalim Aouis, Mohamed Qutb, etc... But for me, all that was finally a disappointment. Let's take the example of Mohamed Qutb, whom I met in 1974 in Saudi Arabia. He had come out of prison in 1973 or 1974 and he was able to install himself over there. I explained to him that I was the editor-in-chief of a review called *Al Maarifa*, which

---

(1) Except perhaps precisely on this context of the rupture with the ITM, regarding which his former colleagues estimate that it is necessary to add his hesitations at having to assume the consequences that could be expected from a confrontation with the authorities, a tendency which his later rallying to the regime would make clearer, but which was already detectable in 1985 in certain parts of his testimony: "And also, the movement risked becoming uncontrollable. Why evolve towards the formation of clandestine networks in the style of the Muslim Brothers who would perhaps evolve towards armed actions that one could not control? Here one did something with the students, there another with the people who worked, there another with high school students and all that grew and became more and more important. With so schematic a spirit one cannot control everything that happens, in a country where the political problems ceaselessly complicate themselves. It is precisely what would happen at the university. In 1978-79, the university became much more important and had much more force to make decisions than the core who directed, from the review, from above. And that is normal. If one had formed a group in the heart of the army... one could have lost control." (...) (Interview with the author.)

appeared in Tunisia. He responded by crying, "You are the valets of Bourguiba...!" I told him that he did not know the newspaper, and that he hadn't read it... How could he know that I was a 'valet' of Bourguiba? I immediately realized that this gentleman did not know anything about what was happening in Tunisia. No doubt he wrote very well—I read everything that he had published, but concerning the reality of the Arab countries, he knew nothing... I had a second disappointment with Aouis. Abdelhalim Aouis was considered to be the theoretician of the Muslim Brothers on the political plane and a specialist on the political history of the Muslim world. I asked him, for example, what the Muslim Brothers advocated as a program for educational reform. He sent me a paper written by the Imam Hassan Al Banna...! The Imam died in 1949... and we were at that time in 1974...! The problems had changed a great deal...! And the same thing happened for the Da'wa, when I met Omar Talmasani. This was a gentleman who had a certain presence and who spoke of many things, but how to say it, it did not correspond at all to what I thought...

Progressively, I began to consider that the Egyptian Muslim Brothers were more a legend than anything else... What one called their method of working seemed to me bit by bit like something completely obsolete that could only lead to disaster... They claimed that they had a large number of members in their brotherhood. They spoke of—between members and sympathizers—three million people. Well, I wonder how a current with so much importance could be dismantled in a few months by Nasser. Dismantled not only materially but also on the ideological plane... A brotherhood of 4,000 members relying on three million sympathizers and in a few months it was possible to imprison them the way one would gather a herd of sheep... There was something that didn't fit... And then, what they wrote was really too general. It was the disappointment there which gave me another way of seeing things. But, of course, the problem was that the literature of the Brothers constituted at that time the essence of our review, *Al Maarifa*. I began on a personal plane to take some distance with respect to those people there, but in Tunisia the movement propagated itself in this form and it was the audience for this type of literature which grew. And with the radicalization at the interior of the labor union, we could not slow down. It was not the moment to make a change in orientation. We felt that the danger from the left was imminent. If I place myself in the position of Ghannouchi, I can understand that it was very difficult for him to change direction at that moment then, when we were living in a complex situation. It is then that I began to use a notion that at the time was completely tabu: "Tunisian Islam." "Tunisian Islam?" What is that? There were some very hard discussions with Ghannouchi: Islam is Islam. There cannot be a "Tunisian Islam!" "One God! One Prophet! One Islam!..." (...) Of course one is against the division of the Arab world, but one cannot not take it into account, one cannot deny it.

We were in fact in a battle against what I called "the new Sufism." It consisted of ignoring the specificity of each Arab country and of only speaking of Islam—in its sole spiritual dimension—in its entirety. That also returned to indirectly attack the Muslim Brothers. Our projects could not have any real impact on society as long as we did not understand the mechanisms of this society, its recent history, its problems and as long as one is not able to translate them, one cannot convert them.

There is an anecdote which illustrates this very well (the divergences as well as the necessity to provide a national anchor point for our action). At the end of the last of the articles that I wrote for *Al Maarifa*, I had attacked Hassan Al Banna by name, and I wrote in substance on this gentleman that he was Dead. Dead, with a capital D. To die physically is not important. But when one is leading an action in which one pulls along a certain number of people and then one is assassinated and the group created is dismantled with astonishing ease, that proves that one is finished, that one is dead. And that the thought in question was not dealing with the real problems of society. And so, one should not resume this strategy, but should instead study it, analyze it, understand why it vanished in smoke... That is what I wrote. As I was editor-in-chief of the review, and I had the possibility of publishing what seemed right to me, I took the manuscript to the printers. But when I received the issue a short while later, I realized that the entire paragraph in which I had spoken about Hassan Al Banna had been cut. It was that which was at the origin of my departure from the review.(1)

Although more nuanced and in fact more realistic in his appreciation of the contribution by Hassan Al Banna and the impact of Nasser's repression, Salah Eddine Jourchi also remembers that the "nationalization" of Islamic action did constitute the first of the great debates which in part served to crystallize the thoughts of those who challenged Ghannouchi. Beyond the affective demythification of the Brothers, there were the questions of the adaptability of their methods to the Tunisian environment:

The questions which Ahmida Enneifer began to ask had internal justifications inside the movement. We had begun to feel since the end of 1976 the fact that we were growing in numbers, but that we were not managing to have a direct and effective influence on the social and cultural environment of the country.

This contradiction between growth and the incapacity of influencing the environment led us to ask if these contradictions did not come from individual religious as well as intellectual training. We undertook a series of activities destined to develop the intellectual side of the movement's members and we began to act more serious in our actions. But after an experience of several months, it became apparent to us that the problem did not lie in partisan questions. The question passed this level. It concerned thought and culture. From then on we began to ask a crucial

---

(1) Interview with the author, cited.

question, as a group, within the Islamic Group: this contradiction and this incapacity to influence our environment, didn't they come from the nature of the culture we were consuming and reading? The question began to be posed of whether as a movement we weren't going through a doctrinal crisis. The question was very dangerous for it shook all our convictions— the spiritual ones as well as the partisan, which is to say organizational and tactical ones. For when we spoke of doctrinal crisis, that meant before anything else that there were doubts about the school of thought of the Muslim Brothers, which had been a model for us. And to say that the Brothers did not represent the strategy and culture we required for the period we were passing through, that implied that we would have to carry out a radical re-examination of everything that touched the Islamist movement.

After that, another question began to be raised: this question had the value of preceding all the others. We had to know in this stage if, we in Tunisia, were living or not in a society which was, as Sayyid Qutb said, a *jahilyan* society. It was an essential question and it unleashed an important debate. It ended in the recognition that we were living in a Muslim society which for historical and social reasons had distanced itself from the sources of Islam as history or as culture or even as ideology. (...) Then we asked ourselves another question. Should our method of Da'wa, and more generally, the modalities of change, be considered as being a divine order, that is to say, could they be found in the texts or was it that each society had its own conditions? Was it not then for us to discover (for each one among us) the method of change and to reattach it to the comprehension of society and its nature and its problems?

That evidently contradicted the ideas of Sayid Qutb. Qutb had, in effect, the conviction that since Islam came from God, the modalities for its transmission to men (*tabligh*) also came from God. During the course of the debate, we (...) we had in contrast established that the method of Da'wa flowed from the conditions of the society, that this was not a divine revelation and that it followed that there was not a universal form of Da'wa which could be applied in all societies, when each had its own characteristics.(1)

In August, 1985, Salah Eddine Jourchi, Abdelaziz Temimi and Kamel Ben Younes, all three dissidents of the ITM, published an internal evaluation of the Islamist action in Tunisia, which as the authors explained in their introduction, was intended to be "the first public attempt to critically evaluate Islamic thought and action."(2) Even if it did not receive the official support of the ITM, which opposed its publication, the report given to

---

(1) Interview with the author, Tunis, July, 1984, and July-November, 1985.

(2) *It is necessary to modify the image that we have of ourselves: internal evaluation of the Islamist action*, Tunis, Maktabat al-Jedid, 1985, 48 pages.

220

the political class to read was the result of a debate in which the ITM had accepted to participate, and it contained a series of propositions on which the consensus had been reached. This call "to reform the image which we have of ourselves," directed at militants of all Islamist sensitivities, usefully completed the enlightening of the internal dynamic of the ITM from 1975 to the present.

The body of the text, essentially a long critique of how Salafism had proved to be sclerotic for the development of Islamic thought, and its anchorage in the reality of Tunisia, was followed by what could be called an operational platform. The signatories invited all those who wanted "to open new perspectives for Islamist action in Tunisia," to adhere.

The first of the necessities was far from being the least instructive. It consisted of admitting in effect that the Islamist movement was in crisis. "It is indispensable before everything else," declared Jourchi, Temimi and Younes,

> to admit the existence of a dangerous crisis.... whose first manifestations go back to 1976, and which has progressively deepened leading to a situation of quasi-intellectual blockage (which is translated by) the absence of any scientific approach to define the contents of the stage which the movement is now going through, to assimilate the transformations intervening at the regional level or world level, and to make the Islamist movement which is organized in a state of a simple pole of attraction, into a pole that emits energies and competence. The non-recognition of this crisis is precisely one of the manifestations of its reality and the principal obstacle to the effective overtaking of the decline which affects all levels of our conscience and our action.

As much a diagnosis of the crisis, the means proposed for getting through it marked a certain rupture in relation to the first strategies. They were articulated principally around three axes: self criticism, political opening and the regeneration of doctrine.

It was necessary first that Islamists, "regardless of who they were," accept to undergo a "profound and complete" autocritique of their past action, and of their doctrine. This critique would not be limited "to a few practices or partisan positions," nor would it "stop at a period in history, of which most of those who demand Islamist Islamism today ignore the different episodes and the different combats." It must on the contrary extend to "the theoretical discourse of the dominant religious thought locally and in the world," and it must set about "dismantling the mechanisms, the instruments of analysis, the conception of existence of the society and the individual." "We affirm that, after having perceived a beginning theoretical resignation (*irtidad*) which tries to embellish Salafism with the virtues of authenticity in making it the unique framework for the reference of Islam, is just when there is a tendency to reduce the crisis which we are experiencing to simple technical causes...of a circumstantial nature." Doing this, the Islamists are asked to strip themselves of all narcissism. "What concurs with the success of this mission of self criticism," the authors of the report emphasize,

> would be that the Islamists abstain from narcissism which has given them the conviction that they are "the" jemaa, that is to say, the nation, in its entirety, in its religious acceptance. They must abstain also from this assurance of being the (only) depositories for the divine message, or to constitute "the" divine movement, which has given them the illusion of being an extra-natural phenomenon.... As if the will of God did not realize itself through the laws of society and of nature, and as if the follower of the jemaa transformed himself in doing this into a receptacle empty of any sediment., or as if we were separated from our environment and exempt from any blemishes.

The end of the crisis passes afterwards with the acceptance of a complete dialogue between the Islamists themselves for one part, and between the Islamists and the other tendencies for the other. This dialogue must bear on the axes that have been defined beforehand,

> from the alternative of civilization and its theoretical and practical implications, which have until then remained in a state of challenge. They will remain so as long as they (the Islamists) are not capable of making a practical rule for every day life and the base of the definition of their theoretical arms.

But the central objective remains that of regeneration of the doctrine. "When one realizes," the authors recognize,

> that the Islamist movements have nothing more in their plans than an assemblage of slogans inherited from a distant past, one admits that what they need before anything else is to proceed to the "crystallization" of a social plan, which is an essentially theoretical task, before going on to acquire a clear vision, which is equally a theoretical task, which necessitates the evaluation (...) of the forces present as well as those (...) of the experiences leading there.

At the heart of this new method of reflection is a clearer anchorage in the concrete local reality. Certainly, underline the authors, "all research must be anchored in Islamic tradition." But it would be serious danger if it consisted of "founding the legitimacy of this thought on only textural and historical work." In fact, "the legitimacy (of the project) depends on its roots in reality and time, which theology knows under the double word "*tahqiq al manat* (taking traditions into account)." And in conclusion, "speaking of the realism of the Islamist project supposes that one starts from real life to change it and improve it, failing which, alienation of the Islamists with respect to reality and history will follow."

In fact, even if the heritage of the great Egyptian Muslim Brothers is far from buried, the spirit of these propositions, (to which Ghannouchi refused to accord too much importance, because as he explained, "the ITM had written similar texts for a long time,"(1) is not foreign to the evolution undertaken by the current. For a long time completely dependent on Egypt's ideological production, the latter little by little proposed the bases for a doctrine contained in the demands and the specificity of Tunisia's national space, in which its history was written, in which it was destined to evolve, and of which it must take into account the demands, or condemn itself to never having a grasp on the real. "In all, we are ten years behind all the other Islamist tendencies in the Middle East," recognized Ghannouchi, interviewed by Abdel Wahab al Effendi, journalist on the review *Arabia*, who was surprised to note that the ITM had without challenge become "the most supple and the most pragmatic of all the Islamist movements in existence, and that one of the specificities was its willingness to objectively study Tunisian society and to fine-tune an Islamic program which would be specifically adapted to it."(2) And, in fact, in taking the measure of this autonomy of the "political space" ignored by the predecessors in the Ulema, the Tunisian Islamists had conceded more clearly than their Algerian or Libyan neighbors several points in the critical analysis of doctrine initially imprinted with this touch of "integrism" which Enneifer denounced. In explicitly adding the pluralist dogma to the spread of their references, in nuancing the most abrupt of their positions on religious freedom, in withdrawing certain critiques with regard to the personal status prescribed by Bourguiba, in actively militating within the League for Human Rights, they had undertaken to give their strategies and their methods an image that broke with their reputation for violence and totalitarianism, which is often still attached to them. Even if, for their political adversaries, the purely tactical considerations are not foreign to this beginning of a metamorphosis, it is difficult to deny today the reality and the importance of these changes.

---

(1) Interview with the author, Tunis, November, 1985.

(2) *Arabia*, August, 1986, page 33.

Mr. Mzali had, in his time, left to the Islamist current a certain free space put in front of responsibilities that it was only partly capable of assuming. In doing this, he had in the short term, no doubt, weakened as much as strengthened it. At least he had led it, and that is perhaps the essential point, to undertake the slow mutation which would lead it to assume—if that were to become the will of Tunisian voters, and only in that event—a part or all of the government responsibilities without the country having to pay the price of a traumatic experience similar to Iran's.

Counter-violence

The brutal return to repression and the amalgamation imposed on the two successors of Mr. Mzali by President Bourguiba has in contrast unleashed the process of radicalization of the movement. The extreme expression of this process was the rupture between the movement in its legalistic strategy and the elaboration, as a response to Bourguiba's extremism of the summer of 1987 during an attempt of armed overthrow of the chief of state. Revealed a few hours before it was put down successfully by the Prime Minister, the attempt, orchestrated by the ITM to accelerate at any cost the arrival of the period after Bourguiba, still remains partly mysterious. If the implication of a circle of military officers is backed up by the 73 arrests which followed in the first days of the new regime and the death under torture of a major in active service, the importance of the institutional implication of the army remains largely unknown. Neither the spokesman of the ITM, who refused logically enough to give any precisions (all the while pointing out that the movement had never blocked any professions from joining) nor the spokesman for the regime, who manifestly tried to minimize the action of the ITM, would permit a clear reconstruction of what had happened. For the officials of the ITM, it was a matter of a preventive counter-violence, that their movement did not want in any way to exploit in order to take power, which, considering the rapport of forces, would have been a poisoned gift.

"It was a Sudanese-style scenario," Salah Karkar, leader of the ITM during this crucial phase of its history (March-November 1987), declared four months later, before going into exile himself in France and Belgium.

"How is it possible to explain what happened?" said Kakar.(1)

---

(1) Salah Karkar, interview with the author in the presence of Habib Mokni, Paris, March, 1988.

224

First of all it is necessary to recall that no part of Tunisian society is excluded from belonging to the Islamist movement, whether they were professors, peasants, policemen or soldier. They are all Tunisians, human beings who need this party. We do not select them by demanding identity cards and throwing out such and such a category of citizen because of their professional training: "You are military? So you don't need Islam..." No, that is not it. Our point of view must be explicit for everyone. As there are businessmen or intellectuals who accept our ideas, well, there are soldiers (...). Our last congress, in December, 1986, had decided to make the maximum effort to avoid confrontation with the authorities (...) Well... Bourguiba... who knew exactly this conception, who knew perfectly that he did not risk losing his position because of the Islamists, but who did not want—he, the secular, he, the without-faith, he, who was against all norms and values of our society—he did not want for Tunisia to come back one day to its values. He considered that the growth of Islamism was dangerous for the future of the country, Bourguiba wanted confrontation. He had said so several times: "I will consecrate my last days to fighting the shanty towns and the Khouanjia." He did not want the Islamic aspect for Tunisia. Absolutely not. Never.

We were against this confrontation with the authorities. But the government, and especially Bourguiba, wanted it. He told his close associates: "If I do not manage to eliminate the Islamists during my days, you, you will never manage to do it." Then they did everything. Everything. You cannot imagine all that happened in Tunisia between March and October 1987. It was the terror. It was people's war. No one was safe. Even in the mountains. Nobody could be sure, if he left his house, even on a mountain, that he would come back and keep a few coins in his pocket. Everyone was hit hard. An old woman of 70 years old, who wore the veil, they went inside to take it off. They did everything. The army, the police, the party militia. Around 150,000 people were chasing members of the movement. With weapons, with sticks, with all the means. And we, we avoided all confrontation. They had really prepared the conditions for a civil war.

The orders given to the militants at the base were to never do anything. One shouldn't forget that no embassies had any problems. No one was caused any problems by our movement. No one had to submit to anything from it. We were very conscious that if we did anything, even in legitimate self defense, the authorities would take that as a pretext to unleash an escalation and to make the situation explode. We, we kept our calm. We were very hard with the people (at the base). "It's necessary not to do anything. Don't give the authorities the opportunity to eliminate the movement." Who would have suffered the consequences? The authorities were in the palace. It is the people who would have suffered the consequences of a civil war. It is for that that we tried not to give an occasion to the regime. But despite that, Bourguiba wanted, regardless of the cost, to do the impossible.

For Habib Mokni, representative of the movement in Paris: "Bourguiba had become a time bomb." It was there, it was set. Everyone saw it. No one did anything to disarm it. It was truly that. Because, what did Bourguiba want? He wanted for one part to liquidate, physically, a political movement. Several dozen people were threatened with death. And for the other part, after that, he wanted to create a climate of civil war. Because it was inevitable. Liquidate Ghannouchi and company, that meant systematically, obligatorily, civil war. There were armed militias prepared for that. And on the other side, there was the movement, which had shown its power, and its force, and its capacity to mobilize the street. To let Bourguiba execute his folly, that was really what would have been the most irresponsible. Since Nouira, everyone said, "Why keep Bourguiba?" Everyone was unanimous, in the interior as well as on the exterior, on the fact that Bourguiba must leave. Even Bourguiba's friends, even his ministers suffered... But no one had budged to push him aside. If the movement was capable of doing it and didn't do it... it would have been because it was crazy!

So, in such a situation, what was it possible to do? France was not there to say to Bourguiba: "No, stop...this is not the right way." One did not find the Parliament, which would have been able to say: "For the first time, I will take a decision..." Neither his Prime Minister, nor his ministers advised him. It was no longer possible. They spoke of 25 killed... I don't know. The League stopped following things. Twenty-five between the riots and those killed by bullets in the street, the interrogations and the two executions.

Tunisia did not have the choice. It did not have the choice. It had two possibilities: either civil war, or the departure of Bourguiba. One had searched for this solution for a longtime, but we would have preferred that it come from somewhere else. We indirectly suggested it to Mzali: "Go ahead. Technically it is possible. You are responsible...You are Prime Minister, go ahead.

Up until the last minute, we delayed. The repression had gone on for seven or eight months though. There were already deaths. Political assassinations. Deaths under torture. But the movement didn't move. And that, that is a supplemental proof that the movement is not violent. It sees its brother, its members, dead under torture and it does not move. That means that our strategy was not that. It is only at the end, because it was not just the movement which was threatened, but the entire country, then it was necessary to move. And in which direction? Not by taking power. That was out of the question, but by removing Bourguiba, because he had become crazy, and by giving political power back to the country.

It was, in fact, the scenario in the Sudanese fashion, in the style of Souar Adhahab (who allowed Niemiery to be overthrown). To eliminate Bourguiba. Not by force. We were very clear on that point. He shouldn't be hurt. Never. And to associate everyone, all the parties. Because we were aware. We were not ready to assume the heritage of Bourguiba. We were incapable of solving the problems of the country. So it was necessary to make everyone participate. To call everyone to assume his responsibilities. To make the country come out of its dilemma, of the crisis. To install a government of public salvation, of national salvation, a parliamentary regime where all the political parties participate in the evolution of the country. It was not conceivable to take power. That is clear. All that we sought was a democratic climate that was more or less favorable to dialogue, to the evolution of ideas and to peaceful change. So, why take power? The strategy of the movement was to eliminate Bourguiba, not as a person, but as a system of decision. And to replace this structure by... let's say the party in power, the Destourien Party, the valuable people in the Destourien Party.... the MDS... the popular groupings... the MUP 1, the MUP 2,(1) the independents... You ask yourself: how would we have made the selection between the good and the bad in the PSD? That is known. They themselves have kept certain ministers and chased others away... Tunisia is not very big. All the people know each other... There are some people who are really fascist, against all liberty, against all democracy. They don't want to discuss. We, we are disposed to talk with everyone. They, they refuse. Sayah, today refused to talk with me. When he was minister, I could understand. But today he is nothing, and he still refuses. Is he objective? Is he sufficiently sure of himself to accept discussion? No. There are a few elements... Skhriri, Sayah... even their colleagues can't accept them. Are these people valuable or not? I think it is a false question. The problem is not people. It depends in my opinion on a strategy, a methodology. No political party can resolve the crisis alone. Either one accepts the method which consists of having everyone participate, and, like that, if one arrives at resolving the crisis, so much the better. If, even with the participation of everyone, one does not manage to resolve it, one will not have a problem there...! All the doors were open... free to whoever wants to criticize. He speaks and shows us. We, that was our methodology. Ben Ali had a very good chance to become a real and responsible leader. It was to govern all of Tunisia by Tunisians. In my opinion, it is the best strategy and the best methodology to succeed. If these people choose this method, they can succeed, why not? If they are going to govern the country alone, they will never make it. And besides, the party, it is a hundred people... who think and who have points of view. The others, the base, they pass from "*Bi rouh bi dem* (by the spirit and the blood) Bourguiba" to "Vive Ben Ali" without transition.

We had a scenario. And things became more and more precise: the men, the personalities, the former ministers like Mzali, like Masmoudi, etc... Like the MDS especially, because it is more or less our ally. It was near the scenario of Souar Adhahab: to give the power to politics. And to permit everyone and ourselves to work in freedom.

---

(1) The Movement for Popular Unity, founded in 1973 by Ahmed Ben Salah, experienced a split between the interior leaders and those who were exiled, which gave birth to the MUP 2 of Mr. Belhaj Ammor. Following that it became the Party of Popular Unity (PUP) and was recognized with the same standing as the PCT and MDS, in the formations belonging to the legal opposition.

Was it our attempt that unleashed that of Ben Ali? It is a question which remains to clarify. The three days, November 6, 7, and 8, 1987, are historic days for Tunisia. Up until now, they have not been clear at all.

Why did one applaud the coming of Ben Ali? Is it that he is our friend? Not at all. We would have liked to have had this Ben Ali two or three months earlier. In that case we would never have thought of a military intervention. And if it was really a question of changing our way of working, then why didn't we go on? Do you believe that Ben Ali was a barrier? Not at all. Never. Never. But our principal problem, and the problem of all Tunisia, of all the Tunisians, was Bourguiba and the unblocking of the situation. Someone came and changed that situation. Well, we approved. Even if we were not completely favorable to the person, but all the same... It was an important stage.

The problem is that Ben Ali did well in the first part of the scenario, but not the second. He pushed Bourguiba aside, but he guaranteed the continuity. That is the difference. The first project was to get rid of Bourguiba and to guarantee democracy. Unfortunately, Tunisia is not mature enough for that. We continue to militate for democracy and change... Tunisia lost. The West lost also. The best occasion to install a true democratic regime and liberty was the attempt by the ITM. It is necessary to respect people. One shouldn't impose their point of view by force. That is a conviction we have.

THE EFFECTS AND LIMITS OF RECOMPOSING THE POLITICAL LANDSCAPE

"By God, the all powerful and merciful." The very first words of the declaration by which Tunisians learned on the morning of November 7, 1987, that the Supreme Combatant had been deposed had a certain illustrative value concerning the event.

Habib Bourguiba had insisted on a repression against the Islamists, which left nearly a dozen dead. A trial concluded on September 27, put several hundred in prison. But the old Combatant, it seems, had felt frustrated with a verdict which would have made "50 heads fall," and had just given the order to his Prime Minister, chosen for his intransigence, to reopen the trial of the leaders of the ITM and to see to it that satisfaction was given. In doing so, he placed his country on the edge of an irreversible fracture, and, in the opinion of observers on all sides, on the eve of a possible civil war.

The care which the new holder of the title to supreme power took to interrupt the repressive spiral in which Bourguibism had engaged showed that the danger had been seen. To calm the game, General Zine al Abidine Ben Ali, former minister of the interior and the ex-chief of the security services, had to forget the ease of a regressive policy that he had for a time gone along with—although like Mohamed Sayah, without excess—and try to carry out a true recomposition of the political landscape. This process had to avoid several snags. First, the slowing of Islamist agitation must not imply that the ITM had been given too much satisfaction on the political terrain. If that were to happen, it would not only risk making the ITM stronger, but it would also risk arousing the reticence of the secular opposition, whose access to the political scene the regime wanted to enlarge in order to obtain its support against the Islamists.

The process of renovating the moribund single party structure and of opening it to "independent" personalities on its "left" implied offering the latter sufficient guarantees. But, there again, the margin of the president, who was outside the PSD himself, remained narrow, since he had to keep himself from too explicitly attacking the privileges of the still active old guard of the Destouriens.

How did one break with Bourguiba and still claim to be following Bourguibism? To change the foundation of the regime, it was a question of renewing the old paradox of "change in continuity" by granting a "state of grace" to all the movements, but in an economic context which left little time for the politicians' recipes to act.

This counter-offensive was undertaken between November, 1987, and June, 1988, along three great axes which, without prejudging the rhythm of the transformations, gave a certain coherence to the government's action. At the end of eight months of reforms, its limits began to show through. In the few awkwardly written pages of the new legislation on parties, the lion of democratic promises gave birth to what appeared to be a mouse.

Cutting One's Losses (la part du feu)

The regime first sought to demarcate itself from the most violent of the symbolic ruptures that had characterized Bourguiba's policies. It tried to do this at the lowest cost possible, which is to say by measures affecting the field of symbolism which the Islamist current had been demanding, but without actually improving the current's status or that of its militants. Without cutting itself off completely from what would remain its principal source of legitimacy, it started a selective reexamination of Bourguiba's heritage, and began in very measured terms to reposition itself.

In the hours and days that followed the forced departure of Bourguiba for his residence in Mornag, 30 kilometers from Tunis, spectacular ruptures were made both with the fallen leader, and his symbols. The national holiday was changed from the day honoring Bourguiba's return to Tunisia, and settled on the actual day of Tunisian independence. Several holidays commemorating episodes in Bourguiba's public and private life (his birthday, etc.) were simply dropped.

After the symbols of the cult devoted to the Supreme Combatant (which in Arabic—*al mujahid al akbar*—implies the use of the adjective *akbar* which is usually applied to God), it was the turn of the symbols of secularism to be brutally called into question.

There was a reintroduction of Islamic symbols ranging from the *bismillah* which from now on would come at the beginning of every public appearance by the president, to the suras of the Koran which often marked the closings. Or the insistence on having television cameras show the general in prayer or making his pilgrimage. Or again, the access of the muezzins to the audiovisual media, the live broadcasting of the Friday prayers, the return of the direction of religious worship from the ministry of interior to the Prime Minister's office, the promise to give the faculty of theology at Zitouna the rank of an independent university and to reinforce the political role of a new Council of the Ulema. All of that was followed up, of course, with a long series of declarations magnifying the role of Arab and Muslim culture, a credo taken to heart by the totality of the political formations, the Communist Party included.

The Relaunching of the Democratic Process

The second axis of the regime's action consisted of giving the state and pluralism the credibility that the storm of 1987 and the aborted political opening launched by the PSD in 1981 had never allowed it to acquire. Parallel to the symbolic satisfactions accorded to the Islamists, the government, week after week, multiplied its measures of political liberalization: the ending of the presidency for life; the abolition of the State Security Court and of the post of public prosecutor; the liberalization of the legislation on holding prisoners in custody; the creation of a constitutional council; the reconciliation with some of the political exiles (Driss Guiga, the family of Mzali, the widow of Ben Youssef, Ahmed Ben Salah himself amnestied after 15 years in exile at the express demand of Ben Ali against the advice of several of his ministers); the union leader Habib Achour, given freedom of movement again and his competitor Mr. Bouraoui invited to reconcile with him; the UGET (General Union of Tunisian Students, victim of constant repression since 1972 when, during its 18th congress at Korba, the leftist students took the majority away from the representatives of the PSD) encouraged to hold meetings in public again and in addition, to attack the positions of the UGTE (the Tunisian General Union of Students created by the Islamists in 1985); the lifting of legal actions against Khemais Chamari, the secretary general of the League of Human Rights; the suppression of fines leveled against the press before November 7; and the adoption of a statute according the press a greater autonomy and providing subsidies to newspapers in the opposition. Not a week passed without the president adding a new element to the process of opening towards the secular political class.

The instrument for collecting the benefits of this operation was the new version of a Destourian Socialist Party, re-baptized at the end of February as the RCD—Democratic Constitutional Union (the Rassemblement Constitutionnel Democratique). This party was destined to extend the foundation of a new regime in the direction of the left and its secular formations.

Once the time for promises had passed, the first tests of the democratic opening were not all that convincing. The partial elections on January 24, which were shamelessly rigged, underlined the importance of the resistance within the structure of the party. Lured by the measures adopted in the days after November 7, the Islamist current had to content itself afterwards with an attitude on the part of the regime that was ambivalent. On the day that Bourguiba was deposed, the dossier of the ITM was, it is true, complicated by a military dimension that incited the government to show an increased prudence.

A New Line of Defense.

A few hours before or after the deposing of the head of state, his Prime Minister-successor had learned of a plot to take by force of arms (an assault on the radio broadcast facilities, and on the Palace of Carthage, then an appeal for a government of national union) that which he hoped to realize himself (or had just accomplished), armed only with article 57 of the Constitution.

The attitude of Zin al Abidine Ben Ali and of Hedi Baccouche was split between the break with repression and the defensive reflex. They had to deal with a current which had just shown that it was also nearly as much at ease in the apparatus of the state, including army and police, as in the streets of the center of the capital, which had been invaded for several months by its demonstrations. Less than two months later, the ITM showed its persistance and the extent of its capacity for mobilization in the university milieu when its candidates in the student union, the UGTE, won 85 percent

231

of the votes cast in student elections and all the seats of the representatives on the university councils.

At first, the State Security court, after several weeks of hesitation, confirmed the verdict of those condemned in absentia (including the death sentence against Ali Laaridh) who had been arrested in the weeks following the verdict of September. A new regulation on the mosques banned their use in principle outside of the hours of prayer by organizations that had not received express authorization. Little by little, at the same time that negotiations were started with representatives of the ITM, the signs of appeasement were, nevertheless, made progressively. At least one contact had taken place in the offices of the ministry of interior between the new president and Ghannouchi, even if Ghannouchi, who was a prisoner, refused to negotiate. On December 12, more than 600 members of the ITM arrested during the preceding eight months (but sentenced after the September trial) and 18 members of the PLI (imprisoned since 1983) were freed. On December 16, the sentence against Ali Laaridh was commuted to life at hard labor. The majority of the militants arrested during 1987 were released. The day of the Eid et Fitr of May, 1990, Ghannouchi was himself pardoned by the President of the Republic, along with 233 other prisoners. Against the promise of a general amnesty, Ghannouchi's movement had been asked to abstain from constituting itself as a political party and to limit its action to the cultural and religious scene.

But the concessions made to the Islamist movement stopped there. The regime did not appear prepared to go further than the cultural terrain. In the meantime, the secular opposition parties, who feared the overflowing that could result from such an attempt "to pull the rug out from under the feet of the Islamists," had undertaken to mobilize themselves and to demand that the regime clearly state the limits of the recentering of its position on religion. On March 18, 40 university professors representing the principal political information, published a long declaration arguing the "necessary separation of Islam and politics" and the obligation to preserve vigorously the acquisitions relating to the code on personal statutes. A few days earlier, an article that was not denied, was published in the Arab-language daily newspaper, *As Sabah*, announcing the opening of debate on an important amendment aimed at the interdiction of the adoption. On March 19, on the eve of the new national holiday, President Ben Ali put an end during a televised speech to the recentering of his cultural policy, defining for the first time the limits within which he intended to situate his action from then on: "There will be no calling into question, nor abandoning of that which Tunisia has been able to achieve to the profit of women and the family. The code on personal status is an attainment to which we are attached and by which we feel attached. We are proud of it, and we draw a real pride from it."

It is in this context that a law on parties whose terms had been carefully weighed was approved in May. It banned the ITM from access to the legitimate political scene. Any party presenting itself as a candidate for recognition must, in effect, in virtue of Article 2, engage itself to defend "all the attainments of the nation, and notably the Code on personal status." Even more effective, Article 3 declared that "no party has the right to refer to itself, in its principles, its objectives, its action or its program, to religion, language, race, or region." Multiple dispositions finally limited, through a tightened play of all kinds of "sanctions" the margin for maneuver of those elected through pluralism concerning the bastions of government. The disposition condemning, thanks to a misprint in the daily *Le Temps* (May 25, 1988), any enterprise at "democratization" (it had meant to say "demoralization") of the nation, underlined, if there was any need to, the limits of reform.

The Return to the Starting Line

Since then, the tendency for caution that has been noticeable in the verbal statements of the regime has been largely confirmed. Four years later, the movement initiated in the days just after the eviction of Habib Bourguiba seems in fact not only to have been interrupted but frankly reversed. The relationship between the regime and its Islamist opposition has taken on all the characteristics of the repression of 1987.

One by one, the political guarantees accorded or promised after the fall of the "Supreme Combatant" have been taken back. The promise to legalize the ITM has been indefinitely postponed. The Movement's newspaper, *Al Fajr*, which was authorized for a while, has been banned once again, and campaigns of massive arrests, justified by hypothetical plots have become the regime's primary mode of communication with its principal opposition.

At the origin of this repressive retrenchment is the failure of Bourguiba's successor to reverse the tendencies inherited from his predecessor. In the mind of Zin Al Abidine, the first electoral test of his mandate was to permit the measurement of the effectiveness of his double strategy of opening towards the secular opposition and of ideologically going around the Islamists. The expected scenario was of an "Egyptian style" controlled democratization, in which a moderate left (which in any case would pose no real threat, since it was already running out of steam) would get some representation in parliament. Such a step would add credibility to the democratic dimension of the Destourian party, which would itself be largely renovated and ready to join its forces to those of the regime in order to face the Islamist surge.

If the official results of the election did not exclude the possibility of a victory for Bourguiba's successor, they, nevertheless, fell far short of the hopes that the government had placed in them.(1) In many respects it appears today that the balloting on April 2, 1989, played a role in Tunisia that was similar to the June 12, 1990, election in Algeria. In short, they confirmed to the regime the difficulty, if not the impossibility, of confronting the Islamists in regular elections unless they wanted to admit the principle of alternating power to the profit of the Islamists. The necessity of adopting methods of dealing with the Islamist movement other than the proclaimed democratic opening had become apparent.

The ITM: from Militants to Electors

On April 2, 1989, during the evening of the anticipated elections, the Tunisian political class was astonished to discover that after the renovated party of President Ben Ali, the second political force in the country was not the so-called secular left but the current that the dying Bourguibism had tried to eradicate, and that its successor had believed it could empty of its powers of mobilization. They had managed to win a national average of 12 percent of the votes (officially, but from all evidence the vote was much more). Even more significantly, they had come close to winning a majority in several important urban circumscriptions (particularly revealing of the evolution of the electorate). The Islamists had begun to harvest the fruits of

(1) Participation in the election was 76.15%, or 2,121,704 out of 2,806,386 registered voters (previous elections had had a turnout of 98%). In the presidential election, Ben Ali obtained 99.27% of the votes. The 141 parliamentary seats, on the other hand, all went to the RCD. The Mouvement des Democrates Socialistes only had 3.76% of the votes. The Islamists won 14% or 300,000 votes, but claimed, with a certain credibility, that their real score was somewhere between 30 and 32% (Mourou, interview with the author, Tunis, May 1989). In Tunis and Ben Arous, these figures which were challenged, still accorded 50% of the votes to the lists of the independents and 65% at the polls in El Ouardia and Kabaria. At Gabes, the brother of Rached Ghannouchi won 27%. In Gafsa and Monastir, the lists won 20%, and at Sousse and Bizerte, 25%. "In the polling places where we were not expelled, the scores sometimes went as high as 70%," (A. Boulaabi and S. Karkar, interview with the author, Paris, August 1991; idem Rached Ghannouchi, interview with the author, London, cited).

234

a pluralist tree that they had been very late in watering. But this success was not any less significant than a profound change that was taking place in the national political scene.

The thousands of votes cast on April 2 went to the independent lists in which the ITM had been authorized to present its candidates and did not all come from student groups. To the battalions of the first student militants, were added little by little sympathizers from the socio-professional class who had more varied backgrounds. The first contact between the activist core and its electoral surroundings accelerated during the period of opening. In a non-Democratic environment, only a limited number of hard-core activists emerge in the media. To assure their existence they are almost obliged to assume a certain degree of confrontation with the political environment. Although they might be well positioned as far as ideology is concerned, the reduced dimension of the militant core does not allow anyone to judge in advance its capacity for mobilization. When restrictions on the freedom of expression are lifted, the circles affected can prove to be much larger than the core of militants during the phase of semi-clandestinity. Once it became possible to show opposition to the government at a relatively low cost, tendencies in public opinion that had been hard to detect under the period of Bourguiba's absolutism became apparent. The universality of the principle that majorities may be silent was reconfirmed. From a larger viewpoint, the ITM did not escape the usual pattern in which the movement overflows the intellectual core of its founders and moves towards the middle classes, first of all in the urban centers, and then towards the quasi-totality of the social landscape. The countryside, more conservative and thus supposedly closer to the universe of religious culture, remained on the other hand (as in Algeria) predominantly loyal to the dominant party. The reasons for this were partly that the Islamist theme always has a tendency to take hold more rapidly in an environment that has come in contact with Western culture, but also because the administrative and police state apparatus, which had served to keep the government's party in power, had a degree of effectiveness in the rural areas that they no longer had in the cities.

To the proselytizing by the mosques and the activism in the universities that it had used in the beginning, the current now added techniques of "social" militancy following the model of the Communist parties in Europe. The lower-income suburbs were systematically canvassed in order to take advantage of the weaknesses of the State policies. The constitution of the Islamist electorate also benefited from the procrastination of the leftist opposition, which was suffering more than the Islamists from the lack of

Bourguibism to react against, and was in the stages of a profound identity crisis. Discredited as a force for protest (its second-in-command, Dali Jazi, ex-secretary general of the League of Human Rights, had accepted a post as ambassador to Vienna and several other militants had more or less chosen a similar path), the Mouvement des Democrats Socialistes (MDS), the spearhead of the non-Islamist opposition, could not pull in the protest votes, and abandoned this valuable field to the Islamists. The non-Islamist opposition subsequently saw its hopes for the future collapse beyond all expectations. The five small formations at its "center" were only able to pull in a combined total of 5.3 percent of the votes, of which roughly four percent were for the MDS. Even if its charges that the results were not accurate were not a priori unfounded (its leading candidate, Ahmed Mestiri, received only six percent of the votes in his circumscription in Tunis), the MDS had clearly become a victim of the effectiveness of the political opening by the president.

The future (cf. infra) Parti de la Renaissance (En Nahda) had manifestly and finally managed to capture the votes of many people who followed a traditional "orthodox" Islam and who had previously been apolitical (which is to say pro-government). Those who, up until then, had never dared to express their preference beyond the reach of the Destourien Party were, in the nascent pluralistic climate, sensitive to the presence on the Islamist lists of a few names "of the old school" (traditional personalities). These figures had been taken on for the occasion, even when, as was the case with the very conservative Sheikh Laroui, they did not really belong to the neo-Muslim current.(1) This abrupt enlarging of its base created some tension at the heart of the party of Ghannouchi in reinforcing the traditionalist component. The prolonged absence of the titular leader of the movement was even attributed by some observers at one time to the intensity of the debates. In retrospect that assessment appears to have been inaccurate.(2) More paradoxically, the recruitment of imams by the regime

---

(1) The RCD, for its part, had recruited the Imam Abderrahman Khelif at Kairouan. He was the same person who had been imprisoned in 1961 after the riots which followed the authorization given to some Western film makers to shoot a remake of the "Thief of Baghdad" in the mosque of Kairouan.

(2) The origin of this prolonged absence which led to numerous interpretations, has since been explained by the principal people concerned. According to Mokni and Karkar, it followed a decision taken in due form by the Majlis al-Shura, which decided that it would be more opportune for Rached Ghannouchi, who had received an unexpected authorization to leave the country, to remain abroad in order to plead the movement's cause, rather than to risk, in the best of circumstances, being

for its lists of candidates (at Kairouan, the RCD responded to the candidacy of a Sheikh by recruiting another one) as well as the new propensity of ministers to juggle with the suras of the Koran, had the effect of legitimizing the use of the religious dialectic in election campaigns, which unintentionally lent legitimacy to the Islamists.

The Return to Repression

The electroshock of the verdict at the election urns was to put an effective end to the debate over the possibility of extending official recognition to the ITM. On June 8, 1989, the Hizb En Nahda (Party of the Renaissance, the new name adopted by the ITM to satisfy the requirements of a law forbidding references to religion in the names of political parties) was refused a license on the grounds that its leaders were still under sentence by the State Security Court that had convicted them in 1987. In its response, En Nahda evoked the "dangerous disappointment" that this refusal generated. It effectively put an end to the period of goodwill which had resulted in the National Pact with the chief of state.

And, in fact, the relationship between the Islamists and the government had once again changed its tone. Unlimited repression was now directed against the leadership core of the movement. The policies of Bourguiba's successor appeared aimed at returning to the former policy of trying to splinter the leadership in order to give more autonomy to the "moderate" wing of the Movement. The president had gone back to being a general. His politics began to reflect little by little his training, that of a man experienced in the techniques of using police, intelligence services and repression.

On the occasion of the national holiday, July 22, Ben Ali clarified his rejection in terms that have more or less defined his attitude since then.

> It must be emphasized clearly (...) that nothing justifies the constitution of any formation as long as it has not defined the model of society that it has in mind, clarified its position vis-à-vis a certain number of primordial

---

deprived of his freedom of movement and/or arrested if he returned. All the same, from the moment he left the country, Ghannouchi ceased to exercise direct executive control over the movement, even though his moral authority remained intact (Salah Karkar and Habib Mokni, interview cited with the author, Paris, August 1991). "The authorities imposed a dilemma on me," the voluntary exile said himself. "Affrontment or exile. I chose the way of a prolonged stay abroad in order to spare the country from the very predictable consequences of confrontation." (Interview with H. Barrada, cited.)

questions concerning civilization and as long as it has not engaged itself to respect the equality, in rights and duties, of citizens and the principle of tolerance and of freedom of conscience conforming to the dispositions of the National Pact. It must also engage itself in an unequivocal manner to respect the clauses of the law on parties and to work for the safeguard of republican institutions, of national independence and of the invulnerability of the country.

On November 7, he reaffirmed the banning of En Nahda and presented the suppression of the ban (in 1979) on the Islamists having their own publication as a necessary preliminary gesture "intended to permit the movement to show its legalism."(1) The increasingly tough stance with respect to the hard core of the ex-ITM doubled with repeated calls to its components who were thought to be favorable to reconciliation. In this vein, Abdelfatah Mourou accepted a seat on the Islamic Superior Council, the first step that would a few months later, during the affair of Bab Souika (cf. infra), lead him to break with his party. The nervousness of the regime showed itself in a certain ministerial instability. On March 3, 1990, the seventh cabinet shuffle since November 7, 1987, permitted Ben Ali to confide the key security posts in the government to his closest collaborators. This was to become the domain in which his political perceptions tended to concentrate. Abdelhamid Escheikh, the ex-chief-of-staff of the military became minister of interior, and Abdallah Kallel (until then, secretary general at the presidency) became minister of defense. Mohamed Charfi, the man who was at

_____

(1) In fact, En Nahda, whose revue (*Al-Maarifa*) was banned from 1979 on, had long ago made a demand for authorization, which was persistently refused, since the Ministry of Finances refused to deliver the receipt demanded by the Ministry of Interior in order to grant the authorization to publish (Ghannouchi in *Jeune Afrique*, cited). In spite of the accorded authorization, the first issue of *Al-Fajr* was late in appearing. No printer would accept the risk of showing solidarity with a group which the regime presented daily as its public enemy No. 1. Its distribution was also limited to 40,000 copies although the speed with which the press run was sold out created the impression that a much bigger public might be reached. Penal sentences followed. On November 10, the newspaper was confiscated because of a common communique of the MDS of the PCT and of the MUP, calling for a reinforcement of the mobilization against the government. Hamadi Jabali, the director of the publication, was convicted on two occasions. The first, on October 6, 1990, for an article by Rached Ghannouchi criticizing the government, and on January 4,1991, after being accused of having "injured the public service of justice" with an article by Mohammed Nouri calling for the dissolution of precisely the same military court, before which Hamadi Jebali and M. Nouri were to be deferred in virtue of new dispositions (articles 50, 51, 68 and 69 of the new code for the Press) in 1988..! A suspension *sine die* was finally given at the beginning of 1991.

the heart of the regime's ideological counter-offensive, was confirmed in his post.

It is a little after this period that a "plan for the fight against extremist religious currents"(1) was adopted. This program, which identified the evil as "not religion or politics, but the liaison that the Islamists made between the two," created the organizational framework, including a secret coordination between various state apparatuses and the party, for a generalized counter-offensive against the primary political challenger. After having underlined the importance of mobilization for the RCD and listed the obstacles,(2) it launched into the counter-offensive. Significantly, it insisted on the danger of a direct confrontation between the chief of state and the Islamists, which might unintentionally give the current more weight. It also proposed to create or reinforce "forward lines of defense" within organizations such as the League of Human Rights and feminist organizations in the heart of civil society, from whom the government should accept "a certain degree of disagreement." The necessity of favoring cultural action over repression was also emphasized. The arrest on December 18 of members of a small group who had arms and explosives and whose chief, Abdelwahab Mejri, was reputed to have declared to the police that he was "in contact" with En Nahda once again lent credibility to the thesis of an "armed Islamist plot." From that point on, it would constitute the heart of the political line of the regime, and, more regrettably, it is true—the horizon of analysis of most of the Arab and Western media, which contented itself from then on too often with paraphrasing the communiques of the ministry of interior on the question. Not that the language of arms was foreign to all the components of the movement. It is very possible and even likely that clandestine channels of importation—notably from France—had been put into place. But, in the landscape in which political violence was undoubtedly initiated by the regime to protect itself against the foreseeable sanction of the elections, the argument of an armed Islamist plot was largely insufficient to

---

(1) "Plan du RCD pour la lutte contre les courants extrémistes religieux" (May, 1990) in *A l'Heure de Tunis*, No. 2, June 17, 1991. The credibility of this document, even though it was made available by those for whom it was destined, does not appear to have been called into question.

(2) Including "the lack of intellectual brilliance of certain low-level officials who were known for their total and unconditional engagement over a long period, and known to be inclined to resort to methods of action dating from before November 7."

justify the fact that repression was erected as the unique style of the government.

On December 26, 1990, Ben Ali resumed the campaigns of massive arrests that had characterized Bourguiba's regime earlier. After the announcement of the dismantling of a network of Islamists in the army, the police and customs,(1) two hundred of the Movement's cadres were incarcerated. Among them, Ali Laaridh,(2) Zyad Doulati and Zakaria Bou Alleg, whom the authorities considered as representatives of the tendency of hard-liners. Hamadi Jabali and Abdelfatah Mourou, whom the government hoped to separate from the Movement, were significantly left at liberty.

At the beginning of 1991, the regime's skillful handling of the Gulf Crisis, which constituted the political backdrop for this period, created the illusion that the Islamists were losing speed. Several errors by the Islamist leaders, who had difficulty communicating with the base of their membership while it was being subjected to unprecedented repression, helped to accentuate impression and comforted the strategists of the RCD, including Mohamed Charfi (Minister of Culture). The government became convinced that it had to mark decisive points against the Islamists while it had time, or it might not get the chance again. Pages of "proof" on the extent of an armed plot were published daily by the press. The repression intensified with five to six thousand arrests, the same magnitude as in 1987.(3)

FROM THE GULF TO "BAB SOUIKA": THE FALSE HOPES OF THE REGIME

With the war in the Gulf, the Bab Souika affair gave the regime a supplementary justification for attaining a new level in repression, and for the

---

(1) The fear of a military coup led President Ben Ali to multiply the individual investigations of his officers, examining the private lives of his former colleagues in order to determine possible traces of sympathy for the Islamist theme. (In many cases the question was asked whether they had served alcohol during their wedding parties.) The fears, it is true, were not completely unfounded, since the ITM had shown on several occasions that no part of the State was sheltered from its capacity for mobilization.

(2) Who had already been arrested on October 27, and released two days later.

(3) For Abderraouf Boulaabi, member of the leadership in exile, the repression was quantitatively superior in 1987, but qualitatively inferior. The regime had obtained a better knowledge of the militant infrastructure of the movement in the interim.

first time in a long time it marked indisputable points against En Nahda. The wave of repression certainly did not manage to stop the Islamist mobilization. It did, however, force Ghannouchi, whose party's leadership had flown into pieces,(1) to concede several important points to the regime which would, once again, believe too quickly in its victory.

Just about everywhere in the Arab world, the necessity for Islamist leaders to create a hierarchy for their sentiments of solidarity and to chose clearly which of two apparently irreconcilable camps they belonged to, contributed to the acceleration of an internal clarification of their doctrine. While the more traditional part of the Movement remained more or less in line with the solidarity imposed by the initial logic of the conflict, or at least to its formal expression (the aggression against the "good Islamist" regimes of the Gulf by the "atheistic" regime of Iraq's Baathist party) and hesitated at distancing themselves from the coalition camp, the more political component of the current, which would at the same time appear to be the immense majority, quickly developed a different reading of the crisis. They saw it as Western intervention intended to break the only Arab military power capable of changing the current "imbalance" in the rapport of forces in the Middle East. This led them to remain silent concerning their immediate solidarities or interests and to support an Iraqi regime whose legitimacy had not been, a priori, clearly established. This vision was little by little imposed equally on the traditionalist component of the current which came out of the confrontation weakened. The "nationalist" component—which appeared to be the only one to be able to mediate between the militant centers of the current and the potential electoral majorities—saw its credibility strengthened. But, doubts, nevertheless, passed through the Movement's leadership structure, whose reaction to the events had been slow and at times disorganized. "It is correct that, for example, in our newspaper, we did not immediately give the crisis the place that it was due."(2) Why?

> Perhaps because we were in a phase in which we were not looking for an increase in tension and confrontation either with the regime or with the Western environment. We were looking more for internal and external support, for a calm from the repression. (...) The communication at the interior of the movement was considerably slowed afterwards. The Majlis Shura continued to function, but the links were long, not just with the

---

(1) A new leadership was elected on May 29, 1991.

(2) Mokni, interview in Paris, 1991, cited.

exterior, notably Ghannouchi, but also simply at the interior of the country.

As soon as a nuance appeared between the declarations, which the media vigorously solicited, they hastened to put them in front and to amplify them.

The fracture which the regime would finally inflict on the movement would not be born directly from the wavering of the Islamists (1) concerning the war in the Gulf, but from a misstep in the face of repression. On February 17, 1991, one of the bureaus of the RCD, that the Islamist militants knew to be at the heart of the repression, was set on fire. The act was not new. Numerous similar incidents, tolerated if not ordered by the party apparatus, had already taken place at several times during the course of the preceding weeks. But this time, one of the two watchmen was killed, burned to death in the office. There were conflicting reports about whether he had been tied up at the time. The episode gave the signal for an escalation without precedent in the repression directed against En Nahda. For the first time, the regime managed to mark points, a fact which is recognized today by the members of En Nahda in exile, even if they contest, with some credibility, the importance given to the episode by the regime.

"Bab Souika," pleads Nejmeddine Hamrouni,(2)

> that was an act of despair that the State knew how to exploit particularly well. It was in February, 1990, during the Gulf crisis. There were numerous demonstrations. The conjuncture was that of very violent confrontations with the police. In September, there was a death of T. Hamassi, in January, that of Salaheddine Babai, hit with a bullet in full in his forehead at Sfax. That also of Mabrouk al Zemzemi. Or again the paralysis of the lower limbs of Ibrahim Lakhiar, who was hit by a bullet in the back. That was the context. As for the facts themselves, they tried to say that these youths had tied up the guardian and poured gasoline on him in order to kill him. But the investigation found no traces of any rope other than a nylon thread which was perfectly intact and untouched by any trace

(1) For an "internal" reading of the divergence in the Islamist movement, cf. notably Ben Nasr Mohamed, "Al-Harakat al-islamiyya wa azmat al-khalij (Al-Nahda, al-Ikhouane al-muslimine fi masr)," *Al Insane* , Paris, May, 1991, No. 4, page 73. For a critical reading of the position of the Islamists facing the crisis, Fouad Zacharia, *Al-thaqafa al-arabia wa azmat al-khalij*, Cairo, 1991.

(2) The second of the leaders of the UGTE union, which was mostly Islamist (but also contained a small Maoist group), authorized by Ben Ali, and then dissolved again during the course of 1991. N. Hamrouni, a medical student, is currently a refugee in Paris (interview with the author, August, 1991).

of a burn. For us, there was intoxication. The State was able to exploit this image to justify the repression against Abdelfatah Mourou and his companions. If a blow from the state had left a thousand people burned, it would not have had the same effect because it would have become an "act of revolutionary violence," but there, it concerned an act of desperate violence and it could affect the social movement as a whole. The State understood that perfectly and perfectly exploited it. It was one of the rare "intelligent" counter-offensives against the Islamists. To understand the impact of Bab Souika, it is necessary to understand the extraordinary impact of the images. In 1987, we had succeeded in calling a strike of 17 days in the Faculty of Medicine, the place where it is undoubtedly the most difficult to organize a strike. Why? Because there was a photo: that of the autopsy of a student, Othman Ben Mahmoud, killed by the police. The strike was only possible because of this photo which we had obtained at the Charles Nicole Hospital. In the affair of Bab Souika, the government exploited the photo of the corps of the burned RCD militant beyond any limits. If he had been stabbed, the same exploitation would not have been possible. If one showed Abderraouf al Arribi on television with the holes in his knees, his burnt hair and the torn fingernail, what effect would that have on people? But those pictures, you don't see them on television. The effect of Bab Souika was lessened on May 8 by the effect of another series of "pictures" against the State, this time: that of Ahmed Belamri and Adnan Said, dead from a bullet in the chest, that of Gellal dead from a bullet in the head, etc. Even if these images were not shown on television, people knew...

In the meantime, the regime had succeeded in marking some essential points. In the waves of repression after Bab Souika, on March 7, Abdelfatah Mourou, called up by the police, was told to publicly separate himself from his movement or to assume the responsibility for an assassination. He knew the skillful exploitation had succeeded in leaving a deep impression on public opinion.(1) Whatever the reasons, Mourou cracked and agreed to announce a "freeze on his participation" in En Nahda and to publicly criticize the recourse to violence of his party.(2) Some of those still faithful to

---

(1) And the impact of which reverberated in the trial of the accused. On May 22, a first verdict sentenced eight people to forced labor for life and 19 others to prison terms. It became more serious in the appeal of June 27 when five death sentences were given, seven more sentences of life at forced labor and 12 sentences of two to 20 years in prison. The prisoners sentenced to death were executed shortly afterwards, the head of state having refused to grant clemency.

(2) For example, in the columns of *Jeune Afrique,* on June 12, 1991, No. 1589, "Rached Ghannouchi always refused to have dialogue. He chose to resort to violence. But there are other Islamists who want to open a dialogue with the authorities. Me for example."

En Nahda claimed that it was simply the incapacity of an individual with little experience in militant action to undergo a new wave of personal repression.(1) It may have simply been the splintering of a personal strategy which had started much earlier. Mourou was joined shortly afterward by several other influential members of the Majlis Shura: Fadel Beldi, Ben Aissa Demni, Labidi and Bhiri. Little by little, Mourou clarified his difference, and openly opposed the line followed by the external leadership (2) and announced his desire to create his own party.

In the wake of this important victory, the regime conquered the last institutional bastions of the Islamists by force. On March 29, 1991, on the discovery of "chemical products intended for the fabrication of Molotov cocktails," and of "tracts hostile to the government" in the offices of the UGTE and several university dormitories, and despite the conciliatory positions that the UGTE had taken throughout the university year,(3) the student-union headquarters, controlled by the Islamists, was dissolved.(4) Between May 8 and May 12, three students were killed by gunfire during confrontations with the police on the campus of Tunis and two others at Sousse and Kairouan. On May 10, 1991, the opposition in exile published a hard communique which was co-signed by Ghannouchi, Mzali and Ahmed Ben Salah. On May 18, in his speech closing the fifth session of the central

---

(1) The thesis adopted by Mokni and Karkar is that the rupture by Mourou and the other members of the Majlis Shura was essentially the result of police pressure, which they lacked the temperament to resist once again. They allegedly "saved their skin" and justified it afterwards by criticisms against the reputed hard core branch of the movement. Mourou supposedly experienced very intense psychological pressure during an interrogation at the end of which he lost consciousness. Among other things, the police had threatened to rape his wife. The use of torture in Tunisia was affirmed several days later by the death in prison of Laaribi, a member of the Majlis Shura, and confirmed in several reports by Amnesty International.

(2) Which has not yet been legalized. On the other hand, Mourou, in spite of his rallying to the regime, was accused a few months later of having sexual relations on the prayer-carpet of his lawyer office, a videotape giving supposed evidence being sent to local and international medias.

(3) In promising notably to exclude strikes from the means of mobilization for one year.

(4) See also Madhbahat, March 8, *Rab'ii al-jéma'at al-tunissiya* (The M assacre of the 8th of May: Spring of Tunisian University), 202 pages, no publisher mentioned, Paris, 1992.

committee of the RCD, the chief of state solemnly renewed the thesis that a plot was underway in announcing the discovery of a new, organized attempt to overthrow the regime.(1) Four days later, a new wave of arrests hit 400 people, of whom a hundred were military with ranks as high as major. On May 24, an international arrest warrant was issued against ten leaders of En Nahda, including Ghannouchi, Habib Mokni, Salah Karkar and Chammam. On June 15, the provincial governors were called on to "face Islamist sedition" and the army on June 24, was told "to preserve the constitutional institutions."

At the same time, the formations of the non-Islamist opposition, which completely boycotted the partial elections in 1990 and the municipal elections on June 11, 1990,(2) have become the object of a limitless kindness from the authorities, and have not been completely unaware of it. If, since exile, Mzali and Ben Salah, who are closer and closer to Ghannouchi, have not made any concessions, the members of the MDS and with them a good number of intellectuals of the old opposition against Bourguiba have been playing the card of renewing relations more and more openly. On April 16, a financing of 80,000 Tunisian dinars was made to six legal opposition parties and promises were given of access to the official media, participation in economic and social councils and diverse administrative facilities. They are notably associated with the regulation of the university crisis, and Mohamed Moadda, successor of Ahmed Mestiri at the head of the MDS has accepted the leadership of a national commission charged with proposing solutions.

One year after the end of the Gulf crisis, it appears, nevertheless, little by little that the government has once again overestimated the impact of its offensive and, a little like Algiers during the summer of 1991, has mistakenly confused the effect of the disorganization that it was successful in provoking in the leadership with damage to the political credibility of the Movement as a whole.

------

(1) A Stinger missile would have been carried from Afghanistan to Tunis where it was to have been used against Ben Ali's plane.

(2) The eve of the historic Algerian election of June 12, 1990, the Tunisian voters went to the polls in a completely different context: All the opposition parties having boycotted the election, the lists of the RCD obtained 98.20% of the seats in 244 out of 246 municipalities... A few days later, an article by Rached Ghannouchi in the newspaper of En Nahda, stigmatizing this situation, was enough to have the paper siezed.

Repression, neither here nor anywhere else, should therefore not prevent the Movement from acceding sooner or later to the responsiblities that its social support allows it to claim.

Chapter 11

ALGERIA
FROM "ISLAMIC SECULARISM" TO ISLAMISM

Long the least structured and complete, the Islamist movement in Algeria, until the political opening in 1988, remained one of the least known in the Maghreb. This lapse has been largely corrected, and Algeria now places at the head of the list for the entire Arab world. The future followers of the FIS were for a long time restricted to clandestine action and only occasionally became known when their cases appeared in court, and then only partially. The FIS were the only ones (except for the case in Libya) to evolve in a strictly monopolitical environment, since the Algerian FLN succeeded until February, 1989, in preserving the monopoly on political expression gained during the war for independence.

Undoubtedly, that is one of the reasons the Algerian movement remained longer than others in the primary phase of affirmation that is part of the growth of all opposition movements, and showed little embarrassment at using in its rare doctrinal expressions a strongly idealized language of rejection. The exclusive character of the Algerian political formula was a factor in this radicalization. It also played this role in the Berberist movement, which also reacted against the authoritarianism of the regime, but the Berbers could not and still cannot pretend to have a national following. Moreover, their relationship with Islamism is far from being merely paradoxical.(1) The Islamist themes tend, therefore, to have the quasi-monopoly of contestation on the political scene. In the "frontist" logic, which has been its strong point, the unique party, even more clearly than the PSD in Tunisia, had, nevertheless, for a long time managed to integrate an active fundamentalist component that was less perceptible from the exterior. Some of the task of regulation was thus handled inside the regime.

---

(1) Given the evidence, the identity content of a religion (Islam) narrowly linked to Arabness does not have the same resonance for populations where Berber culture is perceived as being the ancestral reference. But, with the absence of what was once secular Arabism for the Christians, Islamism is in many ways for the non-Arabs, the best way out of the ethnic ghetto and as such a better way to access universal politics. It is in this sense that Islamism appears, especially in the Maghreb which has no pre-Islamic Christian minorities, to be the sole "political ideology" in the modern sense of the term, which is to say an ideology capable of transcending the cleavages (notably ethnic ones) which have come out of traditional society.

In a society where the destructive effects of colonization took longer to diminish than elsewhere in the Maghreb, the State, which was in effect the political expression of the National Liberation Army, naturally imposed itself as the sole intermediary on the national scene. Its representatives had earned a particularly strong legitimacy in combat and had for a long time received the political dividends from petroleum revenues, which as in the case of Libya had been particularly profitable. Faced with the omnipresence of the State and the lack of any other credible political opposition parties, the Islamist current had a particularly difficult time emerging as a political alternative.

The Voice of the Ulema

Present from the start of independence, the fundamentalist tendency identified itself first with the Association of Ulemas. In spite of its rallying late (1956) to the FLN, it came out of the War for Independence in a fairly good position, while the Marabouts and Brotherhoods, who had compromised with the colonial authorities dropped out of sight for a long time.

The first years of independence corresponded during the mandate of President Ahmed Ben Bella with a period of clarification, in which the rapport of force between the National Liberation Front and the religious establishment, which is to say, the relative predominance of the first over the second, began to clarify.

Without ever distancing itself from the credo so well expressed by Ben Badis,(1) the regime was forced (and succeeded in doing so for 20 years) to prevent everyone, whether individual or group, from gaining any kind of privileged access to the religious scene.

Gradually through conferences, articles in the press or radio broadcasts, in an atmosphere that was more pluralistic than it had ever been since, the parties exchanged arguments, and the doctrine of the Algerian regime began to take form. With the adoption in 1964 at the first Congress of the FLN that was independent of the Charter of Algiers, it became clear that the voices of the secular left (notably those of Mohamed Harbi and Hocine Zahouane) had carried the day. "Muslim Brothers of Egypt, Marabouts, Talebs and Brotherhoods, but also, in a more surprising manner, Ulema and reformers were put in the same sack and renounced, or soon would be," writes

---

(1) "Islam is my religion. Arabic is my language. Algeria is my country."

Raymond Vallin.(1) The labor unions then denounced the "Ulema of evil"(2) with the same virulence as the rural resurgence of Maraboutism.

At the University, the Islamist current was at that time very marginal. "The battles were discussions with the Marxists," Rachid Benaissa recalls today.

We simply asked for a certificate of Islamic civilization, not theology. Only the civilization, which was available in Western universities. In 1964, I was threatened with a revolver for that. Another day, a motion was voted by a General Assembly of students to demand that social sciences and exact sciences be studied "conforming to the Charter of Algiers and at the recommendation of the secretary general of the party, Ahmed Ben Bella." I rose up and asked whether Ahmed Ben Bella understood the law of gravity.... I left the room covered with blood....(3)

The Association of the Ulema made the mistake of linking itself to the Democratic Union for the Algerian Manifesto (UDMA), whose founder, Ferhat Abbas, had just been imprisoned. And Sheikh Bachir, one of the former presidents did not hesitate in denouncing(4) "the risk of civil war" the country was running because its leaders did not seem to realize that the

---

(1) Raymond Vallin, "Muslim Socialism in Algeria," *L'Afrique et l'Asie Moderne*, No. 65, 1965. "The policy consisted less in striking against one side as much as the other, as it did in letting one of these sides propound a policy proclaimed as serving the entire nation," wrote J. Leca and J.C. Vatin for whom, "in accepting the publication in the official press of articles against Maraboutism and brotherhoods, in pronouncing the dissolution of the Al Qiyam Association and arresting several of its members, the governing team— arbitrating behind juridical and sociological fictions about the state and nation—reduced a collective menace, while at the same time providing security to other groups and individuals." (*L'Algérie politique, institutions et régime*, FNSP, 1975, page 414). See also Jean Claude Vatin in "Crise génératrice, maladie infantile ou faiblesse endogène: le FLN algérien, au fil du temps," in *Elecciones, participation y transiciones politicas en el norte des Africa*, Agencia Espagnola de cooperacion internacional, Madrid, 1991, page 133 to 166.

(2) Title of an article of the organ of the UGTA taking aim at Sheikh Bachir Ibrahimi and taking for itself the title of one of his most celebrated articles which appeared in 1950, where he denounced the role of the Church and of Catholic missionaries in the colonial system.

(3) Interview by the author, cited.

(4) April 16, Reuters News Agency; cited by Raymond Vallin, op. cit.

"(...) theoretical base for their actions should be taken not from foreign doctrines, but from Arabo-Islamic doctrines." The observation earned him several weeks under house arrest. When a compromise was worked out, it was on the terrain of the reformist doctrine of "Islamic socialism,"(1) which saw an aseptic socialism—with all mention of class struggle stripped away—receive the guarantee of an Islam whose egalitarian vocation was emphasized. The religious establishment agreed to authorize this "Islamic secularism," (as Henri Sanson put it) with more or less good will, but throughout the second decade after independence this construction did nothing to improve the relationship between the regime and the religious field.

The misrepresentation of this alliance between Islam and the religion of Lenin was principally relayed by the losers in the first skirmishes, Abdellatif Soltani and Mohamed Sahnoun, who are consequently often considered to have been the founders of the Algerian movement. Soltani published a virulent attack on the socialism of Houari Boumediene, entitled "Mazdaqism is the Source of Socialism" in Morocco in 1974. Formalizing the critique of the regime's Marxism, he compared its doctrine to that of Mazdaq, leader of a sect of Persian heretics during the fifth century A.D.who were reputed to be libertine. In attacking the "destructive principles imported from abroad," Soltani situated himself in the right line of the critical re-reading of Western contributions which was being constructed by the Islamist discourse. Faced with the egalitarianism of the State's discourse, its terrain of expression concentrated particularly on the moral sphere so dear to the fundamentalists. It attacked, above all, the degradation of morals as the supreme evil, of which the consumption of alcohol, the mixing of sexes, the lack of consideration for religion or even the cult of pre-Islamic Roman ruins were the expression. And, certain "suspect voices" (Fadila Mrabet for

---

(1) Of which Henri Sanson and Luc Willy Deheuvels permit a better grasp of the contours. Sanson, "The Algerian model," *Geopolitique, No. 7*, 1984, pages 10-12 and 61-69; Deheuvels, "Islam and Politics in the Contemporary Algerian Discourse, a Study of the Review *Al Asala*," to be published, as well as "Official Islam and Islam of Contestation in the Maghreb: Algeria and the Iranian Revolution" in *Renouvellements of the Arab World*, under the direction of Dominique Chevallier, Paris, Armand Colin, 1987, pp 133 to 152. In *The Islamic Secularism in Algeria*, CNRS, Paris, 1983, Sanson evokes notably this "manifest, double desire not just of the state but of Algerian society to have Islam as a transcendent norm or again as a principle of belonging, of reference, of justification, of finality of a part, and on the other hand, to have secularism as a norm for practical affairs, or as a principle of action, with everything that that carries, appeals to independence, to liberty, to reason, to conscience." (page 8)

her work on Algerian women,(1) Kateb Yassine for his iconoclastic humor (cf infra) were the promoters. Put under house arrest after 1981, Abdellatif Soltani died in April 1984, and his burial at Kouba was the excuse for what can be considered the largest Islamist mobilization of the clandestine period (before 1988).

ABDELLATIF SOLTANI:
A MORALIZING FUNDAMENTALISM

Women

These same harmful effects which were produced by the Mazdak sect in Persian society (licentiousness, usurpation, injustice, etc...) are reproduced by socialism and Communism in the countries which are afflicted by them. Injustice and debauchery in all forms are common there. Liberties which call on the good and fight against evil are smothered there, while those who want to do evil or aid it are given complete freedom. Abandoned children are legion, the result of this promiscuity between the sexes instituted under the cover of progressivism, of liberation and emancipation, etc... King Choroes I the Great (Sassanid Emperor of the fourteenth century before Jesus Christ) summed up the results: "The most vile species mixed with the most honorable elements. The low people, who did not have the audacity to reveal themselves before, had access to the most precious women...." [The same today], women go out in the streets with the finery that has been given them, to meet whoever seems good to them, to speak with whom they want, to work in offices or elsewhere. But it is there that the evil and corruption of society hides. It is not just the wives and daughters of rich people and ulema and men of religion who have begun working in business and offices, who thanks to that which God has given to their fathers and husbands have no reason to work, if it is not for love of gain, financial or other; and the woman or the young girl who does not work in an office has become like death. Honor, spirit of chivalry, chastity, modesty, all that has vanished, and the commandments belong to God in the first and last resort.(.../...)

Several newspapers have given to those who defend Islam and its morality a qualification—*Tartuffe*, in reference to a play by Moliére, which does not correspond to reality. The reason for it is that in my Friday sermon on November 5, 1965, I evoked the military parade organized in Algiers on November 1 in commemoration of the revolution of 1954. In this parade, which we saw on television, we had not rejected the force of our army (...). What we denounced, in contrast, and what we insist not be produced again, is that young women dressed in a scandalous fashion were inserted into the middle of the parade.

(1) *La Femme Algérienne*, Paris, Maspéro, 1964.

251

Only a small part of their bodies were covered. In effect, the young woman who represented each of these countries and appeared in front of the troops, wore a miniskirt! That cannot be accepted or allowed to pass in silence. Who should be blamed for it? The one who denounces the inadmissible? No, all the blame should go before any other consideration to the one who brought that young woman here to throw her into this enormous army of young men and in front of the spectators. Her father, who accepted the showing of the body of his daughter and letting her march nearly nude in front of the spectators and cameramen working for foreign television, is just as much to blame (...) The truth is that certain Muslim governments, because of the lack of a sufficient Islamic religious education, are not up to the level of their Umma.

Fadila Mrabet, Kateb Yassine, and the Rocket of Islam

In the group (of those who accuse the ulemas of fanaticism), there is notably a woman and a man who both pretend to be Algerians. The woman blackened a paper a bit with some French and called that a book (*The Algerian Woman*), which she filled with enormous lies and small talk empty of any sense of Islam and Islamic morality. Her intention is to call on the Algerian woman to reject an Islam which is fanatical and archaic because it allows promiscuity between sexes no more than it allows that a woman go where she wants without her tutor (*ouali*) keeping her from it, nor all sorts of other diabolical desires. But it becomes clear from the ideas that she propagates that she is a creature of Marxism, in the service of atheistic pretensions (...) and the name that she uses (Fadila Mrabet) is a borrowed name. As for the man, he is a writer, a novelist who has the habit of decorating his writing with his fantasies and his falsifications in order to attract more readers. But in reality, he is far from understanding Islam. He wrote in a weekly printed and published in Algeria, but French in its language and ideas. It rarely writes of religious events and then only to speak of its disdain for them. It has become insupportable to this writer to see minarets raised over mosques from which the voice of the muezzin calls those who believe in their God to prayer (...) The true believer, hearing the muezzin, is filled with humility, orders his thoughts which have wandered in the labyrinth of the matter of human life, remembers his Lord with deference and respect and makes himself accomplish that which has been imposed on him in his religion. This writer, expressing the hatred that the marks of Islam inspire in him, would like the minarets to be destroyed and leveled until no trace of them remains, and so that he won't have to suffer from seeing them, like the devil suffers when he hears the voice of the muezzins, and since they are the mark of Islam and there is no Islam in him. This writer calls himself Kateb Yacine and this weekly is called *Algérie Actualité*. There appeared an article in it entitled "the Dogs of Douar" (Dogs of the camps) (...) Who are these dogs of Douar in his eyes? They are the muezzin who call the faithful to accomplish the duty of prayer (...). Added to this ironic headline are a minaret and two American rockets in the process of taking off from their launch pads. The caption says concerning the minaret: "A rocket that does not take off." The review that has this headline and these photos is sold in Algeria under the eyes of the authorities. It has not been banned or confiscated (...) the way foreign magazines containing photographs full of impudence and license have (...) For as such they don't touch politics and they meet no objections from the government, even if they mock religion and the beliefs of the Umma. To this atheistic writer and to the many like him, we say: that the minaret is the sign of the mosque and that in Islam is the place where God the creator is adored, but also a place of education, of culture, of teaching, but he undoubtedly ignores all that. How many great men have left the mosque, who illuminated the path of those who walked through the labyrinths of life, who guided them to the safeguard and salvation, such as Emir Abdelkader, the Sheikh Abdelhamid Benhadis and others, whose equal the universities have not been able to produce....(...) The rocket of Islam, this minaret which you mock has destroyed the palaces of the unjust and overthrown the thrones of gigantic tyrants... if only you knew... But where would you have learned, you who have been nursed on the milk of the adversaries of Islam?(1)

Another expression of the fundamentalist current, the Al Qiyam (values) Association has also sought to take advantage of the dividends of the religious elements of the national movement by restraining the operation of the secular parts of the FLN program. Given official stature at its constitution in 1964, the association became known through a series of conferences and by the publication of its moralizing "Review of Muslim Education" (Majallat al Ta'dhib al Islami). A cultural association, it presented itself as the instrument for rehabilitating Muslim values, which in Algeria had been the victim of the double onslaught of "Colonialism and of decadence." If it remained within the narrow frame of "Conversionists," to use the terminology of Bruno Etienne,(2) the doctrinal anchor of its members already placed it clearly in the Islamist movement. Interviewed in 1964 by the review, *Confluent*, its president, El Hachemi Tijani, declared that he was between the reformist line of the Salafis Al Afghani and Abduh, but also identified with the thought of the Lebanese, Chakib Arslan as well as

---

(1) *Al-Mazdaqia hia asl al-ichtirakia* (Masdaqia is the base of socialism), Morocco, 1975, page 33.

(2) *L'Islamisme Radical*, op. cit. Cf also "L'Islamisme au Machreq," *Les Temps Modernes*, Gallimard, March, 1988.

with Al Banna, Sayyid Qutb, Al-Ghazali and with "certain theories" coming from Pakistan.(1)

To differentiate themselves from the classic ulemas, the members of Al Qiyam put in evidence their knowledge of the French language and its values "other than Islam," which is to say Western values, thus participating in the Islamist approach in the sense in which Roy points out "they (Islamists) integrated Western thought to be in a better position to criticize it, while the ulemas purely and simply ignored it."(2) The association, after a long series of verbal skirmishes with the secular left in the unions and universities, suffered a first defeat in 1964 with the eviction of its president from the post of secretary general of the University of Algiers. Soon after, it was banned on September 22, 1966, notably for having sent Nasser a message protesting the hanging of Sayyid Qutb. It was dissolved on March 17, 1970. Close collaborators of Ahmed Ben Bella (Khider, A. Mahsas, Safi Boudissa and M.S. Nekkache)(3) were associated with it. And, another indication of its representation of the tendency at the interior of the State apparatus, the speech of the minister of religious affairs, Mouloud Kassim, never clearly contradicted the line of the banned association. At the same period a similar association, which was hardly known to the outside, Djounouds of Allah,(4) was also dismantled. In March, 1971, the government backed the launching of a review, *Al Asala*, which from then on expressed the government point of view on religious matters. Hailed from its creation by the head of state as one of the cultural elements in his revolutionary trilogy (which also refers to a triple revolution: agrarian, industrial and cultural), *Al Asala* became simultaneously the expression of consensus at the heart of the regime. In a manner that was more ambivalent, it also became the point of anchor for a fundamentalist current, which never completely abandoned its pretentions and to which the head of state made important concessions from time to time, especially concerning Arabization. "One could ask," remarks Deheuvels, "if the review was not simply an instrument of Algerian politics, or if in virtue of a certain autonomy, it hadn't managed to constitute a pole of pressure trying to maintain or accentuate its

---

(1) Which is to say Abou Ala al-Mawdudi.

(2) Op. cit.

(3) Revue *Sou'al* (Questions), No. 5, cited.

(4) Reported by Leca and Vatin, op. cit.

Islamic character."(1) The way to authenticity proposed by *Al Asala* to reestablish a link with past grandeur involved two types of intervention: an exhaustive Arabization based on the sole classical language (any reevaluation of dialectical languages being "rejected as a sin, which would consecrate the isolation of Algeria and a rupture with the past and the Arabo-Islamic patrimony") and a "campaign for moral rearmament of the population by a return to the prescriptions of worship." If it never went explicitly against the government political line (its articles evoking the idea of political fusion of the Arab or Muslim world, were signed by foreign writers), the themes that were developed nevertheless constituted the expression of a well-tempered fundamentalism which Deheuvels(2) emphasized was inscribed in the line of the Badisien reformers.

The Itineraries of Mobilization

It is first of all in the statutes on religious education, whose reestablishment by Ben Bella was contributed to by the Al Qiyam association, that the representatives of the then-diffused current managed to find their first mobilizing themes. The nationalizations of the "Agrarian Revolution" launched by the regime in November, 1971, offered a second terrain for recruitment. The language of religion was used this time to discredit the egalitarianism in the land distribution of Boumediene. Rumors circulated that a prayer made on nationalized land was not valid, and the civil and religious authorities had to be called in to refute these extremely militant religious interpretations. That included the police and justices, who imprisoned the first activists of the new generation (including Mafoudh Nahnah, who would emerge into the light during the riots of 1988). "It should be specified that no religious text prevents application of the Agrarian Revolution," the head of state reminded everyone in 1972. Significantly, the lands which the authorities confiscated from the Zaouias of Oran (and notably the Alaouia of Mostaganem) were not taken over by anyone. No one wanted to run the risk of opposing institutions, which despite (or because of) the secularizing choices of the regime had conserved an astonishing vitality.

"We said in fact," explains Doudi Abdelhadi, one of the collaborators of Mustapha Bouyali (cf. infra), "that this was only a revolution for agriculture, and that it could not in any way bring happiness to the Algerian

---

(1) Deheuvels, op. cit.

(2) Idem.

people by itself. For that we have a religion which takes care of everything, and which shows everything. It leaves nothing to chance, neither that which is small nor that which is grand."(1)

At the heart of the student movement, the agrarian policy was less than was previously thought a line of demarcation for the Islamist current. "To the contrary," says Rachid Benaissa, who thought that the social origin of the first Islamists ought to have incited them, even more than their Francophone colleagues from wealthier backgrounds, to identify with the social objectives of Boumedienism.

> To the contrary(...) We always participated. One of our slogans was: "With the agrarian revolution and against Communism." We chanted that to the tune of an old song that was very well known, which used to raise a ruckus when we traveled in the same bus. We never supported that criticism and we were never called into question on it. We always said that the criticism of the Agrarian Revolution should be a technical one, to criticize its management, and that above all one should not make a dogma out of it. But we never had an attitude of class. On the contrary, we said that we could not be against the distribution of land because we could only benefit from it. Most of us were from peasant origins. We were even more proletarian, in the end, not even proletarian, but frankly without anything.

[On the fringes of this turbulence in the national life, the action of Malek Bennabi, director of higher education, writer and recognized philosopher, constitutes the principle reference for the majority of the militants of the period.]

> Our grandmaster was Bennabi. He had a French education, and it was he who showed me that science should not confuse itself with religion. He had created a center which he called the Center for Cultural Orientation. We held what we called "seances of reflection" there. Bennabi said that he wanted to put on the front of his house: "No one should enter here if he is not an engineer." We did not want to create a doctrine that knowledge depends on faith. We wanted to, as Iqbal says, to reconstruct not just religious thought, but the global thinking of the Muslim. Bennabi was the enlightener, but those who came to him were already ripe and ready. He helped us. We knew, for example, that the solution to the problem of the Islamic world did not come from (the use) of certain political categories, and that it was not within the framework of the national state that we were going to resolve the problem. We knew that the solution was not in an economic approach,

---

(1) Interview with the author, cited.

but we realized that our framework was that of civilization, the cultural framework. (...) and twenty years after, we have the proof that it is the only true support... All the notions of cultural identity are being rediscovered twenty years after having obscured and denied them.(1)

It is on the more explicit terrain of the linguistic quarrel that the fundamentalism of contestation succeeded little by little in making its penetration. The first Islamist student mobilizations were not limited to the Arabaphone movement which in the sixties was only in an embryonic state. "The process started with the Francophones," Ben Aissa insists today.

The four students who in 1967 opened a mosque at university were Francophone. For several years the people listening to us were recruited from the French speakers, and I made my sermons in French. It is also very revealing of this quest for identity. The Arab-speakers only came later. For four or five years, the majority of the faithful were students from the faculties of science, which is to say the Francophones. On the other hand, the other faculties were completely de-Islamicized. It is necessary to understand that at that time, the Arab press in Algeria was more violently anti-Islamic than the Francophone Moujahid.(2)

Frustrated and without professional openings corresponding to an education, which in any case had been devalued by the voluntarism of the policy of Arabization, the students who had followed Arabophone studies little by little identified themselves with the demands for a revaluing of the Arabo-Muslim base, if only because these matched their most immediate professional preoccupations. After entering en masse in the Arabophone curicula which opened without any real planning at the beginning of the seventies, they realized in the second half of the decade, but a little late, that the most lucrative education (notably medicine) was still largely Francophone and was likely to remain beyond their reach. In an employment market which was beginning to show the first signs of saturation, the products of the plethora of literary and law studies were thus the first to form and then enlarge the ranks of the under-employed intellectuals, the category which is in the long term the most dangerous for the stability of a regime. The ultimate terrain for mobilization, which was to permit the true crystallization of the Islamist current, was that of the codification of the personal statute, or the

---

(1) Interview with author, cited.

(2) Idem.

257

laws governing civil life, an area that, contrary to its Tunisian neighbor, the regime had hesitated to broach immediately after the independence. Reluctant to confirm certain latent dispositions of Muslim law (notably polygamy), which a judge could still recognize in referring to custom, the government was still hesitant about making an open rupture with the past. A veritable sea serpent in the legislature for the first twenty-five years after independence, the discussion of the personal statute provided student groups with an excuse for their most violent confrontations. The University of Constantine was the setting in the spring of 1975 for one of them.

During a now-historic Seminar on Family Law, (Qanoun Ahkam al Chakhsia), the cleavage between Francophones close to the Party of the Socialist Avant Garde (PAGS, descended from the Communist Party) and favorable "to the rights of women" and Arabophones demanding the scrupulous respect for Muslim law, was expressed spectacularly. Before a version of the compromise (which still maintained the civil minority of women)(1) could be elaborated in 1984, its adoption was delayed several times, notably after a demonstration of women before the National Popular Assembly, with several heroines of the War of Liberation participating. Those favoring a certain distance from the principles of Muslim law had a chance to examine their ranks after having tried to mobilize the population with petitions. They were mostly from 30-50 years old, almost no youths, and they were above all very few in number.

From Sultani to Bouyali

These were no longer lessons on how to wash one's hands, or to pray or fast. They had become lessons on how it might become possible to live in an Islamic state.(2)

---

(1) In the 1984 legislation, the unequal treatment of women became apparent through the following articles: No. 7, which fixed different ages for marriage according to sex (21 for men and 18 for women); No. 8, which permitted polygamy within the limits fixed by the Koran (four wives); No. 11, "the conclusion of the marriage for the woman is incumbent on her matrimonial tutor who is either her father or one of her close relatives." Article 31 proscribed marriage between a Muslim and non-Muslim. Book II codified a certain number of inequalities in matters of succession. Article 222 gave Sharia law authority over all questions not refered to in the text of the law.

(2) Doudi Abdelhadi, interview with the author, cited.

The passage from protest fundamentalism to Islamism, which is to say the political entry of the protesters against the cultural model promoted by the regime, manifested itself explicitly only at the end of the 1970s. At the beginning of the 1980s, Western embassies and media began to receive a variety of Islamist proclamations, demands and programs intended to break the silence in the media in which the regional government authorities had long preferred to enclose their opponents. The signature of a group, Nidha al Islam, appeared on certain tracts distributed by the Movement for Democracy in Algeria of former president Ben Bella. Starting in 1982, a more credible, "Islamist Movement in Algeria" crossed the threshold of media recognition, although it accomplished that largely because of its dismantlement by the police.

From the first confrontations to a religious establishment anxious to counter its own political marginalization and to stand in opposition to the secularizing socialism of Houari Boumediene, the transition was slow. Abdellatif Soltani, (who had himself come from the cadre of the "conversionists") was no less overwhelmed, and, as was the case with the greater part of the Moroccan and Tunisian Ulema, was partially marginalized by the growing wave of young militants, sometimes more radical, but also intellectually more demanding.

"You greatly magnify the importance of Al Qiyam," Ben Aissa charges today.

> In fact, everything resulted from its being banned. Soltani and Sahnoun were two of the humblest preachers. No one would have talked about them if Algeria had been free. It was the government which made heroes out of them. Who has read *Le Mazdaqisme*? At the time there may have been some readers, but it was quickly put aside.(1)

Among the multiple sensibilities of a diffused and disorganized current, between "Salafists" and "brothers," a recentering gradually shifted towards the latter, who were more political and closer to the oriental experience of the Muslim Brothers, which is to say ready for explicit passage to political action but also ready to use more radical methods than their elders. In contrast to the cases of Tunisia and Morocco, the documentary materials are still partly missing that might help to illustrate the mechanism of this transition in detail and to appreciate its size. But, starting in 1978, the assortment of Algerian movements, while continuing to diversify themselves,

---

(1) Interview with the author, cited.

began to be both politicized and radicalized, and they made a few attempts at creating a structure. The evolution in the method of action, the most exposed part of the process, is the least difficult to observe. Several accounts make it possible to reconstitute the principle internal stages of this slow transformation.

The Impulses of Ben Bella

Released on July 4, 1979, and in voluntary exile since 1980, the first Algerian president, Ahmed Ben Bella, has run the "Movement for Democracy in Algeria" since May 29, 1984. The movement, which for a time at least, received financial support from Libya, propounded several Islamist themes, admittedly with varying degrees of credibility. In the name of its declared vocation of federating the oppositions, the monthly *Al Badil* diffused tracts and appeals to those who considered themselves part of the Islamist scene. After *Al Badil* was banned in January 1987, a number of successors stepped into the breach. They included *Alternative démocratique, Le Changement, November,* and *Libre Algérie,* the publication of the former vice-president of the GPRA, Ait Ahmed, who had founded the Front des Forces Socialistes in 1963. Ait Ahmed had made a tactical accord with the MDA in 1985.

Texts criticizing the regime's drift towards the West circulated through Algeria several times. They were signed by a group calling itself "Nidha al Islam" (the call of Islam). Obligingly reproduced by the MDA's publication without being claimed by any specific group, it seems likely that they were instruments of an attempt by Ben Bella to secure a foothold in the Islamist scene. In any case, the extreme reserve shown in the texts with respect to the first chief of independent Algeria and the ideological approach, which hardly deviates from Ben Bella's line, lead one to believe that that is so.

The MDA often broached certain themes of the Islamists. A tract distributed on May 25, 1985, denounced the "Journey of Surrender" which president Chadli Benjedid had just made to Washington, and which, according to the authors, was the "logical conclusion of a process set in motion by the military coup d'etat of June 19, and followed with less discretion since the death of Boumediene," which had the effect of dispatching Algeria to "rejoin the Egypt of the late Anwar Sadat."

The Lessons of Bait al-Arqam.

It was in 1978 that the first internal expressions of the Islamist current began to appear in the mosques of certain urban centers (Algiers, Oran, Sidi Bel Abbes, Laghouat, etc.). As in the case of Tunis eight years earlier, they took the form of small groups organized for reflection and mobilization and based in mosques where they escaped the direct control of the minister for religious affairs.

> These were no longer lessons dealing with how to pray or perform a fast and all that. No, these were lessons at a high level in which we explained, or we searched for a method by which we could live in an Islamic state... And we also touched on the problems which the Algerian nation was confronting. We spoke about everything. Of all the situations, the economy, of all the aspects of life,

says Doudi Mohamed Abdelhadi,[1] who had a privileged position to witness the birth of the Bouyali group, which he feels he helped inspire on the doctrinal level.

Born in Tunisia (May 10, 1954, at Redayef), and better known under the name of Abdelhadi, the future husband of one of the sisters of Mustapha Bouyali was in fact originally from the village of Guemar, near El Oued. He received his secondary education in Egypt, where he remained until 1975, when he returned to Algeria to round off his education as an Imam and began to militate in Islamist circles of the capital before leaving for France in 1980.

> The first important meeting took place at the beginning of 1979 in the mosque of El Achour. It was attended by a considerable number of the members of the family of preachers (*Ahl al-dou'at*) who had come from both the capital and from numerous cities in the country, from Bel Abbes as well as Djelfa, Hassi Bah Bah and Medea. The objective was to find a form for union. This division of preachers, their dissensions, reverberated against all the members of the group and on the entire base of believers. In fact, each one had his own tendency. One would call himself a Salafi, another one would be for the Muslim Brothers. Another might be for the Jamaat Tabligh, and another for the Jamaat at-Tala'i (the Avant-garde) and still another might be a Sufi. And yet Islam had to deal with all that. It calls for unity; it is unity. In 1975, when I returned from Egypt, I found a situation which was very fixed; there was immobility and passivity. No one bothered with religion.

---

(1) Interview with the author, cited.

Starting in 1976 and 1977, there started to be some Islamic activity in the mosques in general, and in the Baït al-Arqam mosque, where Mohamed Sahnoun and Sheikh Abdellatif Soltani preached, in particular... This beginning was made possible by the problems which confronted society... It was necessary to find a solution, a way out... so there was this start of activity at the Beït al-Arqam, but also in those mosques which called themselves "free mosques," which meant that they were not dependent on the ministry of religious affairs and did not submit to anyone.

In these free mosques, the Da'wa was a free Da'wa, a da'wa where one could talk about everything that was happening in the country, all the truths. And since people always go to where the truth is being spoken, the mosque began to develop. In 1978, the action began to be a true start to structuring. I myself began to give courses and conferences in the mosque of Baït al-Arqam, then I went over to the Ben Achour mosque. Thanks to God, Muslims came from both the capital and elsewhere, from Blida, Medea, or even Hassi Bah Bah, Djelfa or El Asnam.... So little by little the work began, developed gradually. But this action was not organized. There was no solidarity, unity, cooperation nor any coordination between preachers to reach the objectives that we wanted to attain. And that has remained true to our time. There is not a movement represented by an organization, which has a Morchid al-Am (guide), like the movements that exist in Tunisia, Syria, Iraq or in Egypt. Yes, certainly, there is a group of intellectuals, but Algeria's problem is that the preachers, at least the great majority of them, are not up to the level that is required. Let's take the example of Sahnoun, or of Sheikh Abdellatif Soltani, or of Abbasi Madani... and others... which you can count on the fingers of one hand.... if one looks closely, even they do not have the level that is required. They do not have the level of Sayid Qutb or of Sheikh Ghazali, for example, or of Hassan Al Banna, etc. Their culture is limited. Most of them have never left the country. They don't know what is happening in the Islamic world. They do not know what is happening outside of their own world (*kharij al watan*). So their culture is limited: by a lack of books, by a lack of magazines that one can find in France or in America, but which are not found in the country. There are no true thinkers. The University of Constantine? It is only open one year out of two. It hasn't even had the time to give its fruit.

Two years after these first efforts at structuring, there were a few confrontations with the authorities, and four years after that the first violent skirmishes took place. It is no surprise that with the beginning of the 1980's and Khomeini's victory, the mobilization seemed to have grown sufficiently to allow the men who were then leaders, A. Soltani, A. Sahnoun and a student in educational sciences named Abbasi (whose first name was Madani), to risk here and there a few skirmishes with the authorities. Until then, relations with the authorities had maintained a nearly peaceful coexistence. Certainly, some overly violent criticisms against the Agrarian Revolution had earned some preachers (including Abdelhadi, who taught in the region of Djelfa, and a certain Mahfoud Nanah) a few days or even several months imprisonment. But especially after the death of Boumediene, the number-one obstacle remained the Marxist enclaves of the PAGS (the Party of the Socialist Avant Garde), encouraged by the preceding regime. And there, thus, followed nearly four troubled years of diverse symptomatic incidents before President Benjedid's regime passed from suspicion to repression concerning the Islamist activists. On March 19, 1981, at El Oued, a store selling alcohol was destroyed. A few months later, on September 28, the first death of a man occurred at Laghouat. To protest against the arrest of one of them (Said Sayah, a science professor, presented as their chief), about 30 people seized control of a mosque from which they launched appeals for a holy war against the regime. One of the policemen who tried to dislodge them was killed.

In November, 1982, the second major strike by Arabic speaking students, in which Madani played a key role, led to violent incidents inside the walls of the University of Algiers. On November 2, on the campus of Ben Aknoun, Fethallah Lassouli, a 28-year old former sailor, knifed Kamel Amzal, an student from Algiers, during a series of confrontations between "progressives" (who generally belonged to the French speaking sections) and the Islamist "M.B." (Muslim Brothers).

The clashes led to repression (29 arrests and the closing of the prayer areas in the university) that the Islamist movement considered to be very one-sided. A public prayer, held ten days later, was attended by 5,000 people in the courtyard of the central campus at Algiers. A petition drafted by the old Sheikh Ahmed Sahnoun and Abbasi Madani calling for a more intransigent Arabization, including a ban on alcohol and a personal code closer to Sharia Law as well as other demands, was sent to the government. During the following days, other tracts were distributed calling notably for the constitution of an Islamic state in Algeria.

> After my departure from Algeria, they wanted to make a move, to breakout, they sent petitions to demand that the government return to Islam and what God had commanded, or more precisely, the banning of what he forbade: wine, luxury and pleasure. For my part, I was opposed to it, [Abdelhadi says today.] It was not a good method. For we were still in a state of weakness. It's impossible for an unarmed man to face his enemy. It is useless to be in a hurry, for whoever is in a hurry to have something ahead of time risks losing it. It is necessary to train first. Only then, is it possible to make a move, a demonstration, to

show oneself in public, to say everything out loud, all the principles to which we adhere. But for the moment, we are small, we are not yet armed, for the youth are not yet trained. They come out of the mosque after the sermon and only repeat that "Allah is great." That is not the task. The task is to succeed in mobilizing the youth and to make it so that when we say, "In the name of God...." they will begin. There, we will have accomplished our task and we will be able to continue. It all has to be organized. There has to be a beginning and an end for everything. You have to know where you start and where you are going. The prophet organized his troops before going into battle.. But to throw oneself into the street just like that without accomplishing anything....never! But that is what we observed during the meeting of Ahmed Sahnoun and Abbasi Madani at the central faculty of Algiers. Many believers met there but ... to do what? And in the end all that ended in prisons. They arrested this one, sentenced that one, put so many others under house arrest, and all that discouraged the movement. If you want to get started, you have to prepare, to know what you want to do and with whom.(1)

The regime's reaction began to take form. On November 27, Cherif Messaadia threatened "those who use Islam as a tribune to sow doubt on what the masses have gained and to undermine the dignity of those people (manipulated by) imperialism who seek to keep us busy with marginal struggles by exploiting the contradictions in our society."(2) Ahmed Sahnoun Abdellatif Soltani and Madani Abbasi were arrested. Sahnoun, 73, and Soltani, 82, were released eight days later and put under house arrest, but Abbassi remained in prison. On December 3, the head of state, who until then had remained outside the debate, personally implicated himself by announcing to the nation's cadres that he would "not hesitate to take any measure necessary to the defense of the country and the unity of the nation." It is in this context that the announcement was made on December 11 of the dismantling of an organization "which was getting ready to organize armed actions under cover of sectarian and deviant interpretations of Islamic values." On December 11, other members of the same group, which gradually came to be known as the Bouyali, opened fire and killed a policeman while trying to escape a police check. These last confrontations and the discovery of explosives and weapons at the homes of certain fugitives accelerated the change in attitude of the regime. During the month of December, it carried

(1) Idem.

(2) Quoted by F.B. and Hubert Michel in "Chronique politique Algérie," *Annuaire de l'Afrique du Nord,* 1982, Paris, Editions du CNRS, 1984.

out a wave of arrests, and in doing so raised the veil which until then had masked the existence of the Islamist current and led the Bouyali group to finally cross the barrier of anonymity and become known in the media. One of the militants arrested was Ali Belhaj.

Mustapha Bouyali and the "Algerian Islamist Movement"

In 1983, in April, 1985, then for the second time, two years later, in June, 1987, the appearance in front of the State Security Court of 134 and then 202 suspected members of this group, which seemed to have chosen armed action, allowed the movement to partially come out of the shadows (especially with the publication of extracts of a dossier of accusations by the Benbellists of the MDA). The Algerian Islamist Movement, which the friends of Mustapha Bouyali claimed to belong to, was the result of the fusion in 1982 of several small groups that had sprung up in different locations in Algeria. It seemed to have had an incubation period of about three years under the form of a "Group for the combat for the prohibition of the illicit," implanted in Algiers in the mosques of the El Achour and Notre Dame d'Afrique quarters. The group's principle action was to try to coordinate, if not unify, the efforts of different preachers in the country. Veiled criticisms were slipped into Friday sermons. Neo-fundamentalists were dispatched progressively to clandestine meetings in the homes of the most faithful followers, and then to meetings at the national level.

"The appearance of Bouyali on the scene of action, happened suddenly in 1978 in the El Achour Mosque, where I was teaching," Abdelhadi explains.

> Bouyali himself did not have the required level either in his knowledge of the Book nor in that of the Sunna. Bouyali had faith. It is his faith which permitted him to become conscious of the situation in which the country was living. Then the state wanted to kill him, to assassinate him. Even though he was a former Moujahid. And he was known privately and publicly for his uprightness, his faith, his fidelity to his country as well as his religion. And afterwards, he had no choice. It was kill or be killed. He was forced to defend himself, to strike back blow for blow. That is why this group was born. In reality, it was the same as the one at the El-Achour mosque which was created thanks to us and where Mustapha Bouyali came to pray and hear my lessons. Up until this stage, I was thus their professor. Bouyali himself recognized all the time in his speeches that he did not have the required level to exercise his responsibilities. "I am ready," he said all the time, "to give up my place to anyone who says he is more competent."

During the month of July, 1982, three meetings gave the movement a first structure. The "Group of Defense against the Illicit" constituted itself into the "Islamist Movement of Algeria," and Mustapha Bouyali was elected Emir. A former resistance fighter, father of seven children, a well-behaved employee of the National Electric Power Company, a former candidate as deputy, Bouyali, who knew that his life was threatened, entered (in the month of April) into the life of clandestinity after one of his brothers was assassinated by the police. He largely followed the itinerary (even if the personalities were very different) of Sayid Qutb.

For Rachid Benaissa, as for the observers outside of the Islamist movement:

> Bouyali is a banal case which is more the result of police adminis-tration than anything else. They killed his brother.... but he never represented anything. It is only the episode of armed confrontation which turned him into a symbol. That he pulled the rest of the world after him is natural. With us, this type of thing might have been disarmed by arresting the guilty and giving justice to the victim. Instead of that, they covered up the affair. But all that is very marginal in the general process of re-Islamicization. He crystallized all the discontent. Everyone dreamed of escaping from a regime which was stifling... There were many people who were dissatisfied and... impatient for action. That is not what was lacking. For me, it was the case of the revolt of a man whose brother has been killed. This kind of thing could have been defused by arresting the guilty party and rendering justice to the victim. Instead, they covered up the affair. But all that is very peripheral in the process of re-Islamicization.(1)

A first division of tasks took place among the new recruits. The leader-ship core was restructured in several commissions, and a program for action was decided upon, which included operations intended to procure arms and funds as well as influence public opinion and to put pressure on the authori-ties with violence. When the first wave of arrests took place, the members of the MIA got ready to assassinate the prime minister whose car was to be immobilized on December 9, 1982, by a tree on the road of Chrea, which he took to return home. At least this was the account given in documents which Ben Bella's MDA presented several months later, as well as in the charges made by the Security Court. Cherif Messaadia, the second in com-mand of the FLN, was also to be kidnapped.

---

(1) Interview with the author, cited.

On the January 17 and 24, 1982, new arrests struck at the command cell and a militant was killed. Despite the first wave of arrests, while the current as a whole tried to keep a low profile, the members of Jihad Ferhat Mehenni continued to escape the police and managed to put together an impressive stockpile of equipment. After the group carried out a series of actions ranging from the theft of the payroll of a public industrial company to an attack against the police school at Souma, during which a police officer was killed, the police managed to seize 160 kg of TNT, machine guns and other weapons.

From 1982 to February, 1987, with help from a part of the population of the region where he had come from (Larba, near Algiers), Bouyali successfully defied the authorities by appearing regularly in public in certain Algerian mosques. On November 1, 1985, the police carried out an assault against the Douar of Sidi Abbad, in the south of Tessala al Merja, and killed two suspected members of the group.(1) During one of the many chases, an error in coordination led to the death of a dozen police who came under fire from a helicopter belonging to the gendarmerie. Mustapha Bouyali fell on February 3, 1987, in an ambush in the company of three of his close collaborators, including Maamar Touati and Abdessalam Aghrib. Before dying, he managed to kill with his own hand the chauffeur, who had almost certainly betrayed them. Three other members of the group (Boulenouar Taibi, Mustapha Hamza and Abdelaziz Lehoudj) were taken prisoner.

The information, which became available concerning the party of the Islamist trend for whom Bouyali had for a certain time become the expression, confirmed that the Algerian movement at least in the beginning did not represent the most modernist fringe of the movement. The objectives of the group included the bombing of the Union of Algerian Women, the Hotel Aurassi, the Brasserie of Al Harrach and all of the statues and monuments in the capital. While denouncing the Marxism and atheism of the regime, the communiques of the ITM demanded the departure of French cooperants and, in a manner that was more surprising, the return of all the emigrants from the Maghreb. By this approach, the Bouyali brand of Islamists demonstrated an attitude that clearly distinguished them from the ITM in Tunisia and the Jemaa of Abdessalam Yassine, whose position on immigration was diametrically opposed to them.

In fact, the Bouyali group appears today more as an "historical moment" in Algerian Islamism than one of its components. It recalls in this

---

(1) Mahmoud Benomar and Ahmed Klida.

sense the Islamic Party of Liberation in its phase of affirmation, or the radical wing of the Tunisian ITM represented by the small "Islamic Jihad" group, which was partially dismantled in the summer of 1987. Like it, the Bouyali group counted few intellectuals. But the armed option which it had chosen (and which the tendency's majority and "center" were far from adopting) was perhaps nothing more than a reaction to the initial violence that the government had directed towards it.

Beyond the partial view provided by the media window, the Algerian Islamist scene essentially remained atomized for a long time. The regime, which did not hesitate at multiplying religious investments and at anticipating a good number of demands of the Islamist opposition, seemed at that time to have partially succeeded in its attempts at "containment." The nomination of Sheikh Mohamed Ghazali, a former Egyptian member of the Muslim Brothers, to be the head of the great Islamic university of Constantine was a good example of this strategy.(1) There were also certain symbolic shifts in policy such as the adoption in 1976 of Friday as the day of rest, a measure which neither Tunisia nor Morocco have taken yet. The government also launched a vast program at the beginning of the decade of constructing mosques across the entire country. The first verdicts (2) showed that on the scale of the Maghreb, the authorities seemed to want to play a card of rather moderate repression. The verdict of July, 1987, following the first Bouyali trial, showed a relative hardening.(3) But in 1987, the history of the Islamist tendency was only at its beginning. The telltale sign of

_____

(1) "The nomination of Ghazali showed that only the devil was craftier than the regime" said Imam Abdelhadi. "It is curious," said R. Ben Aissa, ironically," that they don't stop repeating to us that Algerian Islam should guard itself against outside influences... and then they look for an Egyptian for us!"

(2) On May 17, 1984, the hundred people arrested during the funeral of Sheikh Soltani were simply released. The first verdict of the Security Court of Medea in the trial of the Bouyali group (104 acquittals and thirty light sentences) was considered very moderate.

(3) Of seven death sentences demanded by the court against close collaborators of Bouyali, four were delivered (against Meliani Mansouri, Abdelkader Chabouti, and Mohamed Amamra) of which only one concerning Djaffar Berkani was in absentia. The police nevertheless killed him the evening of the verdict during a shootout in a suburb of Algiers. Five of the accused were condemned to life in prison, seven others to 20 years, and of 202 suspects only 15 were acquitted. The greatest portion of the troops were hit with sentences ranging from 15 years in prison to one year with a suspended sentence.

October, 1988, would show that neither the ideological counter-offensive nor the first skirmishes of the repressive apparatus had any affect on the mobilizing potential of the candidates, to the relief of the FLN.

The essential, on the eve of the October riots, remained to come.

October, 1988, or the "End of an Era"

In October 1988, a few days of urban disturbances that were not noticeably more violent than previous ones were enough to bring an end to an entire era in Algeria. The riot that led to the quasi-destruction of the FLN had numerous precedents. Why then did this episode take on a new dimension?

First, because eight years after the "springtime of Tizi Ouzou"(1) and two years after the riots in Constantine, emotions going into the crisis were particularly tense. In the days after the dual fall of the price of oil and the value of the dollar, the demographic expansion had pushed the GNP's growth curve below the horizontal for the first time in years. For young people under 20 years old, which is to say nearly 60 percent of the population, doubts had been irresistibly replaced by despair.

The next consideration was the fact that for the first time, public discontent was greatly amplified by the unresolved internal divisions of the regime, which set the supporters of economic liberalization preached by Chadli against the die-hard supporters of a state-controlled economy that had been favored by the late president Boumediene.

The third, and most decisive, characteristic of October resided less in the conditions of the riot than in the repression which the government used to put it down. On the morning of October 6, the government turned to the military to resolve the situation, despite the fact that the resources of the police were far from being exhausted. A state of siege was declared in Algiers and the police withdrew to allow the tanks and heavy weapons of the army to replace them. The resort to repression with machine guns left probably more than two hundred people dead within the next few days. On October 7, the only politically homogeneous procession, that of the Islamists, came under automatic weapons fire at the entrance to the Bab el Oued district. The violence of the repression, which was without precedent since independence, was not only due to the inability of the army draftees to handle a riot. Over a period of days, several hundred demonstrators were repeatedly subjected to physical torture directly ordered by members of the National

---

(1) Serious urban riots took place in April, 1980, in Kabyle.

Army of Liberation. The sole purpose of the torture was punitive. The heart of the October crisis resided there. The protest against repression opened a breach in the ideological shield of the regime's discourse. Through the breach would flow the flood of public discontent that had been held back for too long. The fight against torture became the rallying cry which created a consensus among the opposition movements for the first time. The torture which once had been inflicted by the French colonial occupation had been an inexhaustible source of legitimacy for the FLN. Torture turned back on its children would constitute both an avowal of the failure of these inheritors of the revolution and the most effective weapon in the hands of the protesters against the system. In using, against its own sons, the procedures of the colonial power, the regime failed to realize that it was its revolutionary legitimacy, already undermined by 26 years of monopolizing power, that was in the process of being destroyed.

On October 13, the old Sheikh Sahnoun addressed an open letter to the president of the Republic. Chadli Benjedid decided to receive its author, accompanied by Mahfoudh Nahnah and another cleric whose name would soon become known far beyond the Bab el Oued suburbs: Ali Belhaj. The choice was highly symbolic. The president had just admitted that the Islamists were part of the group that would allow him to renew his contact with civil society. Boosted to the position of quasi-official interlocutors, the inheritors of Sheikh Soltani saw the doors to political legitimacy opening to them for the first time. They had no intention of passing up the opportunity that was being presented.

On October 10, the first political response of the regime was a promise to "limited opening" under the form of a constitutional reform. It was submitted on November 3 to a referendum, and destined to render the government responsible to the parliament, thus creating for the president, in the person of the Prime Minister, a useful political "fuse." The old guard of the FLN, which had shown itself to be peevishly ungrateful, helped permit the president to survive the crisis, even coming out of it with his prestige somewhat reinforced. The resolution of the ideological schism within the party was deferred. The unsurprising results of the FLN's Party Congress on November 27, and his easy re-election to the presidency on December 22, allowed Chadli Benjedid to replace Cherif Messaadia, who had served as the spearhead of his opponents, and General Lakhal Ayat, who had born the brunt of responsibility for the repression.

The process engaged in proved to be nearly without limits. Irresistibly, the juridical universe of partisan monocratism gave way to be replaced by pluralism. The principle milestones are well known. Already shaken by the referendum of November 3, 1988, the system was even more shaken by the new constitution, made public on February 4, 1989, and approved by a referendum on February 23. The double reference to socialism and the dominant role of the FLN were simply excluded. The right to organize labor unions and to hold strikes was recognized. Authorization was granted to create "associations with a political character," which opened the door to multiple parties. Recognizing the new dynamics, the army agreed to withdraw from the Party's Central Committee. Professional associations, unions, leagues and committees, new publications liberated from partisan pressures flourished within a civilian society frustrated from the government's previous denial of autonomy. The bad mood of the party apparatus also manifested itself. The democratization of the official press, which was still largely in the hands of the party, the pressure against civil servants and bureaucrats occasionally affected the credibility of the process, but it could not slow the speed of its application.

The Recomposition of the Political Field

At the heart of the FLN, the end of the reign was not being taken very well. Between the camp of the unconditional followers of this "Perestroika," which was beginning to look more and more as though it were scuttling the ship of state, and the barons of the system who were becoming frightened at the rapidity of their marginalization, the tensions became more and more explicit each day. When Kasdi Merbah, judged too lukewarm in his support for the presidential reforms, was dismissed, the regime brushed up against an institutional crisis. The fallen prime minister, a former head of the military security services publicly voiced doubts about the legality of his dismissal. For a dozen hours, he appeared to want to remain despite the president's will. His successor, Mouloud Hamrouche, was no less prudent in his assessment reforms. He felt it was premature to pick members of his cabinet from outside the FLN, since it was understood that—like he said—the FLN "contained the sensitivities of all the other parties, since the latter had previously belonged to it." In fact, on November 29, the fourth extraordinary Congress of the party was the occasion for a return in force of this hostile tendency to the line of reform. The delegates demanded that immediate elections be held for the central committee, which in principle only took place during the course of the normal sessions of the congress. A. Mehri, the secretary general, stalled for time, but Chadli finally accepted, and, during the night of November 30, the vote went against him. The 1,200 members of the security who were supposed to have, as usual, infiltrated the

271

Congress went against the orders of the president and let the old guard of the FLN back into the leadership organ of the party. Those reelected included Mohamed Salah Yahiaoui and Abdelaziz Boutefliqa (two competitors of Chadli for the succession to Boumediene), Belaid Abdessalam, Ahmed Taleb Ibrahimi and the ex-prime minister Kasdih Merbah (head of the government just after the October riots). Most of the 137 outgoing members were re-elected to their seats.(1) Taleb Ibrahimi had the Congress applaud the period of "Houari Boumediene and the construction of the Algerian state," and Abdelaziz Boutefliqa implicitly proposed his services. The general staff of the army, for once absent from these debates, was not very attentive. What the right hand of the FLN was forced to concede, would the left hand be tempted one day to recuperate?

Outside the sphere of the former unique party, new political equilibriums were beginning to show themselves. One of the translations of this recomposition in depth of the landscape, which moreover was not necessarily the most faithful, was the flowering of a multitude of new political formations, the quasi-totality of which obtained authorization from the administration.(2) If the Jordanian record of 50 parties or the Yemenis of at least 30 were not immediately broken, the threshold of 20 parties was quickly passed, and on the eve of the aborted election of June, 1991, the insignia of the Party of Contemporary Muslim Algeria became the 47th on the list of pretenders to parliamentary power. All these candidates were far from having the same weight. For a small number of them,(3) the authorization corre-

_____

(1) Their number passing (given the departure of the military) to 268.

(2) The recognition would be refused to a "party of revolutionary committees" loyal to Libya.

(3) According to the useful criteria of classification adopted by Abdelkader Djeghloul in "Le multipartisme à l'Algérienne," *Maghreb Machreq Monde Arabe,* March, 1990, page 194. In Arabic, cf. Abd al-Ali Razafi, *Al Ahzab al siyassiya fi al jezaïr, Khalfiate wa haqaiq,* Al Mo'assassa al-watania lil founoun al-matba'iya, 1990, Algiers, 230 pages. On the problematic of the emergence of oppositions in Algeria, cf. F.B., "La longue marche de la société civile, in Algérie," *Encyclopedia Universalis,* 1990. For a list of Islamist formations, cf. Arun Kapil "Les partis islamistes en Algérie: Élements de présentation," in *Maghreb Machreq monde arabe,* No. 33, September, 1991. In this same issue, cf. "Les analyses de Jean Leca, Rémi Leveau et Abdelkader Djeghloul." For the biographies of the principle actors in the Islamist movement, cf. the equally useful *Algérie: 200 hommes de pouvoir* by Louis Blin (dir), Paris, Indigo Publications, 1991, 130 pages.

sponded to a simple exit from clandestinity. That is the case of the Front for Socialist Forces of Ait Ahmed, born in 1963 of the Party of the Socialist Avant-Gard (PAGS), the inheritor of the Algerian Communist Party, which had been dissolved in 1962 and recreated in January, 1966. under its new name. It had rallied to the regime of Boumediene and become a source of powerful leftist protest against Boumediene's successor, Chadli. This was equally the case of the less known Democratic Movement for Algerian Renewal (Mouvement Democratique pour le Renouveau Algerien) created in 1967 by members of the Socialist Workers Party (PST) who opposed Boumediene when he succeeded Ben Bella.

As for the new arrivals, some were the inheritors of a more or less institutionalized mobilization of the past. That was the case for the FIS and the several other formations which would little by little dispute their Islamist monopoly. It is equally the case of the Rally for Culture and Democracy (Rassemblement pour la culture et la Democratie) which, in the style of Ait Ahmed's FFS, seemed to be an inheritor of the cultural movement of the Berbers. Other candidates were more obscure. There was the Social Democrat Party, the National Algerian Party, the Party for Algerian Renewal, the Social Liberal Party, the Union of Democratic Forces led by the former minister of agriculture of Ben Bella, Ahmed Mahsas, and the Mouvement for Justice and Democracy in Algeria (MAJD), created by ex-Prime Minister Kasdi Merbah. There was also the Front for Democratic Algerian authenticity, and a surprising Algerian Party for the Capital Man.(1) Most of these expressed quasi-individual ambitions and never succeeded in making themselves heard in the vast political concert that was in the process of being born.

The Birth of FIS

A series of meetings held by a small circle of sympathizers led to the constitution of a first Majlis Shura and then the evocation on February 21, 1989, during a meeting in the stadium of Bouzarea, of an Islamic Front of Salvation, whose initials would soon attract much of the media's attention. "The idea of creating a religious political party," an organ of the FIS, *Al Munquid*, (2) related,

---

(1) Complete list in Djeghloul, op. cit.

(2) *Al Munqid,* No. 19, page 5, cited by Ghania Sama Ouramdane in "Le Front Islamique de Salut à travers son organe de presse," *Peuples méditerranéens*, No. 52-53, July-December, 1990, page 155-165. The official founding of the FIS

occurred in the mind of Sheikh al Hachemi Sahnouni (a very popular blind preacher) who did not communicate it to anyone, because of the divergences which existed within the movement of the Islamist da'wa. Until the day when he received a visit from Ali Belhaj, who expressed the same preoccupation. Strengthened by this understanding, the two sheikhs spoke to Sheikh Madani Abbassi, who applauded the idea. That is how the contacts began with Algerian (preachers) whose response was either positive or negative.

The real thunderbolt would come only a few months later on September 14, 1989. To the great surprise of a part of the local political class and against the advice of nearly all his Arab counterparts, Chadli, without even waiting for the dispositions included in the constitution against religious political parties to be modified, took the unprecedented step for the Maghreb of opening the gates of the political scene to the Islamist party. Chadli would try to justify the decision by declarations whose lucidity seemingly failed to convince his entire entourage:

> The activities of the Islamist party are submitted to precise rules. If they respect them, we cannot forbid them. We are Muslims and it is important for us to encourage Islam in its just conception, not the pseudo Islam of myths and extremism. If certain people do not look on this legalization kindly, that is their affair. For our part, it is not conceivable to apply democracy to Communists and to deprive the current which preaches spiritual belonging (...). Democracy (...) cannot be selective.

A few weeks later, in front of French microphones,(1) the Prime Minister, Hamrouche, chose to motivate the Algerian initiative thus:

> There is now an experience that is a bit unique in the Muslim world. It is the first time that a state, Algeria, recognizes an "integrist"

---

goes back to a meeting held in the Al-Sunna de Bab El-Oued mosque (whose official imam, Hachemi Sahnouni, often welcomed Belhaj) on February 18. It was followed by another meeting on March 9 in the same walls. The president of the party was then Madani Abbassi, the vice president Ben Azouz Zebda. Ali Bel Haj, another member of the general bureau, although he is considered as the number two, being only one member among others in the bureau. Said Lachi, Mohamed Kerrar, Sahraoui Abdelbaki, Othmane Amokrane, were among the founding members.

(1) January 21, 1990, for RTL.

movement as a political movement. We have chosen this way because we think the best way to master the phenomenon is to understand it, to manage it, to discuss with it. We have chosen the democratic way, the way of wisdom. In leading the Islamist Front, or the Islamists or the "integrists" or the fundamentalists, as you like, to discuss on a democratic plane, we are sure of our argument and our means... Do they have responsible representatives? Yes, of course. I consider the Islamist party is like any other. Officially they have chiefs. They have a spokesman with whom I have discussed matters on two occasions. He is reasonable. He reasons like you or I. Of course one can't judge a party by what it says (...) It is necessary to wait for their Congress to see men who will come out from the base, and it is from that that we will be able to make a deeper evaluation.

The leader of the new movement turned out to be, not surprisingly, Abbassi Madani. He was born February 28, 1931, at Sidi Okba Ibn Nafaa in the southeast of Algeria, is married and the father of six children, five boys and a girl. His father is an Imam. He received a classical Muslim education (*Kuttab*) and courses in theology first at Sidi Okba, and then at Biskra where his family moved in 1941, and where he also frequented the French secondary school for two years. His entry into militancy began through the CRUA (Comité Revolutionnaire pour l'Unité et l'Action/Revolutionary Committee for Unity and Action), one of the ancestors of the FLN, which he joined in 1954 along side Rabah Bitat, and then Ben Boulaid, two of the historic leaders of the FLN. Imprisoned on November 17, 1954,(1) he was freed at independence and resumed his studies for a degree in philosophy at the University of Algiers. He carried out his third cycle on psychology (on teaching in Algeria) and between 1975 and 1978, he received his Ph.D. in Educational Sciences at London.(2) He entered politics to denounce the Marxist dimension in the Charter of Algiers. Close to the Al Qiyam Association (cf. infra), he was a member of the first APW of Algiers from 1969 to 1974. He was known afterwards for having been, in the shadow of Ahmed Sahnoun, one of the leaders of the first confrontations at the beginning of the 1980s. Arrested on December 15, 1982, after the second largest Islamist demonstration in the history of the country at the central faculty of

(1) After having participated in an aborted attempt to bomb Radio Algiers.

(2) On the comparison of teaching systems in French, English and Algerian. He is the author of several studies: *The Problems of Education in the Muslim World, The Family and its Contemporary Problems, The Crisis of Contemporary Thought and the Islamist Alterantive,* and *Epistemological Problems of Historical Knowledge."*

Algiers during the month of November, he was released in 1984 and taught afterwards at the Institute of Educational Sciences at Bouzareah (Algiers). When he becomes president of the FIS, he is 59 years old. He prefers to wear a *gandoura,* larger than the oriental *kamis* favored by the best known of his deputies, Ali Belhaj.

Belhaj, for his part, was born in Tunis in 1956. He became an orphan after his father and mother were killed during the war for independence. In contrast to Madani, his education was exclusively religious. After his schooling he became an Arabic teacher and began preaching. He was imprisoned between 1982 and 1987 during the government's attempts to stamp out the group of Mustapha Bouyali. Those who have had a chance to get to know Belhaj in a less stressful environment than the one that was apparent during his first exchanges with the press, say that he gives more the impression of a mystic than a politician. Equipped with a religious culture that is deeper than Madani's, he also has a theatrical eloquence that Madani lacks. But not having lived outside Algeria and never even having visited a country that was not Muslim, his vision of the rest of the world sometimes tends towards caricature. There is a touch of dogmatism that seems out of date; Islamist leaders like Ghannouchi and Tourabi, who because of their experiences in university or political exile have distanced themselves more from their native universe. The others in the FIS are less known. Benazouz Zebda, the vice president of the Front, but generally considered as the number three in the hierarchy of the party, is the Imam-preacher at the mosque of Kouba (the locality east of Algiers where Belhaj's family lives), one of the two high places for the weekly mobilization of FIS (with the Sunna de Bab al Oued Mosque). A militant nationalist, he has a degree in Arabic letters and is director of the FIS publication, *Al Munqid.*

The Street and the Urns

While waiting to see what they could do in elections, it was in the street that the candidates on the heels of the FLN crisis began to measure their strength. On this terrain, the force of the Islamist camp very quickly became apparent. The first major demonstration by the FIS had the effect of a thunderbolt on the national political scene. On December 29, 1989, to respond to a demonstration of a few hundred women against the Family Code, the brand new Islamic Salvation Front had already organized one of the most important opposition demonstrations in the history of independent Algeria. Several tens of thousands of women, preceding several hundred thousand men, chanting slogans calling for the application of Sharia law, and especially the abolition of co-education, made it possible for the first time to measure the formidable Islamist potential. In the month of April, in a pre-electoral context that was even more significant, the bipolarization of the political scene burst into full bloom during three demonstrations. On April 20, 1990, the FIS repeated its performance of December. Up until the night before, the FLN had tried to cancel this march programmed to take place at the same time that it planned to parade its own troops. The FLN managed to get two Islamists, Sahnoun and M. Nahnah, to back its argument to have the march called off. But the FIS persisted and managed to mobilize beyond any expectations. The next day the casualties were not only in the camp of the FLN. The march had also shattered in broad daylight the limits of Sahnoun and Nahnah's public support, which had clearly failed.(1) "Politically and psychologically, a page has been turned in the country after this demonstration," Sid Saadi, the leader of the RCD,(2) noted lucidly at the time. "The question was no longer if the FLN would stay in power— that was already in the rear view mirror—but to know what would come after it...."

On May 8, it was the turn of the non-Islamist opposition (3) to count its support. Although there was a good showing, the demonstration did not manage to make anyone forget the score of the FIS, which multiplied its rallies throughout the rest of the country. Failing to really open a "second front against the Islamists" (*Le Monde*, May 10, 1990), which would have supposed that the FLN still constituted one, the march of those who were a bit hastily baptized "the democrats" confirmed the state of bipolarization of the Algerian political scene. It still remained for the FLN to take its turn around the track. At the end of a particularly heavy national mobilization, and a large reinforcement brought in by trains and convoys of buses, it managed to bring a respectable number of troops into the streets to fool some of the least alert observers. But the crowd presented here, essentially transported in from the countryside, was more a witness to the capacity of the old-style party to use the apparatus of the State and its means of persuasion than it was of any "ideological" potential capable of actually leading a

---

(1) He would countersign his defeat in not calling clearly for his militants to vote FIS during the June elections, thus missing his place in the victory train.

(2) Interview in *Le Point*, April 25, 1990.

(3) Mobilized by the PAGS, the RCD, the MDRA and the PSD, and the Algerian League for Human Rights, the FFS having tried to find its own niche and called a rally for May 31.

party to victory. To anyone doubting that, what followed made the situation clear. In the meantime, it looked to some as though the secret services had very probably put their talents to the survival of the system. Cemeteries of nationalist militants fallen during the revolution were profaned and covered with inscriptions denouncing, in the name of Islam, the use of tombstones.(1) Attacks against various symbols of popular culture were conducted, and, notably, traditional music spectacles were interrupted by bearded men shouting *haram* (it's forbidden) noisily. Other practices that exceeded the normally defined electioneering, including the burning of mausoleums of saints, which appeared aimed at raising popular piety against the militants of political Islam, left a certain number of observers fairly skeptical. The confrontation between "good Islam" and "bad Islam" would, nevertheless, permit the FLN, a ferocious opponent of the Zaouias and other brotherhoods during the time of the "Agrarian Revolution" to suddenly become their attentive protector. This was not unlike the King of Morocco who had switched to the same role a few years earlier, or Muammar Kadhafi in 1986. And these incidents would fit into an impressive campaign largely orchestrated by the national press and dutifully relayed by the foreign media, and in some cases imprudently included as an element in the problem by certain segments of the academic world.(2)

The day of the opening of the election campaign, division seemed more than ever the order of the day in the ranks of the non-Islamist opposition. The PAGS was unable to present a suficient number of candidates. Several factions argued over the "Berberist cake." Ait Ahmed, who had returned to the country in September, 1989, after a long exile, seemed at first to meet with genuine popular success. But the darling of the French Socialist party, which brought him constant support, had to admit that the impact of his discourse had not really managed to help him escape the ethnic ghetto of his Kabyle origins. Anxious to measure the force present on the political scene before irreversibly positioning himself, Ben Bella preferred, for his part, to

---

(1) These supposed acts of "integrist" violence would disappear as if by magic the day after the election results were published in June. But they would take up again even more strongly, accompanied by attacks on other symbols of the national idea, during the campaign for the legislative elections.

(2) Cf., for example, Ahmed Rouadjia, Islam contre Islam in "Le Fis à l'épreuve des Élections législatives," *Les Cahiers de l'Orient,* 1991, No. 23.

A "first national seminar of the Zaouias" would even be organized in June at Algiers. Cf. Smaïl Haj Ali, "Le premier séminaire national des Zaouias," *Maghreb Maghrek*, No. 132, March, 1992, page 53.

boycott the first elections. Independent lists (especially in the Mzab, where they translated the double identity of the *ibadites* with respect to the FLN and the FIS) constituted here and there a few unknowns. But only the FIS and the FLN were able to present candidates in all the circumscriptions. The "frontal" shock of a clash between the two could no longer be avoided.

A few days before the election, the regime thought that by an ultimate maneuver it could reduce the financial base of the FIS by forbidding contraband, which a few hundred youths (supposedly sympathizers of the Islamist current) had been engaging in for many years. Egyptian light fixtures, ready-made clothes from Turkey, Taiwanese electric appliances and European spare parts were suddenly confiscated at the airport from the young "trabendos" (or contrebandiers). If the measure had any impact at all on the FIS, it was extremely limited. It is more likely that the last minute crackdown only further exacerbated the frustrations felt by a part of the population that lived directly or indirectly from the informal mobilization of the foreign currency in the savings of immigrant workers.(1) This practice had been growing more and more widespread. The evening of June 12, the FIS appeared to be the indisputable victor.

June 12, 1990: The Lessons of an Election

The voting booths during this first free election in the history of independent Algeria produced a flood of ballots, which attested to a very large victory on the part of the FIS. Of 1,551 communes, the FIS had won control of 853. Of 48 *wilayas* (departments), it had won 32. And these first results did not reveal the full magnitude of the Islamist victory. The FIS had won a majority in all the large cities, 64.18 percent of the votes in Algiers, 70.57 percent in Oran, and 72 percent in Constantine.(2) It controlled all the

---

(1) In 1979, when their Egyptian counterparts only sent home $29 million, the Algerian immigrant workers repatriated $211 million. In 1985, the relationship was reversed. Algeria only received $313 million, compared to $3 billion for Egypt.

(2) In six communes, it received more than 80% of the vote. In nine others, from 70 to 80%, and from 60 to 70% in nine others, and 50 to 59% in the six others. In the sole commune of the Wilaya of Algiers where it did not take an absolute majority, its score was still 49.5% (cited by Arun Kapil in "Chiffres clés pour une analyse," *Les Cahiers de l'Orient*, 1991, No. 23, page 41, and Cheikh Slimane, "Les élections locales en Algérie à l'ève du multipartisme Elecciones, participation y transiciones politicas en el norte des Africa," Madrid, Agencia Espagnola de cooperacion internacional, 1991, page 247 to 287).

communes in the wilaya of Algiers (33 out of 33), Blida (29), Constantine (12) and Jijel (28)

Let's first discard the hypothesis that irregularities in the voting could have reversed the rapport of the forces present. At the most, they may have amplified them. The "very weak turn out" (65 percent), which served in the media opposed to the FIS to exorcise the results of the vote should reasonably have been affected by a "qualitative" coefficient, which would have considerably increased the force. For the first time, in effect, one was dealing with an election in which the interests of the apparatus of the State were not identified with only the volume of the participation. As for the discredit that the practices of the FLN had had on previous elections, the voter turnout appeared, in fact, to have been extraordinarily high. The procedure for voting by procuration, which allows a husband to vote for his wife or vice-versa, is not likely to have had much effect either. The procurations are usually used by the head of the family, but it is, nevertheless, unlikely that this provision would have significantly affected the feminine vote. Contrary to what was written so many times by Western observers, there is no reason to support the idea that women constituted in any significant numbers an island of extra territoriality and *a fortiori* resistance vis-à-vis the Islamist upsurge. And when, in a thin urban elite, this might have been the case, nothing showed that these few women had any difficulty in overcoming the legal handicap.(1) Three lessons came out of an examination of the election results:

1. The collapse of the FLN had left it incapable of influencing the voting as it always had done in the past. Worn down by 28 years of monopoly rule, it had been overloaded with violent tensions between the reform camp close to the president and the old-guard of the partisans of the line of Boumediene, who had returned in force during the last party congress. It is likely that Chadli Benjedid would have viewed with a favorable eye (or even, as some maintained, aided) the FIS to obtain 30 percent of the votes simply in order to break the resistance to his reforms by the "orthodox" block of the party. The election on June 12, nevertheless, had shattered these possible subtleties. And, it consecrated the collapse of the party.

---

(1) Reinstated in the new electoral law of October, 1991, the vote by procuration was declared unconstitutional shortly afterwards by the Algerian Constitutional Council.

2. A clear majority of seats was acquired by the FIS, in small part only due to the electoral law which gave the majority of seats to the list of candidates arriving ahead of the others—a place the FLN had clearly hoped to occupy. The result was accentuated by its territorial projection which gave all of "useful Algeria"—the north part of the country—to the Islamists and cast even more doubts on the FLN's score in the south, which is traditionally more susceptible to vote rigging.

3. There was an absence or extreme fragility of alternative formations. Under the banner of the FFS of Aït Ahmed, badly served by his decision to abstain, the democratic theme did not seem to have been capable of leaving its regional Kabyle ghetto. The RCD and the Party of the Socialist Avant-Garde (which literally disappeared from the political scene) also showed that simply supporting the idea of pluralist elections was not enough to win a majority. The "independent" lists finally showed that they were in no way capable of constituting a clear alternative, not even when constituted by dis-illusioned sympathizers of the FLN, as some observers thought they might have been.

FLN Defeat, or FIS Victory?

More globally, the first results would show that the "turn off" effects of the supposedly extremist language used by the FIS and the real and imag-ined practices of its militants concerning women, democracy and human rights were far less of a factor in influencing the Algerian electorate itself than foreign magazines in general, and French magazines in particular, had predicted.

The majority of the voters (between 55 and 82 percent depending on the parameters used) were nevertheless not identifiable with the hard core of Is-lamist themes. On the evidence, the "rejection votes" very likely constituted a strong element in the old single party's defeat (more than "sanction votes," which would not be confirmed in the second round of balloting in a national election). But that does not detract from the fact that these votes can, nevertheless, be considered as contributing to the victory by the FIS. The FIS, in fact, showed itself to be the only party capable of channeling the rejection of the FLN into an election victory—an achievement that was clearly beyond the grasp of opposition parties, ranging from the RCD to the FFS and including the independents. Why were the Islamists successful?

Essentially, because the FIS managed to transfer to its profit the last and most important political resource that the FLN had: nationalism. It accomplished this in a positive sense first of all by exploiting, on the cultural and ideological terrain, the same nationalist themes that the FLN, itself, had once expressed and exploited in politics and economics. It accomplished this also in a negative sense, being able to progressivly identify the political forces arrayed against it with the French-speaking universe, inevitably with France, and a certain social elite doubly condemned for its economic privileges and its cultural proximity to the former colonial power. The verbal clashes between the FIS and European media contributed, in effect, to making the vocabulary of "democracy" and "human rights" seem too close to foreign culture to resist the nationalist contents of the Islamist themes. In the inexorable process of discrediting the secular forces, a paradoxical and not insignificant role was played by France, i.e. the French TV and the political class. With the FIS denouncing France's party, France's haste in defending the "democratic camp" indisputably contributed to disqualifying it at the same time as helping its adversary. The pervasive televised support(1) for the "secular forces"; the abuses of language in denouncing the militants of the FIS, who were certainly "bearded," but not "dirty"(2) since their literalist approach to dogma led them to wash five times a day; the selective aggressiveness of TV newscasters with respect to "the man who frightens France";(3) and the continuing incapacity of TV commentators to distinguish "integrism" from identity references used by all Algerians, helped to turn most of the French attacks into political dividends for the FIS.

The supreme paradox was that the FLN in its battle against the FIS found itself constantly placed in a position of paraphrasing the French media. This opened a number of breaches in its historical legitimacy, which had been founded precisely on its capacity to distance itself symbolically from the former colonizer.

---

(1) It is easy to receive French television in the Maghreb.

(2) This was written by the "envoyé special" of a major French daily, which earned him a suit at the hands of a French Muslim association.

(3) According to a photo caption of Abbassi Madani published on the cover of the French newsmagazine, *Le Point*.

1991: The Aborted Democratization

The opening initiated in October, 1988, seemed destined for a while to reach its natural conclusion: competitive elections accepting the possibility of calling into question the FLN's monopoly over the country. The election of June had shown the capacity of the regime to register a disavowal at the urns. It remained to be seen, of course, whether the regime would agree to resume the test at the national level, and if necessary to suffer the consequences. But the FLN, even though weakened and divided, had no intention of replaying its losing hand at the parliamentary level without reacting. At the very least it intended to try to reverse the spiral of its first political defeat.

The Counter-offensive

The shock of the results in June had numbed the entire leadership class to such an extent that it took several weeks for the counter-offensive to take shape. After having deferred the publication of the results, after having perhaps ceded to the temptation of trying to attenuate their force, the party positioned itself at first on a line that tried both to emphasize the local nature of the first elections and to turn the figures of the defeat into a proof that the elections had been democratic. "If the results were unfavorable to us," the Prime Minister, Mouloud Hamrouche, said in substance, "our defeat attests even more to our desire for a democratic opening than would a victory in which one would have been suspected of irregularity." This was not a plan for reconquest, but, across the axes of the official press, the larger lines of a plan would not take long to become apparent.

Without great surprise, the regime's tactic centered on breaking apart the Islamist camp: To wear down the credibility of the FIS by allowing it to become bogged down in local administration, which would be even more delicate since the financial management of the FLN had particularly degraded the situation and the prerogatives of the mayors to rectify the situation had been spectacularly reduced only two months before the election. To profit after that, from the internal tensions which would inevitably appear inside the FIS when encountering the reality of municipal administration, in order to create and eventually to exploit the divisions in its leadership apparatus. The final tactic was either to develop or create competing Islamist parties capable of diverting at least some of the Islamist dividend towards possible alliances, which would allow a "renovated" FLN to make everyone forget its dramatic counter performance. This program would at least, in part, be carried out.

Up until the end of the month of July, 1990, the FIS was content with criticizing the system, which in the words of Abbassi Madani, worked "like an inverted pyramid, with the head pointed to the bottom." Madani called for the dissolution of the National Assembly, but without fixing a precise date. In his daily routine, he was occupied with a permanent stream of visitors—journalists, diplomats, political messengers, and various foreigners—and began setting about the enormous task of coming to grips with the cumbersome communal harvest.

The FIS and Its City Halls

Hardly a few weeks had passed before news stories began appearing in the national and international press reporting signs of the FIS' presumed inability to keep its "fabulous promises" to the voters. The accounts made it appear that it was encountering a growing disenchantment at its base. Emerging from this concert of protests, were stories of attacks against individual liberties that were supposed to have constituted the main element of the FIS' local policies, and the incapacity of the newly elected officials to respond to economic expectations. In this flood of rumors in the form of accusations, it was for a long time difficult to determine what was really happening. A political generation, at least partly without any experience in administration was taking control of communal structures in a media environment that was exceptionally hostile, and was attempting to work with a central government that remained particularly hostile. All of this was being done with a financial autonomy that was considerably more limited than any of its predecessors. It has since been possible to verify that these catastrophic expectations, which were supposed to lead ineluctably to the electoral collapse of the FIS, should have been seriously nuanced. The few decisions by certain Islamist officials that were seriously contested often turned out to have no real impact on the majority of the electorate as a whole. It is true that some of these decisions, and especially the one concerning the war supposedly declared on Rai music, were often distorted by the government, or simply fabricated by the government press. In other cases the measures had already been taken by FLN communal officials much earlier, and had not aroused any opposition at the time (this was the case notably in the ban on wearing shorts outside beaches, and the closing of certain places serving alcohol).

As for miracles, the FIS certainly fell short of producing any. There was evidence of technical and political errors. There was sometimes a chilly retreat to symbolic measures that were easier to carry out because they did not demand money. This eventually helped to soften the difficulties of handling an economic situation that was beyond the reach of its goals. But had the FIS really promised as many miracles as its "automatic" detractors claimed? To fill the technical demands of the management of the communes, it seemed to have often been capable of mobilizing competent people who were at least comparable to those of the preceding team. On numerous occasions the responsibilities seem to have been assigned to personalities outside the Front who were recognized solely for their competence. In the economic domain, the organization of distribution networks (the Islamic souks), having succeeded in bringing a lowering of prices, even demonstrated how certain technical problems that were reputed to be insoluble might actually be handled at least to a certain extent by mere political mobilization. Week after week, it became clear, in fact, that the balance sheet for the Islamists was far from the catastrophe predicted by the media on both sides of the Mediterranean.(1)

Objective: Division

In the days after June 12, the FLN was not alone in wanting to limit the ambitions of the FIS. The non-Islamist opposition, just as traumatized by its crushing electoral defeat, tried for its part in the first days to launch "democratic forums" intended to try to unify its own ranks. Any observer who had had the time to see the impressive public prayers organized by the FIS at Kouba or Bab Al Oued,(2) and had then a day later managed to stroll

---

(1) See among many others, the example of Salah Derwiche whose assessment of the situation of the FIS is close to that of most commentators: "The FIS has registered a clear defeat in managing the local municipalities (...) One year after the elections, the evaluation is strictly negative: no concrete realizations, the daily problems that the Islamists had said they would take care of have not yet found any solution. (...) For the 'star' of 1990 (i.e. Abbassi Madani) it is the beginning of the decline."

For an academic assessment of the same category, see Rouadjia Ahmed, "Le FIS à l'épreuve des élections législatives," *Les Cahiers de l'Orient,* No. 23, 1991, p. 75.

(2) The first Friday prayer after the electoral victory gave place to massive demonstrations of popular fervor. The voice of Ali Belhaj gave way to sobs several times, a part of the crowd thought it saw the divine hand writing its name

by the Hotel St. Georges where the meager, still highly divided forces of the "democratic" opposition were meeting, would have had difficulty imagining that any evolution in the rapport of forces could be enough to help the RCD or FFS or any of the other parties hoping to stop the growing power of the Islamists before the legislative elections.

The Impossible Return of Ben Bella

There still remained, of course, the unknown represented by Ahmed Ben Bella. Untouched by the electoral defeat, since he had chosen to boycott the communal elections, he seemed for a long time to be a possible wild card which the FLN, or the non-Islamist opposition, or both together, might try to pull out of their sleeve. Ben Bella was consequently the object of attention of most observers for a certain time. On September 28, 1990, after an impressive public relations campaign, the first president of independent Algeria, who had been in exile for ten years, set sail on a boat (rented from Barcelona for the occasion) with hundreds of his followers and representatives of the international press. He clearly hoped that by setting foot on Algerian soil he would be able to turn the results of the June vote to his own profit. And, in fact, the predictions by his most imprudent admirers and of many dreaming of finding in the old politician an adversary capable of standing up to the ambitions of the FIS (1) foretold an "implosion of the FIS" and "a profound recomposition of the Islamist scene."

Events turned out quite different. Ben Bella's discourse proved so opportunistic that it had little effect either on the FIS or on the non-Islamist opposition, and he never managed to turn his OPA into a success. Once he had returned to the country, the leader of the Movement for Democracy in Algeria continued to "sniff the direction of the wind." He wanted to be

---

into a cloud over the sky of Algiers, despite the protests of the militants keeping order who shouted, "That's not what Islam is!"

(1) Hassan Zenatti (France press bureau) had believed over the course of the preceding weeks that the return of Ben Bella had led to an irresitable urge in the streets of Algiers for the "bearded tendency to become defrocked," and this pushed him to predict the inevitable "implosion of the FIS" in the days after the return of the old leader. Numerous observers, including some of the most qualified, predicted that the physical reintroduction of Ben Bella back on Algerian soil would have a much more important impact. Cf., for example, Djeghloul, "Ben Bella's return in Algeria will... necessarily introduce a recomposition of the Islamist movement." (*Maghreb Machrek*, No. 127. cited).

"elsewhere," "above the parties," and to do this he adopted a discourse that was so unfocused that it became ambiguous. While attacking the FLN as "a band of criminals styling themselves as reformers," he declared himself to be violently opposed to the FIS one day, but ready to make an alliance with it the next. He was quick with denials, and then launched trial balloons, then made a discrete invitation.(1) The Gulf War saw him speak out strongly in favor of defending Iraq and stopping straddling the fence for a certain time. But even this issue, on which the FIS had spoken out just as strongly, did not help him to make much impression on the FIS' militants or its electoral clientele. He even found it impossible to appear credible as a future intermediary, just as Mohamed Mzali clearly dreamed of becoming in Tunisia. After a long period of dalliance in the opposition, Ben Bella would terminate his career. He would soon be reconciled with the FLN, which in its time had led him to power. And, he would suffer the discredit of having failed to demarcate himself from the party.

The Islamist Competitors

In the Islamist field, the desires of the regime and no doubt its efforts to inspire a competitor to the FIS produced results fairly rapidly. The creation of the "Front" had not in fact succeeded in organizing the totality of the Islamist potential. Two prestigious individuals, Sheikh Sahnoun and Mahfoud Nahnah, had preferred to remain independent (or in the case of Sahnoun to remain on the sidelines).(2) On the edges of the strictly partisan scene, the League of the Islamic Call, which had constituted the first institution of the Islamist mobilization when it was created under the guidance of Sahnoun just after the 1988 riots, continued to maintain itself as a political interlocutor, distinct from the FIS. After being freed from prison, the old Sheikh Sahnoun was groomed by the government and had returned the investment by taking the side of the possible ally, Nahnah, against Madani on several occasions. Nevertheless, Madani, as the leader of the FIS, had a seat

---

(1) On May 4, 1990, the weekly *Tribune d'Octobre* "did not exclude allying itself with other parties for the defense of those things that are constant in the nation: Islamness and Arabness." After Ben Bella's arrival on Algerian soil on September 28, the tendency was to exclude this idea: "I will not marry myself with a party of the Islamist current. I will not be part of an Islamic alliance."

(2) "They did not wait for us. We were not present," A. Sahnoun declared to an Algerian journalist afterwards. (*Algérie Actualité*, No. 1252, October 12, 1989). On the birth of the FIS, cf. Arun Kapil, cited.

at the League as representative of his party. In spite of the differences that separated them, he kept meeting there with Mahfoudh Nahnah, A. Djaballah, Mohamed Said, etc.

The sharper clashes between Nahnah and the leaders of the FIS had, in contrast, not started overnight. In addition to evident personal rivalries, there were differences which had existed for a long time. Persistent and fairly credible rumors had it that Nahnah had played a role in the Mustapha Bouyali affair that had been much closer to the government's interests than to that of the small group of activists. He was at least suspected of having aided the minister of the interior, after having gained the confidence of the armed rebel and having talked with him, in order to measure the forces present.(1) Nahnah first tried to create an association, Jam'iya al Irchad wal Islah, which he considered to be apolitical, arguing here and there about the inappropriateness of "moving to partisan action."(2) But, after the election of June, 1990, his evident incapacity to influence the greater dynamics of the mobilization of the FIS incited him to change his first analyses, and to enter the electoral arena and create his own party. On December 6, 1990, on the third anniversary of the launching of the Palestinian Intifada, he announced the creation of a party, Harakat al Mujtamaa al Islami, whose initials, HAMAS, recalls the Islamist movement in the occupied territories.(3) (The Intifada had made HAMAS a daily star.) Legalized on April 29, 1991, HAMAS held its constitutive congress on May 29, 1991. On that day it re-

---

(1) Cf. the account of Ahmed Merah, one of the near associates of Bouyali (who presented himself as the military chief of the MIA) published by *Le Nouvel Hebdo*, No. 25, from November 12–18, 1990, page 19, reproduced in Al Ahnaf, Botiveau and Fregosi, op. cit., page 66. Identical rumors are regularly spread in regards to Ali Belhaj, accused for his part of having earned his freedom from prison in 1984 by several concessions to his jailers. Cf. the accusations of one of the fellow prisoners, distributed in the anti-FIS press and reproduced in Al-Ahnaf and others, op. cit.

(2) Cf. notably his interview with the Egyptian Muslim Brothers (*Liwa al Islam*, Cairo, June, 1989) where he declares numerous reasons why it is not a good idea to enter into politics. "Partisan action does not fit the historical period that we are in. The country has just come out of its phase with a single party. Our objectives are not only for the short term. We prefer to progress slowly towards a return to Islam. We will support the Islamic Front with... our advice." The association of Nahnah had a feminine branch that was very active and which demarcated itself from the most literalist declarations of Belhaj concerning the feminine condition.

(3) Harakat al-Muqawama al-Islamiyya (the Movement of the Islamic resistance).

ceived support from the embryonic Mouvement Algerie Musulmane Contemporaine, whose leader, Mohamed Ahmeddine, declared that he wanted to join his party with Irchad to form a new HAMAS. The Algerian and foreign press tried to suggest the image of a moderate HAMAS against a radical FIS. The French newsmagazine *L'Express* (1) even suggested that it had found in Nahnah, "the man who succeeded in creating the synthesis between Islam and democracy." But, the capacity for mobilization of HAMAS (2) could never be compared to that of the FIS. On November 7, 1990, it managed to rally about 15,000 people in Algiers, on the occasion of the 36th anniversary of the start of the armed struggle. In similar circumstances, the FIS would show that it could easily mobilize ten to 20 times as many followers.

Very quickly, the militants of HAMAS, which seemed to have the full support of the FLN, appeared to take on the role of the spearhead in an action to divide the FIS. Battles for control of certain mosques pitted the militants of both groups against each other. The FIS began to get support from some of the smaller more radical groups including the Takfir wa Hijra, or the Jihad.(3)

There were in effect several small but well-known groups in the Islamist movement that did not recognize the FIS' leadership. Takfir wa Hijra (taking the name of an Egyptian group); the usually non-violent followers of the Jemaat at Tabligh; a small group of pro-Iranians who were more or less clearly identified under the name of Sunna wal Charia;(4) those

---

(1) Paying little attention again to the fact that it would provoke on the Algerian scene an effect absolutely contrary to the one it was counting on (cf. *L'Express*, May, 1990).

(2) Who published the review *Al-Naba*.

(3) Thus on May 3, 1991, one of these confrontations, the militants of HAMAS were opposed by the group Takfir wa Hijra, aided by members of the Jemaat at-Tabligh and the Jihad, would leave five wounded.

(4) On January 16, 1990, an armed commando, which would be considered as coming from this group "As Sunna wal Charia," penetrated into the courtroom of the courthouse in Blida, and grabbing the automatic weapon of one of the guards, tried to rescue one of their followers by taking a guard hostage. The gendarmerie attacked, and four members of the commando surrendered. Two were killed as well as the guard taken hostage. The leader of the group, whose name was Nasreddine Khelil, was employed in the Moorish bath of a mosque at Blida. The four other members consisted of two highschool students, one university student and one person who was unemployed. The group was considered to be Shiite and linked

of a hypothetical Jihad party; the group of "Afghans" whose guerrilla experience against the Soviets conferred a prestige which was often disproportionate to their actual training; all conserved a certain autonomy vis-à-vis the FIS. Although they did not particularly want to compete in elections, they, nevertheless, constituted a needle in the foot of the Islamist Goliath. They regularly placed it in difficulty by their activist excesses, which the media usually attributed to the FIS. At the beginning of the State of Siege (cf. infra) a good deal of the internal tensions directed at the FIS would come, it seemed, from divergences on the degree of solidarity that the FIS should assume with respect to this radical fringe.(1)

More serious was the competition from the Mouvement de la Nahda Islamique (MNI), even if its implantation did not seem to pass Constantine, the region of its founder Abdellah Benjaballah, who was originally from Bouchtata in the wilaya of Skikda. Born on May 2, 1956, in very humble circumstances, Benjaballah studied law at the University of Ain El Bey in Constantine starting in 1974, and it is during this period that he declares to have founded the group which 16 years later would give birth to his party. Questioned on several occasions, he was imprisoned twice between 1982 and 1984 and from 1985-1986. From December, 1988, on he gave his movement the juridical base of an association baptized "Al Nahda." On October 3, he obtained the recognition of a party of the same name, the MNI, Mouvement de la Nahda Islamique,(2) whose name recalled the one which the ITM in Tunisia adopted to satisfy the law forbidding political formations from making references to religion.

Other stones in the garden of the FIS: an association legalized on March 26, 1991, under the name, "The League of Ulemas," proclaimed itself the resurgence of the league founded in 1931 by Abdelhamid Benbadis. A Front du Jihad et de l'Unité, and a Hizbollah, directed by Jamaleddine

---

to the pro-Iranian Hizbollah. It was believed to have been implanted in several large northern cities. In the capital, the Shiite groups were supposedly present in the popular quarters on the edges of the city (Climat de France, El-Harrach, Bourouba, Diar al-Jemaa, Dar al-Beida, les Eucaliptus et Notre Dame d'Afrique).

(1) A few days before being arrested himself, Abbassi Madani was said to have refused to help the groups which were dismantled by the police.

(2) The headquarters of the party is at Constantine. Alongside Djaballah (married and the father of six children), there was notably Mohamed El Hadi Athmania (the secretary general, born in 1958) and Rachid Boutheljoun.

Bardi, who is still relatively unknown today,(1) manifested itself by issuing several communiques. The Parti de l'Oumma of Youssef Benkhedda, a former leader of the PPA-MTLD and former president of the Provisional Government of the Algerian Republic (GPRA), created a year before independence, also received approval from the authorities, but it was no more successful than the discrete Parti du Rassemblement Arabe Islamique, led by Ali Zeghdoud, or the Mouvement pour le Message Islamique (Harakat lil rissala al islamiyya, HORAS)(2) in making its voice heard.

The FIS and the Army

Although, like everywhere else, the army experienced in Algeria Islamist penetrations in the ranks of its troops, the General Staff had been identified more than anywhere else with the institution of the FLN and remained closely associated with it. When the army returned to the front ranks of the political scene after an absence of only a few months, though, many analyses ignored this historical relationship. The army was credited vis-à-vis the FLN with a functional autonomy and an ideological identity(3) that in fact it had never had. Since its creation, the FIS had been perceived by the army in much the same way that the FLN had seen it: as a particularly dangerous political challenger, which if it gained power would put an end to the army's reign, and, in doing that, would also end its privileges.

It is in this banal context that the first skirmishes between the army and the FIS have to be seen, and not as the FLN understandably tried to present it, as a hypothetical vocation of the army to be "guardian of democracy," a description hastily and uncritically repeated by many international observers. It was General Chelloufi, a close associate of Chadli, who was the first to drop his reserve in order to attack the FIS, implicitly accusing it of "profiting from democracy, of which the army is the defender" to try to impose its views. The quarrel erupted after the General staff's decision to forbid the wearing of hijjabs in the military hospitals. Ali Belhaj, on April 27, 1990, denounced the ban, brandishing the specter of the infiltration of

---

(1) Cf. revue *Arabies*, Paris, May, 1991.

(2) Directed by Mr. Ahmed Kerfah, who asked for authorization for his party on June 15, 1991.

(3) The army, "traditional defender of the democracy in Algeria," wrote a good number of commentators seriously, only a few months after the bloody repression of the riots of 1988.

the security forces, the dread of the regime: "There are in the army, the police and the gendarmerie, civil servants who adore God, and they will be able to remember that." The Gulf crisis, during which Belhaj multiplied his provocative statements against the military, would raise the level of tension. On January 18, 1991, during one of the largest demonstrations ever organized in Algeria, Belhaj installed himself in front of the ministry of defense and proposed training volunteers to reinforce the collapsing armies defending Iraq, and he denounced "the traitorous and rotten regimes in the Arab world, who buy their arms to make war and then turn them against their populations." Two days later, the leaders of the FIS paraded in military harnesses; the review *El Hidaya*, of which Belhaj was one of the editors, ran a front-page headline saying "The Algerian Army and the War in the Gulf: A lion when it fights (the Islamists), an ostrich in time of war." The tone would mount at regular intervals after that. On April 3, the army weekly, *El Djeich,* published a violent attack "against religious extremism." On April 7, Abbassi Madani, evoking the possibility of resorting to a strike to force the annulment of the electoral law, launched a warning to the Army "if it opposed."

The Return of the Army

Two months before the June deadline, the party-army as unified as ever, began to assess the limits of its counteroffensive. Barring unexpected developments, it risked a repeat of its earlier defeat at the polls. None of the opposition Islamist parties had succeeded in seriously threatening the FIS. The secular opposition (PAGS, FFS, MDA and RCD—the 40 other candidates having only a fictional existence) had not succeeded either in imposing itself credibly. It was even feared that the FIS, which had multiplied its presence in the Kabyle area, might be able to launch a counter-offensive against the FFS of Ait Ahmed from Tizi Ouzou. The few public opinion polls that were available (1) showed that the FIS was not likely to suffer unduly from the supposed failures of the administrations in its communes.

---

(1) The one published by *Algérie Actualité* at the beginning of May, whose credibility should be considered as relative, only gave the FLN a chance of coming out of the second round if it managed to capitalize on the quasi-totality of the votes of the non-Islamist opposition. According to the poll, the FIS would be credited with 33.4% of the votes, the "reformed" FLN with 24%, alone the FFS would emerge with 8%, and the RCD of Said Saadi with 6.4%. HAMAS would only be credited with 2% and the MDA of Ben Bella 0.7%.

For the FLN, once the fragility of the results of its political offensive had become apparent, there was a natural tendency to revert to the semi-legal strategies of the past. In addition, to organized press campaigns, the endangered old Party thus decided to fasten on the tried-and-true device of redistributing voting districts. An old practice in Western democracies, the rearranging of voting districts,(1) or gerrymandering, has always permitted the catering to local weaknesses of the party in power by tailoring the borders of each circumscription with an eye to the rapport of forces on a district-by-district basis. The Algerian legislature, aided or not by French experts,(2) would apply the technique on a particularly massive scale. The south, which was relatively unpopulated, but had remained loyal to the FLN, would find itself endowed through the magic of redistricting with many more electoral circumscriptions than it had ever had before. The heavily populated north with its immense urban areas that were dominated by the FIS, would suddenly find that its circumscriptions were extremely rare.(3) The distortion was so exaggerated that it required ten times as many votes to elect a deputy in some of the northern circumscriptions (like Blida) as it did in some of the circumscriptions in the south.

For the FIS to accept the principle of such a vote would be the equivalent of approving of its own public execution. The tone of the debate began understandably to become considerably sharper. Abbassi Madani demanded a revision of the electoral law, and for the first time insistently attacked Benjedid himself, who he suspected of going back on his word. Madani began

(1) Which for the essential consisted of regrouping the circumscriptions, so that the regions considered taken by the adversary would elect a small number of "bad" deputies, while the regions favorable to the government would see their circumscriptions multiplied to elect the largest possible number of "good" deputies.

In the US the process is called "gerrymandering," after a political boss named Gerry, who redistricted his district in such an outrageous manner that a map of his voting district took on the shape of a salamander. When a critic commented on it, a local wag replied, "No, it is not a salamander; it is a gerrymander."

(2) According to a rumor that is difficult to verify, by officials from the French ministry of the interior.

(3) Although the total number of circumscriptions was 542, only the two large parties were sure to have candidates in all of them. The FFS, itself, was only able to present candidates in 280 circumscriptions.

to demand a presidential election,(1) threatening to boycott the legislative election if his demands were turned down. The few dozen members of the Majlis Shura were, nevertheless, far from being in full agreement on what strategy to follow. On April 27, a coordination meeting between Madani, Nahnah and Benjaballah was held at the headquarters of Sahnoun's Rabitat ad da'wa al islamiyya. The possibility of presenting a common list of candidates, in which two-thirds of the candidates would be from the FIS was not even discussed. Abbassi Madani proposed to start a campaign to postpone the elections and to have the electoral law annulled. Nahnah refused to support that line. On April 23, Abbassi Madani delivered an ultimatum and demanded that the date of the anticipated presidential elections be fixed within a week. On April 23 a call was made for a general strike to be launched for April 25 in order to call for the abrogation of the electoral law. With the exception of the FFS,(2) the non-Islamist opposition parties had also protested against the electoral law. But the other opposition formations, including HAMAS, preferred to distance themselves from the FIS and demand its dissolution.

The first days of the strike appeared to constitute a reverse for Abbassi Madani's strategy. If the municipal services in Algiers were massively interrupted, the majority of the industrial sector appeared to remain indifferent to the FIS's call. And, the media at first announced that the victors of the June election were beginning to encounter the first stages of their decline. Once again this information would turn out to be overly influenced by government sources and would prove to be inexact.(3) It took several weeks to find

---

(1) Re-elected at the end of 1988, President Chadli was in principle supposed to be in office until 1993.

(2) And for cause. The million inhabitants of his fief to Tizi Ouzou, had by the magic of the redistricting of Mr. Hamrouche, obtained the right to elect as many deputies as the two and a half million inhabitants of the city of Algiers.

(3) See notably the guide line of the analysis of F. Ghiles in *Financial Times*, London: "After the strike collapsed, the FIS governing council disavowed its spokesman, thus making bitter infighting public. Moreover, two new fundamentalist parties, An-Nahda al-Islamiya and Al-Irchad wal-Islah have emerged in recent months, creating a climate of often violent competition for the Islamic vote.(...) The credibility of the FIS has not simply suffered from its inability to deliver on promises to find jobs and housing for all. The party also shot itself in the foot during the Gulf crisis, when it first came out in favour of Saudi Arabia and then switched allegiance to Iraq. As a result, the FIS has begun to worry that it might fail to win a majority in the June 27th elections." (6-6-91).

out that the petroleum industry had been hit by the full force of the strike,(1) and that the cost to the national economy had been quite high and that the government would be forced to take any available measures, including political concessions to bring the strike to an end. On May 26 and 28, while the mobilization was expanding, demonstrations hit the streets of Algiers. On May 27, 100,000 people marched through the center of the city. The provinces were also hit with demonstrations.

On May 29, the police began to intervene and clashes grew sharper throughout the first days of June. There were incidents of gunfire between the police and radical groups believed to support the FIS, although the members of the groups were never clearly identified. On June 4 the police deployed itself in order to retake control of the neighborhoods dominated by the FIS (Belcourt and Bab el Oued). The clashes became even sharper and several people were killed.(2) During the night of June 5, army tanks rolled into the capital and at 2 a.m. the head of state declared a state of siege for four months. A new page had just been turned in the history of Algeria. The ANP (Armée Nationale Populaire), which had left the institutional scene barely a year earlier, had just made a spectacular reappearance.

In the confusion caused by the tanks, the head of state announced the delay of the legislative elections and the resignation of Mouloud Hamrouche's cabinet. Sid Ahmed Ghozali, who succeeded Hamrouche, was invited to form a government of "technocrats" from which the FLN was nearly completely excluded. On June 7 the FIS announced the suspension of its strike, and declared that it had obtained the promise of anticipated presidential elections. Having been declared beaten during the launching of its strike, it appeared to have brought down the government and to have won its case for presidential elections. At least at this stage, it appeared to be the victor. But the war which the armed branch of the FLN had just declared against it would not stop there.

---

(1) *Le Monde*, often better inspired, evoked the image of the FIS militants as "hairy beards superfluous in a city that ignored them" (*Des barbus hirsutes à la superficie d'une ville qui les ignorent...*).

(2) The prime minister Mouloud Hamrouche declared one year later that the decision for a massive army intervention was taken "above his head" and that he was not even informed of it. (*Le Monde*, July 13, 1992).

The Counter-offensive

From June 9 to June 30, arrests spilled over from the small radical groups on the periphery of the FIS and began to affect the entire movement. To put it more precisely, the repression, which had been scientifically organized, began to strike at the back bone of the FIS, whose cadres were arrested across the country. On June 21, the military authorities ordered the reinstatement of Republican slogans—"of the people and by the people"—over the city halls held by the FIS. Here and there the mottoes had been replaced by signs proclaiming "Islamic Communes." The army ran into a resistance in some of the more popular neighborhoods of Algiers that quickly made it back down. The disturbances led to another ten deaths and more than a hundred wounded—mostly by gunfire. In this tense atmosphere, Ali Belhaj decided to evoke the necessity for militants to "stock arms." This undoubtedly had the effect of increasing the tension in the Majlis Shura among those who thought the front was pushing its political advantage too far and that it was time to reestablish links with those who had force on their side. On June 26, 1991, hardly more than a year after their election victory, the FIS saw the first breaches open in the unity which had up until then been the key to its success.

Three days after the beginning of the strike, a communique from the Majlis Shura calling for the cessation of the strike had already been denied by Abbassi Madani, who had thus revealed the first hints of the magnitude of the internal divergences of his party. This time the alert would become much more serious. Strongly urged by the regime, three members of the Majlis Shura agreed, in effect, to record a video-tape in which they radically and openly disassociated themselves from the line and methods of Abbassi Madani. "Attention, Abbassi is a danger for the FIS, a danger for Islam. I am leaving the FIS," declared Bechir Fakih. "There are elements in the FIS who want to use all their power and their influence to push the movement towards confrontation," added Ahmed Marani (in charge of social affairs). The challengers of Abbassi Madani did not doubt that they had just given the army the possibility of crossing a new stage in its recapturing of the political scene. It was in this difficult context for the leadership of the FIS, that the army chose in effect to occupy its headquarters in Algiers, and the next day, on June 30, to arrest its principle leaders. Abbassi Madani (1) and

---

(1) Arrested at the siege of the FIS.

Ali Belhaj (1) were immediately charged by a military security court at Blida "for armed conspiracy against the security of the state." The arrests soon reached to the rest of the party's leadership structure and quickly took in eight known members of the Majlis Shura before extending to still others. Each of the successive spokesmen were arrested in their turn. The Front unquestionably underwent a severe shock. The public reaction to the arrests was weak, and the reactions of the militants were disorganized and ineffective. The days that followed the arrests of the two leaders were certainly filled with agitation, but no uprising took place or threatened control by the military. During several weeks, the public prayers were controlled at the Bab el Oued and Kouba mosques, and non-residents were not allowed to enter the area. On July 12, gunfire dispersed the recalcitrant few who tried to reach Kouba. At the end of the month of July, the FIS, divided and disorganized, and the press which had taken to amplifying the slightest division now talking about the formation of a "second FIS," it seemed that the party of Abbassi had lost its battle and that the regime had achieved the principle objectives of its plan for reconquest.

That was without counting the amplitude of the base for mobilization of the FIS. Its infrastructure and leadership had clearly been shaken, but the capacity for mobilization had not been broken, and the arrests had not really had an impact on its potential for militancy. The organizational expression of the Islamist mobilization had been hit, but the themes of the current remained intact. Everything remained to be done, and time would once again turn out more to the FIS' advantage than to that of its adversaries.

Toward the Legislative Elections

In the storm, the FIS had managed to resist on one essential point: it had refused to participate in negotiations in the absence of its two imprisoned leaders whose position at the head of the movement was confirmed at a congress which met at Batna on July 25 and July 26. All those who had publicly expressed their hesitations concerning the leadership outside the movement (El Hachemi Sahnouni, Zebda Benazzouz, Mohamed Kerrar, Saad Mekhloufi et Kamreddine Kherbane), were suspended. The new spokesman, Hachemi Abdelkader, named by the Congress, was arrested by the army a few days later. On August 18, the two press organs of the FIS, *Al Mounqid* and *Al Forkane*, were banned for allegedly having published "appeals for

---

(1) Arrested in the street, while on his way to the television station to record a protest against the invasion of the FIS headquarters.

civil disobedience and violence" and having incited "to crimes and offenses against public order and against the security of the state."

At the same time, some of the lower ranking militants who had been arrested at the end of June began to be released. In contrast, several hundred cadres of the party remained locked up.

The Disappointments that Come from Wishful Thinking

The itinerary that subsequently led to the legislative elections was filled with internal tensions within the Front, which was divided about which strategy to adopt.

The FIS, under the provisional leadership of Abdelkader Hachani, decided to go ahead and participate in the elections. The General staff of the army, for its part, decided not to let the "error of Chadli" (i.e. the legalization of the FIS) lead to an irreversible assault on its interests. From the opening of the campaign, demonstrations in the streets were forbidden. That did not stop the FIS from regrouping its partisans for the time required for several meetings, and reasserting itself in a landscape from which it had been excluded for several months. The most serious incidents in the campaign took place on November 28, when the guards of a frontier post on the border with Tunisia were attacked by a strongly armed group, which took control of the post, killing several people. On December 10, near Qamar, 45 kilometers to the northwest of the city of El-Oued, the Army, which had come to take the situation in hand, left 15 dead, including two of its own, during the dismantling of what the media would call "the group of Taieb Afghani" (34 people).(1) Whether it was a convoy of arms coming from the Polisario (or any other foreign source) and allegedly destined for all or part of the Islamist current or a mere provocation by the military security services to prepare the terrain for a dissolution of the FIS was hard to tell. The affair, in any case, provided the pretext to the chiefs of the army to brandish once again the threat of a dissolution of the FIS on the eve of the elections.

In this landscape of rumors in Algiers, everyone agreed on the quasi-certitude that the army would intervene. The generals had allowed such an atmosphere of contentiousness to develop between them and the Islamists, that in the event of defeat they feared for their physical as well as political survival. The uncertainty concerned only the time when they would make

---

(1) Of which certain members were reported by the Algerian press to belong to a "movement of the Islamic army."

their move—before or after the first round of voting. History seemed to hesitate still. Those who favored an immediate interruption in the electoral process were in a minority. In the limits of their logic, they no doubt didn't want to give the FIS a chance to confirm the extent of its popular base with a stunning success that would mark the army's intervention later with an indelible imprint of illegitimacy. But, as a result of self-intoxication or faulty analysis, the one possibly explaining the other, hardly anyone in the entire Algerian or foreign political and media landscape credited the Islamists with a chance of winning more than 30 to 35 percent of the votes. The only exception was the FIS spokesman who claimed to be certain of victory. The entire length of the campaign, the tone of the media strayed far from analysis. In taking refuge once again in automatic denigration, it had manifestly contributed to its own blinding. Each one convinced himself that the ideological and political counter-offensive of the regime, the outside competition, the pitfalls of communal management, the internal dissensions of the FIS, the role of a completely over-evaluated HAMAS, the "reaction of women," had all contributed to bring Abbassi Madani down from a majority. The general staff and the chancelleries in Algiers seemed convinced that the elections were pushing towards that equilibrium that was the dream of all the leaders in the region: an Islamist party that was domesticated and whose integration in the institutional system would not call the political survival of the regime into question. At the end of a prolonged electoral campaign, "only one thing is certain," concluded the French daily *Libération*, in perfect agreement with its colleagues on both sides of the Mediterranean: "None of the parties present appear on the eve of the balloting to be able to obtain a majority tomorrow."

The FIS Again, and Again the Army

In 48 wilayas, 13 million voters were to designate 430 deputies. In the evening of December 26, the results were the following: of 3,260,359 votes, the FIS had won 188 seats outright on the first round. With 510,661 votes, the FFS arrived in second position and obtained 25 seats. If it had not obtained the one-third of the votes of the FLN, their concentration (for four-fifths) in the departments of Tizi Ouzou and Bejaia, gave it the seats the FLN had not been able to win, thanks to the majority rule. Of 1,613,507 votes distributed over the whole territory (about half that of the FIS), the ex-single party was the great looser. In balloting in 158 circumscriptions, it only obtained 15 seats, and had no chance of catching up in the second round. The FIS, even if it had lost votes compared to the communal elections, only needed 27 seats to control the new assembly. The myriad of other formations had simply disappeared from the political scene. Neither the PAGS, buried since the communal elections, nor the new arrivals to the Islamist scene had managed to capture a single seat, even if their presence was attested to here and there. HAMAS managed to capture only the seat of its leader, Nahnah, in Blida and the possible support of two independants.

On the day after the vote, if the FFS kept a certain political dignity in courageously demanding the continuation of the electoral process, the RCD, which had nothing to lose, openly called for its interruption, and said that it was ready to "paralyze the country" (one could ask with whom) and to "assume all the excesses." A "National committee of safeguard was formed" which the weekly *Algérie Actualité* (1) thought it could credit with the support of around 60 associations and, in a manner that was more hypothetical, the support of "the three million followers of the UGTA."

The FIS, for its part, called on its militants to show "moderation" and "reconciliation" but still did not manage to stop certain members from hardening their tone in announcing the implementation of a government program that did not seem interested in this double objective. Outside the country, if the general Zine al Abidine Ben Ali used the Islamist victory as an argument with which to congratulate himself on the "thoughtful" and "tranquil" democratization, which he felt he had succeeded in putting into operation in Tunisia (something which no Western observers contested), the majority of his counterparts took a more prudent attitude of waiting to see what would happen. The Islamist formations, from Amman to Cairo, and including Sana, naturally exulted faced with what they considered as a confirmation of their own potential and a foretaste of their own victory.(2) The fiction of an Islamist current limited to a small minority of activists, who

---

(1) No. 1369, January 9–15, 1992.

(2) In Cairo, the weekly *Chaab* (Labour Party/formerly Socialist, then of Islamist tendency) at the head of the movement of solidarity with FIS, published a poll tending to show that the vast majority of Egyptians a) think that "the elections in Algeria were really democratic" (91.1%); b) approved of their results (94.7%); and last but not least c) "think that such a practice (free elections) constitutes an experience that is necessary to repeat in other countries." (90.58%). Also in Egypt, see Gamel Eddine Hussein, *Al-Jezaïr fouq borkan*, Cairo, 1992, ISBN No. 977 5 2 25 6, 117 pages, Mourou Mohamed, *Baad 500 sana min souqout al-andalous, Al-Djezaïr t'aoudou ila Mohamed* (Five hundred years after the fall of Andalous Algeria comes back to Mohamed), Al Mokhtar al-Islami, Cairo, 1992, 190 pages.

as such constantly tried to take power by force, was once again shattered. In France, the French Socialist Party, succeeded in seriously "congratulating the good score of the FFS, which avoided a dangerous bi-polarization." Only the extreme right of Jean Marie Le Pen, which, irony of history, had shown actually more knowledge of the Islamist dynamic than all the other French political families together, provoked the dominant opinion by congratulating itself on the verdict of the Algerian polls.(1) In Algiers, from rumors and insinuations, it was becoming less and less believable that there would be a continuation of the electoral process. On January 2, 300,000 opponents of the FIS marched to "save democracy." Ait Ahmed, who had spoken briefly, was acclaimed and everyone started to believe again in a remobilization of the "democratic" camp. The abstentions, which were nearly 50 percent, left a good number of observers with the illusion of a possible counter-majority.(2) In a manner that was more pragmatic, or at least more cynical, others were thinking of a "juridictional" second round, in which the Constitutional Council (after having received 300 demands for annulment of which 174 were from the FLN) might agree to deprive the FIS of its majority. In the shadows, others were preparing a solution that was much more radical. In Algiers, on the evening of January 11, a brief broadcast on national television put an end to the uncertainty. It surprised neither the embassies nor the foreign news agencies.

President Chadli Benjedid evoked the obstacles to following his mission and announced his resignation. He was put under house arrest. In theory it was the president of the National Assembly who should have succeeded him. But, it was quickly learned that Chadli's resignation was only one step in a process aimed at the entire institutional system. It would not stop at the president, but would encompass the entire legality of the constitution. Several days earlier, the head of state had been invited to sign a decree dissolving the National Assembly, and thus creating a constitutional

---

(1) "The Arabs want to become real Arabs again," declared the chief of the extreme right in France. "It is the triumph of the Jellaba over cosmopolitan blue jeans." ... "I see nothing wrong in that."

(2) It is to forget once again that the elections that carried FIS to victory (cf. infra) in the communes and then to its semi-victory in the legislatives were the first in the history of independent Algeria (and in fact in the entire history of Algeria, except for the referendum on independence) in which the state had not stuffed the voting boxes. The 50 to 60% turnout for true elections appears formidable if one compares it to the 10 to 15% turnouts which leaders of "democratic" countries in the region usually get.

vacuum by which the successors would try to justify their entrance on the scene. The president of the Constitutional Council—whose judges had refused to overturn the results of the first round of voting (1)—was solicited and refused to assure any interim presidency. Exit the legality. Enter on the scene the High Council for Security,(2) an institution definitely presented in the Constitution, but only given some meager consultative powers there. The putchists, in the concern to keep a legalistic facade on their intervention, did not stop to worry about such subtleties. On January 14, the High Council for Security, which had self-proclaimed itself to be a legislative body,(3) created by claiming the advice of the Constitutional Council a "High Council of State," which exercised the whole of the powers attributed to the head of state by the constitution. Its members were: Khaled Nezzar, Ali Kafi, Tijani Haddam (rector in title of the Paris Mosque) and Ali Haroun. The mission of the HCE "shall not exceed the end of the Presidential mandate," which is to say 1994. The council was assisted by a "National Consultative Council." The government of Mr. Ghozali, was finally kept. He chose to challenge the legality of the elections.(4) And, iron-

---

(1) Estimating that no more than a dozen, more or less, of the challenges might be justified.

(2) Which includes the Prime Minister (Ghozali), the minister of foreign affairs (Lakhdar Ibrahimi), of justice (Hamdani Benkhelli), of defense (General Khaled Nezzar), and of the interior (General Larbi Belkhir) as well as the Chief of Staff Abdelmalek Guenaizia.

(3) Which stated "that the constitution does not take into account the conjunction of the absence of the popular assembly by dissolution and of the president of the republic by resignation ...."

(4) On January 23, *El-Moujahid* reproduced an interview accorded by the Prime Minister to *La Libre Belgique*: "We have not impeded the elections," pleaded Ghozali. "On the contrary, for the first time since independence, in sight of 200 foreign journalists, the government organized free and clean elections, which are not contested by anyone. But that was not the case for the other parties. When the electoral lists are falsified, when one retains more than a million voting cards, when one has voters cast their votes outside the polling places with ballots that are already filled in, and more serious still, when one organizes a campaign of terror and violates the consciences of people, this is not a clean way to participate in elections. The government on that side was organized so that the two rounds of voting would take place... Only between the two rounds, there was a resignation by the President of the Republic. (*Al Moujahid*, January 23, 1992, page 5).

ically, to take in hand the largely imaginary reticence from France (1) with respect to the coup d'état.

Fairly quickly, the chain of events that had taken place became evident. Benjedid had insisted, despite the counsel of his closest advisers including Ghozali, on following through with the elections. He was prepared, if he lost the elections, to cohabit with an Islamist assembly. In this, he was in a minority position facing both the government and the army. On January 6 or 7, the 181 superior officers who make up the army's command are believed to have expressed a disavowal which had nuances, but which was all the same unanimous.(2) For the authors of the putsch, chiefly General Nazzar, the departure of Chadli would not only block the electoral process but would also allow the FLN to try and reconstitute its political virginity. To perfect the illusion of a new start, the elderly Mohamed Boudiaf, 73, leader in exile in Morocco since 1964 of a Trotskyist-flavored Revolutionary Socialist Party, was persuaded to take up service again and to accept at least the formal leadership of the country. Boudiaf had been condemned to death by Ben Bella, and had never been pardoned by either Boumediene or Chadli. Nevertheless, in spite of his opposition to the barons of the FLN, he could still be considered as a member of the closed circle of the "sons of Toussaint." On January 16 at 2 p.m., the presidential plane brought him back from Rabat. At 10 p.m. he spoke (two hours late, which led some to believe that he had had harder conversations with his employers than expected) from the presidency. "Islam is the religion of everyone in Algeria," he declared. The only false note came from the secretary general of the FLN, a close friend of Chadli, who was opposed to his marginalization and the opening it gave the army and, therefore, condemned the new regime by declaring, "The Constitutional Council has opened the way for a power that is unconstitutional." He was soon called back to a more realistic attitude.

----

(1) An extremely nuanced declaration by the President of the Republic had evoked the utility of "the resumption of the democratic process." Iran, on the other hand, had openly criticized the putsch. Algeria, in recalling its ambassadors from Teheran and Paris, tried to establish a parallelism between Khomeinist Iran and Mitterrand's France — which was ludicrous since France had supported the FLN at each step.

(2) Cf. especially *Libération*. This version of a unanimous support of the army would be denied by the spokesmen of the FIS in Cairo, and a "Communiqué of the Algerian general officers," which was published in the weekly *Chaab*, March 10, 1992, Cairo, never had its origin clearly attested.

A central committee of the FLN convoked at the end of the month of January never succeeded in measuring the extent of the internal malaise and preferred to adjourn without reaching any decisions. In the West, hardly anyone tried to conceal relief at the outcome. Nearly all the Arab regimes more or less explicitly congratulated the new government, except for Jordan which remained relatively discrete. Saudi Arabia chose to normalize its relations with Algiers and to give financial support to the High Council of State. For the Islamist opposition, the results of the elections, the way in which the Algerian military snatched the victory away, the ease with which the supposedly democratic regimes in the North as well as the South quickly accommodated themselves to this turn of events, constituted so much grist for their mill.

The FIS, for its part, denounced the "political piracy," proclaimed that it only recognized the authority that came from the polls in the first round of voting, and called on its militants "to protect the popular choice and to refuse any maneuver aimed at hobbling its will and retarding the process of change." It tried to appeal to the bad conscience of the members of the army. Each declaration unleashed new arrests at all levels of the structure. A new repressive arsenal (1) was put into place. The arrests included some of the newly elected deputies as well as A. Hachani, the successor to Abbassi Madani, despite the fact that he was reputed to be very moderate. The army tried to retake the mosques one by one in order to assign them to Imams sympathetic to the government.

In the style of Tunisia, Algeria had entered into the dangerous cycle of veering toward repression. The state of emergency proclaimed on February 9 for a 12-month period, the dissolution of the FIS pronounced at the beginning of March, then the opening of the detention camps in the southern part of the country where the prisoners would soon be counted in the thousands, little by little extended the failure of the High Council of State.

The internal dissensions of the regime then expressed themselves through the murder of Mohammed Boudiaf on June 29, 1992.(2) The act

---

(1) Especially in the wilaya of Algiers where a decree reserved the sidewalks around the mosques for pedestrians, "regardless of the day and time," etc.

(2) Mohamed Boudiaf was assassinated while inaugurating a cultural center in the town of Annaba, 350 km. east of Algiers, by one of the young officers (Mohamed Lembarek, 26 years old) devoted to his personal security. The plot is often considered to have been prepared by some leaders of Chadli's era, whose economic privileges were being investigated by Boudiaf in an attempt to "moralize" the system. "Boudiaf mistakenly thought he could go to war without

was attributed to the FIS but most probably executed by those who had brought the old militant back to power.

The FIS, after a period of peaceful reistance had, in any case, started a bloody series of murders against policemen and soldiers. At the time (July 12) when Abbassi and Belhaj were sentenced to 12 years in prison, several hundreds of them had been killed. Ali Kafi (successor of Boudiaf at the head of the HCS) and Belaid Abdessalam (prime minister, previously in charge of industrialization under Boumedienc) have tried since then to concentrate on economics, advocating that politics was to be put aside for a certain period of time. This desperate rhetorical attempt has proven insufficient to prevent a dramatic increase in repression. At the same time it gives the regime the means of maintaining itself against the will of a large majority of the population. The repression nevertheless most probably accelerates the speed of the repressive spiral in which the regime is inevitably doomed to disappear.

---

the army," commented a high ranking officer a few months after the assasination. (Interview with the author)

GENERAL CONCLUSION

By virtue of an old political principle, regimes often have the opponents they deserve. Frequently, their successors are the political forces that they, themselves, have largely helped to create.

If it were necessary to hold to this view in order to evoke the near future, pessimism would win out. In the autumn of 1992, there is nothing that leads one to think that the misunderstandings linked to the rise in power of the Islamist challengers to the regime in place are likely to be overcome any time soon. None of the local situations, especially in Algeria, provides cause for much optimism.

A Bilateral Radicalization

To the entire Arab political landscape, the 1991 parliamentary elections in Algeria have in fact transmitted a double message. To the regimes, they have confirmed that no parliamentary elections would protect them from being defeated by their Islamist opponents, since the ability of the supposedly "small radical groups" to mobilize wider compartments of the society has been clearly established. Most regimes have, therefore, both strengthened the prohibition made to the Islamists to accede to the institutional system and intensified a very "preventive" repression against them. This has sometimes occurred (as in the case of Tunis, Algeria and Egypt) without much regard for human rights. To the Islamist troops, the way the results of the elections were dismissed has underlined the poor credibility of the democratic discourse held both by the regimes and their foreign supporters. Inside the movements, it has therefore given more power to the backers of radicalization.

Although Algeria had at one time boasted of being the first Arab country to have a minister of human rights (Ali Haroun, a member of the High State Committee), repression soon became the unique language of communication between the government and the duly elected representatives of the majority of the society. The detention camps have harbored as many as ten thousand militants, whom the Algerian generals decided to extract by force from the political landscape, and whom they still hope to separate from the 3.5 million voters who have cast ballots in their favor during two elections.

Although it has not let the En Nahda movement demonstrate the width of its popular support, Tunis has also played the same repression-game with its opponents. In a country where eleven years after the so called "political opening" by former president Bourguiba not one single seat has been gained by any of the oppositions—Islamist or secularist, the "defense of democracy" nevertheless still provides president Zine Al Abidine Ben Ali's regime with an almost unlimited support from its Western allies.

In Egypt, the already high level of violence has increased during the summer of 1992, as some members of the Gemaa Islamiyya in an attempt to force the regime to reduce the repression against its militants by depriving it of the most valuable tourist income have started assaulting foreign visitors, killing one British tourist and wounding three. The only effect of this highly questionable maneuver has been to heighten the level of an indiscriminate repression. Some villages have been entirely destroyed and hundreds of sympathizers—although absolutely not implicated in the tourist attacks—jailed in detention camps where torture has been repeatedly proven to be used. Long concentrated on the "radical" Gemaa Islamiyya, repression has been extended to the legalistic trend of the Muslim Brothers late in 1992.

As elsewhere in the region, the regime in Cairo keeps refusing any demand for political participation by any component of the Islamist trend. It has long succeeded in doing so, especially vis-à-vis the West, by emphasising the need to "fight against the religious strife" between Copts and Muslims and "preserve unity of the Egyptian society." Western media also tend—sometimes too automatically—to connect any kind of anti-regime violence to its supposed "religious-strife" dimension. In fact, a close look at both the chronology and the causalities of these confrontations reveals that the "religious" factor appears far from being the main source of violence, nor does it appear its principal means of expression. The involvement of Sudan or Iran, used throughout the summer of 1992 by the regime as a pretext, has no higher level of credibility. But it allows the regime to persist in denying access to the institutional system to all of its Islamist opponents, i.e. to the overwhelming majority of its opposition.

Almost throughout the Arab world, various regimes' initial repression is countered by violence from the Islamist movements, creating a dynamic that characterizes the present predicament... and largely determines prospects for the near future.

If the attitude of the Algerian regime is difficult to predict since it partly depends on the reactions of the international community, and especially on the West, it is a less ambitious project to trace the probable limits of its effectiveness. The Algerian leaders may be able to ward off the expression of the political majority that was manifestly demonstrated in the election on December 26, 1991. But how long they can do this will probably be measured in months, rather than years. And they will not be able to alter the balance of forces significantly. It is therefore hard to see how the march of the leaders of the FIS towards power can be interrupted for very long. Having destroyed the backbone of the movement, Tunis can probably face some kind of apparently static situation for a while, although the attitude of the army can, here like anywhere else, influence the process at any time. Like Tunis, Egypt will have to maintain a growing level of repression here and there, and the price of this violence will inevitably be paid by the system some day.

Since Nasser and the crushing of the Muslim Brothers, a great deal of water has flowed beneath the bridges of the Nile, and it is now generally admitted everywhere in the region that attempts to use force to remove a movement from the political landscape, especially when it is supported by a vast majority of the population, is most likely to be insufficient. Nevertheless, neither in the North nor (although more understandably) among the Arab political classes, no one seems in a hurry to accept what seems to be an inevitable cohabitation. Here and there, the image of the entire Islamic phenomenon is still based on a mere extrapolation from the political style of the assassins of Sadat. One pretends to ignore the fact that its social setting has long overgrown the small groups of literalist and totalitarian followers of a "religious discourse" in the strictest sense.

The Algerian voting booths, however, revealed more in a few weeks about the Islamist currents than most of the thousands of pages that have been written concerning them. The Algerian election of December, 1991, was not only conclusive in exploding the thesis of the existence of "small groups afraid of marginalization by free elections" and consequently tempted to seize power by force. It also demonstrated that a crushing majority of women decided to vote for the FIS and with no less deliberation than their counterparts who voted for the secular parties. This expels another common fallacy, the simplistic prediction of an Islamist mobilization "against women." Failing to find a "third force" in the political landscape capable of combating the supposed enemy, external observers have been no less determined to pursue the desperate hunt for a segment of society (women, Sufis, Berbers, militaries?) that could stave off the predictable results of the elections. The most obstinate analysts keep trying to sound out the battalions of abstentionists. Do they exist? No doubt. Do they constitute an alternative majority? Most certainly not. How is it possible to forget that the elections that carried the FIS to its communal victory, and then to its semi-victory in the legislative elections, were the first in the history of independent Algeria (and for that matter in the entire history of Algeria, with the exception of the referendum on independence) in which the government did not simply falsify the level of participation, either through its party operatives, or through administrative ruses? Moreover, nothing suggests that the abstentionists would have acted as anything other than a simple echo chamber for the majority who voted, in other words would have served as anything other than a supplementary reserve of Islamist votes.

Toward Democracy?

When it comes to appreciating the capacity of the political forces to follow the long process of constructing tolerant societies, the only methodological references available must be underlined clearly. In the Arab world today, the line that isolates the "good" from the "bad," the tolerant from the intolerant, the democrats from the anti-democrats, those who defend human (or women's) rights and those who only accord a moderate interest in those directions, etc., is infinitely more sinuous than the dividing line that distinguishes the Islamist currents from the rest of the political scene. Simply being Islamist is most certainly not a guarantee that one will be up to keeping promises of tolerance made by most Islamist leaders. But in the same way, the simple fact of being anti-Islamist (like Saddam Hussein) or Berber, or whatever, is no guarantee that one has a right to claim membership in this "democratic camp" of which the West has all too often automatically accorded the monopoly of representation either to the elites in power or to those "secularist" formations which the Islamist resurgence has irresistibly marginalized.

In conclusion, we will restate the underlying hypotheses of this work: Nearly everywhere in the Arab world today, it is the forces emanating from the vast movement of political Islam that appear to be the leading candidates to replace the regimes linked to the national movements. But this assessment of the centrality of the Islamist forces only makes sense if one avoids giving the label "Islamist" the limited and narrow definition—which we have already tried to show is not operational—of a movement linked to a precise ideology, to a specific program, to modes of action determined and intangible, and eventually to a definite social base. Neither does the declaration of the preponderance of Islamist forces imply the "superiority" of one political theory over another. What we want to say is the simple fact that in the Muslim world, the profound process of reconnecting with the "pre-colonial" symbolic universe, which is the essence of the Islamist resurgence, will more and more affect the entire political chess board. We would suggest that the analyses of the two major processes underway in this region, i.e. of reconnecting the political discourse with the pre-colonial symbolic system on the one hand, and the developing of political attitudes respectful of a pluralisitic culture on the other, ought to be clearly disconnected, or at least that the first stop being automatically considered as a mere obstacle to the second.

To pinpoint the nature of the forces which will assume the leadership of this vast movement more precisely, would in fact require a heavy dose of "clairvoyance," something that is forbidden to researchers. The most that can be done is to underline the direction in which research must concentrate. Rather than focusing on the conditions in which the forces that are too far removed from the process of re-Islamization are in the process of irresistibly marginalizing themselves, it is much more efficient to investigate the internal dynamics of this Islamist resurgence, i.e. the internal dynamic of each of its numerous components as well as the changes in the balance of forces between them.

It is in these dynamics more than anywhere else that one can begin to see the contours of the new forces that will assume the responsibility of directing these societies towards the twenty-first century. Nothing today allows the analyst to assume that they will prove—politically or economically—less efficient than their predecessors.

François Burgat,
translated by William Dowell and François Burgat,
Aix-en-Provence and Cairo,
1992